FORTY MILES A DAY
ON BEANS AND HAY

Forty Miles a Day on Beans and Hay

The Enlisted Soldier
Fighting the Indian Wars

BY DON RICKEY, JR.

UNIVERSITY OF OKLAHOMA PRESS : NORMAN AND LONDON

To the volunteer Indian Wars veteran U.S. regular soldiers whose contributions made this book possible, and to their descendants of this time and times to come who form the sword and shield of the American people.

Library of Congress Catalog Card Number: 62-9952

ISBN: 0-8061-1113-5

13   14   15   16   17   18   19   20   21   22   23   24   25   26   27   28   29

Preface

THIS ACCOUNT of the enlisted men of the United States Regular
Army on the frontier, from 1865 to the 1890's, is not a history of
the Indian Wars (which, to be sure, shaped the experiences of
these men) but a study of the rank and file who served through
the Indian campaigns. The labors, endurance, and combats of
the western regular created the framework of law and order that
made settlement and social development possible. As members
of the Regular Army, these men formed an important segment
of our usually slighted national military continuum, upon and
around which our massive armies have been created in times of
crisis. We need to know more about our military past and the
men who lived it, just as we need to deepen our understanding
of all facets of the American experience.

Few aspects of the frontier past have been so routinely warped
and romanticized as has that mixture of tragic folly, duplicity,

savagery, heroism, waste, and costly establishment of order commonly referred to as the Indian Wars. Now altogether remote from the personal experience of space-age Americans, the men and events comprising the sweep of post-Civil War western military history are customarily written and conceived of as storybook people and situations, outside the mainstream of history. Modern writings dealing with the Indian Wars have tended to portray the frontier regular as a romantic beau sabreur, knighterrant of the West, or brand him as the brutalized and degraded oppressor of noble red men. Neither stereotype comes near the mark—nor closer to the truth than casting the western Indians in the classic mold of noble savages. The frontier soldier was a professional regular, an American or recent immigrant who had enlisted in the United States Army. Synthesizing the thoughts and feelings of these men about their life and service in the West is the objective I have hoped to achieve in preparing this book.

Even in his own day, the rank-and-file regular was psychologically as well as physically isolated from most of his fellow Americans. The people, tired of arms and armies after four years of Civil War, had turned their attention to the mushrooming growth of the American economy and the rise of industrial giantism. Very few regular enlisted men were literarily inclined, and many could barely write their names. Nearly all that has been printed about them has come from officers and others. In order to find out what the regulars had to say about themselves, I found it necessary to consult more than three hundred living Indian Wars veterans. Most of them were consulted in 1954 and asked to fill out questionnaires and write accounts of their army experiences in the West. Many generously entered into lengthy correspondence with me and offered themselves for personal interviews. Wherever possible, then, the old regulars have been allowed to speak for themselves.

Without the material thus provided me, I could not have grounded my book so thoroughly on firsthand sources. To the veterans who participated in this project I owe far more than this simple acknowledgment. Of special significance were the information and the loan of manuscripts and photographs furnished by Sergeant James S. Hamilton (First Infantry, 1876–81); Sergeant Perley S. Eaton (Third Cavalry, 1881–86); Major William G. Wilkinson (Private, Eighth Cavalry, 1886–91); and Brigadier General Reynolds J. Burt, U.S.A. retired, who lived his boyhood at a series of western posts where his officer-father was stationed from 1874 to 1892. All but General Burt have since answered their last roll call. I am also grateful for Congresswoman Edith Nourse Rogers' interest in making it possible for me to locate and write to Indian Wars veterans. The University of Oklahoma Faculty Research Committee made funds available for my investigations. Many people helped me locate source materials, but Mrs. Viola Ransom Wood, National Historian, United Indian War Veterans, deserves my special thanks. Professor Norman Maclean, University of Chicago, was of great personal assistance to me in the crucial, formative stages of preparing the manuscript. The patient, conscientious, constructive manuscript criticisms and personal encouragement of Professor Donald J. Berthrong contributed much to the final character of the book. I am also indebted to Professor Carl Cone, University of Kentucky, who generously lent manuscripts dealing with army life at Fort Ellis, Montana, as of 1871.

Since the writing of history must always be in some degree an act of faith, wherein men and events of another time and set of circumstances are marshaled and partly interpreted through the refracting light of the writer's own experience, training, and self, I will only add that when facts and statements could be tested against contemporary information I made every effort to do it. In many instances when statements could not be verified, due mainly to the lack of any corroborative material, I included them if the internal evidence seemed to justify doing so.

St. Louis County, Missouri   DON RICKEY, JR.

BARRACKS
lived in by a troop of cavalry, about 1890, at Fort Yellowstone.

Courtesy U.S. National Archives

Contents

Illustrations

MAPS

FORTY MILES A DAY
ON BEANS AND HAY

INFANTRY BARRACKS, FORT LEAVENWORTH, ABOUT 1874

A very well appointed and settled post by the standards of the times. Bunks have the four wooden bed boards. The fire apparatus in the center includes an extinguisher, axes, and leather buckets. The "A" barrel held drinking water, and was provided by company funds.

Courtesy U.S. National Park Service

1.

War in the West

THE MORNING OF MAY 23, 1865, saw the nation's capital thronged with citizens and soldiers. Campaign-toughened Union troops, school children, convalescent soldiers and sailors from the hospitals, and eager civilians filled Washington's main thoroughfares, parks, and public buildings. It was the first of two days that men would talk about for years to come, two glorious days focused on national pride and thanksgiving. The war was over, and the victorious armies of the Potomac, of Tennessee, and of Georgia were about to pass in review before President Andrew Johnson and the people.

At nine o'clock General Meade's Army of the Potomac began its march down Capitol Hill toward Pennsylvania Avenue, where the presidential party waited in the reviewing stand erected in front of the White House. Flags and banners fluttered all along the line of march. School children sang and cheered.

3

The crash of blaring bands accompanied the cobble-clatter of mounted officers and the stamp of serried ranks of veteran infantry as the troops moved down Pennsylvania Avenue, past the presidential stand festooned with star-spangled bunting bearing the terrible names of "Vicksburg," "Antietam," "Gettysburg," and others.

The second day of the Grand Review witnessed the passage of Sherman's far-ranging army. Little Phil Sheridan could not be present to lead his cavalry brigades, but Generals Custer and Merritt headed up the mounted column in his place. Custer would ride to defeat and immortality eleven years later at the Little Bighorn, but on this warm day in May, 1865, few Americans, in or out of the army, were much concerned with the potential problems of the Indian military frontier. This was the Grand Review of two hundred thousand victorious Union soldiers. Newspapers and magazines throughout the nation printed columns describing this proud, awesome display of the nation in arms, and universally voiced the prayer that never again would the land be torn by war.

Not all of the federal forces, by any means, could be assembled in Washington for the review, and reporters mentioned in passing that many deserving units of the army were necessarily occupied with garrison and routine duties elsewhere. Where these units were and what they were doing in actuality were not important to those who stood and watched the events connected with the Great Peace. For hours the troops, afoot and mounted, moved smartly in review. The issues between the two sections of a divided nation had been settled on the battlefields. Soldiers seasoned by four years of war could now return to the pursuits of peace, and the nation to the tasks of unity, reconstruction, and agricultural and industrial prosperity.

But this was only the moment of the Great Peace. The reality was of another character. The country had never really been bisectional, north and south: it had three parts after 1803, and there had not been a condition of entire peace in its western

4

domain, which by 1865 extended to the far-away Pacific. There was another race there, and many tongues, those of the Indians, and they knew a great deal about warfare.

As the veterans of the Civil War passed in review, the men of the Seventh Iowa Cavalry and the Eleventh Ohio Cavalry, serving in Colorado and Dakota Territories, were spread thinly, garrisoning posts in eastern Colorado and along the Overland Trail in what is now southern Wyoming. The truth is, these volunteers did not know that the war was over, as powerful hordes of Sioux, Cheyenne, and Arapaho warriors descended on settlements, posts, and trail traffic in the spring and summer of 1865. However, most of the wartime volunteer and state troops, from Kansas, Iowa, Minnesota, and California, were withdrawn from the Indian frontier in the Southwest, from Kansas, Colorado, Nebraska, and Dakota, late in 1865. Active service for the volunteers ended when they were replaced by hastily reorganized regiments of the Regular Army.

At the end of the Civil War, the plains, deserts, and mountains of the West flamed with savage warfare. Another generation would pass before the power of the western tribes was broken. During most of the quarter-century after 1865 the Regular Army was virtually a stepchild of the Republic. National attention was usually absorbed by such compelling developments as President Johnson's struggle with the Radical Republican Congress and the agonies of reconstruction; possibilities of involvement with France over the Mexican question; financial panics and massive labor violence, and the growing pains of a wildly expanding economy. Only the most sensational Indian campaigns received much notice in the older, more settled sections of the nation.

Fairly quiet when the Civil War began, Indian warfare re-emerged in August, 1862, when the Santee Sioux broke out violently in Minnesota. The Santees were finally driven west into Dakota Territory, where their western Sioux kinsmen took up their cause. Troops sent against the Sioux in 1863-64 campaigned deep into Dakota Territory, removing the Indian threat to the border settlements, but leaving all the Sioux ready for large-scale warfare, where before only the eastern Sioux had been serious enemies. By 1865, Sioux, Cheyenne, and Arapaho war parties scourged through most of Dakota Territory, much of Nebraska, Kansas, eastern Colorado, and what is now Wyoming.

On the southern plains the Cheyennes, Arapahos, Comanches, and Kiowas fought Union and Confederate troops alike during the Civil War. Desiring at least an interval of peace in 1864, the Southern Cheyennes negotiated for terms and went into winter camp on Sand Creek, near Fort Lyon in southeastern Colorado. Infuriated, vengeful Colorado volunteer troops tried to exterminate Black Kettle's Southern Cheyennes at their Sand Creek camp November 29, 1864. Already burning brightly, Chivington's Colorado Volunteers had turned the flame of plains warfare into a searing blast, as news of the Sand Creek tragedy spread to the Northern Cheyennes and the Sioux. Indian retaliation was not slow. Raids occurred with ever increasing devastation and frequency. In February, 1865, a combined Sioux, Southern Cheyenne, and Arapaho war party captured, sacked, and burned the settlement of Julesburg in northeastern Colorado.

The Apaches and Navahos of the southwestern deserts and mountains had also been at war with the whites from 1861 to 1864. Kit Carson, leading Union troops as a colonel of Volunteers, quelled the Mescalero Apaches of southern New Mexico, and forced the Navahos to surrender at Canyon de Chelly, Arizona, January 6, 1864. The Navahos were fairly quiet thereafter, but the flame of Apache warfare remained to blight Arizona and New Mexico for another two decades.

Regular Army units were to be sent west after the Civil War and were to find themselves faced with powerful aggregations of hostile tribesmen from the Canadian boundary to the Mexican border and from central Kansas and Nebraska west to and beyond the Rocky Mountains. Government agents would attempt to secure treaties with the hostiles, so that hordes of restless, westering immigrants and gold seekers could settle in and pass through what was still Indian country. The chronology from the moment of the Great Peace to the final settlement of the western frontier was to be long drawn out.

In 1865 a meaningless, scrap-of-paper treaty was negotiated with a few Sioux to obtain white passage and occupation of the Bozeman Trail, from the Overland Trail in central Wyoming northwest through southern Montana to the gold fields of western Montana. Red Cloud's Sioux and their allies relentlessly harried the Bozeman Road and the forts that guarded it from 1866 through most of 1868. Peace treaty commissioners finally assented to Red Cloud's demands and agreed to withdraw the troops garrisoning Forts Phil Kearny and C. F. Smith, abandoning the trail to the Sioux and Cheyennes in the Fort Laramie Treaty of 1868. This treaty, like so many others, bore within it the seeds of later conflicts. Only about one-half of the Sioux agreed to live on the treaty-stipulated reservation, in the western half of what is now South Dakota. The non-treaty Sioux, led by such warriors as Sitting Bull, remained out as free rovers through northern Wyoming, eastern Montana, and the northwestern section of Dakota Territory.

Government peace commissioners met with the southern plains tribes at Medicine Lodge, Kansas, in October, 1867. The assembled Comanches, Kiowas, Arapahos and Cheyennes half-heartedly agreed to live on reservations in what is now western Oklahoma, but many of them took the warpath as soon as the council ended. The Southern Cheyennes raided throughout western Kansas and eastern Colorado in 1867 and most of 1868. In September, 1868, Colonel George A. Forsyth and his specially recruited scouts fought the Battle of Beecher's Island, on the Arickaree Fork of the Republican River, near the Colorado-Kansas border, against Roman Nose's Cheyenne hostiles. Roman Nose fell in the Indians' attempt to overrun the defenders' position on a low-lying sand island in the shallow river. His vaunted bullet-proof medicine had been broken when one of its taboos was violated.

The Southern Cheyennes were dealt another body blow in the late fall of 1868. Lieutenant Colonel George A. Custer smashed the winter camp of Black Kettle's band on the Washita River, in northwestern Oklahoma, in the snowy dawn of November 27. Subsequently, many Cheyennes and Arapahos came in to receive food and live on their reservation during the winter of 1868-69. Major Eugene A. Carr's Fifth Cavalrymen and Indian scouts delivered the final blow to the Cheyennes on July 11, 1869, when the implacable Dog Soldier band was defeated at Summit Springs, Colorado, and their chief Tall Bull numbered among the killed.

Taking office in 1869, President Grant listened to the pleadings of eastern reformers and church groups who were sincerely interested in the welfare of the western tribes. For them, the white man's burden was the responsibility of civilizing the wild tribes through kindness, peaceful persuasion, and education. Unfortunately, the powerful plains Indians looked on warfare as the natural condition of their kind, and they tended to view the efforts of the peace policy advocates as evidences of weakness on the part of the whites. Quaker Laurie Tatum, shepherd to the truculent Kiowas in southwestern Oklahoma, refused to admit that his charges were raiding into Texas and devastating white ranches and settlements until the Kiowas flagrantly boasted of their annihilation of a wagon train near Jacksboro, Texas, in May, 1871. General William Tecumseh Sherman, traveling nearby en route to inspect Fort Sill, Oklahoma, learned all the particulars, and later ordered the arrest of Satanta, Big Tree, and Satank, the Kiowa ringleaders. Agent Tatum, disillusioned and greatly saddened, resigned his commission, and the Kiowas and Comanches came under much closer military surveillance.

In November, 1872, the scene of Indian warfare shifted to the California-Oregon boundary region, when the Modoc uprising broke out and quickly assumed the proportions of a major campaign. The army was compelled to concentrate regiments of regulars and some citizen volunteer units in order to drive the

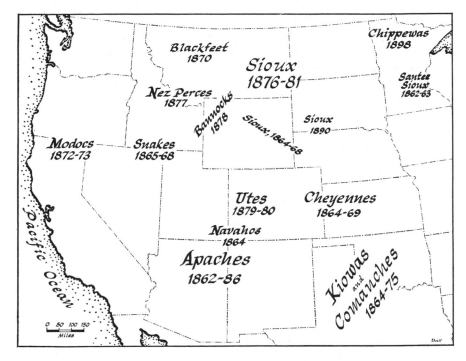

THE INDIAN WARS, 1862–98

9

tenacious Modocs from their stronghold in the lava beds of northern California. National attention was focused on the treacherous murder of General E. R. S. Canby, in April, 1873. Canby had arranged a parley with the Modoc leaders under a flag of truce. When the meeting began, Captain Jack and his hostile lieutenants killed the General in cold blood. Troops and artillery finally dislodged the Modocs, and those guilty of Canby's death were executed.

By the early 1870's white commercial buffalo hunters had made great slashing inroads in the vast herds of the southern plains. On June 27, 1874, a base camp of white hunters at Adobe Walls, Texas, was attacked by a large war party of Cheyenne, Kiowa, and Comanche warriors. Fortunately for the hunters, they happened to be awake when the Indians attempted to surprise them at dawn, and they were able to beat off the assault. In August, 1874, restless Kiowa and Comanche bands broke away from their agency at Anadarko, Oklahoma, and headed for the Staked Plains of the Texas Panhandle. Colonel Nelson A. Miles's column intercepted some of the runaways and their Cheyenne friends in the Antelope Hills of western Oklahoma on August 30, dealing them a heavy blow before most of the Indians were able to make their escape.

The high point of the Kiowa-Comanche Red River War of 1874–75 came when General Ranald Mackenzie found the hostiles' winter camp hidden in the Palo Duro Canyon, south of modern Amarillo, Texas, early in the morning of September 27, 1874. The Indians' village was destroyed, and though only a few were killed in the attack, all their supplies were lost. Most of the Comanches and Kiowas came in and surrendered during the winter of 1874–75. By the end of 1875, the once powerful Comanches had surrendered completely.

With Indian affairs beginning to stabilize on the southern plains by the beginning of 1876, trouble with the Sioux and Cheyennes of the north country again began to assume major proportions. Conflict on the plains reached its peak in the Sioux

War of 1876–81. The Laramie Treaty of 1868 had guaranteed the western half of modern South Dakota as a perpetual reservation for the Sioux. The Black Hills, sacred to the Sioux and Cheyennes and the best hunting country in the region, were part of the reservation. Discovery of rich gold deposits in the Black Hills, by the 1874 Custer expedition, had started a stampede of whites to the new Dakota Golconda, regardless of government attempts to keep the Black Hills inviolate for the Indians. Sitting Bull and his hostiles, who had never concurred in the reservation idea in any case, drew hundreds of recruits to their camps when the reservation Sioux began to leave their agencies in 1875. By the end of that year, the Indian Bureau admitted it had lost control of the situation, and the army was called in to compel all the Sioux and Cheyennes, treaty and nontreaty alike, to turn themselves in at a reservation agency by January 31, 1876.

Winter weather may have kept some peacefully inclined bands from moving toward the reservation, but the vast majority of Sioux and Cheyennes had no intention of bowing to the ultimatum. Columns were sent against them from Fort Fetterman in south-central Wyoming; from Fort Lincoln near Bismarck, Dakota Territory, and from posts in western Montana. Inconclusive actions were fought between General Crook's Wyoming column and the hostiles on March 17 and June 17. On June 25, Custer launched his winner-take-all attack on the combined Sioux and Cheyenne camp at the Little Bighorn. The dashing, newspaper-popular Custer and almost half his Seventh Cavalry Regiment were wiped out by a force of at least twenty-five hundred hostiles. The remnants of the Seventh Cavalry, who had desperately defended themselves five miles from the site of Custer's annihilation, were rescued from a like fate by General Terry's column on June 27. A few days later telegraph wires hummed the message of disaster to a nation whose attention was focused on the spectacular Centennial Exposition in Philadelphia. One hundred years of proud, expansive nationhood was rung in by the shock of disaster on the northern plains.

The Little Bighorn was the beginning of the end for the Sioux and Northern Cheyennes. By the spring of 1877 most of the once powerful bands were harried back to the reservations or defeated in a series of sharp campaigns. Sitting Bull crossed into Canada, where he remained as a threat to the Montana and Dakota border areas until July, 1881, when he finally surrendered at Fort Buford, Dakota Territory.

Sioux war parties were still a very real menace in eastern Montana when the Nez Percé War broke out in the spring of 1877. Refusing removal to a reservation they had not all agreed upon, feeling the press of white settlement in their eastern Idaho valley, the hitherto peaceful Nez Percé were characterized by mounting tension. Some excited warriors killed a few white settlers, and the agony of the Nez Percés began. General O. O. Howard's troops fought indecisive actions with them but failed to halt the Nez Percés' retreat eastward, over the Lolo Trail, into Montana. Colonel John Gibbon's hastily organized column intercepted the Indians in camp on the Big Hole River, August 9, on the western edge of Montana, but could not hold the determined Indians. Looping first southward through Yellowstone Park, then northeast, Chief Joseph led his people across the Yellowstone and Missouri Rivers, halting about one day's march from the Canadian border. Miles's mounted Fifth Infantrymen and companies of the Seventh Cavalry surprised the Nez Percé camp September 30. After a five-day siege, including light artillery shelling of the hostile position, the shattered tribesmen capitulated on October 5. Joseph's surrender speech remains a classic of Indian oratory and pathos.

A year after the Nez Percé War, the Bannocks of Idaho attempted to succeed where the Nez Percés had failed. Troops pursued the runaways through rugged, tortuous mountains and defeated them in a fight on the Clark's Fork River in southwestern Montana, September 4, 1878; the Bannocks then gradually returned to their reservation. September, 1878, also witnessed the start of the Northern Cheyennes' break from their prison reserve in Oklahoma. Removed to the southern Indian Territory after surrendering during the 1876–77 Sioux and Cheyenne campaigns, the Northern Cheyennes were starving and dying of disease in Oklahoma. Determined to return to their eastern Montana homeland, most of them left their reservation and marched north, through Kansas and Nebraska and into Dakota and Wyoming. Struck repeatedly by troops and citizens, only a tragic handful lived through the epic ordeal. Many of the Cheyennes now living on the Tongue River Reservation in southeastern Montana are descendents of those who survived the winter trek of 1878–79.

Barely had Cheyenne matters been settled when smoldering friction between Colorado citizens and the Ute Indians burst into a major frontier war on the obstinacy of Agent Nathaniel Meeker. The agent was killed by his charges shortly after he sent for troops to quell the turbulent Indians. Major T. T. Thornburgh's command was ambushed by the fierce Utes a few miles before reaching the agency. Pinned down and surrounded, outnumbered, their leader killed, the Third and Fifth Cavalry held their position until relief troops compelled the Utes to withdraw. Mediation by peaceful Ute leaders finally ended the uprising, and the Colorado frontier was cleared of potentially dangerous Indians.

In the mountains and deserts of the Southwest the fiercely tenacious Apaches had kept the region alternately smoldering and aflame since the early 1860's. Apache hostilities were almost constant until the late 1880's. In some years raiding was more intense than in others, but the difference was mainly one of degree, for some faction of the Apaches was almost always at war with the whites. By the end of the 1860's, the Arizona Apaches were fairly quiet. This short interlude ended when a posse of vengeful citizens annihilated a peaceful Apache village near Camp Grant, Arizona, April 30, 1870. Some Indians had raided white settlers, but the aroused civilian possemen retaliated on the wrong band. The result was another general flareup of hostilities and a series of army campaigns against the Apaches.

Cochise was finally persuaded to stop fighting and accept reservation life in 1871. During the following year General George Crook's troops hounded other elusive Apaches through the wilds of Arizona's Tonto Basin country. On December 27, 1872, Captain W. H. Brown, leading two companies of the Fifth Cavalry and thirty Apache scouts, struck the Apaches the single most crushing blow they received during their long struggle with the army. Brought to bay in a Salt River Canyon cave, the hostiles fought a furious pitched battle with their pursuers. Only a handful surrendered; seventy-six were killed before the survivors gave up. The Apache country quieted down again after peace was made at Camp Verde, Arizona, April 6, 1873, and Crook was promoted to the Regular Army rank of brigadier general for his achievement. Crook was shifted north in 1875, on the eve of the Sioux and Cheyenne outbreak.

Apache raiding began to increase early in 1876, and by 1879 had become a full-scale border war. Victorio's Mimbreño Apaches were not quieted for another two years. Mexican troops killed Victorio, but old Nana led the surviving hostiles to a linkup with Geronimo in the Sierra Madre Mountains.

In 1881 the attempted military arrest of a troublesome Apache medicine man at Cibicue Creek, Arizona, erupted into a hard-fought action in which a detachment of the army's Apache scouts mutinied and went over to the hostiles. For three more years the Geronimo band terrorized the region, until the recalcitrant Apaches finally agreed to settle on a reservation near Fort Apache, Arizona. An uneasy quiet settled along the Arizona frontier until the façade of peace was shattered in May, 1885. Geronimo and his band of renegades left the reservation and raided all summer. In March, 1886, Geronimo seemed ready to surrender, but negotiations broke off and the hostiles were again on the loose. General Nelson A. Miles assumed command of troops operating against the Apaches in April, 1886. Finally, on the fourth day of September, 1886, Geronimo laid down his arms for the last time.

By the middle eighties, virtually all the erstwhile hostile tribes, as well as those who had stood as allies of the whites, had been confined to specific reservations. Troops were stationed on and near the reservations to overawe the restless Indians and prevent further outbreaks. With the buffalo gone, the Indians became totally dependent on the government and its Indian agents for nearly all their subsistence. New ways, such as farming, were entirely foreign to the but recently unfettered hunters and raiders of the West. Indian culture had been geared to hunting and warfare. Commercial extermination of the buffalo had destroyed the hunting culture, and the government enforced the *pax Americana*, putting an end to ancient intertribal warfare as well as to raids on white settlements. At best, the early reservation period of the eighties was a time of sore trial for the western Indians. Dishonest or incompetent agents, arbitrary regulation of their every move, the steady shrinkage of their lands, and unwise policies aimed at speedily "civilizing" them drove many Indians to desperation.

A minor outbreak occurred on the Crow reservation in the fall of 1887. Agent Henry E. Williamson had needlessly antagonized and alienated the Crows in a series of hasty and ill-advised attempts to force their obedience to his orders. Trouble erupted when Williamson ordered the arrest of Wraps-Up-His-Tail and his followers as a result of their successful horse-stealing raid against the ancient Blackfoot enemy. Wraps-Up-His-Tail, or Sword Bearer, was both feared and respected by the Crows, who were convinced of his mastery of awesome medicine powers. The obstreperous element among the Crows shot up the agency as an act of defiance. The agent panicked and sent for troops to protect the agency and arrest the insurgents. On November 5, 1887, General T. H. Ruger delivered an ultimatum to the Crows demanding the immediate surrender of the troublemakers. When the Crows did not produce them, Ruger ordered his First Cavalry to advance on the village, about one mile from Crow Agency, Montana. Most of the Crows fled to a range of bluffs on the east bank of the Little Bighorn, but Wraps-Up-His-Tail and his handful of hotheaded young men opened fire on the soldiers. One trooper was killed in the skirmish. The rebels soon broke when their leader's bulletproof medicine failed to protect them. A Crow policeman shot Wraps-Up-His-Tail in cold blood, after berating him for having caused so much trouble for his people. A few months later the much-hated Williamson was replaced by a better agent, and the essentially peaceful Crows settled down to reservation life.

Starving on their reservations in South Dakota, the western Sioux grew desperate by the end of the eighties. Word of the coming of an Indian messiah who would right all wrongs and restore the old way of life was eagerly accepted by most of them. Dance was the word; dance back the buffalo and ghosts of the departed. In 1889 and 1890 the Sioux country was swept with the ghost-dance craze. Sensational rumors of impending outbreaks frightened citizens and nervous Indian Bureau officials into demanding the protection of troops. Old Sitting Bull was killed December 15, 1890, when his followers tried to prevent his arrest by Indian policemen, and many Sioux stampeded from their agencies fearing that the army had come to exterminate them. Big Foot's runaway band was apprehended north of Pine Ridge Agency the afternoon of December 28, 1890, and escorted to a campsite on Wounded Knee Creek. The next morning, when the Seventh Cavalry began to carry out its orders to disarm the Indians, a shot was fired in the Sioux camp. Soldiers and Indians went down in swaths as gunfire reached its climax, punctuated by the boom of light artillery. The Indians soon ran for the shelter of nearby ravines, closely pursued by soldiers, and by the afternoon of December 29, 1890 the tragedy at Wounded Knee was over. Regular soldiers would police the Indian country for several years to come, chasing isolated Indian outlaws and serving as occupation troops, but never again would they meet the western Indians in a major action.

2.

Enlistment in the Regular Army

ALL OF THE ENLISTED MEN of the Indian Wars army were volunteers. Each of them, for varying reasons, had seen fit to "take on" of his own free will. Few were educated, many were illiterates, and they have left little behind them in the way of memoirs and recollections. Old War Department records in the National Archives furnish only skeletal information about the enlisted men— that the average age of recruits was twenty-three for first enlistments and thirty-two for re-enlistments. Other sets of figures and statistics are available, but they reflect little of the lives of the men themselves.

In the years from 1865 through the 1890's many recruits were recent immigrants. So many Irishmen were included in the ranks of the Regular Army that General Charles King, the most popular contemporary writer on the subject, repeatedly used the old-line Irish soldier as a stock character. The immigrant recruits came chiefly from Ireland, Germany, or England, with Canada, Scotland, France, and Switzerland furnishing most of the others. Cosmopolitan as the army was, statistics reveal that over one-half of all recruits were native born.

The rank and file of the frontier Regular Army were men of widely diverse backgrounds. Writing of a wagon escort commanded by him in December, 1865, General George A. Forsyth noted that in it were ". . . a bookkeeper, a farm boy, a dentist, and a blacksmith, a young man of position trying to gain a commission and a salesman ruined by drink, an ivory carver and a Bowery tough . . . ."[1]

A large percentage of recruits entered the army from the bottom of the economic ladder, or had fallen from an intermediate rung. As correspondent for *Harper's Weekly* in 1886, Frederic Remington summed up the background of Jack Hayward, one of Miles's Apache chasers, by saying he was "a tall young fellow, born in Connecticut, became bankrupt in New York; did not know what else to do, so he enlisted."[2]

Many of the immigrant recruits had seen service in European armies. For these men, enlistment in the Regular Army offered a familiar haven in a strange country. A Danish immigrant of the early seventies had fought in the Prusso-Danish War of 1864, enlisted in the French army during the Franco-Prussian War, and had been in the French Foreign Legion in North Africa. Landing in New York in the midst of the 1873 Panic, he found no work available, ". . . it was either the soup house, starve, or the recruiting depot." Other immigrant recruits had campaigned with the British forces in India and Africa. A number of Germans who had been conscripts in the spartan Prussian service enlisted in the Regular Army shortly after arriving in the United States. Many recruits enlisted because they found that jobs were scarce

[1] *The Story of the Soldier*, I, 91.
[2] "Our Soldiers in the Southwest," *Harper's Weekly*, Vol. XXX, No. 1548 (1886), 535.

THE WAGON BOX FIGHT

August 2, 1867, near Fort Phil Kearny, Wyoming. Fewer than forty soldiers and wood cutters defended their makeshift position against the onslaughts of at least fifteen hundred Sioux warriors.

Diorama, Jefferson National Expansion Memorial
St. Louis, U.S. Park Service

FORT C. F. SMITH
Montana Territory, 1867. From a sketch by Captain I. D'Isay,
after drawing by Anton Schonborn.

Courtesy General R. J. Burt

for newcomers, and others joined because the five years enabled them to learn English and the ways of a new country.

Financial dislocations, strikes, and the general economic growing pains of the times produced numbers of jobless workers, many of whom became hobos. It was natural that some of these vagabonds should enlist in the Regular Army. Wandering through the midwest, on the eastern edge of the frontier, and in areas of troop concentration, the homeless wanderer was likely to contrast his own condition with that of the soldiers. Laborers, and workers temporarily unemployed, who had nevertheless not taken to the open road, constituted another large segment of recruits. Some sought to escape the tedium and boredom of their occupations, to enlist and get away from it all. Oddly enough, economic opportunity was sometimes the spur to enlistment. An 1886 enlistee, from Washington, D. C., stated that he had joined up because he was "tired of working sixteen hours a day for 50¢ a day." First Cavalryman William Hustede said that he "was working in a grocery store for $2.00 per week—the army paid $13.00 per month." In an era when minimum-wage laws, collective bargaining, the eight-hour day, and unemployment compensation were still years in the future, it is not surprising that unskilled laborers always formed the largest, single, occupational group among recruits.

After holding a variety of odd jobs, Sergeant Samuel Harris, a young Negro from Washington, D. C., enlisted in 1880, so that he could see the West, come home after honorable service, and secure government employment. This man had observed that veterans and men of the Grand Army of the Republic received preference when they applied for a government position.

Every year a significant group of Indian Wars recruits were the romantic young boys, many under the legal age of twenty-one. They were well acquainted with lurid tales of western adventure and army stories, or were fascinated by glimpses of soldiers in natty blue uniforms. Some of these youths had received better-than-average educations prior to joining the army.

Many veterans of the Union and Confederate forces joined the Regular Army after the Civil War. Four years of military and civil upheaval had left large numbers of rootless, restless men in their wake. For many, the army was the only life they had known since leaving home. For some ex-Rebels, there were no homes to return to. The Union veterans who signed up in the Regular Army, after the volunteer forces were mustered out, formed the backbone of the noncommissioned ranks for twenty years after 1865. Not a few of the former Confederates who entered the ranks of the postwar regulars had held commissions in the Southern army. Recalling his 1868 orderly, an officer of the Seventh Cavalry wrote that "this private . . . was a Major of Artillery in the Confederate Army, and born and raised a few miles from my native town, Petersburg, Va. Of course, he was under an assumed name in the U.S. Army."[3]

For many reasons, the Indian Wars army attracted a goodly number of petty criminals and other undesirable, shady characters into its ranks. Writing of his enlistment, a former Thirteenth Infantryman of the 1880's declared that he was certain that ". . . some of the [fifteen] recruits [I joined with] had no doubt served in some penitentiary before enlisting, and I shouldn't wonder that some went back to their old prisons as a haven of rest and decent treatment . . . ."[4] All but two of the original group of sixteen recruits deserted before their five-year enlistments were completed.

The ease with which Civil War bounty jumpers deserted may have established a pattern for the continuance of the desertion problem all through the Indian Wars period. The army was aware of the fact that deserters frequently re-enlisted, and that many former servicemen applying at recruiting offices had been

[3] Brigadier General F. W. Benteen to Theodore Goldin, MS, Feb. 17, 1896, Benteen-Goldin Letters.

[4] Private C. C. Chrisman, Thirteenth Infantry, to General E. S. Godfrey, MS, Nov. 4, 1917, Bates Collection.

discharged under other than honorable conditions. Lacking photograph and fingerprint records, recruiters were often unable to detect undesirable former servicemen. So vexing was this problem that it was seriously suggested in 1876 that all honorably discharged soldiers should be tattooed at the time of separation, to eliminate the problem of re-enlisting ". . . drunkards, obscene fellows, worthless men and deserters . . . ."[5] Years after leaving the army, Charles Kolarik, a former First Cavalry sergeant, said that he had ". . . met many [men] in civil life who deserted, re-enlisted under assumed names and again deserted."

In almost the same category as the chronic deserters and other undesirables were men of shiftless character. Some were derelicts, enlisted by overanxious recruiters. Other poor prospects for shaping into soldiers were men such as the druggist and the preacher's son who enlisted together while suffering from remorse after an extended drunk in Kansas City.

Since the beginning of national standing armies, voluntary enlistees have entered their ranks for a wide variety of reasons. Militarism was not a dominant national ideal in the United States from 1865 through the 1890's, and thus identification with such an ideal was conspicuously lacking as a motive for joining the Regular Army. There was no national conscription to compel service, and rank-and-file army life attracted few who possessed any firsthand knowledge of it as a way of life. Nevertheless, many types of men did enlist, volunteering for a three- or five-year term of service, at a base pay of thirteen dollars a month.

At any of the late nineteenth-century recruit depots one would have found a ragtag assortment of recent arrivals: a mechanic or factory worker tired of dull routine, a farmer with a hankering for frontier life, a restless student tired of his books, a bankrupt businessman, a few shiftless drifters, and some emigrants who could not find work. Many had only the haziest reasons for joining the army. When the deserter inmates of Fort Leavenworth

[5] General J. C. Kelton, Feb. 15, 1876, cited in *The Reorganization of the Army,* 44 Cong., 1 sess., *House Report No. 354,* 133.

Military Prison were asked why they had enlisted, the majority gave no reason except that they had wanted to be soldiers.[6] Some said that they had been out of work, on the verge of alcoholism, wanted a change of climate, were in need of money, had been in some sort of trouble, wanted to go West, or had been influenced by friends. Most enlistments probably resulted from a combination of these and other reasons.

Recruiting offices were maintained in most cities and in many moderate-sized towns. What was more natural for a jobless young worker than to consider enlistment seriously when approached by a recruiting service soldier? After all, as James Maher, an 1889 recruit, remarked, "It was a living." Frequently, after repeated failures to secure employment, the jobless sought out the recruiters of their own volition, considerably easing the recruiting officer's assignment. Statements by men who enlisted in the Regular Army from 1865 through the 1890's indicate that the unemployed constituted about one-half of all Indian Wars recruits. This contributed to the prevalence of high desertion rates. "When things picked up and jobs were available, army life no longer appealed," explained Private Charles Goodenberger.

In addition to those who joined at established recruiting offices, many men were signed up by roving recruiting details sent out by individual regiments. This method of direct recruiting was widely advocated, because men from the smaller towns and rural communities were believed to make the best soldiers. Perhaps rural youths wre more readily impressed by the sight of gilt-buttoned blue uniforms, especially when they observed the effect these uniforms had on the local belles. Life on a late nineteenth-century family farm was often one of unremitting toil for the farmer's sons, and army life offered the prospect of a glamorous change.

There were many handicaps to regular army recruiting during the Indian Wars era. There was, however, one attraction to offer

[6] *Ann. Report, Sec. of War, 1891,* I, 92.

recruits that has not existed since the Spanish-American War—the lure of the frontier West. Many of the younger, more ambitious new men enlisted as a means of satisfying the urge to move west. The nation was being spanned by rails of steel, as the Union Pacific inched across remote expanses. Thousands were taking up homesteads on the prairies, on lands described as the richest in the world. Long trains of range cattle funneled into the mushrooming meat-packing centers, accompanied by swaggering cowboys hell-bent on a good time. Hordes of eager rainbow seekers flooded into the Black Hills and other gold and silver Eldorados. Back east conditions became increasingly stable for farmers and workers. New towns, counties, and states were being carved out of the nation's last and richest frontiers, and many young men enlisted to go west and be a part of what was traditionally the great American experience. At no other time was life on the frontier so romantically and glowingly publicized as during the seventies and eighties. Sombreroed frontier heroes in buckskin were household words: Buffalo Bill, Wild Bill Hickok, Custer, and a host of others. Dime novels proclaimed the wildness and richness of frontier adventure. Adventure, a lure, real or imaginary, that has motivated men since the beginning of time, was one of the chief inducements to enlistment in the Indian Wars army. Few of these adventurous neophytes had any idea of the realities of enlisted service on the frontier, and most of them soon found that their romantic dreams of travel and swashbuckling adventure quickly evaporated in the stern and austere circumstances of western soldiering.

During major campaigns and outbreaks, many recruits were motivated by a desire to get into the fighting. Following the Little Bighorn disaster, the company limit for cavalry was raised by congressional action. The men recruited to fill the expanded, hundred-man companies were designated as "Custer Avengers," and for a brief period enjoyed the same solicitous attentions from civilians that Union volunteers received during the Civil War years.

Enlistment in the military has always been, for some, a way to escape from the responsibilities of everyday living. The Indian Wars army had its share of such men.

A common reason for joining the army was personal trouble at home, but obviously this motive is impossible to estimate accurately. As First Sergeant George Neihaus put it, "Many joined the army because of some misdemeanors at home. Some were good and some were bad, and some were very bad." Perhaps there had been trouble with a girl, or a judge had offered the neighborhood bad boy the choice of jail or the army. Occasionally, an otherwise average man enlisted as an opportunity to "straighten up . . ." from a too liberal fondness for liquor. An 1888 enlistee, who attained the rank of sergeant, said that he ". . . needed the discipline." A Tenth Infantry Sergeant gave his reason for joining the army in 1884 as having been that he had no real home and ". . . many of my crowd were getting into trouble, I wanted to avoid that."

After the close of the Civil War, many youths who had been too young to enlist during the war sought to emulate their Grand Army of the Republic relatives by joining the Regular Army. The Civil War was the climactic life experience for thousands of veterans, and the war stories related by them profoundly influenced some of their young listeners. An enlistee of 1873, Jacob Adams explained, ". . . I fairly ached to get into some action like that I had heard veterans of the Civil War talk about."[7] Many of the boys who enlisted for this reason were later sadly disillusioned. Writing of his enlistment, sixty years afterward, an Indian Wars deserter explained his case:

> I was a boy during the Civil War, there was a army camp near and I guess I soked in some of the game, for later, every time I got Spiflicated I wanted to enlist . . . [I] . . . thought it would be

[7] G. R. McCormack, "Man Who Fought With Custer [Jacob Adams]," *National Republic,* Vol. XXI, No. 11 (1934), 14.

like the volunteers during the Civil War . . . but I found out the mistake. The Regular Army was a tough bunch in those days.[8]

For what must have been a small minority of Indian Wars soldiers, enlistment was chosen as a means of acquiring the rudiments of an education. In one case, an intelligent laborer, thrown out of work by the Panic of 1873, was acutely aware of his lack of learning. He joined the army to learn the fundamentals of mathematics, reading, and writing, and enlarged his vocabulary by studying a small pocket dictionary he carried with him on campaigns. In another instance, Sergeant Theodore E. Guy, a bright but illiterate Polish boy, entered the army in 1889 because he wanted to become a lawyer, but first needed to learn to read and write English.

Many of the younger soldiers joined up simply because they wanted to be soldiers. Military life appeals especially to the young. As one twenty-two-year-old recruit of 1876 phrased it, "I had always had the army fever." Most of those who enlisted for this reason found that the fever ran its course long before the first enlistment was completed. A few, however, remained as career regulars, and served for periods in excess of thirty years. Some recruits had previous military experience in Europe, the state militias, or perhaps the volunteer Civil War regiments. Having acquired a taste for military life, they enlisted in the Regular Army.

For a decade after the Civil War, many regular recruits had served in either the Union or Confederate armies. After the middle seventies, the proportion of Civil War veterans decreased sharply, but down through the nineties almost every company contained one or two long-service veterans who had begun their military careers during the Rebellion.

[8] Anonymous letter to E. A. Brininstool, MS, June, 1935, Fred Dustin Collection No. 316. The letter writer stated that he had deserted from the army after General Crook's "starvation march" pursuit of Sioux hostiles in the fall of 1876, and therefore could not sign his name.

The influences favoring enlistment thus far mentioned were countered, however, by many negative factors, not the least of which was the prevailing public opinion of the rank and file of the Regular Army. Even during the Civil War, civilians had little regard for the regulars. Regular regiments had no political places of origin, no roots connecting them to specific locations, as did the state troops mustered in during the war. When the war ended, and the volunteer and state regiments were disbanded, many people felt that the regulars who remained in service were shiftless men who could not succeed in the competition of civil life. Civilians were likely to be scornful of the regular army soldier. Because of much well-intentioned but incompletely informed eastern publicity, regulars were often accused of carrying fire and sword to peaceful Indians. There was some truth in this view, but, ironically, one of the most shameful examples of military brutality was that perpetrated against the Southern Cheyennes at Sand Creek, Colorado, by Colorado Volunteers having no connection with the Regular Army. Many eastern newspapers were quick to play up any material that put the army in an unfavorable light in its relations with the western Indians.

Among much of the civil population, the judgment "too lazy to work" was commonly passed on those who chose to enlist in the Regulars, and the opinion was not an exclusively civilian one. Relaying an order from the post commander at Fort Meade, Dakota Territory, in 1887, the adjutant required each company commander to compile and forward a roster of his enlisted men showing for each man ". . . his occupation or trade, if he had any, prior to enlistment."[9]

Soldiers keenly resented such attitudes. They realized that "a great many civilians, badly informed . . . , had the very annoying habit of looking down on the regular soldier . . . ." Reporting back to his post upon completion of a regimental detail, one sergeant

[9] Post and Regimental Order Book, Fort Meade, D. T., Jan.–Nov., 1887, MS, Custer Battlefield National Monument Files.

stated that most people believed the recruits were confined to the fort and had no privileges or liberty. This bias against regular soldiers was strongest in the vicinity of the recruit depots at Columbus, Ohio, Jefferson Barracks, Missouri, and David's Island, New York. The heckling of recruits with such bits of doggerel as, "Soldier, soldier, will you work? No indeed, I'll sell my shirt," did little to foster amicable relations between civilians and the regulars.

In the West, civilian attitudes toward the soldiers were usually closely related to the proximity of hostilities or threatened outbreaks. Miles City, Montana, was a good example of this. Until the Sioux and Northern Cheyennes were confined to reservations, the merchants, saloonkeepers and other inhabitants of the town were almost totally dependent on the soldiers stationed across the Tongue River at Fort Keogh. When Miles City became a booming cow town in the eighties, soldiers fell rapidly in public estimation. Later, when the Ghost Dance craze swept the northern plains tribes in 1889 and 1890, and wholesale outbreaks seemed imminent, the regulars quickly became very much appreciated.[10]

Individuals who were in daily contact with the enlisted soldiers in the West expressed conflicting opinions on the qualities of the Indian Wars rank and file. A sutler's clerk at Fort Ellis, Montana Territory, found the enlisted men in 1871, "a rough sort altogether."[11] An officer's widow, whose first husband died with his men in the Fetterman debacle on December 21, 1866, wrote of the loyalty, devotion, and courage shown by the enlisted ranks, mostly recruits, at Fort Phil Kearny, and heartily sympa-

[10] Samuel Hotchkiss, Personal Interview, 1957. This man was a civilian teamster with troops sent from Ft. Keogh to the 1890 Sioux Campaign. He spent much time in and near the fort in the 1880's.

Harry Schlosher, Personal Interview, 1957. Schlosher was a market hunter and cowboy in the Miles City area from 1881 to about 1900.

[11] Peter Koch to "Laurie," from Ft. Ellis, Mont. Terr., MS, Jan. 31, 1871, Letters, No. 27.

thized with them.[12] Mentioning three Seventh Infantry privates in dispatches, a commanding general of the 1876 Sioux campaign said that he hoped the heroism shown by these men would ". . . establish in the public mind a higher and more just estimate of the character of the United States soldier."[13] Another officer, campaigning against the same Indians, showed his opinion of life in the ranks when he relayed his counsel to a young relative considering enlistment, by writing to his mother:

> If he is put off the [rail] road he must not think of enlisting [in] the regular army. He will regret such a move as long as he is in the ranks. I speak of what I know when I advise against such a move.[14]

Perhaps one of the best summations of the realities of life in the frontier Regular Army was offered by the wife of an officer in the Eighth Infantry. Writing of her own and her husband's years in the army, this wife totaled the sum of experiences and applied the old German phrase, "glittering misery," to life in the United States Regular Army.[15] Certainly this must have quickly become apparent to many of the boys and young men who had joined the ranks with heads full of dress uniforms, patriotic parades, and deeds of daring.

Some soldiers enlisted directly into active-duty units at army posts, but the majority experienced their first contact with the Regular Army at a recruiting office. Some entered the office with firm intentions of enlisting. The unemployed farm laborer who walked from northern Iowa to the recruiting office in Minneapolis certainly knew what he was about. The Indiana farm boy

[12] Frances C. Carrington, *My Army Life and the Fort Phil Kearney* [sic] *Massacre, passim.*

[13] General Field Orders No. 5, Dept. of Dakota, Camp at Mouth of Big Horn River, July 26, 1876, Record Group 94, National Archives.

[14] Captain Simon Snyder, Company F, Fifth Infantry, Tongue River, Montana Territory, to his mother, Feb. 5, 1877, MS, Snyder-Ronayne Collection. Hereafter cited as S-R Coll.

[15] Martha Summerhayes, *Vanished Arizona*, 71.

who was turned down as under age at sixteen and again at nineteen had long planned to join the army when he finally did so at twenty-one. Having only the vaguest notions of what life in the Regular Army was like, it is safe to assume that the 1876 enlistee who described his nervous reactions as ". . . a hot streak, a cold streak, and twenty-five or thirty other streaks all streaking it together . . ." voiced the feelings experienced by most of those who presented themselves as candidates for a first enlistment.

Recruiters often asked the candidates why they wanted to enlist. Those giving travel and adventure as their reasons were sometimes offered some straightforward, factual advice on life as a frontier soldier. Most of the time, recruiters were more than anxious to enlist any and all who applied, provided there were no obvious reasons for rejection. They were assigned the task of supplying new men for the army, and their honeyed words and glowing descriptions persuaded more than one casually interested young civilian. "See things as a soldier," and, "get a pension" (without an explanation that one had to serve thirty years in the ranks to be eligible), were common allurements. When few candidates applied, some recruiters were not above assisting underage recruits to falsify their ages.

Not all who applied for enlistment in the regulars were accepted, and especially was this true in times of economic depression. When hard times prevailed, recruiters were offered a much wider selection of candidates. Following the Panic of 1873, less than one out of five applicants was enlisted. Either the recruiters were exercising a considerable degree of selectivity, or the majority of candidates were very poor specimens indeed. The ratio of rejections to the number of those applying, however, remained fairly constant all through the Indian Wars period. Applicants who were obviously under the legal age made up a heavy proportion of those refused, but most rejections stemmed from some physical defect or evidence of disease. Eye diseases, size, character, and being over age were listed as the main reasons for rejection in 1891. In the same year, a rudimentary ability to read, write, and understand English was added to the list of recruit qualifications.

A fairly presentable, sober, and not obviously unfit candidate was required to furnish some basic information. He was told to state his name, age, occupation, and whether or not he had previously served in the armed forces of the United States. For various personal reasons, false answers were often given in reply to one or more of the recruiter's inquiries. Applicants under twenty-one lied about their years, and for the same reason enlisted under assumed names. Sometimes, a promising recruit, even though he was not of legal age, was knowingly signed up. Many recruits had reasons other than age for assuming an army name different from their own. Some served under false names because most civilians viewed enlistment in the Regular Army as socially degrading. Many of the ex-Confederates who enlisted in the Regulars after the Civil War used assumed names. Some company officers knew several of their men by both their real and army names. Some who joined the army under an alias had ample ulterior reason for doing so, as was occasionally demonstrated when a criminal or perhaps a cashiered officer turned up in the ranks. Undoubtedly the practice of enlisting under false names was quite common during the late nineteenth century, and accounted for many otherwise inexplicable disappearances. On this subject, in his 1876 diary, a sergeant of the Fourth Cavalry wrote, "Many a young man has enlisted in the army under an assumed name thinking he would keep it from his family, little thinking what he would have to face on the frontier . . . [many have died] and their whereabouts will forever remain a mystery to their parents."

The recruiter's question about previous service also frequently evoked a fraudulent reply, when a deserter or man who had not been honorably discharged sought to re-enlist. Some lied about previous service because they did not want to be assigned to their old outfits, or simply did not want their officers to know that they were old soldiers.

When he had supplied at least acceptable answers to the recruiter's questions, the applicant was next ordered to strip, bathe, and prepare himself for physical examination. Because there were many unfit applicants, recruiters were directed to be sure that,

> In passing a recruit the medical officer [or contract surgeon] . . . [should] examine him stripped; to see that he has free use of all limbs; that his chest is ample; that his hearing, vision, and speech are perfect . . . [and that he not have false teeth]; that he has no tumors, or ulcerated or extensively cicatrized legs, no rupture or chronic cuteaneous affection; that he has not received any contusion, or wound of the head, that may impair his faculties; that he is not a drunkard; is not subject to convulsions; and has no infectious disorders . . . [especially venereal], nor any other to unfit him for military duty.[16]

Each recruit was again examined upon arrival, from the recruit depot, at the post or regimental station. This second examination frequently revealed that the recruiters had been careless, because many of the new men were medically unfit for duty. In the spring of 1871, the post surgeon at Fort Laramie reported that,

> A considerable number of the recruits recently sent here are unfit for service, many of them being affected with incurable organic disease, for which some of them (under other names) have already been discharged from the army.[17]

Since many recruits were afflicted with such easily detectable disabilities as flat feet, it was obvious to the surgeon that they had not been carefully examined when they enlisted.

Applicants who passed the recruiter's interrogation and the

[16] *Rev. United States Army Regulations of 1861 and Articles of War, to June 25, 1863*, 313. These regulations remained standard until the extensive revisions of the 1880's.

[17] Medical History of Posts, Fort Laramie, 1868–79, MS, Record Group 94, Old Army Section, National Archives, 90.

physical examination were duly enrolled, and raised their right hands in the oath of allegiance. The neophytes were issued ill-fitting recruit clothing and sent to lounge with other recruits, awaiting transfer to a recruit depot, or were allowed to return home until ordered to report.[18] After a sufficient number of new men were enlisted, they were sent to a depot under the care of a recruiting-service enlisted man, who turned them over to the receiving office at one of the depots. Up to this time, the recruits had retained some tenuous connection with their former lives. Adjustment to life as a regular began in the course of a few weeks or months at the recruit depot, where the new soldier gradually began to understand the full meaning of the enlistment oath.

[18] *Ann. Report, Sec. of War, 1891,* I, 82. In the late 1880's, recruits were given a few days to consider the step before taking the oath of allegiance, to lessen the likelihood of desertion.

3.

The Recruit Depots
and Introduction to Army Life

DURING THE INDIAN WARS PERIOD, three major recruit depots were maintained as concentration points, from which active units were replenished as conditions required. Cavalry recruits were sent to the depot at Jefferson Barracks, Missouri. Infantry enlistees were posted to David's Island, New York, and Columbus Barracks, Ohio. Until the early seventies, Newport Barracks, Kentucky, also served in the capacity of assembly point for infantry replacements.

The depots were not originally intended to serve as training centers, and only toward the later years of the Indian campaigns were new men trained for periods of several months at the depots, prior to service in an operational unit. In the years immediately after the Civil War, recruits were trained after assignment to an active unit. The concept of using the depots as intensive training centers was slow to gain acceptance among conservative regular army men. During the seventies, a number of officers recommended retaining recruits at the depots for partial training before assigning them to a line company. At first, only a modest period of ". . . three or four weeks [was suggested], with a view to instruction in the first principles of drill and subordination."[1] It was not until 1890, however, that recruits were normally scheduled to remain at a depot for a minimum three-months training period.

Recruit-depot cadres were composed of officers detailed from line regiments, veteran noncommissioned men, and a sprinkling of re-enlisted privates. Most sergeants stationed at the depots were hardened old-timers. As late as 1884, all the sergeants at the Columbus Barracks depot were Civil War veterans. As might be expected, these hardboiled noncommissioned officers had little sympathy and abundant scorn for the recruits entrusted to them. Some noncommissioned personnel of the depot staff used their positions to swindle, cheat, terrorize, and otherwise mistreat the green recruits.

When the newcomer arrived with his draft at a depot, he was assigned to a recruit troop or company of instruction. Each instruction company was quartered in its own barrack room, where the recruit was allotted a particular bunk. Re-enlisted soldiers, arriving with inexperienced men from recruiting rendezvous, were often appointed temporary corporals and sergeants of the instruction units.

After assignment to a recruit company, the new soldiers had their first taste of army rations, received their issues of uniforms and basic equipment, and settled into their barracks. The depot was big, cold, and impersonal. Its staff of old-soldier noncommissioned men often took delight in embarrassing the neophytes, and recruits who had spent as much as a week in the army were likely to haze the newer soldiers as much as they dared.

For ten years after 1865 most of the articles included in the

---

[1] *Ann. Report, Sec. of War, 1876,* I, 72.

recruit's depot uniform issue were leftovers from the Civil War. Much of this matériel was of poor quality. The basic issue consisted of the navy-blue, wool sack coat with single row of brass-eagle buttons, two pairs of light-blue kersey trousers, two grey or dark-blue flannel shirts, a couple of suits of wrist- and ankle-length two-piece underwear, a caped overcoat of light-blue wool, a pair of rough boots or ankle-high brogans, a forage cap (or kepi), and a leather waist belt with some accouterments.

During the Indian Wars years modifications, additions, and deletions were made and the equipment and uniforms varied from time to time in kind and amount. After 1873, black, wool campaign hats were issued. Few recruits found that their first issue of army clothing fitted them well. Those with the money and the time had their uniforms tailored by the depot tailors. The rough boots and shoes usually rasied blisters when new, and the heavy underwear itched unmercifully in warm weather. Recruits were instructed in the care and maintenance of their uniforms, and ordered to change the woolen socks frequently. Underclothing had to be laundered once each week.[2] With all its imperfections and usual poor fit, the uniform was still an impressive outfit in the eyes of those who enlisted with a longing for adventure and the military life. More than a few must have shared the gratifying experience of an 1890 recruit, John R. Nixon, who stopped to look at himself in every glass and window.

Recruits found that some necessities were not included in their initial uniform issue, and had to purchase them out of the half-pay allowed recruits. To maintain uniforms and arms, the first need was for a cleaning kit, furnished, on credit, by the post sutler, a storekeeper franchised to operate a variety store at the depot. Because the cleaning kits were indispensable and there was only one source of supply, many recruits felt certain that they were grossly overcharged for the articles received, and that some of the depot sergeants and corporals had private

---

[2] N. Hershler, *The Soldier's Handbook*, 53.

Fort Assiniboine •   ✗ BEARS PAW
                          MTN. 1877
      Fort Benton •
      Fort Shaw •

Fort Walla Walla •   CLEARWATER
                      1877 ✗
                         Helena•
      WHITEBIRD CANYON ✗   Billings•
          1877 | BIG HOLE   CANYON✗
                    1877   CREEK 1877
                              Fort C.F. Smith•
                              HAYFIELD FIGHT 1867✗
                              WAGON BOX FIGHT✗
                                      1867
      •Fort Klamath   Fort Washakie•

      ✗ •Fort Bidwell
      LAVA BEDS
      1873   Corinne •
                              •Fort Bridger
      Salt Lake City• •Fort Douglas
                          MILK RIVER ✗
      • Carson   1879

      •Sacramento

San Francisco•

  P a c i f i c
                          Fort Defiance•   • Fort
              Wipple Barracks•   Wingate
                              ✗ BIG DRY
          O c e a n   Camp Verde•   WASH
                          CIBICUE   1882
                          1881 ✗
                      SALT RIVER ✗
                      1872   Fort Apache•
                              Fort Bayard•
              •Fort Yuma   Fort Grant
                          Tucson• •Wilcox
                              •Fort Bowie
                      Fort Huachuca

      0 50 100 150 200
      Miles

THE REGULARS' WEST, 1865–1890's

understandings with the sutler. A veteran 1889 enlistee, who did not publicize the fact that he had served two previous enlistments, wrote that the corporal who escorted his group to the sutler's store at Columbus Barracks must have been in league with the sutler, as he kept piling up excess items, all charged to the recruit's first pay. The veteran knew that the new soldiers were sold at least twice as much cleaning material as they would need. This is one example of the advantages that an unscrupulous noncommissioned officer exercised over recruits at the depots.

Until the early eighties, recruits were expected to learn their place and duties in the army by observation and instruction. Beginning in 1884, however, each man was issued a copy of *The Soldier's Handbook,* a pocket-sized, leather-bound volume containing a variety of information and advice. The *Handbook* also had a place for a list of each man's personal clothing record of items drawn, with the charges, and credits on his clothing allowance, and, in the back, a place for recording each year's target qualifying scores. Regulations and the Articles of War pertaining especially to enlisted men were included, as well as chapters on guard mounting, discipline, physical fitness, detached service, salutes, the care of public animals, the care of arms, post schools, extra-duty and regular pay, and advice on soldierly conduct. Thorough reading and comprehension of the *Handbook's* contents furnished the recruit with a basic knowledge of what the army expected of him during his enlistment, how to take care of himself, and what pitfalls he should avoid.

As transient recruits at the depots, new men did not yet belong to any permanent company or regiment. For that reason, their living conditions and comforts were not adequately supervised, either by officers or noncommissioned officers. The consequences of that neglect were especially evident in the preparation, quality, and quantity of the rations. The stipulated ration of the Indian Wars period was never sumptuous, and, without the self-interested experience of a shrewd old company mess sergeant and the post gardens of most regular establishments, the food at the depots was invariably the worst in the army.

The kitchen sergeant of a recruit company drew rations for his unit every ten days. Issues consisting of salt pork, dry beans, green coffee, brown sugar, Babbitt's soap, and flour were based on the number of men being rationed. The flour was exchanged at the post bakery for bread, on a pound-for-pound basis. Some type of fresh meat was issued twice a week. Rations were prepared by the cooks in the most convenient if not the most palatable manner. Second Cavalryman James B. Wilkinson said that

> At Jefferson Barracks [1882] pork meat was put around at tables the night before for the following morning's breakfast. The meat would be spoiled, turned green, by mornings. Some ate it—others did not, and reported it to the officers. Improvement was only temporary.

From time to time, someone, usually a newspaper editor, would demand an exposé of the food situation at the recruit depots. At Columbus Barracks in 1885, and three years later at Jefferson Barracks, investigations resulted in conviction of many of the noncommissioned staff of shirking duty and cheating on the administration of ration funds. Those convicted were reduced to the ranks and sent to their regiments. "There was quite a shakeup when the Columbus papers informed their readers that Uncle Sam feeds his soldiers on fried mush and sugar," said Philipp Schreiber.

Daily menus at the depots were unappetizing to say the least. Breakfast consisted of salt pork, fried mush, or thin stew that had cooked all night. Strong black coffee was served with every meal. Slumgullion stew was the usual dinner *pièce de résistance*, accompanied by dry bread. Supper most commonly was a meal of dry bread and coffee, with an occasional treat of three prunes. Cold corn bread, sopped with a gravy made exclusively of "hot water and flour," was another depot standby. Not only was the food poorly prepared, but it was almost always insufficient in quantity. One recruit remarked: "Once I went to the dining room after tattoo to steal a piece of bread and was caught. I was lucky not being sent to the guard house." An 1882 recruit wrote years later that

> There is little but nausea in that recollection of slum, dry bread, black coffee and· . . . grapes [stolen from a nearby vineyard]. . . . I was naive enough to believe there was no method of redress. . . . Possibly, it was deemed necessary preparation for what was in the offing—field service against the anti-social redskins.

Samuel Gilpin, a three-enlistment soldier, who had spent some time at Jefferson Barracks, Columbus Barracks, and David's Island, stated that the food served to recruits was equally bad at all three depots. He wrote that the main reason recruits eagerly anticipated their first pay day was because then they would have a little money with which to buy some decent food.

In the barrack room, the recruit found that, perhaps for the first time in his life, he had absolutely no privacy. His assigned living space contained only a bunk and a wooden foot locker. Virtually every moment was spent in the company of his fellows. The bunks were composed of an iron foot and headpiece joined by two stringers, with a series of wooden slats running between the stringers. His mattress was a cloth bedsack, which he was allowed to fill with twelve pounds of fresh straw, once a month. Sometimes the straw was not fresh, but rank hay from the stables. The day before muster, the recruits cleaned and scrubbed the entire barrack, filled their bedsacks with new straw, and even scrubbed the bed slats. In the middle eighties, the slats were replaced with a wire-mesh spring, and the enlisted men were issued thin cotton mattresses and small pillows instead of the straw ticks.

New soldiers were usually mustered for their first pay at the depots, but received only one-half the amount due, as the balance was retained until they joined an active unit. The sutler who had advanced credit on cleaning kits, and occasionally on other items, had first priority at the pay tables.

For several days after arrival, the fledgling soldiers spent their time receiving issues, settling into their barracks, and learning the basic military formations. During these first few days they became acquainted with one another, and found themselves to be an extremely diverse group of men. As always, persons of similar backgrounds and habits congregated together: the farm boys with other farm boys, the temperate with others of their inclinations, and the same with the city men and the sporting element. After a few days, recruits were allowed to walk about the grounds and areas adjacent to the depots. Some of those who had money patronized beer parlors and restaurants, and "there were some bawdy houses near Jefferson Barracks [and the other depots as well] that were patronized mainly by a small rowdy element [among the recruits]." These last were mostly toughs, commonly known in the army as "Bowery Boys."

Only a few days spent at the depots served to awaken the new soldiers to the fact that the easy-going, well-supplied Civil War camps of the state regiments bore no resemblance to the Regular Army's recruit depots—no local girls bringing baskets of food to the patriots, no ice-cream socials in their honor, no officers addressing many of their men by their first names: this was the Regular Army! The recruits quickly found themselves to be in a system far more rigid and austere than any environment most of them had previously known.

Because the depots were not originally intended to serve as training centers, many men, who spent from a few days to three months at the depots, received virtually no military training. Recruits were put to work in fatigue details and on construction projects as often as they were trained in military matters. Commenting on the lack of training at the Jefferson Barracks depot in 1885, Trumpeter Henry Schuldt explained that he was assigned to cook's police, or kitchen detail, as soon as he arrived at the depot. He was detailed to carry food to about fifty guard-house prisoners twice a day, and was allowed no time for drill and instruction.[3]

Like all army posts, the recruit depots observed rigidly organized schedules and routines. Here the neophyte had his first introduction to the daily routines of setting-up drill every morning, fatigue details, formal guard mounting, and all the numerous calls and formations that made up the day at a late nineteenth-century army post. Portions of the daily routine were sometimes found to be quite pleasant, as was the case of the morning ritual of three grains of quinine in an ounce of whisky at Newport Barracks in 1872. The army, of course, did not issue the liquor as an accommodation, but as a preventive of the malarial fevers that sometimes incapacitated recruits.

In the 1860's, newly enlisted men were sent from the depots to their regiments as soon as drafts were filled, with their training limited to a little close order drill, more to keep them occupied than as a training measure. Because few of the new men had any military experience, what instruction they did receive was calculated to teach them subordination, obedience, and their place in the army. One of the first lessons hammered into recruits was the respect and obedience due at all times to commissioned and noncommissioned officers. By disciplining recruits in close order drill, the depot noncommissioned personnel sought to instil in their charges the realization that they were now soldiers and part of a unit. A well-remembered depot sergeant, at Jefferson Barracks in 1882, drove home the fact that the recruits had entered a new life, and incidentally tried to raise their morale, by shouting at them as they drilled: " 'You've only two hours

[3] He wrote that although he received little training at Jefferson Barracks, he had a firsthand view of the disciplinary lengths to which the Indian Wars army was prepared to go. Schuldt stated that he had been detailed to carry food to guardhouse prisoners, and ". . . on the fifth morning they broke out, and the Guard killed three men and wounded 6 prisoners . . . ."

work a day,' he would shout between his 'HIP! hip! hip!' to keep us in step, 'And so you're gentlemen now for the first time in your lives . . . .' "

Realizing that frontier soldiering required a high level of physical fitness, the army adopted setting-up drills to strengthen recruits. These exercises, later termed calisthenics, were conducted every morning at the recruit depots, until the men equated the phrase "setting-up drill" with "aching bones and sore muscles."

When new soldiers were retained for a longer period of time at the depots, and after the inauguration of more formally organized training schedules in the 1880's, they were drilled in close order marching by squads and companies, the manual of arms, and sometimes in the rudiments of the care and use of equipment other than small arms. At Jefferson Barracks, cavalry recruits were instructed in mounted and dismounted saber drill, and in equitation, regular and bareback, as well as in marching and the manual of arms. Transforming some of the raw recruit material into soldiers necessitated training in personal cleanliness, because many of the new men were not accustomed to weekly bathing. As soldiers, they were expected and compelled to keep themselves, their uniforms, and their arms clean.

Most of those who matriculated at a recruit depot in the years between 1865 and 1890 reported that the experience had been unpleasant and rigorous. Some, however, later felt that the time had been well spent. After listening to several Indian Wars veterans grouse about their experiences at the depots and the army in general, one who had passed through three different depots stated that

> . . . to many of us enlistment was the best break in our lives. We learned the virtues of a weekly bath under the supervision of a non-com every Saturday! We learned to walk gracefully across the . . . parade ground . . . head up, chest out, stomach in, arms close to the body, and not swinging like pump handles.

An Eighth Cavalry corporal of the 1880's, Frederick C. Kurz, expanded on the above by observing that his training, while not easy, had taught him ". . . obedience of orders, self-reliance, cleanliness and regularity."

Whether drilled and trained or put to work in fatigue details, recruits soon learned that though the depots might be short on training, they were long on discipline. Missing roll calls, failure to report for drill or fatigue, absence over or without leave, and other misdemeanors usually resulted in speedy disciplinary action. Guardhouse sentences and fines were liberally meted out to those who went astray, and at Jefferson Barracks an institution known as the "bull ring" was a favored type of punishment. The ring, located in the riding hall, was approximately sixty feet in diameter, and was originally intended as a device for training horses and neophyte riders. Defaulters were lined up in single file, on the inside edge of the ring, and ordered to run around it; while the crack of a sergeant's whip counted the cadence until ". . . he finally decided that too much was enough." The running began at double time, and was soon increased to triple time by the sergeant for as long as half an hour. "To youngsters, . . . it was fairly easy, . . . but to the old soldiers just getting over a pay-day booze, fast running was tough discipline," wrote Samuel D. Gilpin.

Because the army enlisted very few specialists during the last third of the nineteenth century, skilled artisans and technicians rarely joined the army in order to practice their trade or specialty. An exception were the telegraph and heliograph operators who enlisted for duty in the Signal Corps. Signal Corps soldiers were the highest rated enlisted men in the army, and were among the first real field specialists of the Regular Army; those who enlisted with experience as telegraphers, received training in heliography and military duties at Fort Myer, Virginia, in the 1880's.

Most newly-joined soldiers were impatient to leave the depots and join an active unit. Some spent only a few days at the depots, depending upon the demands of the service.[4] The length of time spent at a depot varied from a few days to several months. Recruits generally spent more time in training at the depots in the late eighties and early nineties than they did from 1865 to 1880. The new soldier heard that the food and living conditions were much better among the line units and at regular posts. As long as he remained at a depot, the recruit could draw only half the pay due him, and he was not really a soldier until he had joined his company. Men who joined the army to see the West and for excitement were the most eager to leave the depots, but few realized what participation in an Indian campaign and duty on the frontier entailed.

Recruits left the depots in groups of as few as a dozen to as many as two hundred men. Whenever possible, land-grant railroads were used to transport them to their posts. Drafts were commonly in charge of an officer returning from leave or detailed for the duty, but sometimes recruits were conducted by a veteran re-enlistee or noncommissioned man. Usually, they were loaded into railroad cars for the tedious journey to such railheads as Corinne, Utah, on the Union Pacific, for replacements ordered to western Montana posts in 1880, or Yuma, Arizona, for those traveling to Fort Verde and Fort Apache, Arizona, in 1879.

Although land-grant railroads were required by law to furnish transportation to the army, comfortable accommodations were not specified. Replacements, with all their equipment, usually traveled in day coaches, taking turns sleeping in the seats. They were fed in the coaches, and obtained drinking water from barrels placed in the cars. Unpleasant as the rail trip might prove to be, many men viewed the prospect with delight, as a relief

---

[4] Fifth Cavalryman Frank Lovell wrote that in 1872 he had been at the David's Island recruit depot only a short time when men were asked to volunteer for immediate transfer to the Fifth Cavalry in Arizona. Several veteran soldiers tried to dissuade him, but, said Lovell "the rations were so scanty at the barracks, where the commissary was getting rich on the men, that I and several others had decided to go. . . . the food decided us, and we went."

45

from the rigorous depot routines. An 1876 recruit draft, traveling by rail from Fort Leavenworth, Kansas, to Fargo, North Dakota, enjoyed themselves as much as their officers allowed, pulling the emergency-brake cord, pestering the trainmen, and foraging for food at way stops. A member of another 1876 replacement draft, en route from rendezvous in the East to replenish the decimated Seventh Cavalry, bitterly wrote that

> . . . on the way out from New York City, we were in a condition hard to describe; herded in filth, slow trains, no way to rest or sleep [many more men than seats], food doled out at long intervals, no toilets, no water most of the way; all our kits and blankets stolen [with the tacit connivance of those in charge of the draft]. Men jumped off the train at every stop, all the others wanted to.

At the end of a rail journey, recruits generally transferred to wagons, steamboats, or stages for the next leg of the trip. Because their purpose was to guard the isolated areas, few frontier posts were situated on railroad lines during the Indian Wars era.

Disembarking from the railroad cars, replacements were usually met by an escort from the post of destination. A group of twenty new men, bound for the Fifth Cavalry companies stationed at Fort Washakie, Wyoming Territory, traveled from Jefferson Barracks by rail to a point near Fort Laramie, where they were met by an armed Fifth Cavalry sergeant and a six-mule wagon. The wagon carried all the men's baggage and rations on the march across Wyoming, to Fort Washakie, at the western end of the Territory, but the neophyte cavalrymen walked. A recruit later wrote that in 1880 his draft had left the railroad at Corinne, Utah, and "walked six hundred miles to Helena [, Montana]." In the summer of 1872, a draft of one hundred and twenty-five new men, escorted by a few older soldiers and one officer, left Fort Hays, Kansas, en route for Camp Supply, Indian Territory. Each day's march was planned so that some source of water was reasonably close to the evening camping place, and fifteen miles was an average day's march. The men were rationed with the usual hardtack, bacon, and coffee, though the officer in charge, who had the only rifle in the command, shot some game for the hungry recruits. Tramping over the western plains soon taught the new soldiers the importance of conserving water in the dry climates unfamiliar to most of them. A stream was always welcome, as recruits generally carried an empty canteen.

Occasionally, replacements encountered hostile Indians even before they had arrived at their post. In west-central Montana, a group of Seventh Infantry recruits were enjoying an evening swim at the end of a hard day's march. A band of hostiles surprised the swimmers and killed several of them before the guard could drive them off.[5] These men were introduced to Indian campaigning in a way they were not likely to forget.

Not all recruits entered into active duty with their units via the recruit depots. A considerable number enlisted at western and midwestern posts, and those signed up by regimental recruiting parties were usually sent directly to whatever post served as regimental headquarters, where they experienced a rapid introduction into army life, and though they were hazed and guyed by the older soldiers, the officers and noncoms took some measure of interest in them, because they realized that the neophytes would soon be integrated into their own units.

Direct and post-enlistment recruits, wrote General G. A. Forsyth in *The Story of the Soldier,* were usually formed into recruit companies or ". . . put into the awkward squad for a few weeks of preliminary drill and something of an insight into routine army life." The "preliminary drill" consisted of close order marching and the same introduction to professional soldiering given to men who passed through the recruit depots. Only rudimentary instruction was imparted to the new soldiers, for they were expected to learn their trade by observing and emulating the veterans in the companies to which they were

[5] Lieutenant E. E. Hardin, MS.

47

assigned. Because little time was spent in orienting them, they not uncommonly found themselves out on active campaign service less than three months after enlistment. One officer asserted that he was convinced that two hundred lives had been needlessly lost during the Red Cloud War on the northern plains from 1866 to 1868, because the recruits had not been trained in the efficient management of their arms.[6]

"Insight into routine army life" usually meant endless fatigue details, with the new men assigned to all the most unpleasant ones. Those who grumbled that they had enlisted to become proficient in the use of arms and not picks and shovels usually saw their error when ordered to parade for three days with a brick-filled knapsack and other full-marching gear. Other "insights" included learning to accommodate the corporals and sergeants, who not infrequently hazed recruits by coercing them into "heel-balling belts and burnishing equipment." Those who had no knowledge of how the enlisted ranks were rationed soon gained this "insight." Disappointed that fried mush appeared so often on the menu, one 1875 recruit was quickly oriented by a sergeant, who said that he had eaten mush and molasses every day of the twenty-one years of his army career.[7]

The soldier's first loyalty was to his company. When a man was assigned to an infantry or cavalry company, he was almost certain to spend the balance of his enlistment, and perhaps several subsequent enlistments, in the same company.

The President, as Commander in Chief of the Armed Forces, was empowered to regulate the authorized strength of companies, from a statutory minimum of fifty rank and file to a maximum of one hundred. In 1866, infantry, cavalry, and heavy artillery companies were authorized to include 64 privates, while the light artillery companies were to contain 122. Follow-

---

[6] Brigadier General W. H. Bisbee, "Items of Indian Service," in *Proceedings, Order of Indian Wars, January 19, 1928,* 27. This material is from Bisbee's 1866–68 diary.

[7] Ami Frank Mulford, *Fighting Indians in the 7th United States Cavalry,* 7.

ing the Custer disaster in 1876, cavalry companies were expanded to include 100 privates, although actual strength was usually much lower. The small size of most companies made for an increased cohesiveness among the men who served in them. In 1878, an officer of the Fifth Infantry, whose regiment was intensively campaigning against the Sioux and Northern Cheyennes, testified that some companies in his regiment could muster only sixteen men for duty.[8]

A soldier rarely transferred out of the company he joined as a recruit. The men he served with lived in extremely close relationship with one another, and the members of one company usually did not associate with men from other companies. The company tended to be a self-contained social as well as military unit. The privates, noncommissioned men, and officers of a soldier's company were the men with whom he would share nearly all his experiences for the balance of his enlistment. With them he would live, eat, sleep, march, brawl, and possibly die.

[8] *Reorganization of the Army*, 45 Cong., 2 sess., Mar. 21, 1878, *House Misc. Document No. 56*, 246.

4.

Privates, Noncoms, and Officers

SHORTLY AFTER ARRIVAL from a recruit depot, the new men were sent to their companies by the post adjutant. Recalling his assignment to a company of the Seventh Cavalry at Fort Abraham Lincoln in the fall of 1876, A. J. Davis wrote that his recruit draft had been "herded out on the prairie for hours, while the elect [officers] parceled us out to the depleted companies. . . ."

. Having carried his baggage and equipment into the barrack room, the recruit began his acquaintance with the older members of the company, who were usually a motley assortment such as ". . . the Danbury hatter, watchmaker, sailor, counter-hopper, shoemaker, tailors, doctors, lawyers, dentists, pumpkin rollers, preachers, [and] . . . the bowery boy." Some men did not care to discuss their pasts and some were toughs. The new soldier found that his companionship was largely limited to the men of his company, and he quickly learned to live in this re-

A WOUNDED MAN
of General Crook's command, transported by travois, 1876.

Courtesy General R. J. Burt

GENERAL CROOK'S SOLDIERS BUTCHERING A HORSE
when rations gave out on the "starvation march" in pursuit of
Sioux and Cheyennes, September, 1876.

stricted social environment. Even at small garrisons, composed of one company of infantry and one of cavalry, the tendency was for the men of one unit to have little contact with those of another. Lying wakeful in their bunks in the early morning, the infantrymen were likely to chuckle to themselves as one of their number remarked, "There go the sore-asses to chambermaid their horses," when the cavalry troopers attended to their mounts before seeing to their own wants.

The urban-bred recruit who had never left the city or the young farmer who had journeyed no farther than a county-seat town became aware of cosmopolitan attitudes and ideas unknown to him before he joined his company. A Twelfth Infantry bugler of the early 1870's came from a German family that had provided officers for the French and German armies since the time of Napoleon I. While he was serving on the American frontier, one of his brothers was a colonel in the Prussian army. Serving at the same time, but in the Fourth Infantry, was a former member of Mosby's Confederate guerrillas.

Most companies of the Indian Wars contained men who had quite obviously entered the army from a higher social and economic status. Such was the Third Cavalry private, described by his comrade of 1883 as having been ". . . about 30 and hair white as snow. A great Bible student, he was continually quoting from it. He was secretary of B Troop's literary association, and he subscribed for the daily papers . . . New York *Times*, New York *Herald*, Kansas City *Times*, St. Louis *Globe-Democrat, Police Gazette*, the New York *Clipper*, etc. . . ." Although a company usually numbered several illiterate men, there were often others whose education was far above the national average. A Harvard graduate was serving in C Troop of the Eighth Cavalry in 1890, and the holder of a schoolteacher's certificate was soldiering in the Tenth Infantry in 1888.

In the close-knit, almost deadening sameness that ruled the social aspect of an Indian Wars company, the men were quick to pick out salient peculiarities and distinguishing personality traits and to bestow nicknames on each other and the people who made up their world. A recruit who joined D Company of the Third Cavalry in the early eighties, said Perley S. Eaton, soon learned to address his fellows as "Brute," "Nigger," "Josh," "Guts" Guttier, and "Brigham" Young. Several Seventh Cavalrymen were far better known by their appellations of "Soapy" [Myers], "Myers No. 2," "Tinker Bill" [Meyers], "Handsome Jack" [Victor], and "Crazy Jim" [Severs] than they were by their proper names.[1] "Crazy Jim" received his nickname for having been seen killing, skinning, and eating a rattlesnake, an act that struck his comrades as ridiculous. Jim's peculiar eating habits and seemingly derogatory nickname, however, did not diminish the unspoken admiration his comrades had for his feat of retrieving an ammunition-laden pack mule from within the hostile lines at the Battle of the Little Bighorn.[2]

Almost every Indian Wars company contained a few professional privates who had begun their service careers in the Mexican or Civil War. An officer who had known them well remarked that usually they were ". . . sturdy old fellows wearing four to six service chevrons on their arms. They had taken life as it came: Mexico, the plains, the war . . . , and then the plains again."[3] The Civil War had been the climactic life experience for many of these older soldiers, and little else loomed as significantly in their vocal recollections. These old-timers often had a profound influence on the younger men, and as late as 1886 to 1891, at least two Privates of F Company of the Eighteenth Infantry were veterans of the Civil War.

Old soldiers who had served several enlistments in the same regiment and company often expected and received small privileges and considerations not accorded to first-enlistment men.

[1] Judge W. E. Morris, Private, Seventh Cavalry, 1876, to Robert Bruce, MS, May 23, 1928, Custer Battlefield National Monument. Hereafter cited as CBNM. Glendolin D. Wagner, *Old Neutriment*, 51.

[2] Mulford, *Fighting Indians*, 108.

[3] Forsyth, *The Soldier*, I, 130f.

Their officers had a pretty thorough knowledge of these men, and a healthy mutual respect commonly governed their relationships. The finer points of military etiquette and drill ground mannerisms often were absent. Not infrequently, a faithful old soldier who had served several enlistments, but who was unable to perform the arduous duties of a private, was allowed to stay on rather than be thrust out without a disability pension. Sometimes, an officer arranged a pensionable discharge for one of these old-timers for disability in line of duty, rather than have him be refused re-enlistment at the end of his current term of service.[4] The wife of an Eighth Infantry officer described one of the older men in her husband's company in 1878, remarking that "... old Needham was but a wisp of a man; long years of service had broken down his health; he was all wizened up and feeble, but he was a *soldier* . . . ."[5] This is an apt description of many of the long-service men in late nineteenth-century companies.

Old soldiers, often jealous of their positions of seniority, were inclined to indulge in much grousing and grumbling about real or fancied complaints. Such a one, wrote Samuel D. Gilpin, was

> Butts Riley . . . hardly 5 feet tall . . . with 4 enlistments [as of 1885, when the writer knew him in the 13th Infantry] . . . groused at baked beans . . . if they were not cooked army style . . . grumbled at the company cook if plum duff weren't served from left-over bread crumbs more than one Sunday evening in two months. He wanted plum duff every Sunday night, . . . grumbled if his name was put up on the bulletin board for guard duty oftener than once in three weeks . . . he could just about sign his name.

In isolated groups, various members tend to fill definite unofficial but well-defined roles. In a regular company, some men might be singers, others jokers, or leaders in organizing company functions such as minstrel shows and literary societies. Among

[4] Brigadier General E. S. Godfrey, "Jimmy Winn," MS, Bates Coll.

[5] Summerhayes, *Arizona*, 239.

the poorly educated Indian Wars soldiers, those who had received above average educations, and were not otherwise misfits, were often looked to as sources of information. A Seventh Cavalryman of 1876 pointed this up when he said that in A Company, "Howard Weaver was our historian and encyclopedian, and all disputes and arguments were deferred to him for a decision. He was the only one of my comrades whose given name was known to me." When privates proved to be natural leaders, shrewd officers commonly capitalized on their talent by appointing them corporals and sergeants.

A company generally had its share of toughs, gamblers, petty criminals, and men who had a predilection for making trouble. When present in any numbers, the toughs, or "Bowery Boys," commonly banded together and ignored the rest of the company outside the line of duty. A company also usually contained at least one man who was as much a gambler as he was a soldier, and his gambling activities often were the basis of serious trouble, up to and including murder.[6] Soldier moneylenders, who lent at exorbitant rates, such as twenty-five cents for each dollar borrowed, against the surety of the next payday, were also inveterate troublemakers. Occasionally, a company included a thief, or men with criminal pasts who tried to continue their former ways in the army. Although they formed a small minority of the men in a company, their notoriety often colored public and private opinion of the enlisted men in the Regular Army.

Army life has never been conducive to temperance and morality. As Kipling observed, "single men in barracks don't grow into plaster saints." Isolated from the usual types of recreation, influenced by the example of many old-timers and not a few officers, many Indian Wars soldiers took their recreation in forms

[6] Private Eddie Waller, Thirteenth Infantry, 1889–94, Interview, Chicago, Ill., July, 1954. Jack Noon, a soldier-gambler, was shot by the first sergeant of his company, when the sergeant caught him rifling his effects in a tent. Noon was trying to recover what the sergeant owed him in gambling debts; he died several days later, in the care of Private Waller.

as crude as the conditions that frontier duty imposed upon them. Young recruits, naturally, were influenced to some extent by the older men in the company. Commenting on the moral complexion of the Seventh Cavalry in 1871, a recruit said that ". . . most of the 7th were Civil War veterans, much older men than I was . . . they often drank hard, but fought hard too . . ."[7] The same commentary was voiced by a Seventh Cavalryman of the 1888 to 1891 period, when he characterized the men in his company as ". . . good fighters, but mostly heavy drinkers." An occasional spree in a frontier saloon or off-limits "hog ranch" groggery and brothel was not really considered evidence of heavy drinking. A soldier who was classed as a heavy drinker is better illustrated by an 1874 Third Infantryman, who consumed so much liquor in Dodge City, Kansas, that he had no recollection of the long railroad journey to Cairo, Illinois, because he had been in a continuous stupor since boarding the train in Kansas.[8]

When saloons, "hog ranches" and other dispensaries of amoral recreation were close at hand, the new soldiers found that many of their comrades in the company made these resorts their payday headquarters. This picture has often been overdrawn, however, as not all frontier regulars were whisky-guzzling dissipates and ". . . some didn't even drink or smoke. . . ."

Along with the professional privates, gamblers, and hard-living toughs, every Indian Wars company had its share of quiet, serious men. Some of these men occasionally went on sprees or otherwise overstepped the bounds of propriety, without becoming alcoholics or habitual troublemakers. They were subject to the human frailties common to most men. Some of those who gambled away their pay carried small Bibles in their field kits.

Uneducated and illiterate men often took advantage of opportunities to enhance their meager learning. Sometimes, at posts

---

[7] "Sergeant James A. Richardson," *Portland Sunday Times* [Me.], June 27, 1909, Clipping, Package No. 35, Elizabeth B. Custer Collection.

[8] P. M. Ashburn, *A History of the Medical Department of the United States Army*, 103.

too small to support a post school, men having some education assisted others who had none. Recalling Arizona evenings spent in this fashion, First Sergeant George Neihaus, Tenth Infantry, wrote: "A member of Co. B used to come to my Co. . . . I taught him to read and write, in later years, he became a Quartermaster Sergeant." Because the army offered very little in the way of facilities for the men to better themselves, some secured their own books and studied them in the barracks and on campaign.

Although most soldiers spent their money as soon as they received it, some were inclined to save their pay. Men with families often sent most of their money home, rather than waste it at a sutler's store or frontier groggery. Among those who had enlisted to go West, a few carefully saved against the time they would be discharged, in order to make a start in the new country. A good example of this is seen in an 1884 announcement printed in the Billings, [Montana] *Post*. Discussing business trends in Billings, the editor reported that

> Private John Stanley, of the 5th Infantry, stationed at Fort Custer, came over last week, and invested about $1,500. in Billings lots. He has unbounded confidence in the future of Billings, and demonstrates it by investing in the town lots.

As individuals, many soldiers in the Indian Wars period were interested in a wide variety of matters not especially connected with the army. Most companies included a few Masons, who attended lodge meetings as opportunities occurred. Others had such varying avocations as poetry, and the advancement of the Knights of Labor movement.[9] Many cavalrymen became enthusiastic horsemen. Occasionally, an enlisted man possessed some peculiar or bizarre personal interest, such as spiritualism and the occult.

There was sometimes a considerable amount of ill will be-

---

[9] Private H. J. Ciscel, Eighth Cavalry, 1890–93, Interview, V. A. Hospital, Wood, Wisconsin, July, 1954. "Bucky Love recited poetry and talked a lot about Masonic stuff, and Tom Bentley was interested in the Knights of Labor."

tween northern and southern Civil War veterans. Service in the professional Regular Army, however, tended to lessen the prevalence of bad feeling. In 1866, four regiments of Negro troops were added to the Regular Army. They served at many western posts, often with white troops, and though the Negro soldiers were segregated from the others, no trouble arose when Negro and white troops served together on guard or fatigue duties.

Within the company unit, close friendships often grew out of the intimate association of members of a cavalry "set of fours" or an infantry squad, or out of the unofficial "bunky" system, prevalent in all branches of active service. When a recruit joined an active-duty company, he usually paired off with another newly-joined man, or sometimes with an older soldier. On campaign, soldiers generally carried only one blanket apiece. In the high plains and mountain areas this was not sufficient cover, and two men commonly pooled their blankets and slept together for warmth. This practice of sharing usually extended to cooking rations and to fighting together on skirmish lines. In the Indian Wars, a man's "bunky" was his best friend, and if he came to know the history and personality of any man in his company, that man was his "bunky."

Because many men enlisted for reasons known only to themselves, a man's "bunky" was often his only confidant. This was well illustrated by a former Twenty-second Infantryman, when he described his "bunky" as a man of superior education, obviously of Germanic birth and background, who always had plenty of money from sources outside the army. Liking good food, this man repeatedly volunteered for assignment as company cook, because he had a talent for tastefully preparing crude army rations. Seeing his "bunky's" wallet on the floor near his cot, Corporal John Bergstrom picked it up and observed that it was filled with greenbacks. He returned it to the owner, and inquired where all that money had come from. His "bunky" swore him to secrecy, explaining that the money was sent to him regularly by his well-to-do family in Austria, and that he had once been a lieutenant in the Austrian army, but did not want the other soldiers or the company officers to know it.

Individual soldiers naturally had varying opinions and estimations of the men in their own companies. Obviously, those who continued to re-enlist considered their fellows to be at least bearable comrades. Those who served out only one enlistment were often more critical in their appraisals. A great deal depended on the predominant makeup and quality of one's company. Some believed that the average soldier was all right, but recognized that many were men with whom they would not normally have chosen to associate. An interesting commentary was furnished by a man who had enlisted in the Seventh Infantry in 1888, after serving four years in the German army. He wrote that he believed that his Seventh Infantry comrades had been only fair soldiers, that the company officers had been excellent leaders, and that relations between the officers and the enlisted men were very good.

A newly-joined private was quite likely to view his company sergeants, and especially his commissioned officers and the company first sergeant, as occupying positions only a little lower than that of the Almighty. This attitude had more than a slight basis in fact, and all ranks "had to get permission from the 1st Sgt. to even speak to an officer." The first sergeant actually ran the company, and was expected to do so by the company officers. Many privates had little contact with their officers, beyond formal exchanges of military courtesies. Remarking on this situation in 1886, Frederic Remington, special correspondent for *Harper's Weekly* during the Geronimo campaign, wrote that "the personality of many of these soldiers never goes beyond the [first] sergeant's knowledge."

Because the company noncommissioned men were of such importance in every espect of enlisted life, it is worth while to discuss them and their place in the Indian Wars army scheme at some length. If a single word were chosen to describe the noncommissioned officers of the Indian Wars army, that word

58

would have to be—*tough*. Toughness of noncommissioned personnel was not peculiar of course to the Indian Wars army, but was nevertheless one of its most striking characteristics. Most officers left the administration of company affairs in the hands of the first sergeant, who in turn relied on the duty sergeants and corporals. The enforcement of discipline and the awarding of company punishments were often left to the personal inclinations of these sergeants, who frequently prescribed punishments that were humiliating and in many cases actually illegal. In some companies, discipline was maintained by the fists of the noncommissioned officers. Remarking in his diary on a minor infraction of regulations, a First Cavalryman noted that "Sgt. Parrish hit Hall a couple of punches in the mug at supper." In companies containing more than the usual number of toughs, ability as a scrapper was a prerequisite for appointment to noncommissioned status, and a really pugnacious man was sometimes repeatedly reduced to the ranks for some breach of regulations, but then appointed again because he was able to handle the hardest cases in the company without having to call in official assistance.

In a situation where some company officers ignored or condoned disciplinary bullying of their men by the sergeants, it is not surprising that noncommissioned officers occasionally overstepped their bounds and tyrannized over the soldiers. In June, 1880, a sergeant of K Company, Seventh Cavalry, entered a barrack squadroom roaring drunk and proceeded to revile the men, subsequently knocking one of them to the floor with his fist. This was a violation of regulations too flagrant to be overlooked, and the men involved pressed charges against the sergeant, which resulted in a garrison court-martial. Because the offender was generally believed to be a good sergeant, his only punishment was a moderate fine of ten dollars.[10] A private con-

---

[10] Post and Regimental Order Book, Headquarters, Seventh Cavalry, Jan., 1878–Dec., 1881, MS, CBNM, 132f.

victed of a similar offense would have been fined and sentenced to hard labor in the post guardhouse. When a tyrannical noncommissioned man was reduced in rank, the privates whom he had bullied usually made life in the company miserable for him.

In the small, seniority-conscious Indian Wars army, the sergeants and senior noncommissioned men were usually soldiers having long service. In the "Roster of Non-Commissioned Officers of the First United States Cavalry [1894]" the original dates of appointment reveal that almost every one of the sergeants had held his appointment for from ten to sixteen years. Lengths of service previous to promotion are not listed, but it is safe to assume that most had served several years before achieving noncommissioned rank.

All through the seventies and eighties, many of the older noncommissioned men were Civil War veterans, and occasionally men could be found whose careers antedated the Civil War by several years. Such a man was

> Sergt. Bill Irwin [C Company, Second Cavalry], a veteran of 45 years service under Uncle Sam's banner, and all of it served on the plains . . . he is just as stalwart looking now [1884] as he was . . . in 1872.[11]

The long service backgrounds of many old sergeants undoubtedly did little to soften their characters and their attitudes toward discipline. Commenting on the noncommissioned men of Civil War service, a former Seventeenth Infantryman summed up his opinions on the subject in his statement that "old Sergeant McMakin was a Civil War vet, and *he* was mean as hell!"

The practical experience of regular army sergeants who had held commissioned ranks in the state and volunteer regiments during the Civil War was likely to make them superior noncommissioned officers and leaders.

Like the rank and file, the noncommissioned men came from

[11] Clipping, datelined Fort Bidwell, California, Aug. 15, 1884, General A. S. Burt Collection, MSS Div., Lib. of Cong.

widely varied backgrounds. The first sergeant of K Company, First Cavalry, in the mid-eighties was an exiled Russian aristocrat, another sergeant had served in the British army, and a nephew of President Harrison was a corporal in the same company. An Eighth Cavalry sergeant of 1890 received his introduction to professional soldiering as a private in a crack English guards regiment. Previous service in a European army, and sometimes in the defeated Confederate Army, was noted by alert officers casting about for experienced men to appoint to noncommissioned status.

Since there were no photographs or fingerprint files during the late nineteenth century, cashiered officers and others who had resigned their commissions under clouded circumstances, and subsequently enlisted in the ranks, sometimes were given noncommissioned appointments because of their obvious experience. A Seventh Infantry first sergeant of the 1870's had resigned his earlier officer's commission in the Seventh Cavalry, when his infatuation for a Kansas prostitute became a matter of common talk and scandal in the regiment.[12] A former first lieutenant of the Tenth Infantry, who resigned in 1869, apparently preferred military to civil life under any conditions, because he enlisted in the First Cavalry in 1872 and served five years as a sergeant under an assumed name.[13]

Some of the senior noncommissioned officers were well liked by the men in their companies, and frequently a grizzled old sergeant was held in high esteem by the younger soldiers because of the humane considerations he showed them. Occasionally, a sergeant went too far in trying to take care of his men. A First Cavalry private, who had slipped out of his barracks for the night, was apprehended by the guard, after his sergeant had reported him present. The private was fined, and the sergeant was reduced to the ranks for failing to report the soldier absent

[12] Benteen to Goldin, MS, Feb. 17, 1896.
[13] F. B. Heitman, *Historical Register and Dictionary of the United States Army, 1789 to 1903*, Geoghan, John D., I, 451.

at the 11:00 P.M. bed check. The sergeant took the chance that the errant soldier would return undetected. Naturally, such self-sacrifice and risk-taking exalted the privates' opinions of this particular sergeant.

Many of the older noncommissioned men had strong personal ties to their companies and regiments. When his company was ordered out after Joseph's Nez Percé hostilities in the late summer of 1877, a Sergeant McDermott cut short his furlough to take his place in the command. His loss was keenly felt when he was subsequently killed in action at Snake Creek (Bear Paw Mountains), Montana Territory, as "he was liked by all the men in his company, and respected by officers and men throught [sic] the regiment."[14] For another instance, when a sergeant of the Third Cavalry was killed at Fort Washakie, Wyoming, in 1882, the men in his company pooled their money to pay for shipment of his body to his home in Massachusetts. Such noncommissioned men were the backbone of the Indian Wars army.

Though this book is not primarily concerned with the officers of the late nineteenth-century Regular Army, the impact these officers had on the men and the soldiers' attitudes toward their commissioned superiors are important. Basically, all relationships between commissioned and noncommissioned army personnel were governed by the Articles of War, Army Regulations, and such general and special orders as were issued from time to time. The social manifestations of these relationships is commonly labeled the caste system, though the analogy with the Hindu socio-religious caste system is an imperfect one when applied to the relations between inferior and superior Indian Wars army personnel. The relative rigidity of each of the two systems, however, makes the word caste an apt descriptive term. The gulf separating the commissioned officers from all other army personnel was a very wide one. It should be pointed out, nevertheless, that under some conditions the discriminatory

[14] Mulford, *Fighting Indians*, 126.

aspects of the system did not exist, or became inoperative.

As do most American institutions, our military caste system owes much to earlier European models. For this reason, men who had served in European armies found themselves in relatively familiar social surroundings when they enlisted in the United States Regular Army during the Indian Wars years.

Adjusting to the caste system was extremely difficult for many recruits. Some soldiers felt that "the social attitudes of officers toward enlisted men was patterned largely on that of Frederick the Great of Prussia . . . they [acted and lived as if they] were from a different sphere . . . ." Many enlisted men resented the fact that "seldom did an officer speak to a private, except in line of duty." Officers rarely, if ever, mixed with the enlisted men when in garrison. The gulf between the two classes, commissioned and all other personnel, of course extended to obvious matters of pay, types of duty, and quarters. It also extended to the wives and children. Although the number of children was not large at Fort Laramie in the early eighties, separate instruction was arranged, so that officers' children would not have to attend classes with those of the enlisted men and lower-ranked civilian employees.[15]

All armies must operate under a fairly rigid system of organization governing the issuance of orders, responsibility, and lines of authority. The caste system, however irritating to those in the lower ranks, was a necessity. Each class, officers, noncommissioned men, or privates, usually respected the prerogatives and position of the other two, and a feeling of pride and loyalty developed among the members of a company. On special occasions and holidays, such as Christmas, it was customary and almost mandatory that the commissioned officers of a company spend some part of the day with their men, usually in the company mess hall.

[15] Jake Tonamichel, Interview, Medora, North Dakota, Mar., 1957. As the son of the post hospital steward, this man went to the post school at Fort Laramie in the early 1880's.

Company officers sometimes came to have a high personal regard for and genuine interest in some of the perennial privates and soldiers of long service in their companies. This feeling was reciprocated, and the enlisted men often went far out of their way to please or accommodate a favorite officer. A lieutenant of the Seventh Cavalry once offered his company tailor a discharge, because he knew the old fellow could not pass the physical examination for re-enlistment. The man declined the offer, but took the officer's advice on saving his pay rather than frittering it away on sprees. The officer sent the man's savings to an eastern bank, and, in time, a sizable amount was accumulated. When the officer was assigned to West Point in 1879, the old soldier-tailor withdrew all his savings, unknown to the officer, and offered the lieutenant over a thousand dollars to help him get settled in his new post, ". . . because we want you to be among the bist [sic] of them."[16]

Warm personal relationships, but still within the bounds set by the caste system, existed most often between officers and the senior noncommissioned men with whom they worked closely. Sometimes, the ties continued long after either or both principals had left the army. This is seen in a letter of recommendation written in 1901:

> I take great pleasure in recommending Mr. Daniel McGrath, ex-Sgt., 5th Cavalry, for any position for which he professes himself capable.
>
> He is most intelligent, reliable and faithful. He served under my command for ten years and particularly distinguished himself at the Battle of Summit Springs, Colorado [July 11, 1869] where he killed the [Cheyenne] Chief Tall Bull.
>
> He was placed in many responsible trusts and always acquitted himself satisfactorily.[17]

At the time of writing, the author of the foregoing letter was a

[16] Godfrey, "Jimmy Winn," Bates Coll.

[17] Brigadier General E. H. Carr, letter of recommendation, Sergeant Daniel McGrath, MS, Apr. 13, 1901.

brigadier general, who quite evidently had not forgotten his old campaign comrade, Sergeant Dan McGrath.

The reciprocal, healthy, man-to-man relations between officers and their leading noncommissioned men is difficult to evaluate, because few of the corporals and sergeants recorded their estimates of an officer. Occasionally, though, the high personal regard some noncommissioned men had for their officers is reflected in such documents as Sergeant Jacob Vollinger's 1888 letter congratulating his old company commander on his promotion:

> . . . I am very sorry for the Colonel to leave the Regiment the 5th Infantry, but the best friends have to part sometimes.
>
> Colonel I hope you will not think me Presumptuous to address this few lines to you—it is the only way I can express my regard to the Colonel.[18]

The officer to whom the letter was sent had been the captain of Company F, Fifth Infantry, when the regiment campaigned against the Sioux, from 1876 through 1881. When Major Snyder was promoted to lieutenant colonel and transferred to another regiment, his old sergeant did not want him to think he had forgotten him.

The officer–enlisted man caste system was more rigid in the Regular Army during the years from 1865 through the 1890's than it had been in the volunteer and state units during the Civil War, or would be later, during the Spanish-American War. In a few activities, however, class distinctions were ignored, or at least kept in the background. At some posts, field and team sports, such as baseball, were popular among both officers and men, and they played together as team members. The officers who were sports enthusiasts organized and promoted company and post baseball teams, in which they themselves were players. As in other aspects of company life, the personalities of the

---

[18] Sergeant Jacob Vollinger, to Lieutenant Colonel Snyder, MS, Jan. 12, 1888, S–R Coll.

company officers were all important in setting the tone of a unit. If the company officers promoted field sports and track meets, participated in organized baseball clubs, and otherwise entered into the nonmilitary activities of their men, the soldiers were likely to follow the examples set by their superior officers.

Service on the plains and in the mountains, in the broiling heat of summer and the numbing cold of winter, tended to break down the artificial military caste system that in garrison was fairly easy to maintain. Rugged campaigning, in relatively small commands, emphasized the similarities of officer and enlisted man and minimized the differences established by military protocol. Officers who were very military in garrison were inclined to be more tolerant and easygoing on compaign. When officers and men of a company had made repeated campaigns together, equally without shelter from the elements, sharing the same rations, wearing similar clothes, the officer–enlisted man relationships often relaxed.

Combat conditions also tended to ease the caste system. After all, the most insignificant private might at some time be in a position to save the hair of a company officer. On a hot July night in 1866 a lieutenant, conscious that he was approaching a region known to be filled with hostiles, found he could not sleep. As he walked quietly around the small camp, he found that only the sentry was awake, and offered himself as company. The two men paced back and forth, the officer talking to the soldier, telling him of his home and admitting his nervousness and a premonition that he would be killed by the Sioux. The sentry tried to allay his fears, and after a time, the young officer succeeded in composing himself for some badly needed rest. The prospect of danger had leveled barriers that were insuperable back in garrison.

Except in organized sports and during active participation in the Indian campaigns, few opportunities existed for the officers and enlisted men to meet man to man. One opportunity came in the meetings of Masonic and other lodges. Masons quickly recognized one another, and behaved in the manner prescribed by the rules of that ancient order. A Masonic service was conducted by an officer at Fort Phil Kearny in December, 1866, for two Masons, an officer and a sergeant, killed by Indians. At the conclusion of the service, "Captain Brown placed his own [Army of the Cumberland] badge . . . upon the breast of the dead sergeant, whom he had known during the Civil War and to whom he was greatly attached."[19]

The enlisted men had strong opinions about their officers, for reasons that, whether significant or trivial, real or fancied, were of great importance to the soldiers. An officer needed a modicum of professional military competence to win respect, but in addition he had to bear the reputation of treating the enlisted men as human beings. An officer could be quite reserved and military in his conduct toward the enlisted ranks and still be considered a soldier's officer if he was considerate and courteous. Since the Indian Wars army provided little in the way of comfort for the men in the ranks, the circumstances of frontier service naturally fell hardest on them; thus even small courtesies and favors shown by an officer to a private were warmly appreciated. Writing to his fiancée, who lived in a small community near Omaha, Nebraska, a Ninth Infantry private explained his hopes for a transfer by stating that, ". . . Colonel Townsend . . . is one of the finest officers I have ever met in the service—if there is any possibility of getting me to Omaha he will do it . . . ."[20]

Often commissioned superiors could claim no better social and economic background than could many men in the ranks. A trumpeter, describing his 1877 Seventh Cavalry Company, said that of the nearly one hundred men in his company

> . . . we have a printer, one telegraph operator, a doctor, two lawyers, three professors of languages, one harness maker, four

[19] S. S. Peters, Eighteenth Infantry, 1866– , quoted in Carrington, *My Army Life*, 134f.

[20] Private G. W. McAnulty to Miss Lillian Moore, MS, July 25, 1878, Fort Laramie National Monument. Hereafter cited as FLNM.

cooks and bakers, two blacksmiths, one jeweler, three school teachers . . . [as well as farmers, railroaders and laborers].[21]

A former Second Cavalryman of the mid-eighties, James B. Wilkinson, wrote that the officers he had served under were ". . . only fair, there were lots of things they didn't know, and there was a good deal of strife among the officers—one was a known coward." Wilkinson commended the captain of his company as a brave man and a good leader, but qualified the praise by adding that all the men knew he was a heavy drinker.

Officers who betrayed by their bearing their conviction that they were innately superior to men of lower ranks were cordially disliked and considered "stuck-up." Contrasting his unpopular commanding officer with Lieutenant Casey of the 22nd Infantry, in 1890, Corporal John Bergstrom explained that the ". . . C.O. was overbearing, and . . . very unpopular . . . [he] was later wounded by a citizen [of Miles City, Montana, who would not knuckle under to him]." The Lieutenant, on the other hand, was very popular with the men, associated freely with them on campaign, and even sat in as a player in their low-stake poker games. When a Sioux bullet knocked him from the saddle in January, 1891, his loss was keenly felt by the soldiers.

Some officers were unpopular because they showed no consideration for the men in their commands. A former Seventh Cavalryman said of Custer:

> He was a daredevil. . . . But most of the men didn't like him. He was too hard on the men and horses. He changed his mind too often. He was always right. He never conferred enough with his officers. When he got a notion, we had to go. He wouldn't listen to the other officers.[22]

Always, when a few men are given arbitrary authority over others, some will use their authority to tyrannize over those

[21] Mulford, *Fighting Indians*, 57.
[22] R. P. Johnson, "Jacob Horner of the 7th Cavalry," in *North Dakota History*, Vol. XVI, No. 2, (1949), 99.

beneath them. Explaining his opinions of Indian Wars officers to a man who had served as a Seventh Cavalry officer through the Indian campaigns, a former Thirteenth Infantry private wrote:

> My army experience [early 1880's] convinced me that cavalry officers were less afflicted with snobbery than Infantry officers, as I had many an opportunity to observe their conduct with enlisted men. I once saw a shavetail lieutenant but a short time in the regiment put a whole squad of men in the guardhouse because they did not get up and salute him as he passed. It was a fatigue squad, and the sergeant in charge stood up and saluted. . . . In our regiment an enlisted man was a thing apart, and he was given to understand that there was a vast gulf between him and his officers.[23]

The nicknames that the enlisted men bestowed on officers were a good indication of the men's esteem or lack of it. Referring to an officer as "Bull-Dozer" implied that he was overbearing and blustering; the appellation "Jack of Clubs" to another implies that a feeling of camaraderie existed between this young lieutenant and the men in the ranks. Officers who wore glasses were commonly called "Star Gazer," and association with Indian scouts earned one officer the sobriquet of "Crazy Horse." Officer nicknames were usually based on physical characteristics or personality traits, and sometimes enlisted men had more than one slang name for an officer. A tall lieutenant of the Seventh Cavalry was dubbed "Long Soldier" because of his height and "Tony Soldier" because of his fastidious habits of dress. Such nicknames as "Black Jack," "Slicker Bill," and "Fighting Bob" were commonplace, and more than one unpopular officer had to endure the ignominy of "Pansy."

Outstanding incidents in an officer's career were fruitful sources of nicknames, sometimes respectful, sometimes not. After his ruthless, crushing attack on a band of Montana Piegans resulted in considerable popular condemnation, Colonel Eugene

---

[23] Chrisman to Godfrey, MS, Nov. 17, 1917, Bates Coll.

M. Baker was not addressed to his face as "Piegan," but the name was current among the soldiers. Because he drove his men and mounts to the limits of endurance, Custer was well known among his soldiers as "Hard Ass," a name that was euphemized into "Hard Backsides," when reported by the newspaper correspondent Mark Kellogg. Custer's other nickname, "Long Hair," was also widely used, and has been associated with that colorful, if erratic, officer ever since his death.

The officer–enlisted man caste system, irksome at best, permitted almost intolerable oppression when officers were petty and small-minded martinets. The officers of the frontier Regular Army were men of varying experience and training, "some good, some bad." If any of them took pleasure in making life miserable for the men in the ranks, the military structure of the times allowed him to do so with relative impunity.

Enlisted men soon learned which officers were decent and humane and which were tyrannical and abusive. Eighth Cavalry Sergeant Reinhold R. Gast said, "Some of the officers were gentlemen to us—others were rough and hard on the men—nothing would please them." The enlisted soldier's lack of protection from the capricious whims of a harsh officer was an important cause of the extremely high desertion rates.

The soldiers, however, often found ways and opportunities to strike back at oppressors. When all hands were turned out at night to fight a raging prairie fire in 1877, the lieutenant colonel of the regiment began screaming orders and directions. Under cover of confusion and darkness, cries of "Give that calf more rope," "Somebody sit on the Bull-dozer," and "I want to go home to my maw," sounded from among the fire fighters.[24] The last remark was a pointed jeer at the lieutenant colonel for his having returned to embrace his wife when the regiment had left its post on campaign.

While the men detested harsh, mean commissioned officers

[24] Mulford, *Fighting Indians,* 57.

they idolized those who were noted for their kindness and humane consideration. The Seventh Cavalry captain who reduced a sergeant to the ranks for illegal and cruel punishment of a soldier, had the good wishes of all the privates in his company. Later, this loyalty paid heavy dividends when the captain called for volunteers to get water for the wounded and to counterattack the Indians at the Battle of the Little Bighorn.

Reciprocal loyalty between officers and men was vital. Anyone who has ever served in the military realizes that there are occasions when breaches of regulations are best ignored or overlooked. Many a company officer endeared himself to his men by looking the other way and ignoring certain incidents involving the soldiers. When a civilian's prized onion patch was raided by some men of G Company, Thirteenth Infantry, during an Apache campaign, the injured citizen took his complaint to the captain, who ordered the guard to search the camp. No onions were found, and the disgruntled farmer was escorted to the camp limits. "The next night fried onions permeated the air and . . . [the] Capt. sent his dog-robber after some. He enjoyed them very much—and asked where we hid them." This officer knew the importance the men attached to their stolen onions, and did much to build unit morale by acting as an accomplice in augmenting the meager rations of salt pork, hardtack, and coffee.

Enlisted men's concern for a favorite officer showed strongest under the stress of combat and sudden death. Recounting his experiences in the Modoc War [1872–73], as an enlisted man, a retired major wrote of the deep compassion felt for a badly-wounded lieutenant. This officer had always had a decent, cheerful word for the soldiers, and as he lay dying in a temporary field hospital behind the lines, many of his men came back with him, to watch during the night.[25]

Regular officers received their commissions in one of four ways: graduation from the military academy at West Point;

[25] Major C. B. Hardin, "The Modoc War," in *Proceedings, Order of Indian Wars, January 24, 1931,* 43.

direct appointment from civil life; conversion of Civil War volunteer status, usually to a lower regular commissioned rank; and, in rare cases, by entrance as an enlisted man and successful negotiation of a difficult examination and investigation. In the sixties and seventies, many of the company officers were transferred from Civil War volunteer and state regiments. A number were directly appointed from civil life, generally through political influence. As the Indian Wars wore on, the majority of newly appointed officers were West Point graduates, and the army began to commission a very few qualified enlisted men, especially sergeants of proved ability.

Because the direct appointees and Civil War conversion officers were likely to be men of limited experience and qualifications, many soldiers preferred the West Point officers. Some veterans, however, were convinced that the Academy spoiled good men by teaching the officer–enlisted man caste system as if it existed by divine right. Moreover, rightly or wrongly, older soldiers often resented the fact that seemingly callow cadets were sent out to command companies of seasoned campaigners. A Texas Ranger, whose company co-operated with army detachments in campaigns against Apache raiders, remarked that he had personally known ". . . two men who deserted, because their commander was changed from a seasoned frontiersman to an inexperienced cadet—both were good men."

Men commissioned from the ranks, once they left the barrack room behind them, sometimes modeled themselves after the stiffest academy graduates. Others, however, remembered and used their enlisted experiences to good advantage and became excellent officers.

The moral tone of the Indian Wars army, not the highest that our military records can boast, was strongly influenced by the conduct of the officers. In a fairly small post their personal lives were common knowledge to the men. At a time when the army was officially concerned about alcoholism among the rank and file, the sight of their officers reeling and staggering under a load

72

of liquor did not encourage temperance. Nor were attempts to keep prostitutes away from the soldiers and to raise the standards of sexual morality facilitated when a married officer was known and observed to be having an affair with another's wife. Enlisted men were likely to try to emulate their superiors.

Courts-martial proceedings of the Indian Wars era reveal many instances of moral misconduct that would not have been condoned more recently. In reading some of these cases one should bear in mind that they reflect only the flagrant violations, that were actually brought to trial. A fair example is that of a Seventh Cavalry captain, who had long borne a reputation for being extremely foul-mouthed, and who was unpopular both with his men and the other officers. A list of charges and specifications was drawn up against him, consisting of incidents sworn to have taken place between August 1 and the last of December, 1878. It was charged that he had been six times drunk on duty, once as officer of the day, and that he had been absent without leave for two days, on an extended spree in Deadwood, Dakota Territory. His loss of a horse belonging to the United States was added to the charges growing out of the Deadwood escapade. He was also accused of having twice broken arrest and of attempting to persuade the post trader at Fort Meade to lie in his behalf; of drinking with a company laundress, in an ambulance while on the march, and later carousing with her in her tent; and of ordering a soldier to drive him and two laundresses, in an army ambulance, to a nearby road ranch, where he staged another protracted debauch. The charges and specifications noted that all of the officer's violations of regulations and decent conduct were with the full knowledge and in the sight of his enlisted men.[26] The court recommended dismissal from the service, but higher authority commuted the punishment to suspension from command, on half pay, for a one-year period.

[26] General Courts-Martial Orders No. 19, Adjutant General's Office, March 26, 1879, Copy in Historical Research Files, CBNM.

It is not surprising, in the light of such conduct by an officer, that the morality of the enlisted men was not exemplary. There were, of course, company officers whose instructions and personal examples were positive, healthy influences on the rank and file. Only through a clear understanding of the widely varying characters of the men who made up the Indian Wars Regular Army can one interpret its history and strip off the romantic illusions that have usually obscured the subject.

5.

Companies and Regiments

ALTHOUGH EACH REGULAR ARMY REGIMENT was composed of ten
to twelve companies, rarely were all the units stationed at the
same post. During the late nineteenth century, tradition, and the
exigencies of frontier service, made the company the basic military unit. Soldiers lived in company quarters, ate in company
mess halls, participated in company team sports, and were primarily identified with their company. Its strength varied from
time to time, but rarely exceeded eighty men.

At the close of the Civil War, and for about five years thereafter, there was a considerable amount of regimental *esprit de
corps.* The experiences of the war, when operational units commonly contained many regiments and brigades, had fostered
soldier identification with the regiment as well as the company.

Then, following the Civil War, and prior to 1870, the Regular
Army twice underwent reorganizations in which new regiments

were added and old ones merged. Almost one-half of the infantry regiments lost their individual identities, thereby seriously damaging the unit's morale and limiting the soldier's sense of belonging to his immediate company. New officers were added to those familiar to the men, new designations were adopted. The innovations were often unpopular with the inherently conservative regular army soldiers, for, once men have made the adjustment to a rigid military life they tend to object to basic changes in the established system and conditions. A private of the old Thirtieth Infantry wrote to his sister in 1869, complaining of his regiment's merger with the Fourth Infantry; he explained that it just wasn't like the Thirtieth, but that he had only ". . . sixteen months to serve yet, and when that is up they can go to the devil —they won't get this Chile again ill bet."[1] The regular regiments that survived the reorganizations tried to maintain a semblance of regimental loyalty and spirit, although the dispersion of a regiment's companies and battalions to widely separated western posts made this difficult.

Those regiments whose companies were stationed in neighboring posts had some success in keeping alive the older regimental loyalties. The men of the Fourth Cavalry in the Southwest, the Seventh Infantry in the northern plains, and the Thirteenth Infantry in the Apache country, though scattered among several garrisons, had frequent contacts with one another on campaigns. Sergeant T. V. Gibson of the Thirteenth Infantry explained that when his company

> . . . came into [Fort] Wingate from 4 years in the field along the border in Arizona & New Mexico, and the boys at fort [sic] Wingate sure gave us a big blow out, and the band met us on the mountain and the music sure made our hearts glad—we sure were a hard looking bunch when we arrived . . . from old Fort Seldon on the Rio Grande in New Mexico.

These men still had their feeling of cohesiveness within the regi-

<hr>

[1] Lester to Mrs. Stanley, MS, Apr. 23, 1869.

ment and between its companies, despite the fact that they were rarely stationed together.

Nevertheless, a frontier soldier's first loyalty was to his company. Virtually all operations were based on the company unit, or upon a combination of companies. The hardships and campaign experiences of isolated group living and sharing on the frontier exerted pressures that resulted in a high level of company loyalty among the soldiers. Moreover, the noncommissioned men were mostly long-service veterans, and company officers frequently commanded the same units for a dozen years.

With all these stabilizing influences the companies naturally acquired individual characteristics. Some were noted for being good or poor "feeders," others for their habits or group mannerisms. Company A, Seventh Cavalry, in the 1870's reputed to be a wild and unruly outfit, was known throughout the regiment as "the Forty Thieves." Some companies had a reputation for "toughness," others for the high quality of their officers and noncommissioned men. These, in large part, set the style, or tone, of a company.

The sense of personal identification with his company, whether he approved of it or not, was extremely important to a soldier, and for that reason he sometimes objected to a solitary assignment, or denial of his place in the unit by reason of orders. As August Hettinger put it, "The company is everything to a soldier . . . ." The noncommissioned men, after long service in the same company often felt this attachment even more strongly than the privates. When his company of the Fourth Infantry was ordered north against the Sioux in 1867, a corporal, recovering from wounds in the Fort Laramie post hospital, went absent without leave from the hospital and managed to rejoin his unit on the march.

Officers were frequently so completely identified with the companies they commanded that the units were called by the captain's name. Promotion of officers occurred within their regiments, up to and including the rank of major. In the years between 1865 and 1890 there were more than enough officers on the army rolls, and promotions were glacially slow.

Captains and lieutenants had the opportunity to learn as much about the enlisted men they commanded as the caste system and their own inclinations permitted, and some became closely acquainted with their men. Although the caste system, based partly on the belief that familiarity breeds contempt, dictated a distinct separation of commissioned and all other army personnel, some officers and officers' wives came to know the personalities of their soldiers and ". . . learned to know and respect the enlisted men of the American Army."[2] Soldiers fortunate enough to have an officer who was sincerely interested in them, bragged about the fact to the men of the other companies.

Under favorable conditions and effective leadership, company loyalty was an important, positive factor in the lives of the enlisted men. In 1890, the L and M troops of each cavalry regiment were ordered abolished, and the officers and men were scattered among the remaining ten troops. Members of these L and M troops were sometimes deeply disturbed by the enforced change, as witness M Troop, of the Seventh Cavalry. Chosen as troop spokesman, the first sergeant penned a formal letter to the captain, explaining the sense of loss felt by the men:

> We might be separated, but the comradeship among the members will not cease and we dread the day, when we have to leave our quarters, where we have lived in harmony for a long time. . . . We have never broken our reputation and the day we lay aside the letter "M" our record as a "model troop" will always remain and the members will always try and hold on to it.[3]

A soldier's pride in the outfit was one of the most common manifestations of company or troop loyalty. The men were usually proud of their unit's achievements, such as being the

[2] Summerhayes, *Arizona*, 100.

[3] Sergeant Emil Walker, M Troop, Seventh Cavalry, to Captain Francis M. Gibson, MS, Aug. 2, 1890, Gibson-Fougera Collection.

best drilled company in the regiment or holding the highest collective target practice scores. Drill and adherence to military custom contributed to these attitudes, and soldiers were expected to turn out for guard mount and dress parade at isolated, crude frontier posts with the same military smartness and panoply displayed at the older and larger posts in the settled areas. There was often a competitive attitude toward guard mount inspections and dress parade functions, and when a special orderly was to be selected, the men of the companies involved collectively assisted one of their number to win the competition by helping him "heel-ball" his leather accouterments, shine his arms, and groom himself as smartly as possible for the contest. If the company champion won, the triumph was vicariously shared by all the men in his unit.

The relative stability of organization and the permanence of its personnel caused many men to look on the company as their home and family, a feeling that was especially important to the younger, homeless men, and to the old professional privates who re-enlisted in the same units time after time. The captain was usually referred to as "the old man," and, in truth, he was often a man in his fifties or sixties, the patriarch of the company.

Other factors, in addition to living and campaigning as a unit, stimulated a communal interest among the soldiers of a troop or company. Since the usual army rations did not include fresh vegetables, each company usually cultivated a vegetable garden. As mentioned before, team sports were mostly of the intramural variety, in which each company fielded its own team of baseball players, track men, boxers, and other athletes. The company was also the basic financial unit of army supply, and each unit had its own company fund, which was the responsibility of the captain, but was commonly administered by the senior noncommissioned officers. Money was derived from savings in rations, sale of vegetables from gardens, and other sources. The money was used to buy rations and other items not ordinarily furnished by the commissary or quartermaster departments. The company-fund ledger of F Company, Fifth Infantry, for the years 1874 through 1882, reveals that money was used to purchase a wide variety of articles used by all the men in the company. Flour, beef, buffalo meat, vinegar, coffee, bacon, and brown sugar were sold to obtain money for the purchase of eggs, garden seeds, sundries, potatoes, onions, butter, apples, paint, a water cooler, mess gear, a metronome, coffee boiler, newspaper subscriptions, a twenty-two caliber target rifle, and other articles decided upon by the men.[4]

As in a large family, among groups of men living intimately and in isolated situations, clashes are inevitable, and "there was a certain element among the boys that were the cheap tough ones . . . ." Most of the soldiers were congenial enough, but there were almost always a few in a company who made trouble for themselves and their comrades. Trouble between members of the same company was usually resolved by a fist fight. In some units, wrote Sergeant Perley S. Eaton, fighting was held to a minimum, when company officers and the first sergeant did not tolerate it.[5]

Because of the family feeling of many companies, trouble-makers and agitators could be kept in line by pressure from the other members of the unit as well as by the officers in charge. Sergeant Armand Unger explained: "There were a few men called sore heads by the majority—the others made them realize they were in the army . . . ."

Fighting was common, though, often for very petty grievances. Private Harvey J. Ciscel, a veteran of the 1890 Sioux Campaign, recalled that once when he reached for a piece of dry bread, put out by the cooks as a late snack, "Fuzzy Olson, an older man, knocked a piece of bread out of my hand—so I blacked his eye."

---

[4] Quarterly Account Book, Company F, Fifth Infantry, Company Fund, In Account with Capt. S. Snyder, Jan., 1874–Aug., 1882, MS, S-R Coll.

[5] Sergeant P. S. Eaton, Third Cavalry ,1881–86, to Don Rickey, Jr., MS, Nov. 18, 1954. ". . . in my five years in the army I never saw a fist fight in my company, they knew better."

Sometimes fighting between soldiers became vicious, and the rules of boxing were conspicuously absent in "back of the barracks" fights. Bullies frequently tried to assert their physical superiority over those whom they thought they could dominate. Recruits and new men were naturally the ones most frequently singled out, sometimes under the guise of sport. Explaining his own introduction to army fighting, Private Antonio Frascola, a Fifth Cavalry recruit of 1884, related that

> We had a man in our ranks who was something of a prize fighter, named Collins.... [another soldier] got him to challenge me ... [a nineteen-year-old Italian] to a sparring match. When I found out ... I didn't want to back out ... deciding to do the best I could. I struck one blow, landing square on his nose, and Collins did not wait for any more, but ran away. Later, at another time, Collins caught me by the arm and held me and banged my nose.[6]

The arrangement and comfort of troop or company quarters varied widely. Toward the end of the Indian Wars era, when many western posts had become well established, most barracks were constructed of wood framing, sided with sawed lumber. Some, however, were crude log or adobe buildings, small, poorly ventilated, and cramped. No matter what the kind of building occupied as a troop or company barrack, there was a complete lack of privacy for the rank and file. Privates and corporals usually bunked together in a large room, while the sergeants had small cubicles adjoining. Cots, with wooden slats to support the bedsack and later with a woven wire spring, were arranged along the wall, about three or four feet apart, with each man's wooden foot locker in the aisle at the foot of his bunk. When space permitted, an aisle eight to ten feet wide ran down the center of the room. The men were not allowed to have the bedsacks laid

---

[6] Antonio Frascola, Fifth Cavalry, 1884–89, *Indian-Pioneer Papers*, MS, Phillips Collection.

over the slats or spring until evening, and they were usually folded back during the day.[7] The barrack room was generally heated by cast-iron wood stoves, in the center or at each end of the room, and artificial light was supplied by kerosene lamps hung from the ceiling or by candles. A long shelf ran along the wall, about three or four feet above the head of the cots, to hold the soldier's equipment—except carbines or rifles, which were stacked in a special rack in the barrack room. The corporals and older soldiers had the choice bunk locations, near the windows in summer and close to the stove in winter. Having a comfortable bunksite was a matter of great importance to the soldiers.

At meals, the men in each company ate together, seated on long benches, at bare wooden tables. Tableware commonly consisted of a large tin cup and plate, and iron utensils. In the late eighties, the Quartermaster Department supplied heavy, white ironstone china mugs, plates, and other tableware. The mess table was ordinarily presided over by a noncommissioned man, and the senior noncommissioned personnel frequently ate at separate tables, sometimes using special service and table covers provided at their personal expense. At times, money from the company fund was spent to purchase special tableware for all the members of the unit, even to monogrammed silverware.[8]

When several members of a company were discharged at the expiration of service, or casualties thinned the ranks sufficiently, drafts of new men were ordered as replacements. The older soldiers in a company, bound by ties of common experience and membership in the unit, looked on the recruits with mixed feelings. They were glad to see them take their places in the company, but felt some resentment at the intrusion of new personnel into the unit. The newcomers had their own views on the matter,

[7] See photograph facing page 178.

[8] This writer has heard that companies sometimes bought special silverware. He found a silver-plated spoon, bearing the crossed sabers monogram of E Company, Tenth Cavalry, at the site of Fort Custer, Montana, built in 1877, abandoned in 1897.

FIFTH INFANTRYMEN IN BUFFALO COATS
and fur hats and gloves, the winter campaign outfit at Fort Keogh,
Montana. The troopers looked like this when they defeated Crazy
Horse on Tongue River, January 8, 1877.

Courtesy Custer Battlefield National Monument
U.S. Park Service

TWENTIETH INFANTRYMEN SERVING AS GATLING GUN CREW
Fort McKean (Fort Abraham Lincoln), North Dakota, 1877. Few
Gatlings were used in action, and Custer refused to take this one
with him to the Little Bighorn, because its draft team of condemned
horses might have slowed his march.

although most of them were pleased to be sent to a line company at last. Living as casuals, waiting for assignment, recruits were acutely aware that they really didn't belong anywhere. Waiting for assignment to an absent company of the Seventh Cavalry, L. J. Henry, whose draft had been temporarily attached to an infantry company, wrote that as replacements ". . . they [the infantry] nearly starved us—I always wondered that there was not more desertion than there was."

The new soldiers were sometimes not impressed with the appearance and demeanor of the older members of their companies. The new recruit outfit contrasted sharply with the worn and frayed clothing worn by the seasoned campaigners, and the lean hardness of the experienced men probably awed the recruits.[9] They soon learned that life on the frontier was somewhat different than it had been at the recruit depots. The veteran soldiers enjoyed laughing at the newcomers, and hearing the latest eastern news from them.

For several days after joining his company, the new soldier was subject to the sharp scrutiny and silent, sometimes unfavorable, judgment of the veterans.[10] During the first few days in the barracks he was apt to overhear many adverse comments on himself, which he had to bear with good humor. In some outfits, new men were picked on by bullies, and were accepted when they called the bully's bluff.[11] Gradually, as the daily routines went on, the older soldiers accepted the new men as members of the company. In most cases, wrote Private James B. Wilkin-

[9] Mulford, *Fighting Indians,* 26f.

[10] Med. Hist., Fort Laramie, 1868–79, MS, Nat. Arch., 78. A group of 119 recruits were examined by the post surgeon and the post commander, Nov. 15, 1870. The entry regarding these men was generally unfavorable, as they were judged ". . . below average in physique and character." One was covered with scrofula, two were rotting with advanced syphilis, one was a hopeless alcoholic, and one was an epileptic. In November, 1872, another notation recorded the arrival of 54 recruits, ". . . composed of remarkably good material."

[11] Diary of Private B. C. Goodin, Jan. 31, 1893 to July 14, 1893, MS. Goodin was assigned to his company on Feb. 15, and experienced his initiation scrap two days later. He "came out all right."

son, the new replacements ". . . learned from the older soldiers, as their advice was freely given and gladly received." Those replacements who did not measure up were treated harshly, and if several members of a troop or company strongly objected to their presence, they were sometimes encouraged or driven to desert.[12]

In every company recruits were likely to find men who recalled their own earlier experiences, and helped the newcomer to find his place in the unit. Writing from his experience, C. H. Clement recalled how he had wanted to send a letter home to his family, after arrival at his post and assignment to a company. Not having a postage stamp, he approached a veteran trumpeter and asked for the loan of a stamp. The older man looked at him for a moment, and ". . . believing that the lean recruit was broke, proffered the price of several stamps with a friendly smile." These two men became good friends, largely because of this friendly gesture.

Initiation into a company was almost always accompanied by a month or so of hazing. It was usually not vicious, and was mainly intended to test the newcomers and afford diversion for the older soldiers, some of whom took exceptional delight in making the replacements feel ridiculous and uncomfortable. One of the commonest forms of hazing was the dissemination of misinformation to recruits, so that, acting upon it, they would get themselves into minor difficulties or appear foolish. First Cavalry recruits at Fort Grant, Arizona, were seriously told that the "hog ranch" adjoining the military reservation was the source of their pork supply, a story that was taken at face value by the green men. When they were assured that they could collect their "butter allowance" money from the company first sergeant, some tried to do so, to the discomfiture of both the sergeant and the recruits. Occasionally, older men went to some

[12] Unpopular soldiers sometimes found a piece of salt pork and a couple of hardtack crackers in their bunk or blankets. This was a sign to get out, to take the rations and leave the outfit.

pains to play tricks on the gullible replacements. This happened in K Troop, First Cavalry, when one of the veteran soldiers "... took his big US [waist belt] buckle, daubed it with red ink and branded a big US on his hip, then told rookies they were to be branded with a hot iron. He then slipped his trousers down and showed them his brand."

Recruits were often the victims of practical jokes in connection with their assigned duties. Replacements for the Seventh Cavalry were sometimes urged to ride a specially selected, fractious horse, with the stirrups crossed over the saddle, which resulted in much hilarity among onlookers and discomfort if not some hard knocks for the riders.[13] Less extreme forms of duty hazing were such tricks as ordering a recruit to obtain a star and truncheon when his name was posted for stable police. In the same vein, H. C. Durgin, a Thirteenth Infantry replacement of the 1880's, ruefully recalled a bit of joshing he had received, when ordered to split a large quantity of dried peas for split-pea soup. Being new to army ways, he began the task, laboriously trying to halve the hard kernels with a paring knife, until he saw a dozen soldiers laughing at him.

Army life was an entirely new experience for nearly all recruits, and the conditions of frontier life were so strange to them that their imaginations frequently exaggerated their initial experiences. Veterans enjoyed scaring the newcomers with harrowing tales about the Indians, the dangers of the country, and how hard life was for the soldier. New men who fired at skulking coyotes while on guard, or otherwise betrayed their ignorance of frontier life, were the source of much amusement to the veteran soldiers in every company.[14]

During most of the Indian Wars period, the recruit depots provided little training for new men, so that a portion of their first weeks in a line company was spent in preparing them for

[13] Mulford, *Fighting Indians*, 28.
[14] "84-Year-Old Veteran Remembers Buffalo Bill," in *The Happy Harvester*, Vol. VII, No. 3 (1951), 1.

service. Sometimes the demands of campaigning did not allow a training period, and replacements almost completely ignorant of horsemanship and marksmanship were sent out against the hostiles.[15] When recruits arrived for the Third Cavalry, at Fort Bayard, New Mexico, in 1882, they were sent out on active duty with their companies at once, and ". . . learned no more sabre drills, no more foot movements, no manual of arms, no parade ground at 10:a.m. and 2:p.m."

If possible, a company gave its recruits some formal instruction before they were assigned to guard duty or sent out on campaign. They were often drilled at odd hours, when the veteran soldiers in their companies were at leisure or on some routine duty. Each company at Fort Totten, Dakota Territory, sent its replacements off for an hour's drill, separate from the company, at six o'clock, morning and evening, in addition to the company's regular training routines.[16]

New soldiers received only the most basic training prior to assuming their full status as members of the company. In the sixties, and to the end of the seventies, they were drilled mainly in close order movements, the manual of arms, and the military duties and courtesies involved in mounting guard. Not until the late seventies and early eighties did the Regular Army emphasize training in skirmish drills and marksmanship. When target practice finally was given an important place in training, the army took it up enthusiastically, and marksmanship became as much stressed as it had previously been slighted.

In some instances, new men were trained for the type of campaigning that would later be required of them. As early as 1879, Sixth Cavalry replacements were taken on what would later be termed practice marches and bivouacs, to teach them something

[15] Johnson, "Jacob Horner," 77–79. Horner and 77 other Seventh Cavalry replacements went out on campaign with the regiment about one month after enlistment, including one week of waiting at Fort Snelling, Minnesota. None of these men had been trained in horsemanship, and none had received any instruction in the use of their arms. Several died with Custer, June 25, 1876.

[16] Order Book, Seventh Cavalry, 1878–81, 71 *et passim.*

of conditions on active duty in the Southwest. One such practice march was conducted for a party of fifteen recruits. A lieutenant and twenty-five Apache scouts accompanied the new men into the mountains, where simulated skirmishes were held, and the men instructed in the tactics and techniques employed against the hostiles. The Apache scouts knew all the tricks of their hostile kinsmen, and served as excellent "enemies" for the trainees.

Perhaps of as much importance to the recruit as drill was the information he acquired from the older men in the company barracks. From their conversation the neophytes soon learned about a wide variety of subjects, not included in any book of drill or regulations, not all of which had the approval of commissioned officers.[17]

After spending a year or two in a company, most men seem to have made a satisfactory adjustment. They grumbled, of course, about the food and the restrictions of army life, but except for those who chose to desert, the majority became accustomed to the circumstances of their lives and served out their enlistments as regular soldiers.

[17] Forsyth, *The Soldier,* I, 126f.

6.

Routine Duty at the Western Posts

Isolation, boredom, and monotony characterized life at the western posts. Because these frontier forts were intended to serve as focal points for offensive and defensive operations against unsettled hostile Indians, they were usually located in regions little touched by white civilization, where there was little opportunity for normal community relationships. The Regular Army had no rotation plans during the Indian campaigns, and troops frequently were assigned to the same stations for several years. Cut off as they were from everything familiar to them, the men found the necessary daily fatigues and guards extremely monotonous, and welcomed any kind of diversion in what was generally "a rather dull existence," wrote Private W. G. Wilkinson.

Some regiments tried to rotate their companies by having them exchange stations every two years, but the exigencies of the service served to keep some companies at the same posts for many years. Even the more fortunate ones who were transferred from one location to another discovered that the actual travel involved was generally the only real change, for life at one isolated post tended to be much like that at another. Transfers often brought the men into contact with other members of the same regiment, though, and until routine had been re-established, change of post was usually a welcome episode in the lives of the soldiers.[1]

Facilities and quarters were extremely crude at the more isolated posts, where soldiers lived in hastily improvised barracks and huts. Accommodations for the enlisted men were not given priority when improvements were made. Commenting on facilities for the soldiers in 1878, a Fourth Infantry officer wrote that in over thirty-six years of service, he did not remember ". . . ever having seen a bath-house at any of our frontier posts, furnished by the government for the use of the men."[2] As the pressure of Indian campaigning abated, and the western posts became more firmly established, improvements such as the replacing of earth-roofed and adobe barracks with wooden frame buildings were introduced. By the end of the Indian Wars period, some of the larger forts boasted post halls, canteens, schools, and at least adequate living quarters for the enlisted soldiers.

Some frontier posts experienced numerous Indian alarms, and, occasionally, sustained attacks by the hostiles. Soldiers sometimes looked on alarms as welcome breaks in the monotony, but at the most exposed stations these occurrences rapidly lost their romantic color, when the men were turned out two and three times a day to repel attacks on the horse herd or to protect the outposts.[3]

[1] Snyder, Diary, 1878, Jan. 16–Feb. 26.

[2] Letter from Colonel F. F. Flint, Fourth Infantry, Jan. 2, 1878, 45 Cong., 3 sess., *Misc. Doc. No. 56,* 122.

[3] Snyder, Diary, 1876, Dec. 12 through Dec. 14, MS. The building of Fort Keogh, Montana, like that of Fort Phil Kearny in 1866, was attended by constant Indian harassment.

Each day's activities were carried on within the framework of a rigidly organized routine, in so far as conditions permitted. From the sounding of trumpeters' assembly (first call for reveille), until extinguish lights, about 9:30 P.M., almost every hour had one or more calls.[4] The schedule was varied from time to time, but remained essentially the same at all posts during the last quarter of the nineteenth century. The routine generally included three roll calls each day, as well as the daily mounting of the guard, the necessary fatigues, drills, and an evening dress parade at retreat. When not engaged in answering the various calls, attending drills, or working on fatigue details, the men lounged about the barracks, and were generally free to do as they pleased, but were required to remain always within bugle call unless specifically permitted to be absent.

The routine varied slightly from day to day through the week. Mounted drill might be stipulated for some days, and target practice included in the routine of the day following. Fridays and Saturdays were largely reserved for cleanup work, and

[4] Gen. Orders No. 51, Fort Totten, Dakota Territory, Oct. 1, 1879, as written out in Post and Regimental Order Book, Seventh Cavalry, 1878–81, MS, CBNM. The daily routine scheduled in this order is as follows: 5:45 a.m., assembly for trumpeters; 6:00, reveille; assembly (roll call); 6:30, mess; 7:30, fatigue call; 8:00, sick call; 8:55, assembly of trumpeters; 9:00, assembly of guard detail; 9:45, recall from fatigue details (Mon., Wed., Fri.); 9:50, boots and saddles (Mon., Wed., Fri.); 10:00, drill (except Sat., and dismounted on Tues. and Thurs.); 11:00, recall from drill (infantry and artillery); 11:30, recall from drill (cavalry); 11:45, first sergeants' call (for morning reports); 12:00 noon, recall from fatigue (on days when no drills were held), mess; 1:00 p.m., drill for target practice (Mon., Wed., Fri.); 2:00, fatigue call (except Fri. and Sat., when all hands cleaned barracks and other facilities for inspection); 4:15, recall from fatigue; 4:30, stable call (grooming and care of the animals); no evening mess call except by gongs and triangles; five minutes before sundown, assembly of trumpeters, and assembly of entire garrison, except posted guards, in dress uniform; sunset, retreat call, roll call; 8:55, assembly for trumpeters call; 9:00, tattoo, last roll call (soldiers in company formations in front of quarters); 9:30, extinguish lights (note absence of "taps," although this call was in general use); Sun., inspection at 9:00, and if church was held the call was sounded at 10:15.

Sunday's routine centered on the weekly inspection. Through the week, a soldier was assigned to a succession of guards and details. On Monday he might be detailed to stable police; on Tuesday and Wednesday be sent to the rifle range, on Thursday be assigned to kitchen detail for two days, on Saturday be made barrack room orderly, and be granted a mounted pass to leave the post after the Sunday morning inspection.

Guard mount was one of the high points of every day's routine. If the post was a regimental headquarters, the band was mustered to play, and in any case all available trumpeters and buglers formed up to sound off when the new guard relieved the detail that had been on duty for the previous twenty-four hours. Guard was usually mounted in the morning, when the men detailed for the duty assembled in front of their company quarters at the first call for guard mount. They were inspected by the company first sergeant, who marched them to the parade ground, in front of the guard house. At the parade the guard was formed up and inspected by the sergeant major, who announced to the men their assigned details. When the sergeant major was satisfied with the new and old guard formations, he reported to the officer of the day that the guard was formed. The officer of the day proceeded to inspect the guard, ordering them through all or portions of the manual of arms. The passwords were given, and the new guard replaced the old for another twenty-four hour period. The post prisoners were paraded to the left of the old guard during the ceremony. With some minor variations, the same guard-changing routine was observed at each post, no matter how small or isolated.

All except specially detailed enlisted men were liable to guard duty, drawing assignments as their names came up in rotation. When companies were small, or when several men were absent on patrols or other duty, guard turns came almost daily, allowing the men little time for rest.

A soldier was not allowed to remove his clothing or accouterments when on guard duty. If he got any rest at all, it was fully clothed, stretched out on a wooden dais in the guard room.[5] Unless the weather or other conditions required more frequent changes, sentinels were relieved every two hours. Some of the guard were sent out in charge of prisoner work gangs during the day, or otherwise employed in patrolling the area, in addition to manning the established guard posts. Sentinels were posted by the corporal or sergeant of the guard. They were to repeat all the general and special orders, upon the demand of an officer, and render all due military courtesies. The officer of the day usually visited each post at least once on what was termed the "Grand Rounds," at which time he was accompanied by the noncommissioned officers of the guard and an escort of privates. Sentinels called out their post numbers and the time every hour, and sometimes on the half-hour as well.

One of the highlights of guard mounting was the competitive selection of one of the privates of the new guard to serve as the commanding officer's orderly. "Inspection competition was keen," said Sergeant Unger, "the one chosen as orderly received a pass [or at least relief from duty]. Much time was spent polishing and sprucing up for inspection." A company might include one or two noted "orderly buckers," whose expert competition the other soldiers did not try to meet unless the known specialists were not detailed to the same guard. Not only did the orderly generally receive a pass at the expiration of his tour of duty, but he was also allowed to spend the night in his own bunk, rather than on the guardroom dais. He did not stand any sentinel duty nor "chase" prisoners, but spent his time sitting in the headquarters office, waiting to carry orders for the commanding officer. He was allowed to eat ahead of all other soldiers, and often enjoyed small privileges denied to the rest of the guard.

At the end of a twenty-four hour guard detail, the men were frequently assigned to a special fatigue, although this was not

[5] Hershler, *Handbook*, 6f.

always done. They were allowed at least some free time the day after their tour of duty, when their garrison included several companies.

Special guards were sometimes added to the regular garrison guard, and if the pressure of Indian hostilities necessitated almost continuous alternation between guard duty and the required garrison fatigue details, there was no time for drill or relaxation. The visit of a high ranking officer also sometimes called for additional men in the daily guard detail, to observe the formalities befitting the rank of the visitor. When a particularly soldierly-looking guard was wanted, commanding officers might offer coveted passes and duty exemptions to those passing a rigid inspection.[6] From the army's point of view, guard duty was one of the most important duties of a soldier, and most of the training and drill provided for recruits joining an active unit were intended to orient them in this function.

Fatigues have always been a major cause of discontent among enlisted men, especially when they felt that they were serving more as cheap labor for the army than as soldiers. They realized that many of the fatigue details were essential to the maintenance of a post, and that the isolation of widely-scattered small commands necessitated the use of the only available manpower, the soldiers themselves. At the same time, so much of a soldier's duty was connected with labor of some sort, building telegraph lines, constructing roads, erecting buildings, that many men deeply resented what they felt was their exploitation as cheap labor.

After duty in a number of fatigue details, a Ninth Infantry private summed up the general opinion of his fellows when he wrote to his fiancée that he was ". . . beginning to think the soldiers in the Department of the Platte know better how to handle pick & shovel than they do a gun . . . ."[7] Green A. Settle explained

[6] Order Book, Fort Meade, Dakota Territory, 1887, CBNM.

[7] McAnulty to Miss Moore, July 25, 1878.

some of the lengthy and tedious details he had been assigned to, and concluded with the comment that ". . . nothing worries a soldier more than doing the dirty [work] about the post." A detachment of Fifth Infantrymen, stationed at Fort Stevenson, Dakota Territory, in 1877, told some visiting Seventh Cavalrymen that life there was like living in a poorhouse, because they worked hard for bed and board and received only a pittance as salary.[8] "Government workhouse," as a descriptive term for an army post, was in common use among soldiers of the Indian Wars period.

Soldier complaints about fatigue assignments of course were intended to win sympathy. Naturally, some fatigues were more demanding and intensive than others, but many of the more routine work details did not require heavy exertion by the men. A. F. Mulford remarked, "There was always plenty to do, but none of it hard enough to hurt a man. No soldier ever over works." Explaining the place fatigues occupied in the daily post routine, the same soldier wrote that when fatigue call sounded at one o'clock ". . . the different details would proceed to kill time, as they had been doing all the forenoon." This was not true when the men were engaged in essential construction of post facilities, or when they were driven by grim necessity to cut timber for lumber and fuel, build roads passable for supply wagons, and accomplish other high priority projects.

Every soldier, with the exception of the noncommissioned officers and specially assigned men, was liable for fatigue duty as stable police, kitchen detail, room orderly, and a host of other recurring work assignments. Details were announced at company formations, or the men received details from the bulletin board each evening. Short fatigues were welcomed, because the men assigned to them were usually at leisure when their tasks were completed.

The fatigue details connected with construction work, were

---

[8] Mulford, *Fighting Indians*, 72.

arduous and unpopular, especially when a new post was being built in some remote region. A new fort was usually needed because of Indian hostilities, and the soldier-laborers might be continuously on duty every day. Men whose previous experience qualified them as carpenters, stonemasons, or other "mechanics" were allowed extra-duty pay at the rate of thirty-five cents a day, while soldiers classed as laborers received twenty-five cents extra. This was cut to twenty cents in the 1880's. Noncommissioned men were not eligible for extra-duty pay, unless they were acting as overseers of at least twenty laborers. This was unfair to the corporals and sergeants; an extra-duty private often earned more than the noncommissioned officers.[9] Buildings at the newly established posts were usually of log, earth, and adobe. Because of the shortage of skilled workmen, materials, and tools, the construction met only minimal requirements. Lumber was generally too scarce to use for roofing and flooring, and earth was commonly employed for both uses, with the result that quarters offered some protection but little comfort.[10]

Civilians were employed on major construction work when money and workmen were available; even then most of the heavy labor was performed by the enlisted men. When a post had become well established, the crude log and adobe buildings were commonly replaced with frame quarters and other structures of a more permanent nature, again with much labor by the soldiers. Fort Buford, Dakota Territory, was composed entirely of adobe buildings in 1870. By 1872, all the earlier barracks, offices, store houses, and other facilities had been replaced by frame buildings.

Some posts were constantly being remodeled, like Fort Laramie, which was being altered and added to during almost all its forty-odd years as an active station. Comparison of drawings

---

[9] Harbers, "Service Account," in Ashburn, *Medical Department*, 99.

[10] Snyder to his mother, MS, Sept. 19, 1876, S-R Coll. ". . . it is a little unpleasant at first to be smothered with dust every time you walk across the room or whenever the door is opened . . . ."

and pictures of the buildings, at different periods, reveals changes that only a great deal of labor could have effected. This sort of remodeling was not popular with the soldiers, for to them it seemed to have no end and to be merely arbitrary exploitation and busy work. Soldiers were likely to grumble that they "did not enlist to carry the hod," and chant such songs as the one that went: "A dollar a day is damn poor pay, but thirteen a month is less!"

Soldier dislike for such arduous and tedious work as lumbering and logging sometimes went beyond grumbling and resulted in desertions. When the first cantonment was established at the mouth of Tongue River, Montana Territory, in the winter of 1876 and 1877, a great number of logs were required to build even temporary quarters for more than a full regiment of soldiers. Logging for new construction was one of the most important fatigues in areas where timber was reasonably close at hand. A company or two of troops would be sent to what were termed the "pineries," to secure rough logs for construction and enough saw logs to provide timber for working into lumber. The rough boards were fashioned by the ancient saw-pit method, with one man in the pit and another on top of the log, using a long ripsaw, until such time as a steam sawmill could be set up and put into operation. This was backbreaking labor by any standards, and the officer who pitched in and lent a hand with the work, heaving logs, using an ax to trim, or perhaps spelling a tired soldier on the saw logs, earned the affection and respect of his men.

Innumerable police details were an important part of each day's routine at all army posts. Necessary cleanup began early in the morning. As stable police, the calvarymen donned their canvas stable clothes and marched in columns of twos, to water and groom their mounts. Other police details included the cleaning of various buildings and quarters, the disposal of garbage and night soil, and general cleanup around the post. Soldiers have always disliked cleanup details and the men serving on the frontier were no exception. An example of the more unpopular

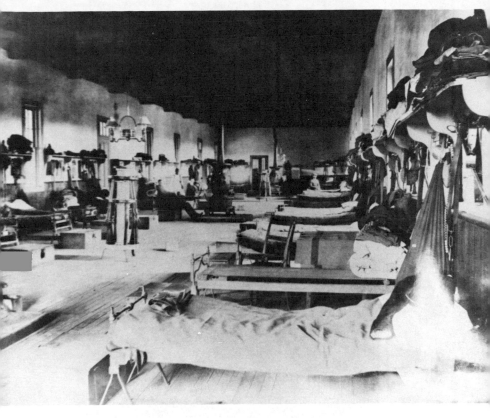

ADOBE BARRACKS AT FORT ROBINSON, NEBRASKA
occupied by a troop of the Ninth Cavalry about 1890. Springs had
replaced the earlier bunk boards in the late 1880's.

Courtesy Smithsonian Institution

SERGEANT PERLEY S. EATON

of D Troop, Third Cavalry, 1881–86. Eaton had this picture taken in his dress uniform. The medal he wears designates him as a sharpshooter. He served at Fort Washakie, against Apaches in the Southwest, and participated in the Battle of the Big Dry Wash, July 17, 1882, on a strenuous Apache campaign in Arizona.

Courtesy Sergeant Perley S. Eaton

sort of assignment was one at Fort Riley, Kansas, in 1888, when a "... large detail was set to pull out sunflowers that almost covered the parade ground. Some of the boys were complaining ... saying 'I came here to be a soldier.' " Men who joined the army to be soldiers saw little connection between soldiering and weed-pulling, wrote Andrew M. Flynn.

The isolation of the posts and the lack of labor-saving devices or engineered utilities made it necessary to employ soldier labor in more than the usual ways. At many stations, cooking and drinking water had to be hauled in barrels from a spring or other source of supply. A daily water-barrel working party hauled empty barrels, filled them, and then took the water around to the cookhouses, barracks, and officers' quarters. Because most of the heating and cooking was by wood-burning iron stoves, the accumulation and maintenance of an adequate fuel supply was another important and continuous fatigue. The scarcity of wood in the plains country often necessitated the establishment of wood camps where timber was available, from which fuel was hauled long distances to the posts. At small posts and temporary camps details of two or three men were sent out to cut a stipulated amount of firewood, which was periodically picked up by a hauling detail from the post. Because of the large quantities needed, wood parties were sent out all the year round, to insure an adequate supply for the cold months of the year. When funds and interested civilians were available, the wood supply was sometimes secured by contract with citizens. This was true also of the hay supply for the horses and mules of a garrison.

Vegetables were not included in the rations issued to soldiers during most of the Indian Wars period, although, the army realized that for adequate nutrition some vegetables must be included in the diet. Instead of attempting to issue them, except in very small quantities and in preserved forms, the army sought to encourage the raising of vegetables in post gardens. Where climate, water, and soil permitted, vegetable gardens were an important adjunct to most frontier posts. Post and company gardens were under the general supervision of the post adjutant or commissary officer, but the on-the-spot supervision was the responsibility of a soldier detailed from each company. Men assigned as gardeners were relieved of all other duty, including guard. One man from each company, though specifically assigned as gardener, could not possibly have done all the work necessary to raise the required quantity of vegetables, and he was assisted by fatigue parties of men from the companies. The fatigue details dug irrigation ditches, hoed weeds, cultivated the crops, and assisted in the planting and harvesting. At some stations each private spent one day a week working the post gardens as part of his regular routine. Like other company activities, gardening often became competitive, with each unit at the post endeavoring to raise the prize vegetables.[11]

Other utility fatigue details were those connected with laying up a store of ice in the winter, when the post was situated near a source of supply. This was hard and unpopular labor, and was usually done by large numbers of soldiers, working for short periods of time. One inevitable detail, universally disliked by soldiers, is that of assisting the company cooks in the kitchen. The men on kitchen detail chopped the stove wood, carried water for the cooks, waited on the men at meals, washed the mess gear and cooking pots, and set the tables three times each day.

Detailing soldiers to some unpleasant extra duty was often a form of company punishment, especially if the duty was performed when the rest of the company was at leisure. A common and time-consuming assignment was that of reloading cartridges. Until the early eighties it was not possible to reload government cartridges, but when modern, replaceable primers were adopted, economy dictated the reloading of all salvageable cases. Reloading became particularly important after target practice was emphasized and encouraged. Soldiers were detailed from each company to refill the cartridges fired by their unit, under the

11 See photograph facing page 115.

supervision of an ordnance sergeant. The fatigue party cleaned, recapped, and replaced powder and bullet in each shell. Although tubs of water were kept close at hand and extreme caution was ordered, accidents did occur. When a careless man blew part of his hand off at Fort Verde, Arizona, in the early eighties, the commanding officer stopped all reloading as too dangerous. In some units reserved as an off-hours, extra-duty punishment, in others reloading ammunition was a regular detail, rotated among the men like other assignments.

In the years immediately following the end of the Civil War the Regular Army was far too small to cope with the upsurge of Indian hostilities. Many of the regulars were green recruits in urgent need of training, but the exigencies of frontier service allowed little time for this vital instruction. The two companies garrisoning Fort Sully, Dakota Territory, in 1866, could not spend time in drill or target practice; hostile pressure kept the troops constantly employed in patrol and guard duty, because there were not enough soldiers to man the post properly.[12] Similar reports came from other posts. No drills were held during the month of September, 1868, at Fort Laramie.[13] Two hours of daily drill were inaugurated at that post in November of the same year, when Indian activities decreased with the coming of winter.

After four years of Civil War, Congress exhibited an attitude toward military spending that in the long run proved to be penny-wise and pound-foolish. New breech-loading small arms, employing metallic cartridges, were issued to the regulars, but the expensive new ammunition was always in short supply. Gatling guns and other new equipments were also being put in service, but in general soldiers were not trained in their use. Put in charge of two new Gatling guns, which formed part of the escort to the Indian Commissioners who met with the southern plains Indians at Medicine Lodge, Kansas, in 1867, a new

---

[12] D. B. Sackett, "Protection Across the Continent," 39 Cong., 2 sess., House Executive Document No. 23, 24, 48.

[13] Med. Hist., Fort Laramie, 1868–79, Nat. Arch., 36.

lieutenant of the Seventh Cavalry believed that his inexperienced gun crews should be familiarized with the use of the guns. Recalling the incident, the officer wrote: "I wanted to have target practice, but was told I would have to pay for the ammunition. The commanding officer refused to authorize target practice for fear he would have to pay for the ammunition, [and the crews never did fire the Gatlings]."[14]

Even when Indian activities decreased, and fatigue details did not demand too much of a garrison's time, indifference on the part of some company and commanding officers seriously restricted the amount of drill and training participated in by the soldiers. Drill was "something unknown" at Fort Ellis, Montana Territory in 1871, and in the opinion of Peter Koch, post sutler's clerk, inspection-day activities were largely limited to the "officers . . . inspecting a few bottles of champagne." With officers apathetic toward drills and training, the rank and file were not inclined to raise the issue. Most regular officers had experienced active wartime commands during the Rebellion, and many of them felt let down and frustrated at being assigned to small frontier commands that offered only the prospect of insignificant skirmishes with savages.

The lack of training troubled some frontier soldiers, such as the First Infantryman assigned to a gun crew manning one of the small cannon that the regiment used during the 1876 Sioux Campaign. Realizing his lack of training, Sergeant Hamilton wrote that ". . . like many of our men I was not adequately trained to handle [the cannon]." A surgeon who accompanied Colonel Gibbon's column from Forts Shaw and Ellis, Montana, during the 1876 summer campaign against the Sioux, noted the results of neglecting training when he gave his opinion of the average cavalryman's qualifications. After spending three months in the field, and participating in the relief of the Seventh Cavalry survivors at the Little Bighorn, the doctor wrote:

[14] General E. S. Godfrey, "Recollections of the Medicine Lodge Treaty Conference, October, 1867," MS, Bates Coll., 1.

... cavalrymen ... as a general thing are about as well fitted to travel through a hostile country as puling infants, and go mooning around at the mercy of any Indian who happens to catch sight and takes the trouble to lay for them behind the first convenient ridge.[15]

Many of these soldiers had not fired their weapons a dozen times a year. On the second day of the Battle of the Little Bighorn, the Reno-Benteen men were ordered to fire only with permission from the officers, because most of them were unable to hit a hostile and merely wasted their ammunition. A lieutenant observed one trooper preparing to fire his carbine, and later wrote that ". . . he pulled the trigger. There was a very perceptible dropping of the muzzle, and a flinch, but no report. He had forgotten to cock his piece."[16]

The Little Bighorn catastrophe sobered the nation, and many people demanded reorganization of an army that permitted raw recruits to be sent against the powerful Sioux. Congress increased the strength of cavalry companies to one hundred men, but the "Custer Avengers" who enlisted in the Seventh Cavalry were hastily assigned to line companies in the early fall of 1876. Many of the Seventh were recruits when that regiment was sent to disarm the reservation Sioux in southern South Dakota. The new men were in pitiful condition when they returned to Fort Abraham Lincoln. Albert J. Davis wrote that he ". . . discovered that none of the new men in my troop could ride at all."

Early in 1878 public and official interest in army training and fitness to combat the hostile Indians finally led to a series of hearings before a subcommittee of the House of Representatives. Testimony, such as that of First Lieutenant Edmund V. Rice, Fifth Infantry, convinced the committee, and many high-ranking army men, that training for campaign and combat conditions

[15] Dean Hudnutt, "New Light on the Little Big Horn [sic.]," *Field Artillery Journal*, Vol. XXVI, No. 4, (1936), 357.

[16] Major E. S. Godfrey, "Cavalry Fire Discipline," *Journal of The Military Service Institution*, Vol. XIX, No. 83 (1896), 258.

would have to be officially ordered and emphasized. When queried on the amount of drill and training in progress at army posts, Lieutenanat Rice replied that to his knowledge, "one-half the posts of the Army have no drills. The companies are so small that all the men are occupied in taking care of the post."[17] The results of this renewed official interest in training were slow in coming, but the well-trained Regular Army of the Spanish-American War actually originated in the training policies and programs formulated in the late seventies and early eighties. Disasters such as that at Little Bighorn, and the costly victory over the Nez Percé at Bear Paw Mountain in 1877, where the troops suffered almost thirty per cent casualties, focused much energy and attention on the problems of preparing combat-ready soldiers.

Some regiments began sending their new men out on practice marches and small-scale war games as early at 1879. This was common practice by the middle eighties, and paid significant dividends in combat and on active campaigns. When troops were outnumbered or surprised by hostiles, the trained men were the steady ones, able to stand fast and counterattack the enemy.[18]

Some regimental and company officers placed as much emphasis as possible on drill even before official interest was aroused after 1878. General Nelson A. Miles was particularly insistent on regular and continuous drills.[19] His practice of drilling the Fifth Infantry, in all kinds of weather and in actual skirmishing, undoubtedly contributed to his achievement of such victories as that of Tongue River, Montana Territory, January 8, 1877. Miles's infantrymen, outnumbered two to one by warriors,

[17] *Reorganization of the Army,* 45 Cong., 2 sess., *House Misc. Doc. No. 56,* Mar. 21, 1876, 246.

[18] "Lieutenant Fountain's Fight With Apache Indians at Lillie's Ranch, Mogollon Mountains, December 9, 1885, and at Dry Creek, N. M., December 19, 1885," *Proceedings, Order of Indian Wars, 1928,* 41.

[19] Snyder, Diary, 1877. July 17: . . .; "battalion skirmish drill, three hours in the morning." March 2: ". . . a cold disagreeable day. Gen. Miles had a row in regard to getting the men out to drill & I had to issue orders upon the subject."

stormed a crescent ridge in below-zero weather and a blinding blizzard, to rout Crazy Horse's hostiles from the field. This band of Indians surrendered shortly after the battle, because they were convinced they could not win against such fighters as the walking soldiers, who combed the country in midwinter and outfought double their own number. When army headquarters finally did focus attention on drill and preparation for field service, regiments such as the ill-fated Seventh Cavalry came in for their full share of it. As of April, 1878, only the post bakers, nurses, cooks, and one room orderly from each company were excused from mounted drill every morning.[20]

No single aspect of training received more emphasis in the late seventies than did small-arms target practice. By contrast, an Eighteenth Infantryman recalled that his unit held no target practice at all during the year 1866, because of the short supply of ammunition. This regiment was campaigning in the heart of the hostile Sioux and Cheyenne country, and held its first target practice in the spring of 1867. In 1872, the army officially adopted a course of small-arms instruction, calling for each man to fire ninety rounds of ammunition at the rifle range, and to participate in drills designed to enable the rifleman to estimate distances correctly. No special emphasis was placed on the subject, however, and the target-practice regulations were generally ignored.

What target shooting there was took several forms. A popular kind of small-arms practice in the cavalry was mounted revolver-shooting. A pile of hardtack boxes was set up to approximate the size of a man. Firing was begun at thirty yards, first at a walk, then a trot, and finally at the gallop. The 1878 rifle and carbine practice was at ranges progressing from one hundred to a thousand yards, with the target having a bull's-eye eight to thirty-six inches in diameter. Recruits fired at ranges of one hundred to five hundred yards, and were expected to achieve scores averag-

[20] Order Book, Seventh Cavalry, 1878–81, MS, 14.

ing about fifty per cent of the possible number of hits. Experienced men fired at greater distances. That some soldiers became proficient riflemen under this system is indicated by the target record of Corporal Henry Beleke, Twentieth Infantry, which shows that at the end of his five-year enlistment in 1887, his six-hundred-yard score, qualifying him as a marksman, totaled eighty-four percent of a possible perfect score.

Soldiers became enthusiastic target-shooters in the 1880's, and took great pride in their skill, and in the marksman and sharp-shooter badges and certificates awarded to soldiers qualifying for them. In addition to shooting at conventional targets, a system of firing at silhouette figures of mock enemies was adopted in the middle eighties. The cutouts were placed at unknown distances, and in all conceivable positions. The number and placement of hits on the figure targets determined the shooter's score. Some units conducted this sort of skirmish drill shooting every week, and most soldiers enjoyed the practice as a sport.

Not all soldiers were enthusiastic about target-shooting three times a week with the forty-five caliber Springfield carbine or rifle. In all-day firing, the recoil of either carbine or rifle could be brutal.[21] An 1887 Seventh Cavalryman, Clarence H. Allen, wrote that soldiers

> . . . had sockets to put over the butt of the carbine, and on top of that we were glad to put paper or anything we could get to keep it from the shoulder. I was black and blue all over the shoulder and down into my chest. I got so I couldn't help flinching and I didn't make a very good score.

In the Thirteenth Infantry, new men shot at targets for two days before an official score was kept. Two pairs of socks padding

[21] The writer has fired hundreds of rounds of .45/55/405 Government carbine ammunition in the model 1873 Springfield carbine. Shooting fifty rounds in a single day produces a marked stiffness in the shooter's shoulder; any more would indeed constitute punishment. With practice, the carbine is capable of quite accurate shooting, at a man-sized target, up to about five or six hundred yards. Until the 1880's, few soldiers were practiced marksmen.

the right shoulder helped one soldier to alleviate the recoil on the second day, but destroyed the shooter's mediocre accuracy. Investigating the reason for such poor shooting, the captain found out about the socks, but only grinned and told the man to try again.

A strong competitive element was injected into the emphasis on target scores when an official policy was adopted in 1879 to award prizes and furloughs to the best shots in each unit.[22] Under the 1879 program, each soldier was to fire twenty rounds each month at the target range. In 1880, competition was organized at the post, department, and divisional levels, with the best marksmen pitted against any and all opponents in the international rifle matches at Creedmore, Long Island.[23] Soldiers were encouraged to spend part of their free time on the rifle range, firing reloaded ammunition, and many men became ardent shooters. By the time of the Spanish-American War, the United States regular was probably the world's best military marksman, compared man for man with the soldiers of any of the world's standing armies.

Even though drill and campaign preparedness were given far more attention in the 1880's, the assembling of many companies and regiments for extended maneuvers was not undertaken until the last years of the decade. The soldiers looked on the maneuvers as a welcome change from the routine of post life. According to Seventh Cavalryman Andrew M. Flynn, the high point of the 1889 war games in western Nebraska came just after the troops were paid in the field. A farmer received permission to sell a load of watermelons inside the camp. Some sold for ten cents, others for a dollar, but the dollar melons each held a pint of whisky. The huckster had no trouble in disposing of his wares, and the soldiers made certain that the secret was not divulged to the officers or the camp provost guard.

Although army-wide focusing on drills and training in the

[22] Major W. A. Ganoe, *The History of the United States Army,* 350.
[23] Order Book, Seventh Cavalry, 1878–81, MS, 121.

1880's resulted in far higher levels of efficiency, the men in some units remained unaffected because of the apathy of their officers. Moreover, the pressure of campaigning against hostiles sometimes allowed only limited time for training activities. In some regiments, such as the Seventh Infantry and Eighth Cavalry, the official policies on drills and preparation were rigidly followed. Private William Hustede, who served in 1890, wrote that he received more continuous and thorough training in the First Cavalry than he had had in his previous three years of service in the Germany army.

The army regulations in force during the Indian wars period stipulated a dress parade every day at retreat. Unlike target practice and skirmish drills, the daily dress parade was held whenever conditions permitted, and most drilling was intended to perfect the soldiers for their part in these formal functions. Drums and bugles sounded the signal half an hour before the time appointed for retreat parade; the adjutant's call sounded ten minutes later. The captains then marched their companies to the parade ground, where each unit formed up in line. Once assembled, the troops were ordered through portions of the manual of arms, roll call was taken, and the results reported to the adjutant by the first sergeants. Orders and assignments were read aloud, and the parade was dismissed by companies. If available, the regimental band played throughout the parade, except during roll call and the reading of orders.

Special occasions were usually accompanied by dress parades. When Fort Keogh was being built near Miles City, Montana, in the spring of 1877, the first unfurling of the garrison flag, on April 13, was celebrated by a full dress parade and an hour of close order drill. Visits of high ranking officials and officers also called for full dress formations. General William T. Sherman's stopover at Fort Keogh in July, 1877, was highlighted by a dress parade and review in his honor, following the General's presentation of the Congressional Medals of Honor to the enlisted men who had been recommended for the distinction.[24] Soldiers were expected to turn out in their most military and formal manner for the visitation of such officers as Generals Sherman and Sheridan. When General Philip H. Sheridan visited Fort Rice, Dakota Territory, each company at the post chose one of its sergeants to compete for assignment as special orderly during the General's stay. In competition with another infantryman and sergeants from the Seventh Cavalry companies at the post, Sergeant Ralph Donath represented his company of the Seventeenth Infantry. After the officer of the day inspected the assembled sergeants and eliminated all but Donath and a cavalryman, he again scrutinized the two remaining competitors. Unable to reach a decision, the officer ordered them to remove first their belts and blouses, then shoes ". . . and thus ended the competition, as the cavalry Sergt. had on civilian stockings and I had on the regulation ones." Sergeant Donath added that, like most soldiers, he normally wore the civilian stockings, but that as an experienced inspection competitor he knew that in such a contest all articles of clothing must be regulation.

The death of an officer or soldier in garrison usually occasioned a full dress military funeral conducted by at least part of the troops at the post. A Seventh Cavalryman, who died of diphtheria at Fort Rice, Dakota Territory, in 1877, was laid out in full dress for viewing by his comrades. A caisson bore his coffin, followed by the dead soldier's horse, with boots reversed in the stirrups. Eight trumpeters played the funeral march as the procession moved to the burial plot. The post adjutant read the burial service at the graveside, an honor guard fired three volleys, and the assembled troops were marched back to their quarters at quick time.[25] The death of a corporal at Fort Laramie in 1869 was attended by similar military honors, with an added

---

24 Snyder, Diary, July 18, 1877, MS.
25 Mulford, *Fighting Indians,* 36.

touch of formal mourning in that ". . . each member of his Company wore a piece of [black] tape elaborately pinned upon the left arm."[26]

The departure or return of commands was another event celebrated with band music and dress parades. Recalling his field service campaigning against Apaches in 1881, Twelfth Infantryman Emanuel Roque said, "when we left Whipple Barracks, the band played 'The Girl I Left Behind Me,' and when we returned, the band came out to meet us and played 'When Johnny Comes Marching Home.'" All the troops at the post turned out in dress formations to salute the incoming companies.

Sunday morning was reserved for dress and semidress uniform inspections. Soldiers were drawn up in single line formations, with leather accouterments polished to a high gloss, arms speckless in the grasp of white-gloved hands, and special shined cartridges in the leather McKeever cartridge boxes on their waist belts. The shined cartridges were never fired, except in a guard-duty emergency. In cold or inclement weather, Sunday morning inspection was sometimes held in the barracks.

On one occasion, a special inspection was ordered as a means of punishing a whole company, at Fort Meade, South Dakota. When the unit did not spring to attention quickly enough to suit Captain "Vinegar Jack" Hennessy, he ordered I Company of the Eighth Cavalry to stand inspection outside the barrack, without overcoats or gloves, in below-zero weather. Nine men became so frostbitten that they required treatment at the post hospital. Penalties were meted out to soldiers failing to pass inspection in the Sunday morning ritual. In January 1869, after an inspection at Camp on Medicine Bluff Creek, Indian Territory (later the site of Fort Sill), for being dirty, three men were ordered to shoulder heavy logs. Three others, of K Company, Seventh Cavalry, ". . . had to carry saddles [marching around the parade

---

[26] Med. Hist., Fort Laramie, 1868–79, 55.

ground for several hours] for not being out to inspection at the first call."[27]

The soldiers sometimes enjoyed escort duty and patrols as breaks in the monotonous post routine. Guarding the traveling paymaster was the commonest escort assignment, one in which the men took pleasure when the weather was not severe. Other escorts were provided for recruit drafts, visiting dignitaries, and special-assignment details such as survey parties. Small escorts amounted to camping excursions for the soldiers in good weather. When the weather was bad, however, in a northern plains winter, guarding the paymaster and other escort duty became extremely unpopular. Convoying the paymaster to troops in the field during the Sioux campaign of 1890 and 1891, eighteen men of the Twenty-second Infantry were on the march seventeen days, sleeping every night on frozen ground; they were able to light only a few fires because of the scarcity of wood in the country through which they passed.

Company self-sufficiency was practiced not only in social and military matters, but in personal services provided for the men. Each company included a man designated as company tailor. The tailor remade issue uniforms, sewed on chevrons and trouser stripes, and repaired the clothing of the men in his unit. He was not ranked as a tailor, nor was he eligible for extra-duty pay and privileges; he earned his extra money in his leisure time. Most soldiers had the company tailor alter the issue clothing to a more stylish fit, and the tailor frequently provided made-to-measure uniforms for the company officers. A company tailor of the Eighteenth Infantry at Fort Phil Kearny manufactured a makeshift carpet for an officer's wife in 1866 by sewing corn sacks together.[28] Most companies had a cobbler also, who repaired the boots and shoes of the soldiers and officers. During the

[27] Diary of a Seventh Cavalry Enlisted Man, Jan. 1 to Dec. 24, 1869, Jan. 10. MS, Bates Collection. Diarist's name is not shown or mentioned.

[28] Carrington, *My Army Life*, 104.

winter of 1866 and 1867, the company cobblers at Fort Phil Kearny made buffalo-hide leggings for the men.

A soldier with some experience and skill as a barber was usually given the post of company barber. Like the tailor and the cobbler, the barber was not an extra-duty man, nor was he exempt from routine duties. On his own time, the barber cut each man's hair once a month and shaved each soldier twice a week. The other men in the company paid the barber fifty cents each month, or one dollar every bimonthly payday. Men detailed as cooks and bakers provided other necessary company services, but without special rank or pay.

Soldiers sought assignment to extra duty for reasons other than the pay. Extra-duty men were commonly excused from some of the drills and guard duty, and were not required to be present at some inspections. Hospital duty, other than as a regularly ranked steward, entitled a soldier to extra-duty pay of twenty cents a day. Men termed farriers, blacksmiths, and wagoners were ranked and paid as corporals, and were not classed as extra-duty men, unless employed by the quartermaster for ten days. With a few exceptions, these men performed the same guard and routine duties as other soldiers. The farrier of a cavalry company was responsible for the general maintenance and proper shoeing of about seventy horses, and was sometimes expected to keep the wagons and ambulance in good order.

The noncommissioned complement of each post usually included one ordnance sergeant, a quartermaster sergeant, and at least one hospital steward. These were older noncommissioned men, and some had lengthy service records. The ordnance sergeant stationed at Fort Laramie in 1879 had served there continuously for the previous thirty years.[29]

The post schoolteacher was entitled to extra-duty pay of thirty-five cents a day. Post schools were maintained to provide the fundamentals of reading, writing, and mathematics for army

[29] Med. Hist., Fort Laramie, 1868–79, 57, 246.

children and enlisted men who were interested in acquiring some degree of education. The soldier-teacher was chosen for his educational background. Teaching the soldiers' and officers' children was not always a pleasant task. At Fort Niobrara, Nebraska, ". . . a soldier by the name of Delany was schoolmaster [in 1887]. He tried hard to make the children learn, but they did not wish to study, and spent all their spare time planning tricks to play upon poor Delany. It was a difficult situation for the soldier."[30] Jake Tonamichel, who attended the post school at Fort Laramie in the early eighties, explained that some soldiers did not welcome assignment as teacher, and that "if the teacher got tired of teaching, he got drunk and [purposely] lost his job." The teacher did not spend all his time as schoolmaster, and he was still liable to guard and other duties at the discretion of his officers. School was not in session the year round, and at some posts the school term lasted only four months.

Until the early eighties, officers and their families were waited on by soldier-servants and "strikers" assigned from the companies. Officers often employed soldiers as cooks for their messes, and sometimes for their families when in garrison. Writing of her 1867 Christmas dinner, the wife of the commanding officer at Fort C. F. Smith commented that "a delicious entree was a venison *paté*, made and cooked by a soldier, a Frenchman by birth, who excelled in making this special dish."[31] Some of the soldiers mildly scorned the officers' "strikers"; for others the added extra pay, freedom from some routine duties, and sometimes a sense of belonging to an officer's family were strong incentives. The conditions of a "striker's" life were ". . . a contrast to the bareness and desolation of the noisy barracks . . . [and "strikers"] sometimes remained for years with an officer's family . . . ."[32] The "striker's" extra pay came from the officer for whom he worked,

[30] Summerhayes, *Arizona*, 261.

[31] Elizabeth J. Burt, "Forty Years in the U. S. Regular Army, 1862–1902," MSS. Div., Lib. of Cong.

[32] Summerhayes, *Arizona*, 90.

and ranged from five to ten dollars a month, depending on the type and amount of work performed.

The regimental band was stationed at whatever post served as regimental headquarters. Bandsmen turned out for all formal parades, but were not usually assigned to routine fatigue and guard duties. Many regimental bandsmen were specially recruited because of their musical ability, and though ranked and salaried as privates, at thirteen dollars per month, they often received extra money from company and regimental funds. They provided music for social functions, and in good weather usually played for an hour or so every evening.

The rank of hospital steward corresponded to that of sergeant or first sergeant, depending upon whether it was first or second class. The steward was assisted by enlisted soldiers detailed from the companies at the post, who served as nurses and cooks, one nurse and cook per company. "No one wanted the job [despite the extra-duty pay, as] . . . the duties the men had to perform did not suit them, so it was hard to get a man to stick to that job."[33] Company officers and first sergeants generally detailed the most shiftless and unpromising privates to hospital duty, as a means of shunting them out of the company, because, wrote General Reynolds J. Burt, few soldiers volunteered to work as nurses or hospital cooks and ". . . the wisecracking, run-of-the-mine enlisted men referred to . . . [them] as bed pan pushers." Assigning the poorest soldiers as nurses sometimes resulted in tragedy. A soldier-nurse drank all the liquor he was supposed to be administering, in measured doses, to a dangerously sick sergeant. The next morning the surgeon found the nurse in a drunken stupor and the sergeant dead.[34]

Officers at the smaller posts had difficulty in finding qualified soldiers for the special assignments of routine garrison life. Writing of his personnel problems while serving at Fort Ellis in 1874, an officer commented: "I had a Commissary Sergeant,

[33] Harbers, "Service Account," in Ashburn, *Medical Department,* 101.
[34] *Ibid.,* 120.

well posted in his duties—and a private in the Company who was a good adjutant's clerk. I also found another private who was a very good Quartermaster's Clerk, and I got a Corporal for Ordnance Sergeant."[35] Detailing men as hospital nurses, clerks, and to other assignments drained company strength, and seriously affected the unit's military efficiency.

Field music, provided by company buglers, trumpeters, drummers, and fifers, was part of the daily routine. A cavalry company usually had three trumpeters, who took turns sounding the calls and acting as orderly-trumpeter. Infantry calls were sounded with both drum and bugle. Musicians were seldom assigned to fatigue and guard duties, and spent much of their time in supervised practice on their instruments.

Of the noncommissioned officers, key personnel in the operation and maintenance of daily life and routine, the company first sergeants were the most important. They acted as executive officers to the company commanders, and controlled discipline and drill. The officers of many units rarely attended company drill. Explaining the importance of the first sergeant, Sergeant Perley S. Eaton wrote, "our 1st and 2nd lts. rarely visited our company—the first sergeant had more to do in running the co. than even the captain." Recommending higher pay for first sergeants in 1891, the *Annual Report of the Secretary of War* described and eulogized them as ". . . the hardest worked noncommissioned officers in the army. . . . responsible for proper care and use of arms, equipments . . . company property; . . . [they are] always on duty. . . . [they] must possess tact, sound judgement, superior intelligence." Generally, the first sergeant was the primary source of authority to the enlisted men in his unit. Third Cavalry Sergeant Perley S. Eaton wrote that the first sergeant

. . . was in full charge of the troop, what he says and does is

[35] Lieutenant Colonel E. E. Hardin, [1874 Seventh Infantry officer], Untitled MS.

backed up by the Captain. . . . there were 6 duty sgts. and 4 corporals in the co., all subject to his orders. He had a room all to himself, called the orderly room, where he slept—he ate with the men in the dining room—he called the roll three times a day—reveille, tattoo, and retreat. He drew all the rations and clothing . . . made out all guard details, stable police, KP, and old guard fatigue—had all the men clean and presentable for Sunday morning inspection—he also made out all orders for detached service . . . [and] visited the sick and wounded in hospital.

The duty sergeants carried out the instructions of their superior noncommissioned officer, and were responsible for such routine duties in the company as making sure that the soldiers ". . . turned out their lights at taps and kept their cots and clothing in order—and no loud talking after taps!"

Sergeants were sometimes very jealous of their prerogatives as noncommissioned officers. A Seventh Cavalry sergeant was reduced to the ranks in 1881, because he refused to act as guard for a prisoner assigned to work in company quarters. This was below the dignity of the sergeant, who stated that, "if Captain Mathey wants me to stand post, he may reduce me to the ranks, for I won't watch him [the prisoner]. I will take him out of the guardhouse, but I don't care where he goes to afterward, and if he goes to hell I won't run after him."[36]

Most officers realized the importance and value of efficient company noncommissioned men. Testifying before a House of Representatives committee, collecting evidence on a suggestion to reduce the pay of noncommissioned officers, Colonel Guy V. Henry stated, "I would rather take $5 a month from my own pay, if necessary, and give it to the noncommissioned officers, rather than have their pay reduced."[37]

Noncommissioned appointments were made by the commanding officer of each regiment, with the advice of company officers.

[36] Order Book, Seventh Cavalry, 1878–81, MS, 207.
[37] Colonel G. V. Henry, Testimony Feb. 14, 1876, *The Reorganization of the Army*, 44 Cong., 1 sess., *House Report No. 354*, 189.

FATIGUE PARTY
cutting ice, Fort Keogh, about 1880.

Courtesy Custer Battlefield National Monument
U.S. Park Service

PRIVATE HENRY BELEKE, LEFT, AND TWO FRIENDS
with prize vegetables grown in the post gardens at
Fort Assiniboine, Montana, about 1885.

Courtesy Custer Battlefield National Monument
U.S. Park Service

The parchment certificates were very formal, nearly as impressive as the commissions issued to the officers. Without competent noncommissioned personnel, the fatigues, drills, parades, and normal routine of army life could not have been continued at the isolated frontier posts.

7.

Material Factors of
Enlisted Life at Western Posts

THE FOOD SUPPLIED TO SOLDIERS largely determines their efficiency, health, and psychological well-being. In 1878 when asked for suggestions on reorganizing the Regular Army, Colonel Henry J. Hunt, Fifth Artillery, stated that he believed one of the most urgent needs was restoration of the soldier's ration to what it had been in 1865, before it was reduced for the sake of economy.[1]

From 1865 through the early 1890's, the mainstays of soldier menus were hash, stew (slumgullion), baked beans, hardtack, salt bacon, coffee, coarse bread, contract-supplied range beef, and some condiments, such as brown sugar, salt, vinegar, and molasses. Trumpeter Charles C. Persons summed up the food

[1] *The Reorganization of the Army*, 45 Cong., 2 sess., *House Misc. Doc. No. 56*, 114.

of the frontier soldiers as "definitely not of the Delmonico type!" Sergeant Perley S. Eaton describes the typical monotonous menus:

> For breakfast we had beef hash, dry sliced bread (no butter) and coffee (no milk); for dinner, sliced beef, dry bread and coffee, for supper, coffee straight—just dry bread and coffee— the food was very poor.

When supplies were low, field rations of salt bacon, hardtack, and coffee were served; for a treat, stewed dried apples or prunes were occasionally included in the menu. Canned tomatoes and canned beans were added to the issue rations in the late eighties.

Transporting supplies to the western posts was a serious problem, especially in the years just after the Civil War. The commissary department relied on dried vegetables, because they lessened spoilage and were light, compact, and easy to transport. A variety of vegetables were "compressed into a large cake, thoroughly dried, requiring but a small quantity for a meal."[2] The dried vegetables were not popular, and did not remain long on commissary supply lists. With supply depots often far removed from the frontier posts, food occasionally ran short. Private Charles Lester wrote that A Company, Thirtieth Infantry, was ". . . living on Buffalow and bean soup," at Fort Kearney, Nebraska, in December, 1867.[3] The soldiers were hoping to have something different from their tiresome restricted diet, at least for Christmas.

Army rations did not include milk, butter, or eggs. Soldiers often used company funds to purchase these items, but at isolated posts, or when company funds were poorly managed, the men were frequently denied these basic foods. Nor did commissary-supplied rations include fresh vegetables, although they were advocated by many officers. Colonel Robert E. Johnston,

[2] Carrington, *My Army Life,* 104f.
[3] To Mrs. Stanley, MS, Dec. 15, 1867.

First Infantry, testified in 1876 that he believed the addition to the daily ration of one pound of potatoes or other vegetables would materially reduce the soldier sick list.[4]

Flour, beans, salt pork, and other staples were issued by the commissary department on the basis of the number of men carried on a company's rolls. Because few companies could muster as many men as were listed on their rolls, the noncommissioned officer in charge of the mess frequently had surplus food to trade to grocers, settlers, or to the commissary department in exchange for nonissue items. Private Charles Goodenberger explained that "the sowbelly (bacon) was not good and the soldiers would trade it for different things to the Indians and others and put the money into a mess fund." The nonissue items obtainable were provided for in 1866 by an act of Congress that permitted the commissary department to supply, at cost, canned fruits, canned butter, and other "small stores" to officers and enlisted men.[5] Sutlers and post traders objected to this practice, for they felt it placed the commissary department in direct and unfair competition with them.

Whether purchased from the commissary department or a civilian supplier, most of the nonissue rations procured for the enlisted men were bought with money from the company funds. Although soldiers sometimes contributed, the mess funds were chiefly derived from the sale of issue rations. Disposition of unit funds was controlled by a troop or company council of administration composed of enlisted soldiers, who met periodically to make appropriations and decide on expenditures. Pickles, fresh

---

[4] *The Reorganization of the Army,* 44 Cong., 1 sess., *House Report No. 354,* 196.

[5] Colonel W. B. Hazen, 1876 Correspondence, Records of the Adjutant General, Document File No. 4271, 1876, Old Army Section, National Archives. Colonel Hazen reviewed the providing of nonissue and "small stores" items by the Commissary Department, from 1866 to 1876, contending that the Commissary catered far more to officers, in supplying "officers' stores," than it did to the enlisted soldiers' needs.

vegetables, turkeys, onions, potatoes, apples, butter, raisins, currants, and spices were purchased to add taste and variety to the issue staples. A form of instant coffee, listed as "coffee essence," was among the specialty foods purchased by F Company, Fifth Infantry, in 1874.[6] Planning to fatten them on mess slops, the same company, in 1877, used some of their funds to buy two live pigs at Fort Keogh. The good food served in F Company, Seventh Cavalry, in 1888 was largely obtained with money from a richer than average company fund, which enabled the soldiers to "get the best the country afforded," explained Sergeant Samuel Evans.

Enlisted men spent their own money to buy extra food from the commissary, or from the post trader or sutler. Sardines, canned oysters, commercial canned beef, and other items were popular delicacies when they could be obtained. Few soldiers could afford to buy much of this sort of food, though, for the cost of freighting the goods to the posts kept prices high. Freighters, who braved very real danger from swarms of hostile Sioux, in 1867 brought potatoes, onions, and butter to Fort C. F. Smith, from Bozeman, Montana. In view of the distance, danger, and demand, the enterprising hucksters unblushingly sold all their goods to the hungry garrison at fifteen dollars a bushel for the onions and potatoes, and two dollars a pound for the butter.[7]

Post and company gardens supplied most of the fresh produce eaten by frontier soldiers. By the end of June, 1869, at Fort Rice, Dakota Territory, gardens were yielding abundant supplies of eagerly anticipated lettuce, radishes, and spinach.[8] In August, the same gardens added cucumbers, new potatoes, and squash to the diet of the garrison. Soldiers frequently took great pride and interest in their gardens. At the more isolated posts, they

[6] Account Book, Co. F., 5th Infy., MS, S-R Coll., 18.

[7] Burt, "Forty Years," MSS Div., Lib. of Cong., 174.

[8] R. H. Mattison, editor, "The Diary of Surgeon Washington Matthews, Fort Rice, D. T.," in *North Dakota History*, Vol. XXI, Nos. 1, 2 (1954), 60f.

sometimes raised their own chickens and pigs, and occasionally kept milch cows for butter and milk.

In regions where game abounded, fresh wild meat was commonly added to the enlisted bill of fare. Soldiers, wrote Second Cavalryman James B. Wilkinson, "hunted buffalo in the buffalo country, and also hunted deer and antelope for the cook," at Fort Assiniboine, Montana Territory, in the early eighties. The area near Camp Supply, Indian Territory, was a hunter's paradise in the early seventies:

> . . . on Sunday the Company Commander would excuse the best shots to go hunting . . . and run the game as near the post as possible before being shot. . . . There were deer, buffalo, wild fowl. . . . The turkeys were shot only during the winter. . . . [sometimes] a detachment of ten men, with a non-commissioned officer in charge and a wagon, would proceed down the Cimmaron [sic] River, and kill whatever they could in ten days and bring it back to the garrison for the use of the troops.[9]

Other natural foods, besides game, were used in many areas. Wild garlic and lamb's quarter were gathered at Camp Supply. Lacking fresh vegetables in 1866 at Fort Phil Kearny, Dakota Territory, soldiers harvested the abundant wild onions growing near the post.

Few had scruples about foraging for food when encamped or stationed near settlements or Indian villages. Twelfth Infantryman Eugene S. DeSparr commented that in the early seventies the settlers' pigs and the Indians' goats were viewed as fair game by the hungry garrison of Fort Yuma, Arizona.

Whatever the source of supply, the management and preparation of food determined the quantity and quality of the meals served to the rank and file. In the management of a company's issued and purchased food supplies, usually one of the first sergeant's functions, experience and managerial know-how were crucial. Eighth Infantryman August Hettinger explained that

[9] Harbers, "Service Account," in Ashburn, *Medical Department*, 100.

... A Company had the worst reputation in the regular army as a feeder. .... No matter what the rations consisted of, in this company you received only hardtack, bacon and coffee. Even beans were considered a luxury. On the other hand, my own company furnished the most substantial meals I ever saw, anywhere. Here ... can one see the value of management, and honestly, the members of one company perpetually went hungry while the next company lived on the fat of the land on the identical same rations.

Boiling was the commonest way of cooking company rations. Beef, soups, vegetables, beans, stews, and even bacon and salt pork were prepared by boiling and simmering. Hash was usually baked all night for the morning repast, and some foods were roasted or fried. The "desiccated" potatoes of the late 1860's looked like coarse brown sugar. A cup of boiling water poured over them made a still-dough that was worked into cakes and fried. Few company cooks had any talent for preparing food and their lack of culinary ability resulted in unpalatable, substandard food for many companies. Major Thomas M. Anderson, Tenth Infantry, advocating teaching new soldiers the rudiments of cooking at the recruit depots in 1878, stated that ". . . nearly as much food is wasted as is used in the Army from the ignorance and inexperience of company cooks."[10] His recommendation had not borne fruit by the end of the Indian Wars period, and the enlisting of men trained as cooks and bakers had not been approved as of 1891, although urged in the *Annual Report of the Secretary of War* every year for the previous decade.

Improper handling and storage, coupled with the crude preserving techniques available in the last half of the nineteenth century, often caused food spoilage, and, consequently, short rations for the troops. Transportation of supplies was slow and irregular. No food supplies arrived at Fort C. F. Smith for several months in 1867, and as Private John L. Talbot remarked, the

[10] *Reorganization of the Army*, 45 Cong., 2 sess., 1878, *House Misc. Doc. No. 36*, 153.

soldiers subsisted for four months on a diet composed almost exclusively of corn and "felt quite mulish about it!"

When rations went bad, the issue salt pork was alive with worms, and the flour and hardtack hosted weevils and other insects. In 1866 ancient bacon, loaded at Fort Reno, Dakota Territory, for the Eighteenth Infantry's march north to occupy the Big Horn country, was found to be so old and rotted that the ". . . fat had commenced to sluff off from the lean, and it was 3-5 inches thick—also full of mice, as was the flour." Finding that much of the barreled salt pork allotted to his troops was rotten, Colonel de Trobriand gave the condemned food to a band of hungry Indians at Fort Berthold, Dakota Territory, in 1868.[11] Remarking on the serving of spoiled pork to the Fort Phil Kearny garrison in 1866, Private William Murphy wrote: "I believe the bacon would have killed the men if it had not been thoroughly boiled . . . [it was] yellow with age and bitter as quinine." Though the quality of rations tended to improve after 1870, substandard, tainted food was regularly reported and condemned at Fort Laramie as late as 1887.

Frontier regulars appreciated better than average food, when special efforts were made to provide it. Recounting his enjoyment of an exceptionally good meal, September 6, 1869, Private Charles Lester, Fourth Infantry, wrote to his sister:

> I ett so much at dinner time that I could hardly waddle about. You may be astonished though to know what I [usually] eat, for a soldier don't generally get the best of grub you know, so I will tell you if it will be of any interest to you [to hear about this special meal]. We had roast beef and potatoes and gravy and apple dumplin. I eat and eat, and till I couldn't—I wont say what—[12]

Though not so crucial as food, their clothing was an important matter to the men. The basic uniform was the navy blue, roll collar blouse, with the light blue trousers, and a campaign hat

[11] M. M. Quaife, editor, and G. F. Will, translator, *Army Life in Dakota, Selections from the Journal of Phillippe Regis de Keredern de Trobriand,* 226.
[12] To Mrs. Stanley, MS, Sept. 6, 1869.

or forage cap.[13] Dress uniforms, trimmed with red, yellow, and light-blue or white piping designating artillery, cavalry, or infantry, were worn only at retreat and on special occasions. The blue undress blouse was discarded in warm weather, and the grey or blue flannel shirt was worn as the outer garment. Because uniform styles underwent several modifications in the seventies and eighties, soldiers in the same company frequently wore slightly different styles of shirts, blouses, and trousers. Being of wool, the issue uniforms were heavy for warm weather, but few soldiers seem to have complained about this. During most of the Indian campaigns, uniforms were available only in one moderately heavy weight of wool, although some soldiers serving in the Southwest were issued blue shirts of varying weights in the late eighties.

Stockpiles of surplus Civil War clothing were issued to regular army soldiers for ten years after 1865. Much of this matériel was of inferior quality, and on the frontier, where supply was a difficult and serious problem, the substandard wartime clothing could not be replaced as fast as the soldiers wore it out. Describing the uniforms worn by the rank and file of the Eighteenth Infantry during the winter of 1866 and 1867 in northern Wyoming, Private William Murphy wrote:

> Our shoes were made of cheap split leather and the shoddy clothes . . . furnished at that time were not any protection. . . . Burlap sacks were at a premium and saved our lives. We wrapped them around our shoes to keep from freezing, for there were no overshoes or rubbers to be had at the fort.

Shoes and cavalry boots, manufactured at the military prison, Fort Leavenworth, Kansas, were the articles of uniform most often complained about. Many cavalrymen substituted Indian

[13] Colonel M. T. Ludington, *Uniforms of the Army of the United States, from 1774 to 1889, passim.* This work contains an itemized description of all uniform articles and a series of colored plates illustrating almost all the enlisted uniforms worn during the Indian campaigns.

moccasins and leggings for the uncomfortable boots. Voicing a foot soldier's complaint, one man wrote that

> The shoes were of very coarse leather, uppers fastened to the sole by brass screws. These were . . . very uncomfortable, but I solved the matter of fit by walking through a creek until the uppers were thoroughly soaked, walked the whole day in them, and so got a foot form and comfort.[14]

The shoes were not only of poor material, but they were fashioned so crudely as to make rights and lefts almost indistinguishable, and nearly as good a fit on either foot. Soldiers generally rubbed soap on their feet and socks to avoid blisters when wearing newly issued shoes. Some officers were genuinely interested in the problem of providing adequate foot wear, and experimented with different styles and patterns of boots and shoes from time to time.[15]

At the foot of his bunk each soldier kept his personal belongings and clothing in a wooden box, packed in a prescribed manner. The boxes were inspected periodically by the first sergeant, and occasionally by a company officer. According to regulations, enlisted men had to wear the prescribed uniform at all times, and were not allowed to modify materially any issue articles, or have any but uniform clothing in their wooden foot lockers.[16] This rule, continuously overlooked in some units, was in others rigidly adhered to. Recalling his life in the Seventh Cavalry during the 1870's, Corporal Jacob Horner said,

> K Troop became known as the "dude company" of the regiment.

[14] Ashburn, *Medical Department*, 113f.

[15] Brigadier General N. A. Miles, to Major Snyder, MS, Sept. 21, 1887, S-R Coll. General Miles asked for a report on the "Waukenfast" shoes made at the Fort Leavenworth prison, adding that he had heard the trial was unsatisfactory. "Will you please give me the facts in the case . . . number of men, whether or not they started with new shoes and what was the result. During the last few years I have given this subject considerable attention and I would be glad to know what was the result of your experience."

[16] Hershler, *Handbook*, 13.

Its members took the white canvas trousers used for stable duty and the troop tailor fashioned them into tight fitting cavalry breeches. The K's wore white shirts and white collars [when off duty or in town]. . . . they made a striking appearance. . . . [The Captain ordered a specially made pair of fancy Napoleon boots that cost him eighteen dollars, but found that they did not fit him.] I bought them from [Captain] Mathey for $12.00. . . . They had gilded spurs. I was very fond of things like that. Almost every soldier in the post borrowed my boots and was photographed wearing them.

Soldiers developed their own styles for wearing the various articles of uniform. Campaign hats were creased, shaped, and dented at the whim of the wearer, and forage-cap crowns, recalled Clarence Gould, were sometimes rakishly "pulled forward so [far] the ornament [on the front of the crown] could be hooked over the visor." In some units, said Sergeant Armand J. Unger, "caps and uniforms were worn in regulation manner—like soldiers!" In practice, enlisted men usually wore the prescribed uniform during working and duty hours, and dressed pretty much as they pleased when off duty.

Uniform clothing was periodically requisitioned by the soldiers, against a modest but generally adequate uniform allowance.[17] Any unused clothing-allowance money was paid to the soldier in a lump sum at the time of his discharge, and many enlisted men managed to save a large percentage of their allowance. Experienced soldiers usually bought uniforms from dischargees, for use in fatigues and on campaign, and were thus able to save up to one-half of their clothing allowance. Veterans seldom drew clothing from the quartermaster department.

---

[17] Hershler, *Handbook*, 57. Enlisted clothing allowances: None in first year, $.094 per day in second year, $.096 in third year, $.089 in fourth year, and $.067 in fifth and final year of an enlistment. The following are some sample prices charged by the Quartermaster Department for uniform articles: wool socks, $.24 per pair; mittens, $.32; campaign hat, $1.79; blue wool trousers, $1.91; shoes, $1.76; blue wool blouse, $2.62; forage cap (kepi), $.80; drawers, $.56, and undershirt, $.48.

Penny-wise soldiers also bought clothing at periodic post auctions, at which condemned quartermaster stores and the property of deserters were sold to the highest bidders. Because articles of uniform represented money, the stakes in barrack room poker games were sometimes socks, drawers, trousers, and other items drawn from the quartermaster.

Some special clothing worn at the western posts was company or quartermaster property, and did not belong to the individual soldiers. Buffalo coats, and leggings, muskrat caps, and fur gauntlets were in this category. The winter buffalo coats were double-breasted garments, falling just below the knee, with large, flat collars, similar to those on naval peacoats. The muskrat caps had flaps that could be lowered to cover the back and sides of the head in severe weather, and were generally worn in a sort of peaked, fore and aft fashion, resembling the overseas cap of World War I. When buffalo coats were stipulated, the fur caps were to be worn with them, and when the heavy, light blue wool uniform overcoats were prescribed, the forage cap and cloth gloves were worn.[18]

Waterproof rubberized ponchos were issued to all soldiers. Though given a trial, rubber raincoats were not included in the usual issue. Rubber-ground cloths had been an item of issue since before the Civil War, and such large stocks of them were manufactured between 1861 and 1865, that Secretary of War Stephen B. Elkins reported that these wartime supplies were not exhausted until 1891.

Like all soldiers, those serving on the frontier were vitally concerned with the amount and form of the salary they received. During most of the Indian Wars period, enlisted men were paid on a basic salary scale ranging from thirteen dollars a month for privates to thirty-four dollars for an ordnance sergeant. Corporals received fifteen dollars a month, duty sergeants seventeen

[18] Circ. No. 8, Feb. 22, 1887, Order Book, Fort Meade, Jan. to Nov., 1887, CBNM, 11.

dollars, and first sergeants twenty-two dollars.[19] During the Civil War, and until 1870, pay had been at a higher rate of sixteen dollars for privates, with noncommissioned officers paid accordingly. Of the basic sixteen dollars, one dollar was deducted as compulsory savings, retained until discharge, and twelve and one-half cents were taken out to support the Soldiers' Home, in Washington, D. C. The Soldiers' Home deduction remained in force all through the last half of the nineteenth century. Congressional failure to renew the special-pay provisions enacted during the Civil War automatically reduced the privates' pay to thirteen dollars per month, a matter of great significance to the rank and file. The desertion of about one-third the total number of enlisted men in the Regular Army in 1872 in part reflects their reaction to the pay cut.

In May, 1872, Congress enacted legislation aimed at adjusting enlisted base pay and deterring desertion by establishing a system of yearly longevity increases amounting to one additional dollar per month in the third year of service, two dollars in the fourth year, and three dollars in the fifth year. All longevity pay was retained until discharge, at four per cent interest. This measure was advocated as a curb on desertion, for it was believed that soldiers would not forfeit their accumulations of money held in trust or on deposit with the paymaster.

A traveling paymaster ordinarily visited each post every two months. Troops were mustered for pay several days in advance of his arrival. Because soldiers were paid at such lengthy intervals, the money frequently burned holes in their pockets, and

[19] Hershler, *Handbook*, 21. Pay scales of enlisted personnel were as follows: sergeant major, $23 per month; quartermaster sergeant, $23; chief trumpeter and hospital steward 3rd class, $20; principal musician, $20; saddler sergeant, $22; first sergeant, $22; sergeant (duty), $17; corporal, $15; blacksmith and farrier, $15; trumpeter, $13; private, $13; saddler, $15; hospital steward, 1st class, $30; hospital steward, 2nd class, $22; ordnance sergeant, $34; ordnance and engineer privates, 1st class, $17, 2nd class, $13; signal corps 1st and 2nd class privates same as in ordnance and engineers.

quickly went to line those of the post trader or sutler. Several officers recommended paying the men once or twice each month, to lessen the intensity of payday drinking and gambling.

The long awaited payday at a western post saw the garrison formed up by companies, the soldiers in undress blue uniforms, but wearing the white cotton dress gloves. Companies were often paid in the order of the seniority of their commanding officers. The rank and file queued up outside the office where the paymaster had set up shop. Each man stepped up to sign the payroll when his name was called, and removed the glove from his right hand. The paymaster counted out the money, which the soldier received in his ungloved hand, at the same time saluting smartly with the other.

The men soon learned that their salaries did not go far on the frontier. In addition to the high prices charged by post traders, sutlers, and frontier merchants, the government's controversial monetary policies worked a hardship on the poorly paid soldiers. Until the resumption of specie payment in 1879, troops were paid in paper "greenbacks," and on the frontier, the soldiers' paper money was commonly discounted at rates of fifteen, twenty, and even fifty per cent in relation to silver and gold.

Family men usually sent some of their pay home, and others tried to save a little. To some extent the army encouraged savings, and soldiers could deposit portions of their pay with the paymaster; such deposits, however, could not be withdrawn until discharge, and few soldiers used this method of saving.

Most soldiers had pledged at least part of their pay long before payday came round. Post traders, sutlers, and civilians catering to soldier trade often advanced credit and when post canteens were established in the late eighties, enlisted men were permitted to obtain canteen checks on credit. Sergeant William Bald explained that most soldiers began their payday activities by "paying off their debts." Some of these debts were to usurious soldier-moneylenders, who charged interest rates as high as one hundred per cent. Other obligations were to the company barber, the company laundress, the company cobbler, and the company tailor.

Many soldiers spent a large part of their pay for extra food. Canned goods, pies, and other foods could usually be purchased at the post trader's or sutler's store, and when issue rations were poorer than usual, a soldier's pay was often "spent . . . to obtain the common necessities of life," wrote William Thornton Parker.

When troops were stationed near a frontier settlement, or when liquor was otherwise available, payday was signaled by a large scale and bibulous celebration by most of the soldiers. Much of their pay was spent at the bars of crude groggeries. Three companies of the Third Infantry arrived at Fort Dodge, Kansas, from Camp Supply, Indian Territory, just in time to make connections with the paymaster in July, 1874.

> The next day was payday and a hilarious time was had. The saloons and gambling houses were wide open and in Kelley and Beatty's saloon, the Officer of the Day came in and ordered the men [back] to camp. One of the men, full of liquor and beer, grabbed the Officer of the Day, took his belt off and threw him under the billiard table.[20]

An army payday was an important event for frontier saloon keepers, gamblers, and others hopeful of securing soldier money. Enterprising civilians often brought "entertainment" to the men, when they could not get into town. Describing civilian interest in selling to troops camped in the Black Hills in 1878, Private George W. McAnulty, C Company, Ninth Infantry, reported to his fiancée that:

> There has been considerable trouble here since payday—men of all descriptions coming out here from Deadwood City with whiskey to sell. Gen. Bradley will not allow any of them within five miles of Camp—he has had several of them arrested and put out of camp.[21]

[20] Harbers, "Service Account," in Ashburn, *Medical Department,* 102f.
[21] To Miss Moore, July 25, 1878, FLNM.

Some soldiers squandered their pay in various kinds of gambling. "Many of the boys would gamble their money away on pay day, then gamble away their extra clothing," wrote Sergeant Perley S. Eaton. Gambling was contrary to regulations, and those indulging in large-stake games were sometimes caught and punished.

Considering the low-quality rations, the often inadequate clothing, the substandard living quarters, and the rigors of life on the frontier, soldiers garrisoning the western posts appear to have been healthier than one might expect. "Our health," wrote Private William G. Wilkinson, Eighth Cavalry, "was excellent, it had to be, because medical attention was conspicuous by its absence."

Civilian contract doctors and commissioned Regular Army surgeons were charged with responsibility for the general health of the garrisons, but little emphasis was placed on matters of hygiene, preventive medicine, and thorough sanitation. Vaccination for smallpox had been practiced for many years in the Regular Army, but when an epidemic threatened at Fort Rice, Dakota Territory, in 1868, the surgeon found that his supply of vaccine was so small that he could vaccinate only eleven men from the two companies at the post.[22] Drugs and vaccines, like many other important articles, might be in short supply, but whisky and quinine were two medical standbys that always seemed to be on hand. At posts considered generally unhealthy, soldiers were routinely given a daily dose of quinine in whisky, as a preventive tonic.

Some commanding officers took more interest than did others in the health of their men. In 1884, at Fort Sully, Dakota Territory, Colonel Richard I. Dodge, believing that regular bathing was conducive to good health, ordered every soldier to bathe at least once a week.[23] Each company commander was ordered

[22] Mattison, editor, "Surgeon Matthews, Fort Rice," in *North Dakota History*, Vol. XXI, Nos. 1, 2 (1954), 57.
[23] S. H. Hoekman, "The History of Fort Sully," in *South Dakota Historical*

to make a weekly report to the Colonel on this matter. Another instance of official interest in hygiene, at Fort Union, New Mexico, in 1884, was the order directing every man to refill his bedsack with fresh straw twice a month, instead of the usual once every thirty days. Police details at all posts inspected and cleaned the company sinks, and the company officers were expected to keep watch over the preparation and serving of food.

Venereal diseases were the most common and widespread serious illnesses among the rank and file at the western stations. Some venereal disease was brought to the frontier forts by soldiers transferring from recruit depots and eastern stations, but most infection probably resulted from contacts with Indian women and frontier prostitutes. Hoping to remove the source of venereal infection at Fort Custer, Montana Territory, in 1886, the commanding officer urged the immediate creation of a large and well-defined military reservation, segregating his men from the nearby Indians. Stating his case to Departmental Headquarters, Department of Dakota, Colonel N. A. M. Dudley wrote that "the class of Indians that settle round a post have a large number of worthless, lewd women along, who are more or less diseased. Two-thirds of the inmates of the post hospital have been placed there by the effects of diseases, contracted with these Indian women."[24] General Tasker H. Bliss remarked that venereal disease was so pervasive in the 1870's that "it was a common saying [in the Regular Army] that [post surgeons] had nothing to do but confine laundresses and treat the clap."[25]

Diseases stemming from dietary deficiencies were common afflictions suffered by the rank and file. Scurvy frequently ravaged the garrisons of poorly supplied posts. Almost one-third of the garrison of Fort Stevenson, Dakota Territory, was incapacitated by scurvy in 1868, when seventy-nine cases were reported

Collections and Reports, Vol. XXVI, 1952 (*The Madison Leader*, South Dakota State Historical Society, 1953), 267.

[24] To Adjutant General, Dept. of Dakota, MS, June 9, 1886, Nat. Arch.

[25] Quoted in Ashburn, *Medical Department*, 112.

among the 246 men at the post. An epidemic of scurvy broke out among the soldiers at Fort Phil Kearny, Dakota Territory, in the early spring of 1867. The men grew weak, and many lost their teeth. The post surgeon prescribed wild onions as an antiscorbutic, and "the scurvy gang was ordered out to eat them," recalled William Murphy. At the more firmly established posts, gardens generally supplied fresh vegetables to prevent scurvy and kindred ailments.

Army posts, like other late nineteenth-century frontier communities, occasionally suffered outbreaks and epidemics of diphtheria, typhoid fever, and influenza. Asiatic cholera swept through the West in the late 1860's, causing more soldier deaths than did combat. From 1866 to 1868, the Seventh Cavalry lost thirty-six men killed by Indians, six men drowned in the line of duty, and two missing in action. In the same period, the regiment lost fifty-one men who died of cholera.[26]

Rheumatic ailments were another common affliction of frontier soldiers. Shortly after returning from the Sioux Campaign of 1890 and 1891, Private Harvey J. Ciscel, Eighth Cavalry, found himself almost unable to move one morning at Fort Meade, South Dakota. He went to see the "strictly regulation" doctor in the morning, but was refused treatment because he did not have a "sick slip" from his first sergeant. His company commander saw him in bed in the barracks that afternoon, and, believing the soldier to be shamming, ordered a corporal to take him to the guardhouse. Two of Ciscel's comrades took him from the corporal and carried him to the hospital, where he subsequently spent five months in bed. Doctors such as the one encountered by Private Ciscel were all too often met with in the frontier Regular Army.[27] A man dangerously ill with typhoid fever in 1883, remarked that he believed his recovery was almost miraculous, for he had been "nine days without medical treatment."

[26] Major E. A. Garlington, "History of the Seventh Regiment of U. S. Cavalry," MS, CBNM, 2f.

[27] General Bliss, in Ashburn, *Medical Department*, 112. "To tell the truth,

Routine soldier illnesses and injuries were treated with "iodine, alcohol, quinine, castor oil, morphine, Blue Mass pills [containing finely divided mercury as the active agent], mustard plasters, and flaxseed tea and plasters." Carbolic acid, developed and urged as an antiseptic by Sir Joseph Lister in the 1860's, was in use in the post hospital at Fort Laramie as early as 1870. Ether and chloroform were used as anesthetics. Sergeant James S. Hamilton stated that he knew of at least one time when a mortally injured First Infantryman was intentionally given an overdose of drugs, to put him out of his misery.

Medication given to the rank and file was "principally laxatives," according to Fifth Cavalry Sergeant Armand Unger. Blacksmith Frank Heidelberger characterized the medical services in the Sixth Cavalry as restricted mainly to "epsom salts and iodine" for virtually all ailments and injuries. "Quinine was prescribed for everything [in the Seventh Cavalry]," wrote Corporal Louis Courville. Hospitalized soldiers were usually given specially cooked rations, including vegetables, eggs, butter, and milk, when they were obtainable.

No dental care or services were provided for regular army soldiers. The post surgeon pulled teeth when necessary, and itinerant civilian dentists occasionally visited the larger posts.

Like soldiers in all times and places, the frontier rank and file sought to use their duty assignments, favorable connections with officers and senior noncommissioned men, and whatever degree of native shrewdness they possessed to lighten or avoid unpopular duties. Some soldiers were very adroit at "working the angles" to their personal advantage. This was generally admired and accepted by the soldiers, so long as it did not result in hardships for the rest of the men. The hospital steward at Fort Laramie was discovered by an official inspection party in 1875

most of the line [officers] did not regard them [medical officers] highly . . . , some of them, like line officers, lived too narrow and isolated lives, used too much alcohol, as did many men of their day, and occasionally met disaster in that line."

to have quartered his wife and child in one of the hospital rooms, and his wife had been drawing pay as a hospital matron without performing any of the duties of the position.[28] Soldiers assigned to skilled and semiskilled extra duty at Fort Totten, Dakota Territory, in 1881, were leaving their extra-duty jobs and working for civilians during post work hours, a situation that resulted in the issuance of special orders when the commanding officer heard of it.[29]

Relief from routine guard and inspections, aside from the pay involved, made some assignments very attractive. Some of his comrades envied the company gardener, wrote Thirteenth Infantryman C. C. Chrisman, because, "he never did any soldiering." Working for the officers in the rooms of the post canteen reserved for their use was a way to procure food, liquor, money, and favorable connections. Private Harvey J. Ciscel said that a knowledgeable soldier could reap many benefits, because he was privy to much that the officers did not care to have discussed. "The Captain," said Cisel, "told me I knew how to keep my mouth shut. I was in and out of the officers' club plenty, after the lights were out too, I saw plenty, but knew enough to keep quiet." A soldier's attempt to use an assignment to personal advantage was recounted by Sergeant Theodore E. Guy, First Cavalry. When Guy was a corporal, during the 1890 Sioux campaign, he was assigned a fatigue party to construct a temporary guardhouse out of baled hay. One of his men, a noted drinker, placed a bale that could be removed, in the guardhouse wall. He had managed to obtain a bottle of bootleg liquor, and expected to be placed in confinement.

Cooks, bakers, saddlers, and other specialists often used their positions to earn extra money. In 1867 the post baker at Fort C. F. Smith had the foresight to arrange somehow for the transportation of his personally-owned barrel of dried blackberries to that isolated post.

[28] Med. Hist., Fort Laramie, 1868–79, MS, Nat. Arch., 175.
[29] Order Book, Seventh Cavalry, 1878–81, MS, CBNM, 194.

He made and sold pies to the soldiers at seventy-five cents each. The pie trade, together with the [officers] laundry [washed by his wife], proved so lucrative that a sum was accumulated sufficient to buy a home for his family upon their return to the East.[30]

When soldiers at the western posts had money to spend, someone was usually able to supply the demand for extra foods. Arguing for the abolishment of the company laundresses in 1876, General I. N. Palmer stated that not only did they charge too much for their services, but most of them preferred "to make leathery pies to stuff the men with at the next payday."[31] The rank and file did not object to such small-scale private enterprise, but they bore no love for the avaricious sharpers among their own ranks who sold tobacco won at poker to nicotine-starved soldiers at ten dollars a pound.

A common way of "working the angles" for personal gain was the theft of army property and supplies. Arms, food, clothing, and ammunition were most frequently stolen. The first sergeant of D Company, Seventh Cavalry, used his position to steal rations from his unit in 1876 and 1877. The men in the company hated him for it, because they, not the army, suffered.

It was against regulations to sell uniform clothing to civilians, but the practice was a common one. The blue wool trousers, flannel shirts, footwear, and underclothing were in great demand among settlers, cowboys, miners, and other frontiersmen, who could usually buy them cheaply from soldiers. A Seventh Cavalry private was fined five dollars at Fort Totten, Dakota Territory, in 1880, for deceiving his company commander by drawing boots, shirts, and trousers that he did not need, and selling them to civilians.[32]

Apparently most soldiers did not view conversion and pilfer-

[30] Burt, "Forty Years," 162.
[31] To Committee on Military Affairs, Feb. 8, 1876, 44 Cong., 1 sess., *House Report No. 354,* 54.
[32] Order Book, Seventh Cavalry, 1878–81, MS, CBNM, 140.

ing of government property as actually stealing. Undertaking to tell the truth about frontier soldiering, as he had seen it, a veteran of the Seventh Cavalry and of the Signal Corps wrote, "I found rascality from the top all the way down to the second-class private [a Signal Corps rank]. I was learning fast. I was never found out. Some of the poor boys [who were] went to Leavenworth, some committed suicide." This statement was published in 1929 as part of a long letter to the editors in the National Indian Wars Veterans' newspaper *Winners of the West*. The editors, themselves Indian Wars soldiers, subtitled the article, "Truth Once Known to Thousands, Seldom Told."

To a soldier food, clothing, pay, health, and possibilities for manipulating circumstances to his personal advantage are always important.

A veteran of the mid-twentieth century, far removed in time, and with the conditions of his life vastly altered by technology, may still find that some aspects of Regular Army life at the western posts can strike a responsive chord.

8.

Discipline and the
Frontier Desertion Problem

Discipline, the foundation of military authority, is essential to the efficient functioning of any military unit, and for maintaining order. Discipline refers to the training of soldiers to comport themselves in a prescribed manner, but it also means to chastise or punish. In the unenlightened Regular Army of the late nineteenth century, the latter meaning was the one generally applied.

On the frontier, where mere maintenance of isolated garrisons was a major achievement requiring the combined efforts of all a command's personnel, discipline was vital to survival, and however inadequately trained and supplied it may have been, the frontier Regular Army suffered no shortage of disciplinary fervor. Discipline regulated garrison life and enabled ranking officers to carry out campaign plans by making soldiers steady and responsive in the face of campaign hardships and in combat.

Regular Army discipline was founded upon the Army Regulations and the Articles of War, in which were codified the thou-shalt-nots of enlisted behaviour and the punishments for infractions. Fear of punishment was the basis of discipline.

The Regular Army contained undesirable men, who probably would have caused trouble in any environment; yet the most frequent single source of disciplinary problems was liquor. The restrictions of military life, the physical hardships of frontier soldiering, oppression by tyrannical superiors, and isolation, all contributed to the disorientation attending service on posts far removed from familiar surroundings. This psychological disturbance was experienced by thousands of young Americans in the far-flung theaters of World War II.

The character of the raw, frontier communities increased the problems. The civilian population of these western goldtowns, cowtowns, buffalo hunters' rendezvous, and end-of-track railroad villages were notorious for low moral standards. Murder, mayhem, and violence of every description abounded in the West, and in varying degrees soldiers serving in such an environment were influenced by it.

Discipline was always a primary concern, even when arming, clothing, training, feeding, and housing the frontier soldier were given slight attention. The Articles of War, embodying most of the disciplinary admonishments and warnings for the rank and file, were ordered read and "published" to all troops at least once every six months.[1] Commanding officers, intent on driving home the importance of the Articles, sometimes ordered them read to their men as often as twice a month.

In the Articles, officers were instructed to exercise their authority firmly, but "with kindness and justice . . . [and] superiors of every grade [were] forbidden to injure those under them by tyrannical or capricious conduct, or by abusive language."[2] If these instructions were ignored, an enlisted soldier was permitted

[1] Hershler, *Handbook,* 39.
[2] *Ibid.,* 5.

by Article Thirty to make formal complaint of mistreatment, by pressing charges against a superior through his commanding officer. The burden of proof, of course, rested upon the complaining soldier, and if the charges in his appeal were judged "groundless and vexatious," the appellant was to be punished at the discretion of the court-martial convened to hear his claims. Few soldiers availed themselves of this avenue of redress, and for all practical purposes, they were at the mercy of their commissioned and noncommissioned officers.

Some humane officers did not tolerate oppression of the rank and file. Colonel Henry B. Carrington, Eighteenth Infantry, was such a commander. Abhorring brutality, the professor-soldier issued an order called "Bully 38" by enlisted men. The directive, originating at Fort Phil Kearny in 1866, was ". . . occasioned by the brutal striking of a soldier by his sergeant and some profane endorsement of the sergeant by his own lieutenant."[3] Spelling out his instructions on the subject, Carrington wrote:

> That perversion of authority on the part of non-commissioned officers which displays itself in profane swearing, verbal abuse, kicks and blows, and which violates every social, moral, and military principal, will be dealt with in the most decided manner . . . [swearing] can never command respect. It never will prompt a cheerful obedience, where the soldier retains a spark of manhood, though he may implicitly obey the very letter of the order given. . . .
>
> Whatever (not his own act) degrades a man, destroys the soldier, and it is perfectly compatible with strict discipline and the highest order of military subordination, to command that the personal rights of the soldiers will be held as sacred as those of officers.

Captain Frederick W. Benteen, Seventh Cavalry, was another officer who did not condone bullying. Writing of what he felt had been interference with company discipline, a sergeant, who had been the object of Benteen's censure, explained:

[3] Carrington, *My Army Life*, 111.

I tied a man up by the wrists at [Fort Rice, Dakota Territory, 1876] . . . for cutting a halter strap from one of the horses in the stable, and the man was afterwards confined to the guard house by order of Captain French [who, as revealed by the court-martial records cited in footnote 116, Chapter IV, had little regard for regulations himself] . . . . This man reported on the sick list the next day.

We had a new doctor appointed at the time . . . . He wrote a report to the post adjutant in regard to this affair, and I knew then what to expect. I was ordered before a court martial of which Captain Benteen was president . . . . I plead guilty to illegally suspending this man by the wrists, and I was reduced to the ranks. The proceedings were read out . . . before an undress parade.[4]

Some high ranking officers recognized the crucial importance of protecting the rights of the rank and file in the process of maintaining company discipline. Capricious or malicious misuse of authority destroyed unit morale. Believing the matter to be extremely significant, General Christopher C. Augur, commanding the Department of Texas, issued a lengthy general order on the subject in 1872. General Augur was most emphatic in calling attention to the commissioned company officers' responsibility to prevent noncommissioned men from tyrannizing over the men in their units.[5] Some company commanders wisely restrained

[4] Sergeant John Ryan, Seventh Cavalry, 1866–76, to Mrs. Custer, MS, Sept. 6, 1909, Package No. 38, Custer Coll.

[5] General Orders No. 19, Headquarters, Dept. of Texas, Oct. 27, 1872, File No. 5924, 1876, Box 1156, Nat. Arch. ". . . too many company commanders habitually *leave* (not even intelligently *entrust*) the discipline of their companies in the hands of irresponsible non-commissioned officers. There is no point in the discipline of a company in greater danger of abuse, nor one requiring a more persistent scrutiny on the part of the company commander, than the manner in which non-comm. officers exercise authority. . . . Ill regulated or abused, it furnishes more cases for courts martial than any other one cause, except perhaps desertion, of which it is the great promoter. . . . an indiscrete, capricious and trifling [noncom.] . . . will cause more discontent and trouble in a company than the best company commander can allay. . . . It is a mistaken

overzealous sergeants and corporals, reserving for themselves the disposition of serious disciplinary problems.

Discipline, like other elements of company life varied from one unit to another, and depended a great deal upon the personalities of the company commanders. In the final analysis, the legal rights of an enlisted man were the responsibility of his unit officers. Conscientious officers protected and upheld these rights, but some regular officers did not "recognize the fact that enlisted men have any rights or attributes to be respected."[6]

Administered by commissioned personnel, the frontier Regular Army, as a matter of policy, frequently supported tyrannical officers against the complaints of the rank and file. A newly-joined Seventh Cavalry second lieutenant arbitrarily ordered a private to leave the sutler's store and repair to retreat assembly ten minutes before the appointed time. The soldier refused, asserting that he was within his rights and would appeal to his company commander. Angered by this reply, the lieutenant ordered the man taken to the guardhouse. When the case was heard by a garrison court-martial, the soldier was fined one month's pay, not for his refusal to go to the parade ground for assembly, but for his insubordinate attitude.[7] Another soldier was told to shoot to kill any prisoners attempting to escape from the guardhouse. The enlisted man refused to do so without a written order, which the officer declined to give.

Soldiers expected little justice when haled before a court-martial. Many felt that "the man was [considered] guilty before being tried!"[8] "Rarely," remarked Private Clarence H. Allen,
view that it is essential that non-comm. officers must always be sustained, right or wrong . . . ."

[6] Mulford, *Fighting Indians,* 57.

[7] General Orders No. 13, Apr. 11, 1881, Order Book, Seventh Cavalry, 1878–81, MS, CBNM.

[8] Private W. G. Wilkinson, Eighth Cavalry, 1886–91, to Don Rickey, Jr., MS, Aug., 1954. Wilkinson served as a major in World War I, and had considerable experience with the administration of military justice. He emphasized that enlisted men, in his experience, received little impartial justice in courts-martial during the 1880's.

was impartial justice meted out to enlisted men in courts-martial!

Regulations specified the rights of enlisted men confined in the guardhouse by order of an officer. As an extension of the *habeus corpus* limiting arbitrary imprisonment, it was stipulated that all guardhouse prisoners were to be released each day at guard mount, unless the commanding officer specifically decreed otherwise, or written charges were preferred against the offender.[9] There was nothing to keep a commanding officer from repeatedly "decreeing otherwise," and this article was easily circumvented. Soldiers awaiting courts-martial were customarily confined until tried or released by "proper authority." All soldiers tried by courts-martial at Fort Meade, Dakota Territory, from 1878 to 1887, were confined in the guardhouse until tried.[10] Soldiers accused of capital crimes or offenses against the person or property of a citizen had to be surrendered, on demand, to civil authorities.[11]

When ordered to stand trial in a court-martial, an accused soldier, if he could state a convincing objection, was allowed to challenge the fitness of a commissioned member of the court. The court itself judged the weight of a soldier's challenge to one of its own members. If the accused "stood mute," refusing to enter a plea, the court proceeded as though he had pleaded not guilty, thus guaranteeing at least the semblance of a trial. Should a commanding officer or member of the court request a continuance of a case, the trial could be postponed for as long as sixty days, while the accused remained in close confinement. The soldier was not represented by a formally appointed counsel. His interests were supposedly protected by the member of the court acting as judge advocate. The judge advocate acted as prosecutor for the United States Army, but the Regulations ordered that after a plea had been entered, "he shall so far con-

---

[9] *Rev. U. S. Army Regulations of 1861 and Art. of War, to June 25, 1863,* 39.

[10] Order Book, 7th Cavalry, 1878–81, MS, and Order Book, 7th Cavalry, 1882–87, MS, CBNM, *passim.*

[11] Hershler, *Handbook,* 35.

sider himself counsel for the prisoner as to object to any leading question to any witness, and to any question to the prisoner, the answer to which might tend to criminate himself."[12] How well the prisoner's rights were protected depended entirely on the judge advocate.

Courts-martial had extremely wide discretion in prescribing punishments. Thirty-two of the thirty-four Articles of War relative to enlisted offenders left their punishment to the judgment of the courts. This was partially remedied in 1891 by a presidential executive order that prescribed limits of punishment for various categories of convictions.[13]

The traditional garrison courts-martial handled the vast majority of trials of enlisted men until the adoption of the streamlined summary courts in 1889. Summary courts were easily convened, and were intended to safeguard the rights of soldiers previously subjected to arbitrary company punishments. In practice, the summary courts merely made it easier for an officer or noncommissioned officer to have a soldier court-martialed. Men were tried in summary courts for unbuttoned blouses, missed roll calls, and other minor infractions that had traditionally been punished within the company. In 1891, "the actual number of different men tried [by summary courts] was about 45 per cent of the command [in the Department of the Missouri]. [14]

Desertion was by far the most prevalent serious military crime during the last half of the nineteenth century. Recapitulating the Regular Army's desertion losses, Secretary of War Stephen B. Elkins reported that one-third of the men recruited between 1867 and 1891 had deserted. Until the World War I, desertion was not considered an especially dastardly offense, and many civilians in the West sympathized with deserters. The Regular Army's main object in condemning and curbing desertion was to end the loss of government-owned property that deserters

[12] *Ibid.*, 38.
[13] *Ann. Report, Sec. of War, 1891,* I, 324.
[14] *Ibid.*, 332.

usually took with them. Moreover, desertion, by making replacements necessary, greatly increased the cost of recruiting and training men. Definitions of what constituted desertion were sometimes quite rigid. In recent years, a soldier has had to be voluntarily absent from his unit for a period of at least thirty days, and intend to remain absent indefinitely, before being classed as a deserter. In 1875, a Seventh Cavalry private was convicted of desertion after absence from military control for one day, but of more importance to the army was the fact that he had stolen a carbine and ammunition and sold them to a civilian.[15]

The Regular Army had suffered heavy desertion rates for so long that some officers considered the malady incurable. Asked for his recommendations on the problem in 1878, Judge Advocate General W. M. Dunn could only suggest stiffer regulations against gambling, and more stringent discipline for drunken soldiers. Many years passed before officer boards, convened to investigate desertions, were instructed to "minutely investigate" the causes of desertion. The army focused considerable attention on the desertion problem in the 1880's, and, in 1890, finally took some important, positive steps to deal with it. For the first time, soldiers were given the option of purchasing a discharge. Men with three years' service could request a thirty-day furlough, and at the end of that time apply for a discharge. They were thus provided with a legal method of leaving the army two years prior to the expiration of an enlistment.[16] At the end of 1891, the army, with the hope of cutting desertion rates by improving the soldiers' food, finally added one pound of vegetables to the stipulated daily ration. Because enlisted men were generally confined while awaiting courts-martial, another new regulation was pro-

15 Muster Roll, Company E, Seventh Cavalry, Apr. 30–June 30, 1876, Private William Davis, CBNM.

16 *Ann. Report, Sec. of War, 1891,* I, 63, 67f. It was reported that three times as many soldiers took their discharge at the end of the optional three-year period than remained for the full five-year enlistment.

mulgated, ordering trial by summary courts within twenty-four hours of confinement. All of these measures were steps in the right direction, but their administration depended largely upon the inclinations of the officers.

By the later eighties, the army had developed a sincere interest in determining the causes of desertion. Secretary of War Elkins reported that an 1891 survey among the 194 deserter-convicts in the military prison at Fort Leavenworth, Kansas, showed that liquor and general dissatisfaction were the two major causes, and tyrannical superiors the most often reported specific reason for desertion.[17]

"Bad officers are sure to spoil good soldiers," wrote Trumpeter Ami Frank Mulford in 1878, and "I believe the principal cause of desertions is the manner in which many of the harsh officers treat enlisted men."[18] Musician James D. Lockwood, Twenty-seventh Infantry, supports Mulford's opinion in his acount of service in the West from 1866 to 1869. His unit was en route to the Big Horn country of northern Wyoming, in 1866. As they marched along the North Platte River, in Nebraska, one of the privates dropped out of ranks to buy some milk at a stage station. A mounted officer rode up to the man and began cursing and beating him with the flat of his sword, ordering him back to his place at once.

> The soldier obeyed his orders to the letter, as far as making haste to catch up with the command, and obtaining his loaded gun . . . carried in his absence by a comrade, he again fell back towards the rear of the column; as the officer came riding up, the

---

[17] *Ibid.,* 93. The 194 deserters interrogated as to why they had deserted gave the following answers: generally dissatisfied, 42; liquor, 67; trouble, 14; sickness, 9; claimed innocence, 6; homesick, 9; tyrannical superiors, 31; induced, 1; no cause stated, 14; to get married, 1; lack of food, 1. Three of these men had previously been sentenced for desertion. Some more specific reasons given for desertion, perhaps lumped in the "trouble" or "general dissatisfaction" categories, were: fear of punishment, debt, overwork, women, and "shunned by comrades."

[18] *Fighting Indians,* 56f.

soldier . . . cocked his rifle and deliberately aiming at his heart, pulled the trigger, but the cap alone exploded . . . . The soldier was instantly overpowered and disarmed [and in the morning was found missing from the guard tent].[19]

Another instance of oppression-inspired desertion was related by two runaways, to a coworker in a New York lumberyard in the 1880's. One of the men exlpained that they had enlisted in the Seventh Cavalry in the early 1870's, having acquired a taste for army life during the Civil War. The defectors said that an I Company sergeant had tried to beat one of them, who bested the noncommissioned man in self-defense. The captain, when the matter was immediately reported to him, being a little drunk, aimed a blow at one of the men with his cane. Certain that retribution would be swift, the two soldiers deserted at once.[20]

Discussing the reasons for mass desertions from the Seventh Cavalry in 1869, retired Brigadier General Frederick W. Benteen cited Lieutenant Colonel George A. Custer's harshness. In the

> . . . summer of '69 Gen. Custer had in use a hole deeply dug in the ground about 30 x 30 feet, by about 15 feet deep, entrance by ladder, hole boarded over: *this was the guard house,* and a man even absent from a call was let down. [There were so many of them] I don't know how the prisoners laid down.[21]

Strictness on the part of an officer was more bearable if he was a proven leader of long service, but youthful West Point graduates who modeled themselves along the same lines were quite another matter. Experienced soldiers sometimes deserted rather than serve under them.

Many desertions were directly traceable to measures of economy. When regular army base pay was reduced in the early seventies from sixteen to thirteen dollars per month for privates,

[19] J. D. Lockwood, *Life and Adventures of a Drummer-Boy,* 135.

[20] Statement by Fred Dustin of Matters Relating to the Seventh U.S. Cavalry Before the Battle of the Little Bighorn, Jan. 31, 1932, MS, Dustin Coll.

[21] To Goldin, Feb. 14, 1896.

"hosts of men deserted."[22] In the West, where labor was always scarce and wages for almost any kind of work were considerably higher than in the East, many defectors left the ranks to earn more money. Spring was the favorite season for deserting. Construction work was resumed along the railroads, in the mining regions, and in the new communities, and travel was faster and easier. Gold rushes and widely publicized mineral discoveries frequently infected soldiers with the same get-rich-quick fever that burned in the hearts of civilian prospectors. General George Crook's troops, attempting to police the gold-bearing Black Hills in 1875 and 1876, were accompanied by newspaper correspondent John F. Finerty. He saw the desertions mount, as "our soldiers . . . overcome by the moral epidemic [of gold-hunger], deserted by the squad to join the . . . [gold-seekers]."[23] Custer City, Deadwood, and other Dakota Territory mining centers were thick with men who had deserted to join the stampede to the diggings.

For some, the circumstances of enlisted soldiering became more than they were willing to endure. Some could not bear the loneliness of life at a frontier post. Discussing First Cavalry desertions from Fort Grant, Arizona, Private Nathan Bell explained, "We were stationed so far from any town [twenty-eight miles from Wilcox, Arizona], and on a desert . . . and the boys [who deserted] wanted to get back to civilization." Utterly exhausted and seriously ill after participating in General Crook's "starvation march" campaign against the Sioux and Northern Cheyennes in the fall of 1876, one self-confessed deserter wrote that the experience had led him to depart at the first opportunity ". . . when I had enough, I quit."[24]

When companies of the Twenty-third Infantry were assembled at Fort Garland, Colorado, to launch a campaign against the hostile Utes in May, 1880, Private Wallace E. Bingham wrote

---

22 Harbers, "Service Account," in Ashburn, *Medical Department,* 127.
23 *War-path and Bivouac,* 41.
24 Letter to Brininstool, June, 1935, Dustin Coll., No. 316.

that "it was found at roll call that one-third of the command had deserted," the morning after arriving at the rendezvous. These infantrymen dreaded what they believed would be a grueling mountain campaign. Some may have been influenced by reports of the fighting qualities displayed by the Utes the previous fall at the Battle of Milk River, Colorado.

Continued exploitation of soldiers as cheap manual labor rankled many enlisted men and motivated some to desert. Several desertions from Fort Randall, Dakota Territory, were attributed by Corporal Herbert Martin to the commanding officer's assigning soldiers to labor on his pet bathhouse project. The bathhouse was being built over a hot, sulphur spring, which the commander wished to make available the year round to officers and their families.

Inability to adjust to military discipline and routine caused some regulars to desert. "A lot of fellows from the citys and eastern slums could not stand the discipline," wrote Private Louis Ebert, Sixth Cavalry, "some left the first payday, if in walking distance of a settlement." Discussing desertion by disillusioned youths who found the Regular Army very different from expectations, an 1876 soldier told the story of a young recruit, who enlisted in the early seventies, and wrote his mother that he detested life at his assigned western post. "One day she got a letter, opened it, read it and burned it . . . never mentioned the boy again. He never wrote again. She seemed to fade away and died soon after."[25] First Sergeant George Neihaus penned a short but poignant comment on this general type of deserters, when he described them as, "tired of army life, some homesick, yet most had no home to go to."

Enlisted men facing courts-martial, or expecting punishment for some breach of regulations, sometimes preferred desertion to enduring the consequences of their transgressions. An extreme case of this sort occurred in 1891 at Fort Walla Walla, Washington, when a citizen-gambler murdered a Fourth Cavalryman.

[25] *Ibid.*

148

His aroused comrades, believing the murderer would escape punishment, took him from the county jail and killed him. Efforts by civil and military authorities to bring the lynchers to trial resulted in forty-five desertions from the Fourth Cavalry companies stationed at the post.[26]

Soldiers who did not conform to the accepted standards and patterns of the regular company they were assigned to were sometimes encouraged to desert. "Those who did not fit in went over the hill—deserted," wrote First Cavalryman Thomas E. Gutch. "In most cases, they were men whom the army could well do without," said Private William G. Wilkinson, Eighth Cavalry.

The commonest method of desertion was failure to return from authorized absence. Soldiers planning to desert "would take passes and never return," wrote Sergeant James S. Hamilton. Some carefully schemed their defections, occasionally securing assistance from civilians. A sergeant of the Third Infantry was attacked by a band of desperadoes, near Fort Dodge, Kansas, in 1868. The attackers tried to free the deserter whom the sergeant was escorting to the fort.[27] From the evidence, this deserter must have attempted to use his connections with the lawless element in the neighborhood. Another soldier planning to desert from Fort Keogh in 1890 lacked civilian accomplices and counted on financing his flight with the money won foot racing. The man was a noted sprinter, who deliberately "threw" a race in order to get heavier betting odds on his next contest. "I am going to walk away with this race, and then walk away," he told Corporal John Bergstrom. The plan succeeded and, having acquired a sufficient stake, the man disappeared a day or so later.

[26] *Ann. Report, Sec. of War, 1891*, I, 330. Sergeant Reginald A. Bradley, Fourth Cavalry, 1889–94, was at Fort Walla Walla in 1891, and recounted many particulars of the case in a personal interview with the author, San Francisco, Oct., 1954.

[27] Adjutant General, U. S. Army, *Decorations of the United States Army, 1862–1926*, 32. The sergeant in this case was awarded the Congressional Medal of Honor for retaining his prisoner and repelling the attack.

One of the best examples of a well-planned desertion was reported to have occurred in the Seventh Cavalry in 1868.

At one post in Colorado the 1st Sergeant, after tatoo roll call, went into the barrack room and dispatched thirty men for detached service and had the . . . [men rationed and armed] for a period of days. The Sergeant mounted the detachment, marched them quickly out of the Post, and when some distance away marched rapidly till about thirty miles from the Post, then he halted the detachment and informed them that they were all deserters and it was every man for himself, said Goodbye and started South to the mining regions. Two or three at once turned back, returned to the Fort and gave themselves up and told the story of their desertion. . . . many of these [deserters] who were captured said that they had enlisted for adventure and to get transportation to the West.[28]

In 1885, a sergeant discovered the plans of two would-be deserters from Fort Washakie, Wyoming Territory, when he learned from some Indians that they had sold pack horses to the men to carry provisions and equipment for their unauthorized journey. Because there was no effective state or federal law enforcement in Yellowstone Park at the time, the defectors had planned to route their escape through the Park. Horses and arms were the most frequently stolen government properties, but some deserters took only their arms.[29]

Some who intended to desert waited until they were ordered out on campaign or other field service, and then took off with their mounts and equipment. Private William White, Second Cavalry, noted such desertions in his 1876 diary. Shortly after leaving Fort Ellis, Montana Territory, two men left Colonel John Gibbon's column.

[28] Godfrey, "General Sully's Expedition Against the Southern Plains Indians, 1868," MS, Bates Coll., 1.

[29] Diary of the Seventh Cavalry Enlisted Man, MS, Bates Coll. Desertions from K Company noted on January 7 and Feb. 28.

Renals, who was serving out a sentence, was out with a 4 inch gun, and Clark of L. Co. was sentry over him, they drove the team down in the brush and left to parts unknown. All hands was mounted but no use. They was not found.[30]

In the spring of 1877, striking forces, composed mainly of Fifth Infantry companies, were sent out from Fort Keogh on campaign against the Sioux and Northern Cheyennes. Some of the men apparently did not relish the notion of arduous campaigning, and, being equipped for travel, "several men deserted in heavy marching order."[31] When Third Cavalry companies stationed at Fort Washakie, Wyoming, were ordered to Arizona in 1882, some of the soldiers deserted from the column on the march. "They took their horses, saddles, [field equipment], carbines and revolvers—some deserted because they didn't like soldiering, others because they didn't want to go to a hot climate," explained Sergeant Perley S. Eaton.

The mounts and equipment were essential for travel, and could be readily converted to cash in any frontier community. Desertion from a force in the field was most common when troops were operating near the Canadian and Mexican borders, along railroad lines, or near communities where deserters could lose themselves among civilians.

Though the seriousness of the desertion problem was readily admitted, the Regular Army followed few consistent policies aimed at discouraging the defections and apprehending the defectors. Some measures were sporadically adopted. In the spring, when desertion was at its peak, unscheduled roll calls were taken at odd hours of the day and night. "Sometimes during the night, the Captain or a Lieutenant would come to the Company quarters with the First Sergeant, and go from bunk to bunk, (waking up those asleep), and require each man to give his name."[32] Such special checks increased the likelihood that un-

---

[30] Diary of William White, Second Cavalry, 1876, MS, April 3.

[31] Snyder, Diary, Apr. 29, 1877, MS.

[32] Mulford, *Fighting Indians*, 56.

authorized absence would be quickly discovered, and tended to discourage deserters, who had counted on a start of several hours before any pursuit could be sent after them.

The majority of deserters were never caught. Usually no widespread search was conducted, because there were no integrated communications or law-enforcement networks. In the West, commented General Reynolds J. Burt, "the general opinion was that ranchers were disposed to cover up such men," and rarely volunteered information or admitted any knowledge of them to detachments sent in pursuit. When conditions permitted, however, details were sent out after deserters. Most defectors made good their escape, for a few days' pursuit, in vast reaches of unsettled country, rarely resulted in captures if the deserters had a head start of ten or twelve hours.

Enlisted Indian scouts were generally the most successful at tracking deserters, especially when motivated by rewards. The seriousness of deserting was demonstrated to Private Frederick Fraske and some other Seventeenth Infantrymen, when they saw one of three deserters brought back, "stretched over a mule," at Fort D. A. Russell, Wyoming.

Since desertion was not classed as a particularly dastardly crime, soldiers who had remained loyal themselves sometimes sympathized with those who had run away. The diary of First Cavalryman B. C. Goodin, at Fort Grant, Arizona, mirrors that attitude: "March 17— . . . Six cases of desertion [from the six companies at the post] detachments out after them, hope they don't catch them." When available, the telegraph was used to transmit information on deserters to nearby United States marshals. Few soldiers took pleasure in the sight of a runaway's return in manacles, with one of these marshals. The rank and file believed that hope of collecting the reward, rather than a sense of duty, was the real motivation. Especially noted among soldiers as an informer and collector of deserter bounties was a peace officer near Miles City, Montana. He accosted newly-discharged Corporal John Bergstrom, who, still wearing his army hat, shirt, and trousers, was working on the railroad. Shown the discharge, the lawman refused to believe it, and Bergstrom had to fight him to keep from being taken in.

Rewards paid for capturing deserters varied from about thirty dollars in the late sixties and early seventies to the sixty dollars authorized in 1891. Deserters were keenly aware of the interest shown by some civilians in collecting the reward money. A soldier deserting from Fort Dodge, Kansas, in 1870, met a citizen wagon train about twenty-five miles from the post. The civilians attempted to capture him for the reward, and the soldier committed suicide rather than be taken back.[33]

Apprehended deserters were customarily kept in close confinement while awaiting courts-martial or transfer to prison. As they were often assigned to prisoner work details outside the guard house during the daytime, to make escape less likely they were generally "kept in ball and chain," or otherwise shackled, explained Corporal Louis Courville. Shackled prisoners, said General R. J. Burt, "could walk only with difficulty," wearing a short length of chain or a bar shackle fastened from one ankle to the other. General Burt explained that when freedom of movement was restrained by ball and chain, "the blacksmith forged an iron ring around the prisoner's ankle . . . [to which] a 25 pound iron ball" was attached by a five- or six-foot length of chain. Shackled prisoners sometimes suffered excruciating pain. "You could hear the screams of the men being shackled a mile out on the prairie," said Private Harvey J. Ciscel in his account of the treatment accorded Eighth Cavalrymen who had deserted during the Sioux Campaign of 1890–91. The army justified such measures by arguing that some prisoners were desperate, hardened criminals, requiring maximum physical restraint to prevent their escape.

Deserters and prisoners charged with other serious crimes were heavily guarded. Guards were under orders to prevent

---

[33] Otis, *Surgical Cases,* 37.

escapes at any cost. Sentries allowing prisoners to escape through negligence were confined in place of the escapee. "Ellis made his escape out of the [Ft. Grant] guard house," wrote Private B. C. Goodin. "Brown of our troop shot at him but did not hit him. Brown in guard house on acct. of it."

During the latter third of the nineteenth century, arrested deserters commonly served out the unexpired balance of their enlistments, in addition to the time spent in confinement, or their remaining enlistment time was added to the court's prison sentence. In the late sixties and early seventies, so many regulars deserted that a sort of general amnesty was authorized in 1873 to those who voluntarily surrendered. General Orders Number 102 of that year stipulated that deserters who presented themselves would be normally restored to duty, but would be required to serve in addition the time lost while absent. Apparently this order was not considered a very strong inducement for few deserters took advantage of it. Men who had absconded with government property were still liable to court-martial on charges of stealing.

Commenting on a deserter who surrendered himself, Private Roman Rutten, Seventh Cavalry, wrote of First Sergeant Farrell, "who . . . was then [1876] going by the name of Gilmore. He deserted afterwards, gave himself up and was permitted to re-enlist but lost all previous service [for longevity pay and retirement purposes]. Farrell served through the Civil War as a Capt. of Volunteers."[34] Fourth Cavalryman George W. Winnie deserted from his outfit May 5, 1885, and surrendered himself to authorities March 17, 1886. He again deserted and re-enlisted in the Second Cavalry, at the Presidio, San Francisco, from whence he was again sent to Arizona on campaign against Apaches. He was not tried for the second desertion, but the matter was resurrected years later, when he was denied an Indian Wars pension because of it.

[34] To Sergeant Ryan, March 26, 1911, Package No. 36, Custer Coll.

In the years just before the Civil War, desertion was customarily punished by flogging, marking, and dishonorable discharge in a garrison ceremony calculated to impress the beholders. Flogging was legally abolished August 5, 1861, but other outmoded and semibarbaric punishments remained in force. From 1865 to 1870, deserters might be sentenced to confinement at hard labor, dishonorable discharge, loss of all pay and allowances, and to be "indelibly marked [tattooed] upon the left hip with the letter D, one and-a-half inches in length."[35] Branding had been abandoned as a method of "marking" only a short time previously. The customary prison sentence was two years at hard labor. Mitigating circumstances sometimes led to reduction of the sentence to one year, and, in aggravated cases, the term was set at three or four years. Restraint, by permanently attached ball and chain, was frequently decreed for deserter convicts during the term of their sentence.

Disciplinary problems related to the abuse of liquor, violence and felonies, moral deviations, military crimes other than desertion, and the usual and unusual punishments awarded in connection with them, will be considered in the following chapter. The views of the rank and file on methods of discipline, and on various crimes and misdemeanors provide additional insight into the realities of frontier soldiering in the post–Civil War West.

[35] Headquarters, Dept. of the Missouri, *General Court Martial Orders, 1869, passim.* See also *ibid.,* 1870, *passim.*

9.

Crime, Vice, and Punishment

LIQUOR, RELEASER OF INHIBITIONS AND DESTROYER OF ORDER, has been, to some degree, a major disrupter of military discipline in all armies. On the frontier, with its dreariness and isolation, the problems caused by excessive drinking were more than usually severe. So pernicious were the effects of alcohol that, according to Private James B. Wilkinson, "it was the curse of the army."

Some enlisted men drank moderately; others spent virtually all their money on liquor. Many officers, too, were known as heavy drinkers.[1] First Sergeant George Neihaus remarked that drunkenness was not only common among the soldiers and officers, but that the post chaplain at one fort was known among the men to be an excessive tippler.

[1] Anson Mills, *My Story*, 150, and Lieutenant Colonel O. L. Hein, *Memories of Long Ago*, 100. Both authors were officers through the Indian Wars era.

Soldiers obtained liquor, beer, and wines from the post traders or sutlers, and, later, beer and light wines from the post canteens. Any nearby supply of intoxicants, if not securely guarded, was considered fair game by the rank and file, and soldiers sometimes went to great pains to steal it. A small barrel of whisky was stolen in 1881 from a citizen's store by troops camped nearby, on the Uncomphagre River in Colorado.

> The night they [companies of the Fourth Cavalry] arrived, two men of Co. C & one from D. Co. [Twenty-third Infantry] sawed some logs and stole a barrel of whiskey from the storeroom of the settler's store. They could not get it away that night and it laid all day in the sagebrush, in plain sight, while searchers were combing the hills & river bottoms. . . . [The next night,] after taps the barrel was carried to the kitchen of C Company, blankets hung over the windows, then it was opened, and the contents of the barrel put in bottles, jugs, or anything that could be gotten, and hid. Company C's breakfast was cooked with the barrel staves the next morning.[2]

In regions where prices were high, soldiers often resorted to selling and bartering clothing and other equipment for liquor, although the offense was punishable by court-martial. Occasionally the civilian entrepreneur trading liquor for army matériel was outsmarted by his customers. When a train transporting companies of the Seventh Cavalry to the theater of operations in Dakota stopped at Beatrice, Nebraska, in late 1890, many of the rank and file sought to obtain liquor from civilians. Private William J. Slaughter related that

> . . . Colonel Forsythe, seeing some of the boys heading for the Stock Yard Hotel, ordered a guard stationed at each door to keep soldiers from entering. The proprietor, not to be outdone, had three or four men carry a couple of quarts of tangle-foot apiece and sell it on the quiet to those who had money, and when

---

[2] W. E. Bingham, Twenty-third Infantry, 1880–85, "Early Days on the Frontier," MS, 16.

the money ran out he had them swap a quart for an army blanket.... They saw he was throwing the blankets into a room behind the bar and, climbing through the window, threw them out to their comrades who carried them away.

The army tried to suppress excessive drinking chiefly because drunken soldiers were neither willing nor able to perform their duties. In Dakota Territory in the late seventies, soldiers and an officer, assigned to escort a paymaster from Fort Berthold to posts further up the Missouri River, left on a cold, wintry day: ". . . they came back . . . that same night, having been relieved of all their funds by two lone bandits. The officers were all more or less intoxicated so that when covered by the bandit's guns they made no resistance and the bandits got away without firing a shot. That night I heard the ambulance driver [who had transported the detail] chuckling over the whole affair."[3]

Intoxicated enlisted men were, of course, far less tractable and inclined to accept military authority than when sober. An officer, attempting to arrest three drunken soldiers, in Austin, Texas, in 1870, was pummeled and beaten about the head with a heavy cane, while lying on the ground.[4] He died several days later from the effects of skull fractures and severe concussion. "There was a May Day celebration [in the late 1880's]," said Eighth Cavalryman William G. Wilkinson, "and many of the men got drunk, with numerous fights . . . the Corporal had a fight with a sergeant and threw him out the window of the orderly room." The corporal was so drunk that he later could not recall the incident, though he was court-martialed and given a dishonorable discharge.

Fist fights and free-for-all brawls frequently broke out among enlisted men when liquor was available.[5] The fighting some-

[3] Rev. James F. Walker, "Old Fort Berthold As I Knew It," in *North Dakota History*, Vol. XX, No. 1 (1953), 40.

[4] Otis, *Surgical Cases, 1865–71*, 117.

[5] White, Diary, MS, Jan. 21: "Sullivan and Gilbert tried their hand at sparing. Both being under the influence of drink, and wound up by Tim getting in the guard house."

times ended in murder and manslaughter, when whisky-maddened men of violent temperament became embroiled. Noting the results of one vicious Donnybrook, Private William Bald, First Cavalry, said that ". . . Corporal Taylor had his head split open with an axe at the [whisky] ranch better known as the White Elephant." In command of a detail sent out on a twenty-four-day scout early in 1879, Captain Simon Snyder noted in his diary entry of February 20: ". . . Indian scouts drunk and very quarrelsome. Had I not arrived upon the scene when I did to quell the row, one or more of them would have been killed."[6] An extreme example of trouble between drunken scouts and soldiers and civilians is an incident that took place just outside Fort Grant, Arizona, in 1893. An Apache scout, who had previously won the Congressional Medal of Honor, went berserk and ". . . tried to clean out the ranch and Lennon [bartender] shot him with a shotgun as he came in the door with a cocked Winchester."[7] In view of past services, Sergeant Rowdy was "buried with military honors [the following day]. Lennon was acquitted by the coroner's jury."

Alcoholism is the almost certain consequence of continued excessive drinking. Many a frontier regular fell victim to liquor addiction. The alcoholic officer or soldier unable to control his intake of liquor was a serious morale and discipline problem. During the decade of the 1880's, a ratio of almost forty-one for every thousand men were hospitalized as alcoholics.[8] In an era when only the most severe cases were treated, for manifestations such as delirium tremens, this average of one out of twenty-five is evidence of an extremely serious situation. For some reason, the ratio was much smaller among the four regular regiments of Negro troops, in which only a little over five and one-half cases of acute alcoholism were reported for every thousand soldiers. Studies of alcoholism reveal no definite correlation between

---

[6] Snyder, Diary, 1879, MS.

[7] Goodin, Diary, Jan. 31, 1893–July 14, 1893, MS, March 31.

[8] *Ann. Report, Sec. of War, 1891*, I, 593.

prevalence of the malady and service on the frontier. The lowest ratio of all the posts in the army was that of Fort Custer, Montana, where only three and a fraction cases per thousand men were reported. Perhaps much depended on the morale of a company or regiment, and little on the location of the posts.

Enlisted men naturally were influenced by the examples set for them by the officers. When a commissioned superior was known to be a hopeless alcoholic, the men he commanded may have been inclined to emulate him. At least, the alcoholic officer was not likely to promote temperance among his soldiers. In at least one instance, though, the tragic death in delirium tremens of a young lieutenant served as a hard-hitting object lesson to the rank and file.[9] An officer displaying alcoholism was sometimes removed from the view of enlisted men, as a matter of taste and policy. Dr. Holmes O. Paulding noted in his 1876 diary that a bibulous captain "has been at [Fort] Ellis on a spree and had the jimjams. Dr. Shaw *kindly* installed him in my quarters [while I was absent on campaign], where he proceeded to break up mirrors and furniture."[10]

Punishments for drunkenness depended to some degree on the seriousness of the case, and to a large extent upon the inclinations of the officers or court-martial imposing them. A private, convicted by a garrison court of being drunk and missing stable call, at Fort Totten, Dakota Territory, in 1881, was fined five dollars.[11] Another soldier, found drunk at retreat formation, was fined three dollars. For drunkenness, in addition to fines, short guardhouse sentences might be ordered. In the field, drunken soldiers were frequently punished by being forced to march dismounted at the rear of a column. Aggravated drinking by noncommissioned men was commonly punished by reduction

[9] Sergeant Eaton, to Don Rickey, Jr., MS, Nov. 27, 1954. Eaton detailed the death in 1883 of a Third Cavalry lieutenant, due to alcoholism and the officer's sudden withdrawal from liquor. The official obituary stated that the officer had died "during a temporary mental aberration."

[10] Diary, March 28, 1876, MS.

[11] Order Book, Seventh Cavalry, 1878–1881, MS, CBNM.

to the ranks. Private William Bald, C Troop, First Cavalry, noted that "Sgt. Wright, while drilling recruits, went off reservation and got all hands drunk. Sgt. under arrest . . . . [and that] Sgt. Wright was read off at retreat, one year [in confinement], $120. [fine]."[12] Unorthodox punishments for drunkenness were sometimes brutal. Private William Murphy stated that he had seen a drunken soldier "spread eagled," or staked out, at Fort Reno, Dakota Territory, in 1866. Chronic drunkards were sometimes given undesirable, "bobtail" discharges, with the "character" section clipped from the document. Clipped or "bobtail" discharge papers were a positive indication that the recipient had not been honorably released. Some officers had favorite punishments for problem drinkers.

> Custer [said his soldier-servant, John Burkman] had a way of punishing soldiers at Ft. Lincoln for bringing whiskey into camp. He got tired of stopping their pay from them as that did not seem to stop it. So he made them carry [actually wear] the vinegar barrel for 5 to 10 days. Just so there feet and heads would show.[13]

The gathering momentum of a nationwide temperance movement was felt in the Regular Army. In June, 1865, the Secretary of War ordered that whisky no longer be made available through the subsistance, or commissary department. Enlisted regulars participated in temperance organizations to some extent, and the International Order of Good Templars maintained branches at several western posts. Organized as an abstinence movement in 1851, at Utica, New York, the Good Templars spread over the United States, Canada, and Great Britain by the end of the sixties. Its members personally pledged total abstinence from the use of any and all alcoholic beverages. Some post commanders promoted the work of the Good Templars, as a means of

[12] Diary, Sept. 18 and Oct. 24, MS.

[13] I. D. O'Donnell, Notes taken in conversation with John Burkman, enlisted servant of Lieutenant Colonel George A. Custer, I. D. O'Donnell Collection.

curbing liquor problems among the rank and file. Discussing temperance and moral betterment movements in the Regular Army of the seventies, First Infantryman John E. Cox explained:

> One of the earliest attempts was the organization at Ft. Randall of a Good Templars' Society to combat the fearful influence of the saloons and gambling dens. It was in 1874. Sgt. Keeler and Captain Eli G. Apley came to me [to propose it]. . . . In the barracks store Keeler stood on a box, commanded the attention of the men there assembled and announced an organization meeting at the Odd Fellows' Hall. The announcement was greeted with jeers and we were doubtful of the outcome. But on the next night 18 men responded. [I was elected Chief Templar] . . . of perhaps the first temperance society in the army of the northwest . . . . The officers of the garrison gave hearty support . . . particularly Col. Lugenbeel . . . . The lodge became a sort of corrective agency. When a soldier got drunk the Commander would suspend sentence on conditon that the offender joined the Good Templars and took the abstinence pledge.[14]

The Good Templar lodges usually provided some sort of non-alcoholic clubroom, where soldiers could read, play cards, and generally relax. Members who broke their pledges were voted out of the lodges, though some of of these, who later repented their lapses, were readmitted.[15] Post commanders often made a building available to the lodge, and furnished the organization with materials to improve their quarters.

Frontier soldiers sometimes supported essentially civilian temperance movements. "In the summer of 1877," wrote First Infantryman John E. Cox, "a temperance convention was held at Miles City, attended by hundreds of soldiers, officers . . . and government employees. They met in a hall made by posts set in the

[14] John E. Cox, "Soldiering in Dakota Territories in the Seventies: A Communication," *North Dakota History*, Vol. VI, No. 1 (1931), 78f.

[15] White, Diary, MS. White was a Good Templar, having membership in the lodge at Fort Shaw, Montana Territory. He mentions many meetings, and several cases of members breaking their abstinence pledges. The lodge hall was often used by the troops for social functions, such as dances.

ground with a dirt roof. An Indiana man, a government contractor, made the principal address."[16] Most of the military personnel who attended were stationed at the newly established Fort Keogh, two miles from Miles City.

To encourage temperance, post commanders often limited the amount of liquor post traders and sutlers could sell to enlisted men; for example, the trader might be allowed to sell no more than three drinks per day to each soldier, and then only at three different times of the day. Infraction of these rules was a frequent cause of contention between merchants and commanding officers, who, in some outfits, carefully supervised the available supply of liquor. Sergeant James S. Hamilton said that "to buy a bottle of whiskey [in the First Infantry, from 1876 to 1881,] an order had to be obtained from the Capt. and this bought only a pint, which was purchased in a sutler's store."

Officially, the Regular Army wished to curb liquor abuses. The strictness with which its policies were carried out, however, depended in large measure upon the personal inclinations of company officers and post commanders. Hard drinking could not be suppressed among the rank and file, so long as it was common among their commissioned superiors.

The motives for murder and manslaughter were many and varied, but cases involving liquor were the most numerous. In 1884, at Fort Bidwell, California, General R. J. Burt, as a boy, witnessed an incident of potential violence that was the result of inhibitions and repressions unleashed by drunkenness. He wrote, of a cavalryman:

> He stood at the top of a barracks flight of stairs with a loaded carbine in his hands. He reviled the non-commissioned officer (in charge of the quarters) who was at the foot of the stairway, finally yelling, "Come on you son of a bitch and take me!" The . . . Sergeant leaned quietly against the railing . . . interjecting a phrase or two. . . . all the yelling [by the private] was no use.

16 "Soldiering," *North Dakota History,* Vol. VI, No. 1, 79.

This continued until the effects of the whiskey wore off. The Sergeant then mounted the stairway, took the carbine, and ordered, "Get your blankets."

Describing what the soldiers felt was a dastardly killing, in 1878, Private George W. McAnulty, C Company, Ninth Infantry, wrote:

> . . . deceased was in the act of separating . . . [two brawling sol-
> diers] when young Clark the murderer came up behind his vic-
> tim and struck him a crushing blow on the back of the head . . . .
> They had the prisoner at Headquarters this morning . . . he will
> be sent to Cheyenne City [Wyoming] and turned over to civil
> authorities—he is under a strong guard here, they are afraid the
> soldiers will attempt to lynch him.[17]

The officers had good reason to be apprehensive. About six months earlier, when a sergeant was murdered by one of the men in his detachment, the killer was "lynched by the men of his company the same evening."[18] Perhaps the vigilante justice often resorted to by frontier civilians influenced the western regulars, who, contrary to all military discipline, executed one of their own number.

Violence was far more widespread on the frontier than else-where, and in the army was frequently manifested as opposition to military descipline. Officers and noncommissioned men, as the upholders and enforcers of discipline, were the usual victims of mutinous and rebellious soldiers. A second lieutenant of the Fifth Cavalry was murdered May 11, 1881, by a soldier in the detachment he commanded.[19] In 1866, an Eighteenth Infantry-man's attempt on the life of a harsh officer failed only because

[17] To Miss Moore, July 26, 1878.
[18] "Med. Hist., Fort Laramie, 1868–79, MS, Nat. Arch., 224. Dec. 15, 1877: "1st Sgt. J. H. Van Moll, Co. A, 3rd Cav., was assissinated by Private Kennedy, same company, near Silver Spring Ranch, Wyo., Terr."
[19] *Twelfth Annual Reunion of the Association of the Graduates of the United States Military Academy, at West Point, N. Y., June 9, 1881,* 2nd Lt. Samuel A. Cherry, 49.

his rifle-musket did not fire when the hammer struck the percussion cap.[20]

Lawless men, who had enlisted in the regulars, sometimes committed murder and other acts of violence while in the army. A young Seventeenth Infantryman from Georgia always carried a derringer pistol, on a string down the back of his neck, said Private John C. Ford. He finally used it to shoot a comrade in the back. A first sergeant shot a soldier caught rifling his effects, while on campaign in southeastern Oklahoma, in 1889. Pointing up the relative cheapness of human life, Private Harvey J. Ciscel told of the murder of one of his comrades, stating that the man had been killed for his shoes alone, and the body thrust into a snowbank.

Even basically law-abiding soldiers were probably influenced to some extent by the rawness of the frontier environment. On many occasions tragedy was narrowly averted. Indicative of the prevalence of violence among men who ordinarily would not have resorted to it, is Sergeant Perley S. Eaton's account of a heated argument between two commissioned officers. "My first sergeant" wrote Eaton, "jumped between two Lieutenants, that were going to shoot each other with revolvers, and disarmed them—they might have accidentaly shot him."

Self-destruction, also, was all too common in the Regular Army. Loneliness, boredom, and alcoholism, among other causes, contributed to a relatively high suicide rate. An investigation of the suicide problem in 1891 revealed, according to War Department reports, that the ratio of 76 suicides per one thousand men, from 1879 to 1888, was three times as high as the ratios reported in the British and Belgian armies, and twice as high as the ratios reported in the intensely disciplined Prussian forces.[21] Exposure of a homosexual relationship was the direct cause of one soldier suicide in 1878.[22]

---

[20] Lockwood, *Drummer-Boy*, 135.
[21] *Ann. Report, Sec. of War, 1891*, I, 595.
[22] Godfrey, "General Sully's Expedition," Bates Coll., 4.

Some companies included a sneak thief or two, who stole from their comrades. Forced as they were to live in very close proximity to each other, soldiers viewed such pilfering as a heinous crime. To steal the meager possessions of a comrade was to assume the status of a pariah, and those caught at it generally received some rough handling before the matter was officially reported. Some units were virtually free of petty theft.

Stealing food, or some form of government goods, did not carry the stigma associated with stealing from one's fellows. Theft and sale of government property was widespread. Firearms, ammunition, food, equipments, and clothing were most readily converted to unauthorized use or sale. To curb the illegal disposition of arms in the Department of Texas, General Orders No. 19 was issued in 1872. Observing that "it appears from the proceedings of Boards of Survey, that arms are continuously being stolen from Company barracks," General Christopher C. Augur directed officers to secure all arms in special racks, or put them in the keeping of a completely reliable soldier.[23] A Sergeant Graham was placed in charge of his company's Colt revolvers in 1876. Twenty of the revolvers were stolen, and the Sergeant claimed they had been taken by two deserters. An intensive investigation was ordered, and Sergeant Graham himself deserted from Fort Brown, Texas, before the matter was cleared up.[24] The new, model 1873 Colt forty-five caliber revolvers had not long been on the market, and civilians paid soldiers premium prices for them. Commercial firearms often cost more than an Indian purchaser could afford. "Some of the soldiers would sell their guns to the [friendly] Indians," stated Private Charles Goodenberger.

The sale of army rifles, carbines, and revolvers was not considered especially serious by the rank and file, except when a man stole another soldier's arms in the process. The company commander held each man accountable for the weapons issued

[23] General Orders No. 19, Dept. of Texas, Oct. 22, 1872, Nat. Arch.
[24] "Captain Chilson, 8th Cavalry," Misc. Doc. File, 4080, 1876, Nat. Arch.

to him, and those who lost them paid heavily for their careless-ness.[25] Many soldiers unobtrusively marked their arms as a means of positive identification in the event they were stolen. Rifles and carbines were marked under the butt plate, under the trigger guard, and on the stock under the barrel; revolvers were marked on the inside of the wooden grips.

The more avaricious and daring of the soldier-criminals were occasionally tempted to undertake serious burglaries or even armed robberies. In 1881, Twenty-third Infantryman Wallace E. Bingham described how he foiled a plot to rob a paymaster. He had been assigned to guard the money in a tent, while the pay-master took some of the cash to pay soldiers in a camp about a mile away. Bingham said:

> . . . I sat down on a camp chair back in the tent, where I had a good view. It wasn't long before I saw two soldiers sneaking through the brush, about 150 yards away. They kept looking at the tent, at the same time trying to keep out of sight. I waited until they got in a more open place, then stepped out through the opening. The breech lock of my rifle caught the cartridge. I put it [the hammer] back and came to a "ready" and commanded them to come out in the open. Then I recognized them—two C Company men, but "bad eggs."

He told them to clear off, and they did. According to Bingham, one of the men had been dishonorably discharged from the British Army; the other later deserted. Just before leaving he admitted to Bingham that the two would-be robbers had planned to kill the guard and escape to South America with their loot, but Bingham had seen them too soon.

Frontier regulars were frequently involved in violent riots and other disturbances that originated among civilians. "During a row in Miles [City] after the celebration of the 4th [July, 1882] a colored man . . . struck a soldier . . . a blow over the head with

[25] General Orders No. 43, July 11, 1868, Nat. Arch. A soldier "losing" a Springfield breech-loading rifle-musket was to be charged $50.00 for each weapon lost, about double the actual cost of these rifles.

a stick . . . fracturing his skull and inflicting such injuries that he has since died."[26] A private of the Seventh Infantry was fatally stabbed in a civilian groggery, forty-five miles from Fort Laramie, during a civilian brawl in 1883.[27] The shotgun killing of the Apache scout Rowdy also took place in a privately owned and managed "hog ranch." Violence involving regulars could result in courts-martial under military law, or entangle enlisted men with civil law-enforcement authorities. Negro regulars were sometimes the special object of peace officers' attentions, which led to numerous brawls and a few gun battles between soldiers and civilians.

Men had plumbed the depths of vice and sexual depravity centuries before the Indian Wars era. Some frontier soldiers may have explored these matters for themselves, but it is doubtful that any new discoveries were made.[28] Moral deviations were not new to the army, although they were not usually published or discussed in late-Victorian society. Soldiers have always been numbered among the prostitute's best customers, and the frontier regulars were no exception. Concentrations of troops always attract the purveyors of vice. In the 1880's, a presidential order, meant to lessen vice among enlisted men, instead compounded the problem.

Toward the close of President Rutherford B. Hayes's administration, advocates of total abstinence pressured the President into signing an order forbidding the sale of whisky at all military establishments. Informed that they were not allowed to buy liquor at the post trader stores as before, the rank and file re-

[26] *Billings Post,* July 15, 1882, 4.
[27] Med. Hist., Fort Laramie, 1880–84, MS, Nat. Arch., 175.
[28] Sergeant T. E. Guy, First Cavalry, 1889–92, told of an incident he witnessed in which some of the soldier "sports" in his company conducted an orgy in an off-limits brothel and saloon. A nude prostitute postured to accommodate the "sports," standing in the center of the table around which the soldiers were drinking. Of his own low moral level and that of others in his company, another Indian Wars regular said, "I lived a disgraceful life as a kid in the army!"

acted by switching their patronage to the "hog ranches" that
mushroomed just outside the military reservation limits. Totally
unsupervised, the "hog ranches" sold the men whisky of the
poorest quality, took their money in gambling, and provided
them with the vilest and most diseased whores.[29]

Frontier soldiers availed themselves of the companionship of
prostitutes to about the same degree as cowboys, miners, and
other western civilians, but were limited by their slender pay, as
usually "they did not have money enough," explained Private
William G. Wilkinson. Because the rank and file could pay little
for the favors of "red-light" women, those whose clientele were
principally soldiers were generally not the reigning beauties
of the demimonde. Perhaps unduly biased by their views on
soldiers in general, the open-range cowboys of the 1880's, claimed
that "a prostitute's standing in her profession depended on her
clientele and, . . . when a woman went to the dogs, she went to
the soldiers, the lowest level in the customers' scale."[30]

Writing of the Tenth Infantrymen he had known in the middle
eighties, First Sergeant George Neihaus said that there was only
a "fair amount" of consorting with prostitutes by the men in his
company, and that because it was only "7 miles to a little Mexican town, soldiers used to put dummies in their bunks for check
roll call." Corporal John Bergstrom remarked that many Twenty-
second Infantrymen formed liaisons with Indian women while
out on campaign in the winter of 1890 and 1891. This practice
was more common in some areas than in others, and was sometimes a serious cause of trouble.

Posts situated near settlements were sometimes visited by
enterprising prostitutes. Noting one such occasion, at Fort Ellis,
near Bozeman, Montana, in 1876, Private William White's diary
entry for February 8 stated that, "after supper the Frenchy lady

[29] Forsyth, *The Soldier*, I, 141.

[30] M. H. Brown and W. R. Felton, *The Frontier Years, L. A. Huffman, Photographer of the Plains*, 145.

made her appearance at the fort. The sequence was Ousel got put in the guard house and she was sent home."[31] Some prostitutes were patronized by soldiers from particular units, among whom they enjoyed a certain following and special favor.

Post and company commanders held varying opinions on methods of controlling the "social evil." Some did their best to keep their men away from diseased whores. According to Private John C. Ford, a few accommodating women accompanied his unit on the march, riding in a wagon at the rear of the column. "Everybody," said Ford, "knew this, including the Captain." Men who had relations with these women were inspected each morning by the doctor. Perhaps the unit commanders considered this arrangement of controlled availability preferable to unsupervised contacts with free-lance prostitutes.

At isolated garrisons or during intensive campaigning soldiers had few opportunities to indulge in heterosexual promiscuity. Venereal disease rates for the entire army, from 1880 to 1890, show that about eighty out of every thousand men contracted some form of venereal infection.[32] The artillery and recruits suffered the highest incidence of infection, which indicates that possibilities of diseased contact were higher in the settled areas garrisoned by the artillery and in the vicinity of the recruit depots than they were on the frontier. Virtually all artillery units were stationed at seacoast forts, guarding the nation's major port cities.

Homosexualism, when one attempts to discover its prevalence and significance, is always one of the most elusive moral deviations. In the late-nineteenth century, the subject was so taboo that although it must have existed to some degree among the thousands of frontier regulars, almost no evidence of it has come to light. An exception is the well-documented account of a "Mrs. Nash," who held the post of company laundress in the Seventh Cavalry. Always heavily veiled, this person remained with the

[31] Diary, Feb. 8, 1876, MS.
[32] *Ann. Report, Sec. of War, 1891*, I, 593.

regiment, married to a succession of soldier-husbands, from 1868 to 1878. She did not leave the service when her "husbands" were discharged, and in 1878 was cohabiting with a corporal at Fort Meade, Dakota Territory. The corporal accompanied his unit on an extended campaign in the summer of 1878, and "Mrs. Nash" died during his absence. When some of the garrison ladies went to lay her out, the shocking truth was revealed. "Mrs. Nash" was a man![33] The corporal's comrades ridiculed him unmercifully, and, unable to bear their scorn, he committed suicide with his revolver. Here is evidence of a series of homosexual liaisons, embracing a period of ten years, which must have been known to many of the rank and file. Though sociologists inform us that homosexualism is more prevalent among the highly educated and leisure classes than among the lower elements of the socio-economic and cultural scale, it existed to some extent among the enlisted men serving in the frontier West.

Purely military crimes and misdemeanors engaged much of the attention and disciplinary efforts of the Regular Army. Having sworn to abide by the Army Regulations and the Articles of War, soldiers were frequently guilty of misdeeds of omission as well as commission. Under civil law, the citizen must have committed an illegal act before he could be brought to trial, but, under military law, the soldier who failed to carry out any standing or special orders could be tried for neglect of duty. Like punishments for other infractions, those for neglect of duty varied widely. Remarking on the failure of a comrade to turn out smartly for guard detail, a Seventh Cavalry blacksmith noted in his 1869 diary that "Private Curley is tied up all day for not being clean on guard mount."[34] In 1878, at Fort Rice, Dakota Territory, a private who missed stable call and retreat formation was fined five dollars.[35] For compounding failure to attend

---

[33] Godfrey, "General Sully's Expedition," MS, 3f. Other letters, in the Bates Collection and Custer Collection, confirm this account.

[34] Diary of Seventh Cavalry Enlisted Man, Feb. 24, 1869, Bates Coll.

[35] Order Book, Seventh Cavalry, 1878–81, 32.

stable call by being drunk, a First Cavalryman was ordered to the guardhouse for ten days.

Corporals and sergeants convicted of shirking duty were usually reduced to the ranks. Two Seventh Cavalry corporals were broken January 11, 1869, because, "they would not come out to roll call in time this morning," wrote a member of K Company.[36] Neglect of duty took many forms, and one sergeant was fined a month's pay, in 1881, for allowing the post horse herd to stampede while he was in charge of the stable guard.[37] A private who had made himself comfortable on guard by sitting down was sentenced to seven days in the guardhouse, at "hard labor."[38] A sergeant lost his stripes in the First Cavalry for failure to report a soldier absent without leave from the 11:00 o'clock bed-check roll call.[39] Occasionally neglect of duty had serious consequences. Assembled at Fort Fetterman, Wyoming Territory, in 1876, the Fifth Cavalry was camping just outside the post.

> A member of the guard had placed his carbine in a wagon, and in taking it out, it was discharged. [The bullet killed a soldier sitting nearby.] . . . The culprit had failed to eject the cartridge when he came off guard. He was tried by a . . . courtmartial for neglect and gross carelessness, was sentenced to be dishonorably discharged . . . and to serve a term in military prison.[40]

Soldiers could be court-martialed or otherwise disciplined for breaches of regulations and the Articles of War, ranging from murder and desertion to "profanity" and "reproachful or provoking speeches."[41] Insubordination was one of the more serious infractions. An officer charged Fifth Cavalryman Antonio Fras-

[36] Diary of a Seventh Cavalry Enlisted Man, Jan. 11, 1869.
[37] Order Book, Seventh Cavalry, 1878–81, 203.
[38] *Ibid.*, 201.
[39] Diary of Private William Bald, C Troop, First Cavalry, July 25, 1893, MS.
[40] Colonel H. W. Wheeler, *Buffalo Days*, 151.
[41] Hershler, 28–30, 34. The following Articles of War were included in the *Handbook* as especially applicable to the rank and file: 16, selling or wasting ammunition punishable by court-martial; 17, selling, losing, Government mounts, arms, clothes, etc. Offender to suffer stoppage of pay, up to one half the amount

cola with insubordination in disobeying the order not to fire guns in camp, while in the field in the Indian Territory. A sergeant, who knew the facts in the case, reported the details to the commanding officer at Fort Reno; it was the accusing officer himself who had fired the shot.[42]

Discipline in some regiments categorized very minor lapses as military insubordination. For laughing in ranks, explained Sergeant Grandison Mayo, Twenty-fifth Infantry, the miscreant was ordered to march double time around the parade ground for fifteen minutes, with his rifle held at port arms. In the Eighth Cavalry, said Sergeant Reinhold R. Gast, "a soldier refused to go on kitchen duty [claiming it was not his turn]—he was made to sleep on a cold, bare floor—with no food but bread and water, for three days [in the guardhouse]." An insubordinate First Cavalryman was sentenced to fifteen days in the guardhouse and a thirteen dollar (month's pay) fine.[43] A Seventh Cavalry private, at Fort Totten, in 1880, was ordered by a corporal to get some sawdust for the squadroom floor. The soldier refused, saying, "Go to hell, you red-headed son of a bitch!"[44] The fine of ten

due, or by courts-martial decreeing fine or imprisonment; 20, disrespect to Commanding Officer, punishable by courts-martial; 21, striking or threatening a superior, punishable by death, or as decreed by a courts-martial; 22, mutiny, same punishment as Art. 21; 24, "forays" and quarreling, punishable by confinement; 25, "reproachful or provoking speeches, . . . who so offends shall be confined, and required to ask pardon of the party offended, in the presence of his commanding officer"; 32, absent over leave, punishable by courts-martial; 33, absent from parade or other formation, punishable by courts-martial; 35, "failure to retire at retreat," same punishment as Art. 33; 36, "hiring duty," same punishment as Art. 33, though this was very common; 38, drunk on duty, court-martial, *but*, no branding, "marking," or tattooing as in former times; 39, sleeping on sentinel duty, death, or other courts-martial sentence; 40, "Quitting Guard," or leaving assigned station, punishable by courts-martial; 42, "Quitting post in the face of the enemy," same as Art. 40; 53, profanity—officers were to be fined one dollar for each offense. Enlisted men to be fined one-sixth of a dollar, and if the offense was repeated, confined for twenty-four hours. All fines collected for profanity were to be used for the benefit of sick members of the offender's company.

[42] Frascola, *Indian-Pioneer Papers*, Phillips Coll.

[43] Bald, Diary, Sept. 2, 1893, MS.

[44] Order Book, Seventh Cavalry, 1878–81, 113.

dollars from his private's pay, may have led him to ponder the results of insubordination, even to a corporal. Insubordination was frequently punished through summary court-martial, after the adoption of those streamlined courts in 1889. Since repeated convictions by summary courts automatically resulted in a "bobtail" discharge, at least one soldier sought to turn repeated insubordination trials into the discharge he coveted.[45]

Shirking duty and malingering, termed "gold-bricking" in more modern times, was a common form of disobedience of orders. When soldiers assigned to working parties absented themselves, they were usually not punished harshly, except in repeated and aggravated cases. A Seventh Cavalry saddler grew weary of laboring in his company garden, at Fort Totten, during the harvest of 1879. He waited for a good opportunity and slipped away to the post trader's store, where the corporal found him sipping a glass of lager. The corporal promptly ordered him back to work, whereupon the thirsty trooper refused to go, saying, "I am going to have my beer."[46] For shirking duty, and insubordination, the saddler paid with a ten dollar fine and a month in the guardhouse.

Besides failing to report for working parties, or refusing to perform some assigned duty, soldiers found other ways of shirking. Corporal John Bergstrom explained that many Twenty-second Infantrymen practiced deceit by maintaining their heavy campaign gear in constant readiness. Knapsacks were stuffed to make them appear filled with clothing and equipment. Extra field shoes were supposed to be placed in such a way that only the soles and heels were exposed. Some men cut off the uppers to lighten the pack without showing that the equipment was incomplete.

[45] Private Richard F. Watson, First Cavalry, told of a soldier named Cooper, an Englishman, who was deliberately insubordinate in hopes of being discharged. When his sentence was decreed as confinement instead of a "bobtail" discharge, Cooper attempted to escape, but was caught and sent to the prison at Fort Leavenworth.

[46] Order Book, Seventh Cavalry, 1878–81, 87f.

Many shirkers reported themselves sick in an attempt to escape unpleasant assignments or get time to recover from a hangover. Malingering soldiers sometimes tried to obtain medical-duty excuses in order to go on a spree. Such pretence is not peculiar to frontier regulars, and has been tried by hosts of military personnel in more recent times. As always, most of the shirkers were detected in their deceptions. Soldiers scheming for "quarters" assignments in the Seventh Cavalry were often suffering from the aftereffects of excessive drinking. They felt bad enough, but were actually able to perform their duties. Hangover shirkers were customarily given castor oil, jalap, "anything to keep them moving . . . administered in good big doses," after which they were detailed to some unpleasant extra duty.[47]

Discussing successful deceptions on the part of shirkers and malingerers, Trumpeter Ami Frank Mulford wrote:

> Then there was McCurren, who was shot in the hand [in the fight with the Nez Perce, Bears Paw Mountain, October, 1877] and had also lost a finger, and always told the Surgeon [in the hospital at Fort Abraham Lincoln] that the hand was so stiff and sore he could not use it, yet as soon as the Surgeon had crossed the parade to his quarters, he would grab a broom and go through the manual of arms without flinching. *He was stiff and sore for a discharge,* and he got it too![48]

Such a case was not common though, for many genuinely incapacitated frontier soldiers were retained in the ranks, because soldiers discharged as injured in the line of duty were eligible for pensions, which the parsimonious Regular Army did not favor.

Aside from those involving drunkenness, regulations governing unauthorized absence and absence over leave were the ones most frequently broken. Violators were customarily given short guardhouse sentences or fines. "But the fines," said Corporal

---

[47] *Fighting Indians,* 44.
[48] *Ibid.,* 132.

Louis Courville, "usually went to the troop funds, and we got the benifit of it." Men who missed the eleven o'clock bed check, or were otherwise absent without specific authority, ran the risk of being charged with desertion, for the Articles of War stipulated that "any soldier found one mile from camp, without leave in writing" from his commanding officer, was subject to court-martial on suspicion of desertion.[49] Nocturnal visits to "hog ranches," garrison women, and nearby settlements occasioned most of these unauthorized absences. Sergeant Reginald A. Bradley told of a captain who complained that he had heard someone, probably a soldier, trying to gain entry into his quarters one night, while Bradley was on guard. The Sergeant mollified the officer, claiming he had been faithful and diligent in his duty and denying that he had heard anyone attempting to *enter* the captain's house. What he did not tell was that he had seen a soldier *leaving* the house in question, through the window of a female servant's room, and in fact knew all about the affair.

Minor infractions of regulations and breaches of discipline were usually punished within the company. Extra duty, extra guard assignments, restriction to quarters, and unpleasant fatigue details were imposed. For more serious violations, garrison and summary courts-martial levied fines and ordered guardhouse sentences. Fines ranged from two to sixty dollars, or even more, although most pay stoppages were for sums up to and including thirteen dollars. In the late eighties, money collected in fines was customarily turned over to the company fund, and used to provide recreation facilities. Prior to that time, all fines assessed against soldiers were sent to the Soldiers' Home, in Washington, D. C. Court-martial convictions frequently carried guardhouse sentences in addition to fines. The slang phrase, "a month and a month," so often heard in garrison courts, specified loss of a month's pay and a thirty-day stay in the guardhouse. A Third Cavalryman, convicted of calling his captain a bastardly son of a bitch, was given six months in the guardhouse and a

[49] Hershler, *Handbook*, 31.

fine of sixty dollars. "He had to do all the dirty work around the post, under guard, for six months, except Sunday, and was kept locked up in the guard house every night," wrote Sergeant Perley S. Eaton.

Confinement to the post guardhouse was usually for periods of a few days up to six months. Ten days in the "mill" was a common punishment for drunkenness. As Private Clarence H. Allen put it, "A certain type [of men] would go into town and get drunk—they were put in the guard house." Stiffer guardhouse sentences might specify all or part of the term to be "in solitary confinement on bread and water diet." Prisoners were commonly shackled while serving out their sentences. During the day prisoners were assigned to such fatigues as garbage and trash disposal, under the charge of guard details.

Enlightened prison reform had not yet spread to regular army guardhouses at the end of the Indian Wars era. The Fort Laramie guardhouse was described by the post surgeon, in 1868:

> The basement room is [about twenty-five feet square] of rough stones, whitewashed, has one door and a window towards the river [heavily barred with wagon tires] and on the opposite side at the top two small windows for ventilation. A couple of [small] cells are partitioned off [with heavy planks and solid doors] in the south side for refractory prisoners.

> The prisoners are all kept in the basement room which contains no furniture. There are ten prisoners at present [twenty-one in November, 1868]. The basement room is not warmed [as in the guard room on the first floor]. . . . The prisoners have no light.[50]

Guardhouse prisoners were not supplied with bunks, chairs, or other basic furniture. Prisoners brought their blankets with them when ordered to confinement. They ate, slept, and frequently performed all the necessary human functions in the

---

[50] "Med. Hist., Fort Laramie, 1868–79," MS, 7, 39.

guardhouse. By the late eighties, the climate of reform that pervaded army thinking on other facets of enlisted life led to official interest in guardhouse conditions. Some officers favored separating youthful minor offenders from the repeater "mill birds." As of 1891, however, prisoners were still not allowed bunks, mattresses, reading matter, or such pastimes as checkers,[51] and in most guardhouses still slept on the bare floor, or on a wooden banquette, or dais.

Long-term sentences, prior to 1874, were customarily served in various state and federal penitentiaries, such as that at Detroit, Michigan. Terms usually ranged from one to four years, with a few for longer periods. Most military convicts were deserters, but men convicted of murder, manslaughter, serious theft, and other felonies were numbered among the prisoners. They were generally sentenced to hard labor, which meant heavy construction, or work in the prison's shoe, harness, pipe, carpenter, broom, or tin shop.

The United States Military Prison, at Fort Leavenworth, Kansas, was established in 1874. It was an austere, thoroughly regulation establishment, where prisoners were subject to strict, hair-trigger discipline. It supplied a large portion of the army's shoes, cooking utensils, harness, and other matériel that could be manufactured economically in its shops. Convicts were not paid for their labor. Each, when released from prison, was given five dollars, as a start in civil life.

Prison sentences, and many other courts-martial decrees, made mandatory a dishonorable discharge at the end of the prisoner's punishment. Men dishonorably discharged from the western posts were sometimes drummed out of the fort in a ceremony witnessed by the garrison.[52] Old soldiers, who for some reason, usually drunkenness, fell afoul of military law, were usually the

---

[51] *Ann. Report, Sec. of War, 1891*, I, 327.

[52] Mattison, "Surgeon Matthews," *North Dakota History*, Vol. XXI, Nos. 1–2 (1954), 29. "Private Melburn . . . was drummed out of the service at 2 p.m. in execution of sentence of Court Martial [Dec., 1869]."

BARRACK ROOM OF K TROOP

Third Cavalry, Fort Elliott, Texas, 1885. The seated sergeant is
Perley S. Eaton and the young soldier with arms folded across his
chest at the right is Private John Hubbard. Both men, in 1954, gave
firsthand information on their army experiences.

Courtesy Sergeant Perley S. Eaton

COMPANY OF FIFTH INFANTRY IN WINTER POST
dress, probably at a guard mount ceremony, at Fort Custer
or Fort Keogh, Montana, 1887.

Courtesy Corporal Frank B. Knight

ones punished with "bobtail" discharges. Younger, first-enlistment troublemakers frequently wanted nothing so much as a discharge, any sort of discharge, and to them a "bobtail" was as good as any other form of release. Professional re-enlistees, on the other hand, had elected to make the Regular Army their home, and sending one of them out of the service was a harsh punishment. Chronic "mill birds," drunkards, and shiftless soldiers were also shunted out of the army with an undesirable discharge, to avoid wasting government funds subsisting them in guardhouses and prisons.

Brutal, humiliating, painful, degrading, and sometimes sadistic punishments, traditional or improvised, that were frequently imposed prior to the Civil War, received much unfavorable notice during the Rebellion. Flogging was abolished in 1861, and other cruel punishments also were declared illegal, thanks to pressures from civilians imbued with wartime enthusiasm. When the war ended in 1865, the nation lost its earlier, emotion-charged interest in the Boys in Blue, and the Regular Army lapsed to some degree into its former methods of disciplining refractory enlisted men. On the frontier, a self-willed martinet, commanding an isolated garrison, was not subject to much control from higher authority. A harsh or sadistic officer could order disciplinary measures supposedly outlawed and actually illegal. That possibility was recognized in General Orders No. 7, Headquarters of the Army, of February, 1866, which stated that ". . . treatment of enlisted men by commissioned officers, will be particularly investigated, with a view to preventing harsh and arbitrary treatment and illegal punishments."

That the orders prohibiting brutal punishment were not universally followed is attested by a letter written from Fort Ellis, Montana Territory, the day after a payday, in February, 1871. Describing the treatment of prisoners, the sutler's clerk wrote:

Mulford, *Fighting Indians*, 38. Dishonorably discharged soldier was "escorted out of camp by a guard . . . [1876]." The band usually played "The Rogue's March," or "Poor Old Soldier," on such occasions.

. . . they have some [prisoners] tied up by their thumbs, some by the arms, ala spread eagle; one fellow, whom they couldn't manage any other way, bucked and gagged and laid out in the snow four hours; a most severe and almost cruel punishment; but he deserved it richly.[53]

The clerk's letter raises two questions: what would he have considered a really cruel punishment, and, what was the nature of the last prisoner's offense? Perhaps he had offered violence to the clerk, while the latter tended bar in the store on payday. In any case, the 1866 general order, though not rescinded, does not seem to have restrained the post commander at Fort Ellis from administering old Regular Army chastisements.

In apology for such treatment of the rank and file, and yet partly in defense of regular officers, Colonel O. L. Hein, himself an Indian Wars campaigner, wrote that

Various forms of savage physical punishments continued to be inflicted upon the enlisted men . . . for several years after the Civil War, and as late as 1871 within my personal observation; but such instances were rare and exceptional, and generally at the insistence of officers of foreign birth in the army, and who had risen from the ranks. In after years all forms of harsh and degrading punishment were strictly forbidden.[54]

Other evidence seems to indicate differently. Perhaps Colonel Hein did not see much of this sort of thing, but others did.

The punishment or, more precisely, torture, termed "spread eagle," was one of the most common of the vicious punishments inflicted on frontier regulars. It was witnessed in 1866 by Private William Murphy, Eighteenth Infantry, who penned a graphic description of the "spread eagle":

At the guard tent [on the march to the Big Horn country of northern Wyoming], four stakes were driven into the ground; and the drunken soldier was stretched out full length and tied to

[53] Koch to "Laurie," MS, Feb. 21, 1871, Letters of Koch, No. 29.
[54] Hein, *Memories*, 25.

them. This was called the "Spread Eagle." Sun beating down on him, flies eating him up (in eyes, nose, mouth, ears). It was reported that he died . . . . [I] heard they started the same thing at Fort Reno [Dakota Territory] a month or two later and caused a riot or mutiny. The commander gave the soldier his discharge as a compromise.

At Fort Phil Kearny a few months later Murphy saw one of the later-day applications of another "old Army" punishment. A drunken soldier was ordered turned out, he was branded, his head was shaved, and he was drummed out of the post.

The style of "spread eagle" described by Murphy was the usual one.[55] A variant method was trussing an offender up on the spare wheel of a caisson, in the rear of a marching column. Through the latter seventies and early eighties the incidence of "spread eagling" rapidly declined, and some outfits were notably free of such punishments. The practice had virtually disappeared by the nineties, although Seventh Cavalry Quartermaster Sergeant Dorsey E. Phillips (1893 to 1898), stated, "I was Sgt. of the guard, [when] two prisoners were very unruly, and were ordered by the officer of the day to be spread eagled."

"Bucking and gagging," like the "spread eagle," was outlawed and all but ended by the nineties. This punishment consisted of tying a man up so that he could not move and placing an effective gag in his mouth. The wrists were tied to the ankles, so that the victim was doubled up. This barbaric punishment was sometimes inflicted for such infractions as "not being clean on guard mount," but was generally reserved for more serious offenses.[56]

[55] David L. Spotts, *Campaigning With Custer and the Nineteenth Kansas Volunteer Cavalry*, 135. This is mostly the author's 1869 diary. March 1, he witnessed a "spread eagle" ordered by a West Point graduate, at Fort Sill, Indian Territory: "He made the man lie on his back, spread out his arms and legs, then drove a stake at each hand and foot and tied his hands and feet to stakes." Sergeant Eaton explained that "sometimes when a soldier got drunk and got so bad that you could do nothing with him, I have seen them make a spread eagle of him, also they sometimes tied him to a wagon wheel."

[56] Diary of a Seventh Cavalry Enlisted Man. Feb. 24, 1869: "Private Curley is tied up all day for not being clean on guard mount."

Men might be subjected to this ordeal for as much as a whole day at a time. Some Kansas Volunteers found a regular soldier "bucked and gagged" at Fort Sill, February 28, 1869. The man had lain in the same restrictive posture for some time, for "he was unconscious, and his eyes were wide open and staring . . . for we hurried and took the gag out of his mouth and unloosened him so he could breathe, but it took some vigorous rubbing to bring him to."[57] This example of regular army discipline as practiced in the Seventh Cavalry, was totally unacceptable to the ninety-day volunteers.

Suspending soldiers by their thumbs, wrists, or arms, was another of the older punishments that gradually died out. Prisoners were tied in such a way that only the tips of their toes touched the ground or guardhouse floor, a punishment more suited to medieval Europe or the Far East than to late nineteenth-century America. Commenting on the severity of such measures, Colonel Hein wrote:

> Mrs. Cavanaugh, a post laundress, threatened to kill the First Lieutenant . . . with a knife, because he had ordered her husband, the troop blacksmith, to be tied up by the thumbs . . . [for being drunk at evening stables]. This was the last instance of the infliction of brutal punishment upon a soldier, within my remembrance.[58]

Sergeant John Ryan, Seventh Cavalry, admitted having illegally suspended a soldier in 1876, and other incidents, not known to Colonel Hein, undoubtedly took place.[59]

One of the commonest traditional improvised punishments was ordering offenders to march about carrying a heavy weight, usually a rail or stout log. This was not nearly so harsh as the methods previously described, but could be a grueling ordeal. In 1871, Peter Koch wrote to his mother that eight to ten men

[57] Spotts, *Campaigning With Custer*, 134.

[58] Hein, *Memories*, 67f.

[59] To Mrs. Custer, MS, Sept. 6, 1909, Package No. 26, Custer Coll.

could be seen carrying heavy logs on their shoulders, walking up and down in front of the guardhouse. "They make them carry them sometimes," said Koch, "till they cannot stand any longer, but it doesn't do much good . . . they will get drunk again the next day."[60]

Occasionally frontier regular officers devised their own off-beat punishments. An officer of the Tenth Cavalry had two quarreling troopers whip each other with mule whips, and when one of them later tried to shoot him, the officer made the man a sergeant for showing his courage.[61] In some regiments a sadistic, mean, or emotionally unbalanced officer could impose his own inimitable penalties with relative impunity.

The percentage of oppressive officers was probably somewhat higher in the frontier Regular Army than it has been in more recent years, but intensely harsh, cruel, and overbearing ones were always in the minority. After thirteen years of regular service in the West, Second Cavalryman Joseph Kuhn observed that the vast majority of officers he had served under, from 1882 to 1895, "were efficient and fair and of good moral fibre." Kuhn, like many other Indian Wars soldiers, felt that while discipline was sometimes strict, it was fairly administered. Most of the rank and file would probably have agreed with Sergeant Perley S. Eaton's summation that "as long as you behaved yourself and performed your duty as a soldier, you got along all right."

Others of the enlisted men believed that discipline and punishments were too strict and harsh. Some qualified their statements by conceding that perhaps the character of the men and the circumstances justified heavy-handed authority. "The discipline," wrote Sergeant Samuel Evans, "was some good for the many young fellows who were inclined to be rowdies. They were held in check and when their time was up, they were really respectable citizens." It may be that a term of service in the Regular Army exercised an educational and beneficial influence on un-

[60] To "Mother," MS, Feb. 14, 1871, Letters of Koch, No. 28.
[61] Wheeler, *Buffalo Days*, 252.

ruly youths, who, in a much later day, would be termed "juvenile delinquents."

Of course, the rank and file held a variety of opinions on the highly controversial subject of discipline. After serving four years in the German forces, Private John G. K. Bangerd enlisted in the Seventh Infantry, in 1888. He compared the two armies, and stated that he believed that Seventh Infantry discipline was fair, and not too demanding. Two other men, who served with Bangerd in the same regiment at the same time, said that they felt that strictness and harshness had been the keynotes of discipline.

"The words military discipline," wrote Seventh Cavalryman Albert J. Davis, "have covered a multitude of tyrannies." Like the Greek tyrants of old, many of the frontier regular officers were benign in the exercise of tremendous arbitrary authority, but the lack of uniformity in discipline and punishments was resented by enlisted soldiers. Capricious, subjective administration of discipline, and the fact that the men convicted of the same offenses, and having equal records, were often not given equal punishments confused and irritated the soldiers to no end. The rank and file did not respect military justice that smacked of favoritism.

10.

Recreation, Relaxation, and Outside Interests

LIKE ALL MEN, frontier regulars needed to unwind and relax when off duty, and the crushing boredom and monotony of post life in the West made the need for healthy recreation all the more acute. Individual officers sometimes attempted to provide recreation leadership and facilities for the enlisted men, but the army as a whole showed little interest in the problem until the late eighties. As a result, men stationed at remote posts tended to become lethargic and stale, and many sought temporary oblivion in drink. Months of inactivity were depressing and psychologically deteriorating, and probably bred more serious trouble than any other single factor.

The principal barracks relaxation was visiting and talking among themselves. Since the army did little to provide rest or recreation, enlisted regulars improvised most of their own amusements. The diary entries of Private B. C. Goodin, C Troop, First

Cavalry, for a month at Fort Grant, Arizona, shows that he was on mounted pass for half a day, and spent the rest of his off-duty time reading in quarters, "strolling," playing cribbage, singing and dancing in quarters, attending an "entertainment" in the post chapel, and playing jokes on his comrades in the barracks.[1] No form of athletics is mentioned, though several sports were popular.

The leadership of some officer or noncommissioned man was needed to popularize sports; someone had to organize teams, events, and competition to "get the gang going." In companies lacking such leadership the men participated in very few sports. "When they were through with mounted drill, sabre exercises, revolver practice, and dismounted skirmish lines [drill]," wrote Fifth Cavalry Sergeant Armand Unger, "most men had experienced all the exercise they wanted." In other outfits, athletics were encouraged and were popular with all the rank and file.

Foot racing, jumping, weight-throwing, horseshoe pitching, and field sports were particularly enjoyed by frontier regulars. Of these, foot racing was most common; the usual race was the one hundred yard dash. First Sergeant George Neihaus remarked that he had been a noted runner in the Tenth Infantry, and was able to run the "100 yards in 10 seconds."

Like many other soldier enterprises, field sports were often a company endeavor. Members of the same unit coached and otherwise assisted their company champions in competition with other companies and with civilians, and demonstrated their unit loyalty by betting heavily on the outcome. Recalling a race between a company athlete and an Indian runner, Fifth Cavalryman Antonio Frascola said:

> We met up with an Indian who thought he was a foot racer. [In the Indian Territory, in 1887.] We had a bugler who could run one hundred yards in nine and a half seconds. They made a

[1] Diary, March 5–April 1, 1893.

match, the winner to get $50.00. Kelly, the bugler, beat the Indian foot racer five yards.

A speedy civilian turned the tables on the soldiers at Fort Laramie in the late 1880's, as General Reynolds J. Burt related:

> One day there appeared a tall, lanky non-descript civilian who discretely talked about foot racing. A match with him and our best man was arranged. They ran the 100 yard dash, the stranger ran away from the soldier, with no effort at all. The stranger faded out over-night [as much money had been wagered, and the soldiers were looking for the fleet-footed civilian].

Baseball was next to foot racing and field sports in popularity. Many units had company ball teams, on which the officers played with their men. The teams competed with others stationed at the same post, and all-post teams sometimes played those from other posts, and civilian teams from nearby communities. Colored soldiers of the Ninth Cavalry companies and their white comrades of the Eighth Infantry, played on the all-post team, at Fort Robinson, Nebraska, in the middle eighties.

Baseball equipment was purchased with money from the company funds, for no athletic gear was provided by the Regular Army. General Andrew S. Burt, according to his son, Brigadier General Reynolds J. Burt, zealously promoted baseball at the several western posts where he was stationed from 1866 through the 1890's. The son pitched on the Fort Washakie, Wyoming, nine in 1889, and, sparked by the enthusiasm of the officer-player, the team received the wholehearted support of the garrison. The best equipment was purchased, and a complete set of fine baseball uniforms was secured for the players. Post enthusiasm was dealt a sharp blow, however, when a sergeant deserted, taking all the new uniforms with him.

Though not so popular as baseball and field sports, boxing was one of the more common athletic recreations among western regulars. At large posts, company pugilists were matched in well-attended bouts fought in the post hall, or in a large building fitted up for the occasion. Soldiers took little interest in the companion sport of wrestling, but matches were held at some posts.

Cavalry outfits were enthusiastic horse racers. Special mounts were occasionally maintained for this purpose alone, to compete against other companies, Indians, and civilians. In regions where wild game was plentiful, the men sometimes went on extended hunting trips, and a few were ardent anglers. Football, still in its infancy as a national sport, enjoyed only a limited popularity. When played by frontier regulars, it was more likely to be rough and tumble than to have any scientific maneuvering and execution of complicated plays.

Without any sort of service-wide athletic policy, organized sports were engaged in as much as a method of gambling as for the enjoyment of the game. Few post commanders were personally interested in promoting an athletic program.

Singing for pleasure, although not so common in the regulars as it had been among the Civil War volunteer troops, was still one of the relaxations enjoyed in the frontier army. "We had some singing," said Second Cavalryman James B. Wilkinson, "and always one or two could entertain, such as tap [and clog] dancers and singers." Soldier preference ran to ballads, and, as Private George Whittaker wrote, "the more sentimental the better." The average regular company was composed of men in their mid-twenties and thirties, past the age to care much for group singing. A company, however, usually had a few noted singers, who sang mainly for their own pleasure, but whose performances were appreciated by the other men. Occasionally a talented trio or quartet was called upon for impromptu entertainment. In the Negro regiments (Ninth and Tenth Cavalry, Twenty-fourth and Twenty-fifth Infantry), singing, at work and during leisure time, was more common than in the rest of the army. The son of a frontier officer recalled one instance when an entire Twenty-fifth Infantry company harmonized on a series of melancholy spirituals, after the unit had been confined to quarters by an exasperated officer. After listening to the melodious laments, the officer relented and lifted the restriction.

Civil War songs were favorite soldier ballads all through the late nineteenth century. "Marching Through Georgia" and the bold strains of "The Girl I Left Behind Me" were particularly liked. The song most closely associated with the frontier regulars was most appropriately titled, "The Regular Army, O." Two New York vaudevillians, Harrigan and Hart, seem to have introduced, or at least popularized, this lilting ditty in 1875. Sung to a tune very similar to the old Irish melody, "Dear Old Donegal," the song was quickly adopted by the regulars. With almost as many respectable or unprintable versions as "Mademoiselle from Armentières" of World War I, its root variety was as follows:

> There was Sergeant John McCaffery
> and Captain Donohue,
> They make us march and toe the mark,
> in gallant Company "Q,"
>
> Oh the drums would roll, upon my soul,
> This is the style we'd go,
> Forty miles a day, on beans and hay,
> In the Regular Army O.[2]

Some of the soldier-composed verses referred to specific campaigns:

> We wint to Arizona
> for to fight the Injins there;
> We came near being made bald-headed,
> but they never got our hair.
>
> We lay among the ditches,
> in the yellow dirty mud,
> And we never saw an onion, a turnip or a spud.

[2] Words by Ed. Harrigan as edited with additions and glossary by Don Rickey, Jr., and published by Wm. A. Pond & Co., 1962. Company Q referred to the group of men serving guardhouse duty.

Oh we were taken prisoners
  Conveyed forninst the Chafe;
Oh he said, "We'll make an Irish stew,"
  the dirty Indian thafe.

On the telegraphic wire
  we walked to Mexico,
We bless the day, we skipped away,
  From the Regular Army O.[3]

One of the more pointed, yet printable, soldier parodies concerned General George Crook's well known anxiety for the welfare of his pack train:

But twas out upon the Yellowstone,
  we had the damndest time,
Faith, we made the trip wid "Rosebud George" [Crook]
  six months without a dime.

Some eighteen hundred miles we went,
  through hunger, mud, and rain.
Wid backs all bare, and rations rare,
  no chance for grass or grain.

Wid bunkies starvin' by our side,
  no rations was the rule;
Sure twas ate your boots and saddles, you brutes,
  but feed the packer and the mule.

But you know full well that in your fights,
  no soldier lad was slow,
And it wasn't the packer that won ye a [general's] star,
  In the Regular Army O.[4]

Another regular army song that evolved out of the Indian campaigns was "The Dreary Black Hills." Probably a miners' song, the soldier words described the dangers of campaigning against the powerful Sioux:

[3] *Ibid.*
[4] *Ibid.*

> Boys stay at home, stay at home if you can.
> Stay away from the city that's known as Cheyenne.
> For Sitting Bull's there, also wild Comanche Bill,
> And he'll sure lift your scalp in the dreary Black Hills,
> And still we keep marching, to the dreary Black Hills.

A song that was sung to some extent by western regulars, but that is believed to have originated long before the Civil War, was "Home Boys, Home":

> There is the Adjutantee, the worst of them all,
> He stands upon the parade ground, before the "first call."
> If you should look crooked, or either crook a limb [or crack
>   a smile],
> Its "Corporal, do your duty, put the beggar in the mill!"
>
> Oh, its home boys, home,
> Its home yez ought to be.
> Home boys, home, in your own countree,
> With the ash and the willow tree.
> They're all growin' green,
> In North Americkee.

Army ballads were often earthy and sometimes obscene. Some of them may still survive, in modified forms, on the lower levels of American culture, but, if so, they are not identifiable as originating during the post-Civil War Indian campaigns.

An example of the soldier folk song, dealing with a soldier subject, and not popular outside the army, was one entitled, "Riley's Gone to Hell, Since Down the Pole He Fell."[5] In regular slang, to "go up the pole" meant voluntary abstinence from liquor. Modern parlance would call it "going on the wagon." The ballad describes the horrible results of the unfortunate Riley's lapse from cold-water grace.

Besides army songs, frontier regulars sang many old Irish,

[5] Brigadier General R. J. Burt, U.S.A. Ret., recalled singing this song at a western army post in 1884. He picked it up from a career sergeant in his father's command.

English, German, Scotch, and American folk songs. The quasi-folk melodies of Stephen C. Foster were among those frequently heard at the western stations, as well as popular songs of the day, usually sentimental ballads such as, "Mother, Kiss Me in My Dreams," "Susan Jane," and "Little Annie Roonie."[6] Soldiers stationed in the Southwest occasionally sang Mexican songs, such as "La Paloma."

Of the musical instruments played for barracks amusement the banjo, guitar, violin, and mouth organ were especially enjoyed. "There was always someone who could play an instrument, and especially the guitar and accordian," wrote Private George Whittaker. The music was "crude, not too much talent," said Sergeant William Bald, "just a banjo and a couple of violin players."

Much of the small amount of church activity at the western posts was related to the singing of hymns, such as the Sunday evening singing promoted by the religiously inclined commanding officer of Fort Phil Kearny, Dakota Territory, in 1866.[7] At larger and longer-established posts, such as Fort Leavenworth, Kansas, said Samuel D. Gilpin, much of the interest in church participation was centered around singing by "a choir made up of the Bandmaster and four privates of Troop B, 3rd Cavalry . . . at 8 P.M. for the hour's service [in 1882]."

Regular soldiers have never been distinguished for their interest in religion. As Private C. O. Norman put it, the religious life of the average regular was "mighty poor." First Infantryman James S. Hamilton agreed that "there wasn't too much religion. . . . though some men carried bibles [in their haversacks]." A priest came to visit the Roman Catholic soldiers once each month, when First Sergeant George Neihaus' company of the Tenth Infantry was stationed in the Southwest, but "religion at no time was mentioned [among soldiers]." Fourth Cavalry-

[6] Mulford, *Fighting Indians*, 92.
[7] Carrington, *My Army Life*, 102.

man W. B. Jett commented that he "never knew but one soldier who professed to be a Christian." Formal religion was apparently not a very significant factor in the lives of rank and file regulars.

Chapel and church services were conducted regularly at some posts, and while enlisted men were welcome to participate, the services were held mainly for the benefit of the officers and their families.[8] At some stations, the post commander supplied the pulpit for lack of a clergyman. Post Chaplains seem to have exercised little influence on the soldiers, and some of them were not respected by officers or soldiers.[9] Testifying before the House Military Affairs Committee, in February, 1876, Colonel Guy V. Henry said of the regular chaplains:

> The men look to them for a good example, and they do not receive it as a general thing. . . . I am sorry to say, that I think chaplains are not of much account in the Army. They are generally old men who do not exert a good influence. . . . the men will have nothing to do with them. At Fort Russell they have a chaplain . . . [and out of a garrison of over three hundred and fifty men] I do not think I ever saw over ten soldiers in the chapel on any one Sunday.[10]

Some soldiers, nevertheless, did participate in church services. Fifth Cavalry Sergeant Armand Unger said that the interdenominational services held in his command were fairly well attended by the enlisted men. A high estimate of twenty per cent attendance at Fort Custer, Montana Territory, was reported by Cor-

[8] Jerome Thomases, "Fort Bridger: A Western Community," in *Studies on War*, 130.

[9] First Sergeant George Neihaus wrote: "Our Post Chaplain (Tenth Infantry, 1884–89) had service on Sunday—then he spent the rest of the week indulging in liquor." Corporal Louis Courville, Seventh Cavalry, 1889–91, commented: "There was a chaplain, but the soldiers rarely visited him."
Lieutenant Colonel Hein in *Memories of Long Ago*, page 86, describes the 1871 Camp Verde, Arizona, chaplain as an ignorant, itinerant lay preacher, "unattractive in person and manner."

[10] *Reorganization of the Army*, 44 Cong., 1 sess., *House Report No. 354*, 148.

poral Frank B. Knight. Perhaps the inducement of relief from duty and Sunday morning inspection, as offered at Fort Rice, Dakota Territory, in 1878, motivated a considerable number of the church-going soldiers.[11] In any case, evidence reveals that the Regular Army did little to advance the spiritual life of its rank and file, except through the efforts of individual commissioned officers who were religiously inclined.

In 1866 an act reorganizing the Regular Army required the maintenance of school facilities for enlisted men at all permanent stations. For a minority of soldiers, the elementary education provided at some of the western posts became an engrossing outside interest. The educational legislation of 1866 did not specify the means of providing education for the rank and file, and the facilities at most stations in the late 1860's and 1870's were similar to those at Fort Laramie. In 1868, the post surgeon reported that, "a school is kept by the Post Chaplain for the children of the Post and in winter, also a night school for such enlisted men as wish to attend."[12] Not until the 1881 revision of the Army Regulations were the required educational opportunities for soldiers specified. Officers were directed to encourage school attendance actively, and to provide the opportunity, although enlisted participation was always purely voluntary.[13] In the 1880's and early 1890's, regularly scheduled evening classes, generally two hours in length, were held. Instruction was provided either by an officer, or by a qualified enlisted man. His assignment as a post teacher, said Eighth Cavalryman William G. Wilkinson, so aroused his interest in learning that he took a discharge in 1891 in order to attend college.

The enlisted men's school curriculum was composed of basic reading, writing, arithmetic and a little geography and history. Many of the rank and file had entered the army unable to read and write, and the opportunity to learn was very important to

11 "Circular, April 19, 1878," Order Book, Seventh Cavalry, 1878–81," MS, 17.
12 "Med. Hist., Fort Laramie, 1868–79," MS, Nat. Arch., 9.
13 Hershler, *Handbook*, 14.

some of them.[14] First Cavalry Private William Hustede said that he had learned English at Fort Assiniboine, having enlisted as a young recruit, fresh from Germany. Attendance at post schools was rarely very large. An average of only ten soldiers a year took advantage of the post school at Fort Bridger, Wyoming, during the 1880's.[15]

More advanced and specialized instruction was offered in the 1880's, to men seeking a noncommissioned rank. Selected privates and noncommissioned men were instructed in "the school of the soldier," and courses proceeded through the basic "tactics."[16] "These evening courses," wrote Sergeant Reinhold R. Gast, "were an opportunity to advance one's education. . . . I, myself, took advantage of this [and was appointed corporal and sergeant]."

Post libraries and reading rooms, available to the rank and file, existed at the larger western posts all through the Indian Wars period. Describing the Fort Laramie library facilities, in 1868, the post surgeon wrote:

> There is a post library in the adjutant's office containing about 300 old, nearly worn out books. A number of papers and periodicals are subscribed for from the Post General Fund and kept in the library room to which the enlisted men have access.[17]

Some troops and companies had library clubs and "literary societies," to which the members paid a small fee as their share in the subscription fund, and sometimes the post sutler was

[14] E. E. Hardin, Untitled MS on Indian Wars in the 1870's, 26. "At that time [1874] there were many men in the regiment who could not read or write." Commenting on elementary education for enlisted First Cavalrymen, Sergeant Bald (1892–95) wrote: "A teacher taught reading and writing, some fellows could read and write very little."

[15] Thomases, "Fort Bridger," *Studies on War*, 129.

[16] Orders No. 7, Jan. 10, 1887, Order Book, Fort Meade, D. T., Jan.–Nov., 1887, MS, CBNM, 1. "A school for Non-Commissioned Officers and such Privates as Troop and Company Commanders may select . . . . Tuesday of each week . . . 6:30 to 7:30 p.m. . . . 15 pages will be given at a lesson."

[17] "Med. Hist., Fort Laramie, 1868–79," MS, 1.

assessed a small fee, by the commanding officer, to pay for sub-scriptions.[18] London *Punch, Appleton's Weekly, Galaxy, The North American Review, Colburn's United States Magazine,* and *Blackwood's Magazine* made up the subscription list at Fort Sully, Dakota Territory, in 1868. One might suspect from the titles that the choices were made by the commissioned offi-cers. More popular reading was the *Detroit Free Press,* sub-scribed for by Company F, Fifth Infantry, at Fort Keogh, Mon-tana Territory, in 1877.[19] *The Army and Navy Journal,* remarked Sergeant Perley S. Eaton, was subscribed to by almost all post and company libraries. Periodicals available for enlisted men's reading at Fort Bridger, in the 1880's, included *Harper's Weekly, Puck,* the *New York Herald,* the *Salt Lake Tribune,* and the *San Francisco Examiner.* Indicative of soldier selection was the sub-scription to the *Police Gazette* ordered in 1882, by Company B, Third Cavalry.

Library facilities were appreciated and used by some of the men. "My recreation," wrote Private Martin Anderson, "was mostly in the [Fort Riley, Kansas] library studying. I spent most of my spare time to learn English [as a young Danish immi-grant]." Many of the rank and file never set foot in their post or company reading rooms, observed Private Harvey J. Ciscel, as they preferred to spend their free time in town and at "hog ranches."

Small variety and minstrel shows occasionally relieved the tedium of post life. "Once in a while," recalled Sergeant Rein-hold R. Gast, "from the outside, a minstrel show passed through." The frontier regular, hungry for entertainment, welcomed even the most mediocre traveling troupe. Performances were held in the post hall, a large storehouse, or whatever space could be found to accommodate players and spectators. A stage and seats

[18] Hoekman, "Fort Sully," in *South Dakota Historical Collections,* Vol. XXVI (1952), 264.

[19] Snyder, Diary, 1877, MS. Oct. 27: "First *Detroit Free Press* for Company F arrived."

were improvised, and the entertainment-starved garrison usually turned out as nearly en masse as its duties permitted. Soldiers heard songs from the music halls of St. Louis, Kansas City, and other cities, and deeply appreciated the offerings.

Thrown upon their own resources for entertainment, western regulars worked up stage shows using whatever talents the garrison afforded. Minstrel shows were one of the most popular form of soldier-produced entertainments. An amateur minstrel troupe at Fort Keogh, Montana Territory, gave a performance in February, 1877, only a couple of weeks after the bitter Crazy Horse campaign.[20] Although the garrison was quartered in crude, uncomfortable log huts, and living conditions were extremely difficult, the morale of the men was excellent. A minstrel show performed at Fort Stevenson, Dakota Territory, in 1871, was not so well received by the garrison, for the soldier audience repeatedly hooted and booed the players.[21]

The production of soldier theatricals depended upon the desire, ability, and talent of someone in the garrison to generate interest among the men and organize the show. Enthusiasm frequently replaced talent, but some of the productions were quite elaborate. A Sergeant Mooney produced and took part in a minstrel-type variety show, at Fort Bidwell, California, in 1884. The Sergeant had lined up and rehearsed a dozen or so soldiers in a series of acts, in one of which he and the ten-year-old son of the post commander sang a duet entitled "I'm in Love With Biddy Magee."[22] The commanding officer and his wife, invited to attend the performance, were "astonished" at the sight of their son on the stage, but took the incident in stride. The officer was popular with his men, and they knew they could presume upon his good nature. Amateur theatricals were not covered

[20] *Ibid.*, Feb. 19: "The minstrel troupe gave their first concert this evening."

[21] Mattison, "Old Fort Stevenson," in *North Dakota History*, Vol. XVIII, Nos. 2–3 (1951), 72.

[22] Brigadier General Burt was the ten-year-old boy who sang this song with Sergeant Mooney in the variety show.

anywhere in the regulations, and soldiers sometimes took advantage of the fact.

The presence of soldier families in garrison frequently increased community interest in amateur entertainments, for the wives and children of the posts thoroughly enjoyed the singing, clog dancing, and other talents exhibited in the variety shows. "One time," wrote First Sergeant George Neihaus, "I took the part of a deserter, was dressed up in a suit, all stripes, and sang a song—'They Dressed Me Up In A Suit of Soldier Clothes, With Numbers On My Back.'" What would now be called "little theatre" groups were sometimes organized. Soldiers produced skits and short plays, either original or chosen from the melodramas of the day. Interest in amateur garrison entertainments indicated healthier morale than existed at stations where no such enthusiasms developed and instead garrisons had lapsed into partial or complete apathy.

Dancing was moderately favored as recreation. Formal dances were held infrequently for the enlisted men, few of them had any experience in the finer points of ballroom amenities, and what little they knew of the subject had generally been acquired in the army. The regimental bands stationed at headquarters posts enabled their garrisons to have more dances than did others, but according to Sergeant James S. Hamilton, impromptu jigs and square dances were often staged in company quarters to the music of banjo, harmonica, or violin. Dancing was enjoyed to some extent even at the most isolated posts. Writing of his service at Camp Supply, Indian Territory, in the early 1870's, Private H. Harbers recalled that "dances were given bymonthly [sic] by the companies and the strongest drink that we could get would be lemonade, and that was made by use of the extract."[23] There were always "too few ladies," said Private Louis Ebert, and thus any female who attended a soldier hop could count on dancing every german, waltz, or polka that was played. Women sometimes did not come even if they lived nearby, be-

[23] Harbers, "Service Account," in Ashburn, *Medical Department*, 100.

cause of civilian disdain of soldiers. Enlisted regulars at Fort Ellis, Montana Territory, invited many town girls from Bozeman to a dance held January 4, 1876, but when none of the girls put in an appearance, "they contented themselves by dancing with the laundresses until first call for reveille."[24]

With female dancing partners always in short supply, and sometimes nonexistent, western soldiers often held "stag" dances. Earthen, puncheon, and sawn lumber barracks floors resounded to the stamp and skip of heavy boots and brogans when frontier regulars unwound in an all-male dance. Seventh Cavalryman Ami Frank Mulford explained his enjoyment of "stag" dances in 1877, writing that such dances were "when we have all the fun by ourselves and no officer to bother us. We dance all the popular dances and take turns being the opposite sex."[25] "We had dances with the soldiers, and made women up," said civilian army teamster Sam Hotchkiss. "Ladies" at these dances were identified by a handkerchief or white cloth worn on the upper arm.

Soldier organizations, and especially the Good Templars, occasionally sponsored dances for the rank and file in their meeting rooms,[26] and enlisted men who enjoyed dancing sometimes formed clubs to promote it.[27] Of such a club at Fort Ellis, Second Cavalryman William White's February 4, 1876, diary entry notes that "the dance club had a dance in the Good Templars' hall. It lasted until after reveille."

At large posts, and at those located in or near major population centers, enlisted dances were held regularly. Posts such as Forts

[24] White, Diary, Jan. 4, 1876, MS.

[25] Mulford, *Fighting Indians*, 47.

[26] Diary of a Seventh Cavalry Enlisted Man, MS, Bates Coll. Fort Harker, Kan., Dec. 24: "A big ball is to be held in the Q.M.D. storeroom by the Good Templars of this Post. I Expect they will have a good time."

[27] Handwritten dance invitation, in possession of William Bald, First Cavalry Sergeant, 1892–95, North Wildwood, N. J.: "Fort Grant [Ariz.] February 9, 1893, The Merry Gliders of Fort Grant desire the pleasure of your Company at a dance to be held at the Post Hall, February 14, 1893."

Riley and Leavenworth in Kansas, Fort Laramie in Wyoming, and Omaha Barracks in Nebraska, staged social dances for the rank and file of their garrisons that sometimes were as formal and elaborate as officers' balls, with engraved invitations and fancy, printed programs.[28]

Drinking can hardly be considered an approved form of recreation, but certainly it was an important relaxation and pastime for many frontier regulars. Although some drank little or not at all, large numbers were accustomed to heavy drinking, and many spent most of their pay for beer and whisky. The army's general attitude was one of tolerance, because officers realized that liquor provided an escape or, at least, an artificial and temporary amelioration of the dull, hard, and lonely lives of the men.

Beer was always a favored beverage. It was customarily sold in quart bottles packed in straw-filled barrels. Post traders and sutlers generally charged fifty cents to one dollar for a quart of beer;[29] later the post canteens sold it at the lower price of eighteen to fifty cents a quart.

Until President Hayes' order abolishing the sale of whisky went into effect, in March, 1881, hard liquor was legally sold by post traders and sutlers by the drink and by the bottle. Ten cents per drink was the usual price. Bootleg whisky was sold to soldiers at Fort Berthold, Dakota Territory, for one dollar a half pint in 1877.[30] An inferior grade of legal whisky cost only thirty cents a half pint at "the widow's," a privately owned groggery, near Fort D. A. Russell, Wyoming. Some men pre-

[28] Elaborately printed dance program, in possession of James B. Wilkinson, Private, Second Cavalry, 1882–87, Warnock, Ohio. This was a formal, dress uniform affair: "H Troop, 2nd Cavalry, December 25, 1884, Fort Spokane, Washington."

[29] "How E. M. Locke Saved Command of Captain Clark From Massacre," in *Rocky Mountain Husbandman*, Vol. LXVI, No. 4 (1942). Beer, brought to celebrate payday at Fort Peck, Mont. Terr., sold at one dollar a bottle in 1879.

[30] Mulford, *Fighting Indians*, 73.

ferred to drink their whisky straight, but it was frequently mixed with sugar and water to make a variety of hot and cold toddies. Rock and rye was a favorite cold weather drink with many men, commented Sergeant Armand Unger.

Liquor was hard to obtain in some areas, and it could not be legally sold at posts located on Indian reservations. In the Apache country of the Southwest, "soldiers made fire water out of mescal, they called it Indian Fire Water," wrote Ninth Infantryman Christ F. Feil. Recalling his own experience with mescal, First Sergeant George Neihaus said, "I drank Mexican mescal once, was tied up for two days and never drank again in my life." Grain alcohol and Jamaica ginger, two liquor substitutes of the roaring twenties, were sometimes imbibed by frontier regulars in the seventies and eighties. The semipoisonous ginger must have produced the same crippling "jake leg" among those who drank it that it did fifty years later when consumed during the era of national prohibition. Drinking alcoholic whisky substitutes, always dangerous, was sometimes fatal. Two cavalry sergeants, sent on a scout in South Dakota in 1890, "accidentally drank some wood alcohol," and died from its effects, recalled Eighth Cavalryman J. M. Glenn.

Before the middle and late eighties, most alcoholic beverages consumed at the western posts were purchased from post trader or sutler stores. The sutler system antedated the Indian Wars period by many years. The sutlers were franchised by, and unofficially to, particular regiments, moving with their organizations from one station to another, and supplying soldiers with goods on campaign. Originally, the sutler had a private arrangement with the regiment's commanding officer, a situation open to many abuses. The post traders who replaced sutlers in the seventies and eighties were licensed by the War Department to operate stores at specific posts. Virtually all sutler and trader stores had an officers' and a soldiers' bar, and often a billiard table or two. Post traders were subject to the supervision of the commanding officer, and some, "whose only interest was to sell poor whisky and inferior goods [to the garrison] at high prices," bore careful watching.[31]

Post commanders regulated the trader's store hours, stipulating "a reasonable hour at night [for closing]."[32] Traders operating within the jurisdiction of the Department of Texas, were in 1872 to remain closed all day Sunday, after nine o'clock in the morning. Gambling was supposed to be forbidden in all trader establishments. Through his control over the trader, post commanders could to some extent regulate the amounts of beer and whisky sold to the rank and file.[33] Believing that the consumption of liquor was getting out of hand in 1870 at Fort Winfield Scott, Nevada, the commanding officer forbade enlisted men to enter the trader's store.[34] On the other hand, "General Miles concluded to open the Sutler's bar to enld. men" at Cantonment Tongue River, in January, 1877.[35] A board of officers, appointed by the post commander, set price limits on the trader's goods, but differences between what the officer-purchasers considered a fair price and what a trader felt he had to realize often caused much bad feeling. Traders were constantly penning grievances to the War Department in Washington, and the trader at Fort Laramie committed suicide after a "council of administration" reduced his prices, in July, 1880.[36] As a rule, post traderships were coveted plums, and the rank and file generally looked on traders as parasites.

Because many officers and government officials believed that the post trader system worked ineffectually and with little advantage to the western garrisons, a system of nonprofit, self-

[31] Forsyth, *The Soldier*, I, 138.

[32] "General Orders No. 19, Dept. of Tex., Oct. 22, 1872," Nat. Arch.

[33] "Med. Hist., Fort Laramie, 1868–79," MS, 39. Post Commander's authorization: "allowing sale of a moderate amount of beer daily to the soldiers, but counseling the officers to use their best endeavours to avert drunkenness."

[34] Hein, *Memories*, 62f.

[35] Snyder, Diary, Jan. 25, 1877, MS, S-R Coll.

[36] "Med. Hist., Fort Laramie, 1880–84," MS, Nat. Arch., 28.

supporting canteens was inaugurated in the middle eighties. By 1889 wherever they were practicable, canteens replaced the post traders.[37]

> The pleasant canteen, or Post Exchange, the soldier's club-room, was established, where the men could go to relieve the monotony of their lives. . . . the tone of the post improved greatly; the men were contented with a glass of beer or light wine, the canteen was well managed, so that profits went back into the company messes in the shape of luxuries heretofore unknown; billiards and reading rooms were established . . . . The men gained in self-respect; the canteen provided them with a place where they could go and take a bite of lunch, read, chat, smoke, or play games with their own chosen friends, and escape the lonesomeness of the barracks.[38]

Since they were not intended to make large profits for an entrepreneur, the canteens easily offered soldiers more for their money than did the "hog ranches" and other unhealthful pleasure resorts.[39] The men were allowed credit in the form of three or four dollars worth of five-cent canteen checks each month. "The beer was good," said Corporal John Bergstrom, "and only five cents a glass." In some canteens, beer was sold only with lunches, explained Private John Gibbert, to lessen the chance of a soldier's "getting a skin full" on an empty stomach.

The food available at the canteen was a major attraction, and many soldiers spent a large percentage of their pay for "counter eats." Extolling the virtues of the Fort Custer canteen, Colonel N. A. M. Dudley wrote that the pies, cakes, sandwiches, and canned delicacies stocked by the canteen enabled "the soldier to live almost sumptuously."[40]

The regulars, living as they did in a rigidly organized, rou-

[37] *Ann. Report, Sec. of War, 1891,* I, 77.

[38] Summerhayes, *Arizona,* 259.

[39] Forsyth, *The Soldier,* I, 136. Canteen beer glasses: "always the largest found on the market . . . ."

[40] *Ann. Report, Sec. of War,* 1891, I, 77.

tined environment depended for most of their recreation and relaxation on special occasions, when regulations were slightly relaxed and conditions were propitious. The most welcome of those occasions was the regular bimonthly payday, a joyful time for men who had been short of money since the last payday. Like children, the younger men tossed coins in the air and juggled them gleefully.

Sutlers and traders carried on a heavy whisky business immediately after payday, and high spirits rose still higher. In 1871, payday at Fort Ellis, Montana Territory, was ". . . a perfect pandemonium in the saloon, it was crowded all the time, everybody drunk and trying to outtalk everybody else. Every few minutes somebody would get knocked down, and occasionally a free fight shook the whole house."[41] The guard regularly filled the "mill" after the garrison was paid, and there was a marked increase in demands for the services of the post surgeon. Of a payday at Fort Laramie on July 29, 1870, the surgeon wrote that the troops were paid in the afternoon, and "as a necessary consequence, the number of patients in hospital was at once increased, with nothing however more serious than a broken rib or two, several sprains, and bruises with a few scalp wounds . . . payday casualties."[42] Less serious, but even more common than physical injuries, were the numerous hangovers the following day. Second Cavalryman William White noted that "some of the boys got up with large feeling heads," after the usual payday spree in 1876.[43]

Besides the hard drinking bouts, payday inaugurated a brief period when a soldier "lived like a king, ate ham and eggs, paid his wash, his barber, his canteen check, played a little poker, [and perhaps] shot craps for a few days," wrote Seventh Cavalryman John R. Nixon.

At frontier stations, celebrations attending the Fourth of July

[41] Koch, to "Laurie," MS, Feb. 21, 1871, Letters of Koch, No. 29.
[42] Med. Hist., Fort Laramie, 1868–79, MS, 7.
[43] White, Diary, Jan. 28, 1876, MS. Jan. 28.

made it one of the year's outstanding special occasions for the entire garrison. All guards and duties not essential to post security and maintenance were customarily suspended and "the day was devoted to manly sports such as baseball, races, etc."[44] Field sports and games were arranged more for participation than as spectator events. The post surgeon's concise account of the 1880 Independence Day activities at Fort Laramie states that the observance began with "35 guns at noon . . . [followed by] wheelbarrow, horse, slow mule, sack, and foot racing . . . [and ended with] fire works in the evening."[45] In 1887 Fort Keogh's Fourth of July program lists: three-legged race, wheelbarrow race, two hundred yard foot race, sack race, fat men's race, slow mule race, greased pig contest, and greased pole climb. The winners received purses of five dollars each.[46] Team prizes for the tug of war and skirmish were ten dollars. The soldiers greatly enjoyed such a field day of boisterous sports. Competition was intense and strenuous, with much raucous coaching and cheering of company champions.

Civilians and military units from neighboring posts often joined forces to celebrate the Fourth. Observing the day in camp on the Mexican border, during the 1885 Geronimo campaign, "Company A [Thirteenth Infantry] met a cowboy baseball nine [in competition] for two barrels of beer from Milwaukee," wrote Samuel D. Gilpin. The soldiers won, and hospitably shared their beer with losers and spectators. Milwaukee beer was a rare treat for regulars camped along the arid Mexican border.

Although the Fourth was universally celebrated as a festival day at Regular Army posts, special events were not always scheduled and when no program was planned, the men marked

44 Med. Hist., Fort Laramie, 1868–79, MS, 94.
45 Med. Hist., Fort Laramie, 1880–84, MS, 29.
46 Program of events, Fort Keogh, Mont. Terr., July 4, 1887, S-R Coll.: "Fun! Fun! Fun! . . . 10:00 a.m. Grand Procession of all Contestants [lists races and prizes]. . . . The pedigree of each mule [in the slow mule race] will be given by Hon. Chas. Brown, Miles City, who will also be the starter of the race. . . . Skirmish Match—At one p.m. on the Rifle Range . . . ."

the day in their individually chosen ways. Private B. C. Goodin's diary entry for July 4, 1893 is probably a good average reflection of this:

> Came off guard at 9:00, went on mtd. pass with Bald and some others. Went to the White Elephant [saloon], only stayed a few minutes, from there to Cutter's store, got refreshments, went to the hog ranch, stayed a little while and came back to post. 44 gun 12 pounder salute—big time in qts. all afternoon and evening.

No special occasion outshone the Christmas observance. Plans were laid far in advance, and soldiers "filed away whiskey orders [authorizing purchases] and stored away the article itself for some time . . . in view of the approaching festival."[47] Regulations were usually relaxed, and guardhouse prisoners, serving sentences for minor infractions, were sometimes released in honor of the day. Festivities began on Christmas Eve. In his diary entry for December 24, 1868, Surgeon Washington Matthews notes that at Fort Rice, Dakota Territory, "a number of enlisted Germans having formed a German [singing] Society at the post, their first entertainment was given this Christmas Eve. It consisted of songs and supper and the drinking of a weak, homemade beer. The officers of the Fort were all invited."[48]

Christmas Day was one of general rest, relaxation, and recreation. On December 25, 1877, fine weather permitted the garrison of Fort Shaw, Montana Territory, to enjoy field sports in the morning, which were followed by a large dinner in the afternoon, and officer visitations to company quarters in the evening.[49] Some sort of special observance was the rule at even the most isolated posts. Lacking Christmas decorations, and supplies of all kinds, the Fort C. F. Smith garrison nevertheless enjoyed "a grand feed of [elk, bear, mountain sheep, and deer]

[47] Mattison, editor, "Surgeon Matthews," *North Dakota History*, Vol. XXI, Nos. 1–2 (1954), 29. "A Christmas celebrated chiefly by the amount of whiskey drank at the post."
[48] *Ibid.*, 28.
[49] E. E. Hardin, Diary, MS.

meat, at least, for their [1867] Christmas dinner."[50] At all posts a special dinner was served, accompanied by table delicacies rarely enjoyed by the rank and file. "On holidays [Christmas and Thanksgiving]," said Sergeant Reginald A. Bradley, "we had a good dinner of turkey and all that goes with it, but, this was not supplied by the Government; it was paid out of the company fund." The nuts, raisins, fruits, turkey, puddings, and cigars distributed at Christmas were not included in regular army issues of the late nineteenth century.

Thanksgiving, Washington's Birthday, and Memorial Day were frequently observed by the suspension of all but essential duties for the day. Special anniversaries, such as post establishment days, battle anniversaries, and presidential inaugurations, were sometimes celebrated with special events. On the twentieth anniversary of the Regular Army's occupation of Fort Laramie, August 12, 1869, "Ordnance Sergeant Leadogar Snyder, who was a member of that [1849] detachment and has since been on duty at this post, celebrated the event by a display of fire-works in the evening."[51] New Year's was celebrated in the time-honored way with such bibulous revelry as circumstances and individual commanding officers allowed. To liven up the occasion at Cantonment Tongue River, Montana Territory, December 31, 1876, the commanding officer assembled the Fifth Infantry band on the parade ground at midnight, and "the band played the old year out and the new in."[52]

The enlisted man found opportunities for rest and recreation mainly during short passes that authorized him to do as he pleased, for a day or two at a time. Furloughs were rare, although commanders had authority to grant furloughs for up to five per cent of unit strength. Travel difficulties and isolation materially lessened the desirability of furloughs in the West, but occasionally men received them. Private James B. Wilkinson recalled a

[50] Burt, "Forty Years," Burt Collection, MSS Div., Lib. of Cong., 164.
[51] Med. Hist., Fort Laramie, 1868–79, MS, 57.
[52] Snyder, Diary, Dec. 31, 1876, MS.

two-week furlough, granted to him and to a few other Second Cavalrymen, at Fort Assiniboine, Montana Territory, for having recaptured a herd of stolen horses for the Royal Northwest Mounted Police in the middle eighties.

Gambling has been a soldier pastime for centuries. Some among frontier regulars squandered all their pay in gambling. The favorite games were three-card monte, "seven-up" (a type of fantan), "high-low-jack," "honest john," and "black jack," with poker the most prevalent of all. "Stud horse poker and draw poker," were especially popular, wrote First Sergeant George Neihaus. Dice games were played to some extent, generally as "craps," but were not so common as card games. Most soldier gambling was for small stakes, tobacco, and clothing. Thirteenth Infantryman John G. Brown explained that one- and two-cent pieces were often used as poker chips, as "1¢ and 2¢ coins had no value in New Mexico [1879–84]." In many companies, on the other hand, there were a few "poker sharks," who were semiprofessional gamblers, and playing might be for high stakes and involve big money. Such men occasionally ran faro banks and other house games, in which their comrades regularly "bucked the tiger" after each payday.

In the army all forms of gambling were illegal. The average low-stake barrack room games, however, were usually not rigidly policed. The semiprofessional, big-money games were another matter, and when the "boss gamblers" organized a game, it was generally held in a place safe from official interruption. Brigadier General Reynolds J. Burt, who as a boy had "kibitzed" many big games in the early eighties, described the habits of the serious gamblers:

> When the [payday] money was collected by a few of these [semiprofessional gamblers] they played in an obscure room in the back of the post trader's store or in some off-the-beat empty warehouse where officers were not likely to look in. These boss gamblers, little known except by a freelance youngster, who

went unnoticed, were well schooled soldiers and did their military duty well.

Realizing that soldiers' pay burned holes in their pockets, and that many were inveterate gamblers, civilians sometimes operated gambling devices and games of chance exclusively for soldier patrons. Corporal John Bergstrom stated that when several companies of the Twenty-second Infantry camped for three months up Tongue River, Montana, in 1890, civilians set up roulette wheels and faro banks in tents nearby. Of course, soldiers visiting frontier communities generally availed themselves of whatever recreation was offered, which usually included gambling houses in addition to saloons, restaurants, and brothels.

Since card playing was probably the most popular off-duty diversion among western regulars, several varieties of games were played purely for amusement. When soldiers had no money for poker and other gambling games, they played euchre, whist, casino, cribbage, and pinochle.

Membership in Masonic and other lodges provided outside recreational interests for a minority of frontier regulars.[53] The International Order of Good Templars was probably the most widespread. The Odd Fellows established lodges at a few western garrisons, where officers and enlisted men met as equals within the confines of organization rules and rituals.[54] Grand Army of the Republic posts existed at some army establishments, and some Civil War service regulars maintained memberships, but, since the posts were organized along military lines, they

[53] Cox, "Soldiering," *North Dakota History*, Vol. VI, No. 1 (1931), 68. "At the time of the [Custer] fight I was still stationed at Fort Randall. I had gone to Springfield, about 40 miles away, with other soldiers to be initiated into the Masonic lodge. We knew the news [of the Little Bighorn] would mean great excitement, if not a general Indian uprising. . . . The lodge officials induced us to tarry long enough for a hurried initiation."

[54] *Ibid.*, 79. Echo Lodge No. 2, Odd Fellows, was active at Fort Randall, S. D., in the middle 1870's. Officers mingled with the rank and file members in this lodge.

were probably dominated by their officer-members and therefore not very inviting to the eligible rank and file.

The jokesters and wags to be found in every company provided sorely needed comic relief from the grim, austere living conditions, and bolstered their comrades' spirits with their practical joking, clowning, and broad humor. They frequently used other soldiers as foils. A lovesick Third Infantryman, stationed in the Cheyenne-Arapaho country of what is now Oklahoma, in 1874, continuously lamented his absence from the side of his "Malvina," wrote Private George App. Knowing of the lover's concern, his comrades began constantly asking him, "What will poor Malvina do when she finds out you have lost your scalp?" The cry of "Oh Malvina, I've lost my hair," became a standing joke in Company D. After Private Eddie Waller accidentally bayoneted his first sergeant's calf, while on guard duty at Fort Sill, in 1889, shouts of "Who killed the Sergeant's calf? Eddie Waller, Eddie Waller," rang out for days around the post. Waller had demanded the password from a figure hulking up at him out of the night, and, receiving no reply, had executed an accurate lunge that impaled the hapless stray on eighteen inches of triangular bayonet. It was one of his first experiences on guard duty, and the old timers had "jobbed" him with Indian stories.

Favorite stories about officers, noncommissioned men, and "characters" among the rank and file were oft-told tales of the barracks. In 1870 the repartee of a popular captain of Company F, Seventeenth Infantry, became a favorite story among his men. The officer approached a large Indian, at Grand River, Dakota Territory, and asked him his name. The Indian answered that his name was "One Hundred." Staring fixedly at the warrior, the Captain, a large, fat man, replied emphatically, "Well, my name is Two Hundred!" The name took, and the captain was "Two Hundred" to his men forever after. The same officer, while helping his soldiers carry poles for the construction of a temporary redoubt, cheered his laboring men with shouted cries of "another load of poles," said Private Patrick Boland. The

CROW INDIANS
captured in November, 1887, during the Crow uprising,
guarded by soldiers.

Division of Manuscripts, University of Oklahoma Library

COMPANY K, FIFTH INFANTRY
ready to march out of Fort Davis, Texas, 1889.

*Courtesy Custer Battlefield National Monument
U.S. Park Service*

soldiers enthusiastically adopted the phrase, and it soon came to mean re-enlisting for another hitch in the regiment. A Sixth Cavalry captain and his trumpeter, in 1885, furnished a frequently repeated barracks story that grew out of the officer's order to the trumpeter to sound the first call "at peep o' day." The soldier took this to mean daylight, and accordingly did not sound the call until relatively late in the morning. The captain came storming out of his tent, strode up to the trumpeter and said, "Damn it! Don't you know there are three lights in the morning? Peep o'day, break o'day, and broad daylight!" The trumpeter's comrades never tired of asking him if he knew what time it was in the morning, said Terrance J. Clancy.

Soldiers also repeated humorous stories about the great and near great. Writing of "Buffalo Bill" Cody and "Buffalo Chips," the white scout killed at the Slim Buttes fight, September 9, 1876, one of General Crook's 1876 campaigners related that "when General Sheridan was in the West he asked for Buffalo Bill, when this Bill [a friend of Cody's] said he was B.[uffalo] B.[ill] while he was gone, as a joke. Sheridan looked him over and said, Buffalo S— more likely . . . and the name stuck."[55] The name of the scout, euphemized as "Buffalo Chips," remains in the literature describing the Slim Buttes engagement.

However great their enjoyment of stories and humorous repartee, the favorite form of humor among western regulars remained the practical joke. Recruits were easy victims, although humorous deception was also practiced on noncommissioned officers and on each other. The Springfield carbine was considerably lighter than the "long Tom" infantry rifle, and for this reason carbine cartridges were loaded with fifty-five grains of powder instead of the seventy grain charge intended for the rifle. The rifle shells looked the same as those for the carbine, but firing the seventy grain ammunition produced very heavy recoil in the carbine. "When someone slipped a long Tom cart-

---

[55] Letter to Brininstool, MS, June, 1935, Dustin Coll., No. 316.

ridge in on you [in target practice] . . . you thought the sky fell in." wrote Seventh Cavalryman John R. Nixon. This was one of the oldest and most popular practical jokes among regular cavalrymen.

When Seventh Cavalry units were stationed with some infantry in Kentucky during the early seventies, several cavalrymen stole some infantry uniform blouses and went foraging at night on nearby farms. Complaining farmers informed the commanding officer that the culprits had been wearing infantry uniforms, and, acting on this information, the post commander ordered the infantrymen to extra kitchen duty.[56] Not only did the enterprising horsemen acquire the vegetables they sought, but they also succeeded in playing what was considered a very funny joke on their infantry comrades.

At Fort Yuma, Arizona, in the early seventies, Trumpeter Eugene S. DeSparr had placed himself in a compromising situation by shooting an Indian's tame goat. He avoided detection and played a joke on the company cook at the same time.

> "I saw a deer coming to the river every morning for a drink," said DeSparr, "when I was sounding first call for reveille. So one morning I went down and shot it. When I lifted it up, I saw it was [a friendly Indian's] . . . goat. I dragged it up to the Fort and shoved it under the cook's bed."

The commonest practical jokes on the frontier, perhaps, were the many variations on the "Indian scare" theme. Most often played on recruits, the following example was staged for the benefit of a noncommissioned officer at Fort Assiniboine, Montana, in 1890:

> One night in the dead of winter and just before taps, [recounted First Cavalryman Clarence Gould] one of the men came to the orderly room and told 1st Sgt. Hawks there was an Indian squaw out back of the Bathe House, a detached building in the rear of the quarters. Hawks immediately investigated, found the

[56] Wagner, *Old Neutriment,* 50.

facts to be as stated, and suggested to the squaw that it was warmer in his quarters, but something went wrong with his plans, for the Indian announced in gutteral English, "Me no squaw, me buck!" and drew a butcher knife from his blanket and commenced cutting circles in the air too close to Hawks' head for comfort. It is needless to state, that top pusher made the orderly room in ten seconds flat, and . . . [the Sergeant never did know] that his Indian friend was none other than Shorty Grant, a Trumpter of his own troop, and the knife was a long bladed breadknife from the troop kitchen.

Soldier humor, as well as other forms of relaxation and recreation, was much the same as that enjoyed by civilian frontiersmen. The frontier environment affected the army rank and file much as it did the civilians who came West. Like those of his citizen counterpart, the western regular's amusements were direct, strenuous, and often boorish. Perhaps this was a reaction to his austere living conditions and the harsh realities of the Indian campaigns that were his reason for being on the frontier.

11

Campaign Preparation, Equipment, and the Hostiles

REGULAR ARMY ORGANIZATIONS, stationed in the West to control and pacify the mountain, desert, and plains Indians, carried out almost innumerable patrols, police actions, and campaigns. For most of the Indian Wars period, the majority of western regulars were in the field. Many units spent over one-half their time marching and countermarching in Indian campaigns. From 1869 to the end of the frontier era, the army was limited by law to a maximum strength of 25,000 men, including those required for southern Reconstruction duty or immobilized as coastal fortress garrison troops. Charged with responsibility for overseeing vast expanses of unsettled country, sometimes occupied by hostile Indians, from Texas and Arizona to the Canadian border, and from the Missouri River to the Pacific coast, the army spread its effective strength so thinly that troops were compelled to campaign over large areas.

The majority of Indian campaigns occurred in the spring, summer, or early fall, when travel was easiest. Some of the most important campaigns were conducted in winter, however, when the ponies of hostile Indians were weak. To force the Indians to submit, it was first necessary to catch them, and this required long and arduous campaigns, sometimes planned well in advance, as segments of major operations, but sometimes carried out as reactions to hostile initiative. When courier or telegraph announced an outbreak, planning-level officers issued orders sending soldiers out on campaign, much as a fire marshal dispatches men and equipment to control a sudden blaze.

Just at sundown, September 17, 1877, word reached General Nelson A. Miles, at Fort Keogh, Montana Territory, that Joseph and his Nez Percés had eluded General Sturgis' Seventh Cavalry, at Canyon Creek just north of the Yellowstone, and were driving toward the Canadian line and a linkup with Sitting Bull. Miles at once issued orders sending out the mounted battalion of the Fifth Infantry. The men were to be ready to march by sunrise, and "all was commotion from the time the order was recd., and no sleep for anyone."[1] All night, soldiers received issues, packed equipment, prepared their mounts, and readied themselves for the dawn assembly.

Less well prepared for field service were several companies of the Twenty-first Infantry, at Fort Douglas, Utah, in 1890. A telegram arrived on New Year's Eve, ordering the Twenty-first to the Sioux country, in South Dakota. Most of the rank and file were whooping it up in nearby Salt Lake City, and, as Private Louis P. Terhune explained, "it was pretty nearly all night before they got us together," for the railroad journey to Fort Robinson, Nebraska. Garrisoning Fort Yates, North Dakota, regulars of the Eighth Cavalry abruptly received campaign orders as they lounged in quarters at the end of a December day in 1890. The Ghost Dance craze was sweeping the Sioux reserva-

---

[1] Snyder, Diary, 1877, MS.

tions, and when "1st Sgt. Kennedy came into quarters and called out, 'get ready for ten days,'" it came as no surprise to the soldiers, said Private William G. Wilkinson. The Sergeant designated ten men who were not required to go out, and though they kidded their alerted comrades, all of them later voluntarily joined the detachment. As an 1877 Seventh Cavalryman explained, the men preferred to go on an active campaign "than to remain in quarters and be abused by stiff-necked officers."[2]

Notice to move out on campaign always created excitement among the rank and file. When orders arrived November 25, 1890, posting the Eighth Infantry to the Sioux agencies, from Fort Robinson, Nebraska,

> . . . most of the soldiers started a jollification at the canteen [wrote Private August Hettinger], the officers also laid in a supply for strictly private use . . . [most of which was later stolen by the enlisted men], the Quartermaster came to me and said that two of his gallon jugs had been found empty, and he asked me to take care of [a full] one . . . which I managed to get through to the Rosebud Agency by putting it in a nosebag and filling it to the top with oats.

Rumors of impending orders circulated constantly among frontier regulars, as they have among soldiers since time began. Indian outbreaks, reported "massacres," and word of action were the rumormonger's stock in trade. Some soldiers felt that facts and plans were purposely withheld. Writing to a friend, about the possibilities of a Sioux outbreak in 1890, Sergeant George B. DuBois, F Troop, Eighth Cavalry, told his correspondent that ". . . the enlisted men are kept as ignorant as possible." Explaining soldier interest in developments among the Sioux, DuBois said, "I am personally acquainted with some of the chief [ghost] dancers and I would like to see the dance (from behind a big rock)." Men sent out against the hostiles believed they were

[2] Mulford, *Fighting Indians*, 58.

entitled to be informed of their commander's plans; repeated, tedious marches, that seemed to have no purpose or apparent effect on the over-all campaign, bred dissatisfaction and grumbling.[3] Regulars endured hardships and short rations easier when they understood their necessity.

Soldiers who expected to be ordered on campaign duty carried out official readiness instructions, and made private preparations of their own. The blue undress uniform worn in post was the usual campaign clothing. Special field-service uniforms had not yet been developed, but for campaign wear, frontier soldiers frequently modified and added to regulation issues. In 1876, newspaper correspondent John F. Finerty, in describing General George Crook's troops, explained that "on an Indian campaign little attention is paid to uniform."[4] Western troops provided their own broad-brimmed campaign hats before they were added to the regulation issue, and some men substituted long-wearing buckskin trousers for those of light-blue wool. The campaign hat was favored over the regulation kepi, or forage cap, and when issue hats were not available, at Fort Rice, Dakota Territory, just before the 1877 summer campaign, "each man had to buy his own campaign hat from the sutler, at a good price."[5] Experience was a valuable guide in advance planning for field service. Writing of his participation in the Sioux winter campaign of 1890 and 1891, Private Walter C. Harrington explained that one of the older sergeants in his company, having experienced other winter campaigns, had the foresight and influence to provide himself with eight blankets, instead of the usual one blanket per man.

In anticipation of combat with hostile Indians, frontier regulars developed a keen interest in their arms. Several varieties of rifles, carbines, and hand guns were issued for field service prior

[3] Snyder to his mother, MS, Oct. 15, 1876, S-R Coll.
[4] *War-path and Bivouac*, 52.
[5] Mulford, *Fighting Indians*, 59.

to the army's final standardization on the forty-five caliber Springfield and the forty-five Colt in 1873.[6] Even after the issue of the forty-five caliber weapons, some soldiers believed they were indifferently armed. "We could have been better armed," wrote 1876 campaigner James S. Hamilton, "it was fortunate my unit was never engaged in [serious] . . . combat." Actually, the forty-five caliber Springfield rifle was superior in range and accuracy to all but the best commercial weapons, and only a handful of warriors were equipped with powerful, long-range rifles. Repeating arms might have given the soldier the psychological advantage of a greater feeling of security, even though the issue, single-shot Springfield was superior in power and accuracy. Most soldiers were not good enough riflemen to make optimum use of the Springfield's capabilities before the upsurge of interest in marksmanship in the eighties.

Because of the serious consideration they gave to their arms, western regulars sometimes provided themselves with weapons they thought were more effective than those issued to them.

[6] The army decided to adopt breech-loading, metallic cartridge small arms at the close of the Civil War. Spencer, Henry and a few other metallic cartridge arms had been used to a limited extent during the war. Muzzle-loading, fifty-eight caliber Springfield rifle-muskets, firing the conical "minie ball," were the standard infantry arm until enough of them had been altered to breech-loaders to retire the older weapons from service between 1867 and 1869. The Springfield remained a single-shot rifle, but its range, accuracy, and loading speed were much increased. It was manufactured in fifty caliber until 1873, when the caliber was reduced to forty-five to achieve better ballistics. The Spencer, in use by some cavalry until the early 1870's, was a seven-shot repeater in fifty or fifty-six caliber, but its ammunition was often substandard, and its range was only half that of the Springfield. The Henry, forty-four rimfire, metallic cartridge repeater, and forerunner of the Winchester, was likewise not as long ranged or accurate as the issue weapons. Until 1874, the army used a hodge-podge of altered Springfield and Sharps rifles and carbines, Spencers, and numerous trial breech-loaders. None of these arms tested as effectively as did the 1873 model Springfield rifle or carbine. The Springfield remained the standard issue weapon until the repeating Krag rifle was adopted in 1892. The 1873 model Colt forty-five became the most popular hand gun in the West after its adoption by the army. It replaced all altered and percussion Colt and Remington revolvers by the end of 1874.

This was especially true before the adoption of the forty-five caliber Springfields and metallic cartridge Colts in the early seventies. Soldiers frequently added to their personal armament by purchasing revolvers and knives with their own money.

Military arms and equipment that proves of little or no value in field service will always be "lost" or otherwise discarded by soldiers. The cavalry was equipped with the saber, in addition to the carbine and revolver, but the cumbersome edged weapon was of such limited utility that it was rarely carried on active Indian campaigns after the early seventies. By the time a cavalryman was close enough to deliver a saber stroke, he was likely to be bristling with arrows and liberally punctured with Indian bullets.

Most sizable campaign columns had light artillery or Gatling guns. The Gatling, however, was a new weapon, and some commanders, Lieutenant Colonel George A. Custer for example, did not consider it worth the trouble of transporting it in the field. There was a good deal of justification for this view. The Gatling was heavy, the barrels fouled rapidly and became inaccurate with black powder ammunition, and with no provision for cooling, the weapon quickly heated up and became subject to jamming. Basically, the Gatling gun was an efficient weapon when the enemy would oblige by coming up to where it was emplaced, but Indian warriors were seldom so accommodating. The Seventh Cavalry's commanding officer in 1867 thought so little of the Gatlings, that he would not even authorize ammunition for target practice.[7] The artillery included in larger columns was an important weapon mainly because of its psychological effect on Indians, but Sergeant James S. Hamilton pointed out that the infantry soldiers usually assigned to gun crews were not adequately trained to make efficient use of the guns.

Because the years from 1865 through the early 1890's were

[7] Godfrey, "Medicine Lodge Treaty Conference," MS, Bates Coll., 1.

a period of change and transition in the Regular Army, soldiers used a wide variety of equipment.[8] Much matériel remained on hand at the close of the Civil War, some of which was still being issued when the Indian frontier ceased to exist. For that reason, some cavalry units continued to use the extra-wide carbine slings for many years after a new model was adopted in 1874, and several varieties of loop cartridge belts were used in 1890, although the 1876–77 and model 1881 belts were supposed to have been replaced by the model 1885 webb ammunition belt developed by Anson Mills.

Each man was expected to prepare his own rations in the field, in a two-piece, tin mess kit, consisting of a folding-handle frying pan and a shallow plate. Some soldiers did not like the issue cooking gear. Private James B. Wilkinson wrote:

> We had an outfit for cooking. . . . soldiers discarded these and bought their own at the sutler's store—skillet (small) and quart tin cup. The tin cup was used for making coffee. Everything was cooked in the skillet; salt pork, par-boiled, if water was available, then cooked in the skillet. Hardtack was soaked in water, then fried in the grease, after the pork. Brown sugar was sprinkled on the hardtack. Not a bad meal.

Wilkinson added that experienced soldiers generally begged a few fresh onions and potatoes from the cook, just before leaving the post, as they "helped give variety to the diet." If soldiers knew well in advance that they were going out on field service, commented Fifth Cavalry Sergeant Armand Unger, money from the company fund was spent to purchase a variety of foods to add to the issue rations of hardtack, salt bacon, dried beans, and green coffee in the bean.

[8] Research has not been done on the complex history of the many equipment changes tried and adopted by the Regular Army during the Indian Wars era. It is a field by itself. Some of the changes are noted in a series of Ordnance Department Memoranda published from 1865 through the early 1890's. A few articles have been written on the subject, the best of which is that of J. S. Hutchins, "The Seventh Cavalry Campaign Outfit at the Little Bighorn," in *The Military Collector and Historian*, Vol. VII, No. 4, (1956).

When orders were received to take the field in major operations, a great deal of work had to be accomplished before troops left their station. Ordered to assemble with the rest of the regiment at Fort Abraham Lincoln, in the spring of 1877, Seventh Cavalry companies at Fort Rice, Dakota Territory, overhauled all saddles, bridles, and other horse gear, reshod four hundred horses, received issues of new equipment, and packed all personal and company property for storage, in two days' time.[9] All of the stipulated forty-eight hours were needed to accomplish the task, with no time left over, and soldiers and officers worked around the clock.

Regular troops sent out on lengthy campaigns generally went in what was termed "heavy marching order." For the infantrymen, this meant a regulation burden of about fifty pounds.[10] Heavy marching equipment customarily included the knapsack, or back pack, half a "dog tent," extra shoes and clothes, rations for several days, and up to one hundred and fifty rounds of forty-five caliber rifle ammunition. Cartridge belts held about fifty rounds, the rest of the extra ammunition was carried in the haversack, knapsack, or clothing pockets. When the conical Sibley squad tents and sheet iron stoves were taken, they were transported in army wagons. Heavy marching order for cavalry included much of the above mentioned matériel, plus horse

[9] Mulford, *Fighting Indians,* 58f.

[10] Lieutenant W. B. Weir, "Infantry Equipments, Ordnance Notes No. LXVII," in *Ordnance Notes, Nos. 41–67,* 532. Full field equipment, infantry, 1877:

sixty rounds ammunition and belt	5.40 lbs.
overcoat	5.25 lbs.
blanket (gray wool)	5.13 lbs.
rubber blanket (ground cloth)	3.00 lbs.
Springfield rifle and sling (bayonet omitted from this list)	8.40 lbs.
extra clothes	2.00 lbs.
full canteen (one quart)	3.84 lbs.
five days rations: ¾ lbs. meat and 1 lb. hardtack per day	8.75 lbs.

The author of the article recommended use of the horseshoe blanket roll instead of the knapsack, and elimination of the triangular-bladed bayonet for western field service.

221

accouterments, and it was packed upon the trooper's mount instead of on his person. Cavalrymen also sometimes carried ten to fifteen pounds of grain as feed for their horses. Long marches were tiring for cavalry, but with the burden of full field kit, they could be torture for foot soldiers.

Companies and detachments sent out in anticipation of imminent contact and combat with hostiles, usually went in "light marching order," to increase the soldiers' mobility and striking power. Light marching order, ruefully commented Trumpeter Ami Frank Mulford, meant "no tents, no extra clothing, no supplies."[11] General Field Orders No. 2, Headquarters in the Field, Department of Dakota, August 10, 1876, spelled out "light marching order" for a force being sent in pursuit of the Sioux, following the Little Bighorn disaster:

> No tents whatever will be carried, no company property, no cooking utinsils, except tin cups, no bedding [except one blanket per man] . . . 100 rounds of ammunition [per man] . . . . Each mounted man will carry on his horse four days rations. Every infantry officer and man will carry with him two days' cooked rations . . . . No enlisted man capable of doing duty will be left behind.[12]

Companies of the Fifth Infantry, ordered against the Sioux and Cheyennes, in Montana Territory, in July, 1876, took "only a blanket, shelter unit, pr. of shoes and one change of under clothing for each man . . . ," besides the necessary arms, field rations, and ammunition.[13] When soldiers camped at Crow Agency, Montana, in 1887, were ordered to prepare for immediate action against a party of Crow insurgents, each man was instructed to carry only his arms, one hundred rounds of am-

---

[11] Mulford, *Fighting Indians,* 93.

[12] General Field Orders No. 8, Dept. of Dakota, Camp on Rosebud Creek, Aug. 10, 1876, MS, S-R Coll.

[13] Snyder to his mother, MS, July 30, 1876, S-R Coll.

munition, canteen, and "2-days cooked rations in the haver-sack."[14] The cooked rations referred to meant broiled or fried bacon and hardtack.

Stripping troops of surplus equipment was the subject of considerable study during the middle seventies. Findings usually recommended that soldiers should carry less weight in the field. The knapsack was slighted in favor of the blanket roll, while soldiers preferred loop cartridge belts to clumsy leather cartridge pouches, and it was recommended that all accouterments be designed to obviate chafing and binding. First Sergeant George Neihaus wrote that his company commander would not allow his men to carry more than thirty pounds in field equipment during the Apache campaigns of the middle eighties.

Campaign experiences resulted in some significant modifications of field equipment from 1865 through the end of the frontier period. Traditionally, the Regular Army had not embarked upon major campaign operations in winter, but during the Indian Wars some of the most successful campaigns were carried out in the teeth of the bitterest western winters. Special winter clothing was found to be essential, if troops were to be employed against hostiles in the season when the Indians were least able to elude columns sent against them. The wool overcoats and cloth headgear customarily issued as cold weather clothing were not sufficient. Taking a leaf from the Indians' book, regulars adopted almost ankle-length buffalo coats, buffalo overshoes, fur gauntlets, wool face masks, and muskrat hats. Marching to attack Crazy Horse's village, up Tongue River, Montana Territory, in January, 1877, General Miles's foot soldiers bore little resemblance to the popular conception of United States regulars.

> When dressed in their blankets and furs, [the soldiers] looked
> more like a large body of Eskimaux than like white man and

[14] Report of Major Simon Snyder to Assistant Adjutant General, Dept. of Dakota, Dec., 1887, MS, a pencil rough draft of Snyder's report of the action at Crow Agency, Montana, Nov. 5, 1887, S-R Coll.

U. S. troops, and when they wore their woolen masks over their heads it was impossible to distinguish one from another.[15]

Muffled against the below zero cold, Miles's regulars moved against the hostile village and routed double their own number of Indians in a pitched battle, January 8, 1877. Buffalo coats and special winter clothing became standard issue in the Army.

During the Civil War, the Union Army experimented with mounted infantry as a strategic force. In the seventies the practice of mounting foot soldiers on horses and mules, to enable them to achieve the mobility essential in Indian warfare, became increasingly more common. Mounted infantry could move as fast as Indian war parties, especially when riding captured Indian ponies.[16] During the five years following the Battle of the Little Bighorn General Miles developed the mounted infantry techniques that were an important factor in the ultimate defeat of the Sioux and Northern Cheyennes. In the Southwest, explained Twelfth Infantryman Emanuel Roque, the company in which he served was sent into the field against Victorio, in 1881, mounted on the spare horses of the Sixth Cavalry. Some of the troops engaged in rounding up the mutinous scouts and Apache hostiles after the fight at Cibicue Creek were mounted "gravel pushers."

Mounting foot soldiers on horses and mules generally required

[15] Beyer and Keydel, editors, *Deeds of Valor*, II, 227. This work lists all, and describes many, of the acts for which the Congressional Medal of Honor was awarded, from the Civil War through the Spanish-American War and the Philippine Insurrection.

[16] Special Orders No. 41, Yellowstone Command, Cantonment Tongue River, May 14, 1877, MS, S-R Coll. Several companies of the Fifth Infantry were ordered equipped as "mounted infantry, using the Indian ponies recently captured [Lame Deer's village, May 7, 1877] and such horses as may be procured: The saddles and other horse equipments captured will be used for this purpose . . . . Only light field equipment will be used." This mounted battalion camped just outside the Cantonment, and sometimes on the opposite, north bank of the Yellowstone River, to be in immediate readiness whenever Miles decided to order them out. The mounted battalion existed until 1881, when Sitting Bull surrendered, and proved its worth as an extremely mobile task force against the Sioux, Cheyennes, and Nez Percés.

considerable persistence. Ordered in February, 1877, to equip and mount 150 Fifth Infantrymen for a five-day scout out of Fort Keogh, Montana, Captain Simon Snyder noted in his diary entry for February 14:

> After a good deal of fuss and worry I got the men mounted upon the mules at 1 P.M. for the purpose of drilling them in cavalry tactics. As may be supposed, the sight was as good as a circus, and the way several of the men were thrown was a caution. Upon the whole however the drill was a success. We finally got away about 6:30 P.M.[17]

Several articles of routine issue field equipment were added to the individual regular's campaign outfit from the late sixties through the middle eighties. All ammunition was carried in loop belts after 1876, the campaign hat, first black, then grey, was added, and canvas leggings were issued in the late eighties. Before leggings were furnished, foot soldiers stuffed their trousers into stocking tops and tied them round with string, for warmth and to keep out dust, mud, and snow. Navy-blue shirts replaced the earlier grey flannel issues in the late seventies and early eighties, and experimental issues were made to supply soldiers with shirts to correspond with climatic conditions. By 1898 the Regular Army had adopted a field-service uniform of khaki-colored twill. Perhaps the wearing of the older brown canvas fatigue suits, for campaign service, in the late 1880's and in 1890, was one of the earliest attempts at authorizing a utilitarian campaign outfit.[18]

Enlisted regulars on the frontier had varying opinions on the causes of the Indian troubles. Some thought that foolish and overbearing white civilians provoked much of the friction that ultimately flamed into soldier-fought campaigns. Seventeenth Infantry Sergeant Ralph Donath remarked that much of the

---

[17] S-R Coll.

[18] Soldiers campaigning in the Southwest during the 1880's are believed to have been the first to wear the brown canvas fatigue clothing as a campaign uniform in the field.

trouble between whites and the Sioux, from 1876 to 1881, was the result of the ruthless greed of a few civilians. On campaign in southern Colorado in 1880, Twenty-third Infantryman Wallace E. Bingham's command very nearly clashed with many times their own number of warlike Utes following the wanton murder of an Indian by a white "greenhorn." The civilian was drunk and had only recently come from the East, where his conceptions of Indians and frontier life had been molded by blood and thunder "frontier stories." He wanted to "get him an Indian." Bingham stated that civilian peace officers arrived in time to avert a pitched battle, and surrendered the killer to the Utes, who exacted payment for the murder by taking the life of the killer. The soldiers camped nearby believed the Indians were in the right, and felt no sympathy for the easterner who had nearly sparked an outbreak. A Thirteenth Infantryman, serving in western Oklahoma in 1890, believed that most of the trouble that sent small units of soldiers out to keep peace among the Kiowas, Comanches, Southern Cheyennes, and Arapahos stemmed from mistreatment of Indians by white cowboys.

Many enlisted regulars believed that dishonest and inept Indian agents, and miserable mismanagement by the Bureau of Indian Affairs and civil government in general, were the root of many Indian campaigns. "We saw the Nez Percé reservation taken," wrote Sergeant James S. Hamilton, "these Indians had schools, churches, and fair homes and were happy and prosperous. They were transported to a sage brush, barren area where they could hardly exist." Commenting further on injustices to the western tribes, Hamilton included soldiers in his remarks, writing, "I saw our own army personnel steal from the consignments which were supposed to go to the Indians." Having observed the work of the Indian Bureau in Wyoming and on several Apache reservations, Sergeant Perley S. Eaton stated that he felt the cheating and greed of dishonest Indian agents was the source of most Indian discontent in the early eighties. First Sergeant George Neihaus, who also served in Apache campaigns, explained that "the Indians were promised lots of things, and they were betrayed: then the Indians went out to raid the settlers. I feel the Indian agents, many times—not all—were the cause of a great deal of unrest."[19] The same opinion was expressed by Sergeant John H. Barron, in his remarks about the abortive uprising at Crow Agency, Montana, in November, 1887. This was only partly true in the Crow case. The agent was indeed incompetent, but things would not have boiled over had not a young Crow trouble maker tried to set himself up as master of the reservation.[20]

Several men who campaigned against the Sioux in 1890 and 1891 were convinced that bad faith on the part of the Indian Bureau and its agents, coupled with starvation among the Indians, were the real causes of the outbreak that culminated in the Wounded Knee disaster. The rank and file believed the Indians understood completely that they were being cheated. Sergeant Charles Johnson, Eighth Cavalry, wrote that he had seen underweight beeves palmed off on the Northern Cheyennes

---

[19] Sergeant Neihaus had no sympathy for Geronimo and his band; he said that the soldiers belived they were really Indian hoodlums and outlaws, parasites on their own people.

[20] The Crow name for 1887 agent Henry W. Williamson was "The Crazy White Man," as they believed he was mentally unbalanced. The agent could not handle a young Crow-Bannock named Wraps-Up-His-Tail, whom the Crows distrusted, but at the same time respected and feared because of his powerful medicine. The restless faction among the Crows insisted on raiding horses from their old Blackfoot enemies. Williamson tried to arrest Wraps-Up-His-Tail as the ringleader, Crow young bloods defied the agent and shot up the agency, whereupon the agent, in a panic, summoned troops for protection. The insurgent young men refused to surrender when soldiers surrounded the Crow Agency on November 5, 1887. Firing broke out when the troops advanced on the Indian camp, but ceased when Wraps-Up-His-Tail and his chief lieutenant were shot. Most Crows felt this was the best thing that could have happened. This information is drawn from interviews with elderly Crow men and women, some of whom were in the camp when the fighting began. This affair is an almost classic example of trouble growing out of Indian unrest among the reservation-bound young men, the incompetency of an Indian agent, and a perhaps too hasty belligerency on the part of the military.

in 1890, through the connivance of a dishonest agent. "At the time," said Johnson, "graduates of Carlisle School . . . were around, and commented [to non-English-speaking Indians] on what was taking place." Private Henry Backes, Tenth Infantry, said that he and his comrades, who were ordered to a Moqui (Hopi) village, near Fort Defiance, New Mexico, in 1891, believed that the threatened outbreak resulted from "the dishonest treatment of the Indian Agent."

The Indian's primitive barbarism, reacting to restrictions and changed conditions he did not agree with nor understand, was believed by some western enlisted men to have caused much friction between the Indians and the army. The roving northern plains tribes grew restless when confined to reservations, observed Second Cavalryman James B. Wilkinson, and persisted in their old horse-stealing habits. Wilkinson, like many other soldiers, felt the directives of the Indian Bureau that emanated from Washington were often very foolish, and were unworkable on the frontier. Unhealthy influences on the part of Indian medicine men were charged as a basis of some uprisings. Corporal Frank B. Knight explained that the trouble at Crow Agency in the fall of 1887 was believed by the soldiers to be mainly due to the hostile machinations of the medicine man Wraps-up-his-Tail (Sword Bearer). The same view of Indian restlessness and hostility was expressed by some of the regulars sent to the Sioux country in the early winter of 1890. Medicine men were thought to be stirring up trouble among the near desperate Sioux through the medium of the ghost dance and announcement of the imminent appearance of the Indian messiah. Considering Indians to be unstable and barbaric at best, western regulars universally believed that trouble was bound to follow when Indians secured liquor, and that to some extent trouble was actually "brought about when young Bucks obtained whiskey."[21]

21 Sergeant William Bald, First Cavalry, served in the Apache country. Of Indian unrest, Bald observed, "we thought they were not getting an even break—and they weren't."

Some Indian trouble was ascribed by the rank and file to the Indians' innate "cussedness," treachery, and love of strife. Sitting Bull was generally viewed as an archconspirator, whose fondest wish was war, and whose greatest pleasure derived from the contemplation of slain and mutilated whites. Fifth Infantryman Luther Barker stated that the Lame Deer Fight, May 7, 1877, was triggered by Sioux treachery. Barker wrote his description of the affair: "We called it the Little Muddy [Creek]. . . . Lame Deer and Iron Star rode up to Gen. Miles in a friendly way, and when near they called out 'How, John' and drew their guns and fired at the General, but killed his orderly." There are several versions of how the Lame Deer Fight began, but this is the account accepted by the soldiers.[22]

Before the government arrived at a consistent policy for forcing the western tribes to remain on assigned reservations, soldiers were often disgusted with the vacillating "peace policy" of the United States. Failure to control the Indians, so that major campaigns to compel submission would be unnecessary, exasperated regulars who knew they would have to fight the hostiles and reservation runaways. Explaining the matter to his sister, in 1869, Private Charles Lester, H Company, Fourth Infantry, wrote from Fort Fetterman, Wyoming Territory, that the Sioux ". . . come in here when it is cold weather and pretend

[22] An Indian version of how the fight began comes from Mr. John Stands-In-Timber, elderly and educated Cheyenne historian, who lives at the action site, Lame Deer, Mont. According to Stands-In-Timber, Lame Deer and his head warrior Iron Star rode up to parley, outside the Minneconjou Sioux camp, with General Miles. Big Ankles, a nephew of the chief, rode just behind them. He was a nervous, excitable young man. Just as the parley opened, Big Ankles aimed and fired his rifle at Miles, but killed his orderly instead, whereupon the soldiers returned the fire, Big Ankles was killed, and the action opened in earnest. This account tallies in general with the soldiers' view that Indian treachery sparked the shooting, varying mainly in the matter of who actually tried to kill Miles. The real difference is in how the act was interpreted. The soldiers saw it as deliberate treachery by the Indian leaders, when actually the young Indian acted on his own, contrary to his chief's wishes. Discipline was rarely effective among plains Indians.

to be friendly and when it is warm . . . they go on the warpath [with the full knowledge of Indian Bureau officials]."[23]

No matter what reasons soldiers gave for Indian outbreaks, the fact that hostile operations resulted in weeks and months of hard campaigning for themselves was enough to arouse animosity toward the "Reds." In June, 1876, General Alfred Terry told his troops that they would return home to Fort Abraham Lincoln as soon as Sitting Bull's hostiles were rounded up. "I wish for mine part," wrote Seventh Cavalry Trumpeter Henry C. Dose, to his wife, "we would meet him tomorrow. Sergt. Botzer and me come to the conclusion, it is better anyhow to be home baking flapjacks. When we get home we will pay up for this, and bake flapjacks all the time."[24] Trumpeter Dose baked his last flapjack sometime before the afternoon of June 25, 1876, when he fell at the Little Bighorn.

Regular soldiers usually do not feel the intense animosity toward an enemy that is often displayed by wartime volunteers and citizen-soldiers. Warfare is their business, and they understand that professional enemies are in the same trade, but on the opposite side. Indian campaigning, however, differed from so-called "civilized" warfare of the nineteenth century. The enemy were savages, who neither gave nor expected quarter, who tortured, mutilated, and ravaged helpless enemies, and generally refused to stand and fight pitched battles where regulars could come to grips with them. Propaganda literature, depicting Indians as bloodthirsty murderers, was avidly devoured by the American reading public, including soldiers, throughout the nineteenth century. Having had very little personal, firsthand experience with western Indians, frontier soldiers distrusted and feared them for the same reasons that men have always feared what they do not understand. Some regulars, such as the men of the Seventh Cavalry, of which half the roster were killed by the Sioux in 1876, had what they believed were

[23] To Mrs. Stanley, MS, Oct. 17, 1869, FLNM.
[24] June 8, 1876, MS.

good reasons for holding grudges against Indians. "The Seventh Cavalry," wrote Private Jesse G. Harris, "just didn't like Indians —you can take that from me!" Put more bluntly, Seventh Cavalry Corporal Louis Courville's statement that "the only good Indian is a dead Indian was the general attitude [of the regular soldiers in 1890]." Courville heard that Indians treated white captives brutally, but added that he never saw any instances of this himself.

Men filled with propaganda, and involved in what they and the general public tended to view as something of a crusade to redeem the West from savagery and to avenge the victims of Indian outrages, were inclined to consider all Indians the same —hostile, or potentially so when the opportunity arose. The steamer *Durfee* was transporting several companies of the Fifth Infantry to the Yellowstone country in July, 1876, when a band of Indians was seen moving away from the north bank of the Missouri River, near Fort Buford, at the mouth of the Yellowstone. The steamer was quickly nosed into the riverbank, and a company of soldiers advanced toward the Indians in skirmish order. The northwestern plains had been in a turmoil since Sitting Bull's thousands had defeated Custer a month previously, and the region was full of hostile war parties. When the infantrymen surrounded the Indians, they proved to be a small band of friendly Arickarees. "I never saw men so crazy for a fight as mine were when we gained the rear of the Indians' camp," wrote Captain Simon Snyder, "and it was with the greatest difficulty that I restrained them from [firing] . . . on the poor Indians."[25] To these regulars, the Arickarees, some of whom had scouted for the army against the common Sioux enemy, looked the same as the hostiles they had come to fight.

Barbaric Indian treatment of prisoners and enemy dead was one of the principal factors conditioning the frontier regulars' thinking on the tribes they campaigned against. "Men returning

[25] Letter to his mother, July 30, 1876, MS, S-R Coll.

from campaigns said the Indians were cruel and tortured our [men captured by them, who were] . . . killed and scalped," wrote First Infantryman James S. Hamilton in 1876. The rank and file, said Third Cavalry Sergeant Perley S. Eaton, believed Indians usually killed their prisoners outright, but older soldiers told him they had found brass-eagle buttons in heaps of ashes, indicating that soldier captives had been burned to death.

Many enlisted regulars had firsthand knowledge of Indian savagery. An entire column of the Eighteenth Infantry witnessed the brutal killing of two soldiers, near Julesburg, Colorado, in 1866. The two men had taken a light wagon out to cut some hay. At some little distance from the command, a party of warriors surrounded and cut them off. As described by musician James D. Lockwood, the "hellish demons [killed them] . . . almost in the presence of a hundred friends, and in less time then it takes to read this . . . they were stripped of their clothing, mutilated in a manner which would emasculate them, if alive, and their scalps torn from their heads."[26] A few weeks later, Lockwood shot an Indian from behind in cold blood, as the warrior quietly sat his pony near the Bozeman Trail. Savagery begets savagery, and the civilized white man could kill as wantonly as any plains warrior. Private Charles Lester wrote his sister, in April, 1867, that a war party had caught and killed two soldiers, near Fort Kearney, Nebraska, "and scalped them and cut them in pieces besides." Lester and his comrades were not inclined to overlook such events when hostile prisoners fell into their hands.

Trying to explain soldier reactions to Indian atrocities and mutilations, First Sergeant Martin J. Weber, Fifth Cavalry, wrote to a correspondent that "some of the things the Utes did [1879] was horrible, not fit to print."[27] The late Victorian sense of propriety did not countenance publication of shocking, obscene mutilation details. However, soldiers who saw them prac-

[26] *Drummer-Boy*, 143.
[27] To Mrs. V. R. Wood, Feb. 7, 1940, MS, United Indian War Veteran Files, San Francisco, Calif.

ticed upon the bodies of other regulars, women and children, and civilian frontiersmen, could not help having their attitude toward Indians heavily influenced by the experience.[28]

Having heard of or seen the hostiles' handiwork on the persons of their white enemies, western regulars frequently paid them back in their own coin. John F. Finerty, who marched into the heart of the hostile Sioux country, as a correspondent with Crook in 1876, described the regular rank and file attitude toward Indians in his account of the desecration of an Indian grave, on Crazy Woman Creek, in northern Wyoming. Two Ninth Infantrymen were overheard discussing a wooden scaffold burial:

"Hello, Sam what in hell is that?"

"That—oh that is the lay out of some damned dead Indian. Lets pull it down. Here boys, each grab a pole and we'll tear it up by the roots." . . . within ten seconds the Indian tomb was helping to boil the dinner of the 9th Infantry.[29]

Of his comrades' reaction to the discovery of another Indian burial place near the Yellowstone River, during the 1876 Sioux campaign, Second Cavalryman William White states in his diary entry of February 25: "The boys set fire to a tree where a Indian was buried, and they cremated him."[30]

Soldier retaliation for hostile barbarities extended to the living as well as the dead. When three Indians, believed to have murdered and tortured civilians, were released after a short stay in the Fort Sill guardhouse, "they were taken a few miles away

[28] Two types of Indian mutilations considered "unprintable" in the late Victorian era are described as follows:

Notes Taken by I. D. O'Donnell in Conversations with John Burkman, Custer's striker, MS, I. D. O'Donnell Collection, CBNM—"The Negro scout Isaris [Isaiah] had about a dozen arrows shot in his breast and a picket pin through his balls."

"Med. Hist., Fort Laramie, 1868–79, MS, Nat. Arch., 192, Oct. 10, 1876, a citizen killed Oct. 8 was brought into the post—"smally piece of scalp taken and an arrow pushed up anus."

[29] *War-path and Bivouac*, 83.

[30] MS, in possession of William Watt, Crow Agency, Mont.

from the Fort and turned loose," said ex-regular Martin D. Schenck, "but the general supposition [among the soldiers] was that they did not get very far away."

Attitudes of regulars toward Indian enemies were not always governed by animosities and hatreds bred of fear, distrust, and atrocities. The progressive Nez Percés, who did not scalp or mutilate white enemies, and who had lived at peace with the government for many years prior to 1877, were not looked upon as were the Sioux and Cheyennes. "None of us felt very hostile towards them as they were good Indians but our orders were to go after them," explained Seventh Infantryman Homer Coon. Even the ferocious Apaches were not hated by some of the regulars who campaigned against them. Commenting on formerly hostile Apaches, First Sergeant George Neihaus wrote "the soldiers did not hold hard feelings about the Indians. I could always make friends with them, when they were treated right." Immediately following action at Crow Agency, in November, 1887, First Cavalry soldiers rounded up the frightened Crows and brought them back to the agency. "We even helped them to erect their tipis and to pacify them," said Sergeant John H. Barron.

Soldier gestures of peace and friendliness toward captured or surrendered hostiles were not always taken as they were intended. Describing an 1891 example of this, Private Walter C. Harrington wrote:

> A strapping private from Indiana by the name of Carter and I were walking on the [Rosebud, South Dakota,] Agency grounds one day when we passed a fine appearing young squaw, I raised my cap; like a flash and without a sound she made a slash at me with her knife. Carter caught the movement before I did and gave me a shove: she missed me.

Harrington added that he was later told the woman's husband had been killed at Wounded Knee.

Rank and file opinions on the fighting qualities of hostile Indians ranged from healthy respect to fear-breeding awe. After weeks of grueling campaigning in 1885, Sixth Cavalry regulars met the surrendered Apache war leader, Nana. "He was a very old man, short, fat and wrinkled," wrote Terrence J. Clancy, "we all wondered how such a man could stand the awful strain and hardships that this Apache had to endure." Sergeant James S. Hamilton stated that the regulars he knew, from 1876 to 1881, in campaigns against the Sioux, Cheyennes, Nez Percés, and Apaches, believed "the Indians were good fighters."

The Utes and the Nez Percés were viewed as especially dangerous and competent enemies. During the 1879 Ute campaign, a macabre soldier joke revealed something of the regular's opinion of the hostiles' abilities. Two soldiers were talking:

"Got a comb and brush?"

"No, when we get over and have a brush with the Indians [Utes] they'll fix your hair for you!"[31]

Sergeant John B. Charlton, who fought seven pitched battles and many skirmishes with Indians, from 1870 to 1880, ranked the Utes as the best-armed and most dangerous foe he had encountered.[32] After the battle and siege at Bear's Paw Mountains, where Joseph's Nez Percés finally surrendered in October, 1877, the troops involved knew they had faced a worthy band of foes. The Nez Percés were as well armed as the soldiers, exhibited great courage, skill, and tenacity, and had in fact associated so long with whites, that they fought more like white troops than did any other western Indians.[33]

Fear of the hostiles occasionally passed the point of instilling prudence and caution in the enlisted men and turned some into craven shirkers. A column of four hundred Third Cavalrymen,

---

[31] Maria Brace Kimball, *A Soldier-Doctor of Our Army*, 104.

[32] Carter, *Old Sergeant's Story*, 145.

[33] Correspondence of Edward S. Godfrey, Vol. I, MSS Div., Lib. of Cong. This is a MS of General N. A. Miles's Report to Dept. of Dakota Commander Alfred Terry, Oct. 17, 1877, detailing the Battle of Bear's Paw Mountains, Sept. 29 to Oct. 4. The report states that the Nez Percés were all well armed, knew how to use long-range rear sights on their rifles, and were superior to the Sioux as fighters.

camped at the Cimarron Crossing on the Santa Fe Trail in July, 1867, was surrounded by harassing hostiles. "Many of the men who expected to be detailed for guard duty reported at sick call in order to avoid duty," wrote William Thornton Parker. The shirkers feared that Indian infiltrators would murder sentries under cover of darkness. Twenty-third Infantryman Wallace E. Bingham stated that one-third of his command deserted from Fort Garland, Colorado, in May, 1880, when the outfit was ordered to take the field against the Utes. When the Eighteenth Infantry marched north, to hold the Big Horn country of northern Wyoming and southern Montana, in 1866,

> . . . new recruits deserted in unusual numbers in . . . fear of Indian troubles, much increased by wild stories from straggling volunteers from the upper country (some deserters later claimed they were abandoned)! The Civil War men, inured to hardships, remained steadfast and faithful.[34]

Indian armament was a touchy and highly controversial matter in the 1870's and 1880's. Much sensational propaganda clouded the subject, and many citizens and soldiers believed the hostiles were armed as well as or better than were the regular army soldiers sent against them. Some believed the government and unprincipled traders supplied potentially hostile tribes with firearms that were superior to army issues. "We were told that . . . Winchester rifles had previously been issued by our government to the Indians for shooting buffalo," said an 1876 First Infantryman, James S. Hamilton. "Indians had better rifles than our own men," thought Hamilton, "when they were disarmed at Standing Rock they had cap and ball Colts plus various kinds of rifles, but for the most part they carried good Winchester rifles." Few hostiles actually did own and understand the use of arms superior to the issue Springfields, but In-

[34] Bisbee, "Items of Indian Service," in *Proceedings, Order of Indian Wars, January 19, 1928*, 24.

dian possession of some Winchester repeaters was considered an important point by regulars.

A Pawnee scout, who served against the Sioux and Cheyennes in 1876 and 1877, and had fought them as blood enemies before enlisting in the army, said that only about thirty per cent of the hostiles he saw owned modern, metallic-cartridge firearms.[35] Scout Rush Roberts added that the hostiles were not usually very good marksmen.

Most western regulars agreed that hostile warriors were not generally dangerous marksmen, except at point-blank ranges. "Indians fired point blank," explained Private William G. Wilkinson, "soldiers used the [long range rear] sight and wind gauge, which the Indians knew nothing about." Springfield, Henry, Winchester, Sharps, Spencer, Remington, and other metallic-cartridge, black-powder weapons were capable of fairly accurate long-range shooting, provided the shooter understood the uses of the elevating-leaf rear sight, bullet drift, and the effect of wind on bullets.

Under some conditions, warriors were better marksmen than the rank and file regulars, from long practice in the type of mounted fighting they thoroughly understood. Shooting from a running horse, Indians were occasionally better point-blank, snapshooters, than were the army adversaries. This was not often a very significant factor, for warriors rarely made frontal assaults that brought them within the short ranges they preferred. Long-range Springfield rifle and carbine fire usually kept the hostiles at distances beyond their normal abilities as riflemen.

Soldier views on hostile Indians, field equipment, and campaigning in general quite naturally affected their performance and conduct in the field. Regardless of variations of opinion on other factors, the rank and file of the Regular Army agreed that

[35] Scout Rush Roberts' Pawnee name was AhreKahrard. He is mentioned by name in Luther North's writings about the Pawnee Battalion's part in the Dull Knife-Mackenzie fight of November 25, 1876.

campaigning against the western tribes was arduous, exacting, and time consuming. Indian campaigning, as First Sergeant George Neihaus put it, "was a war of who could last longest."

12.

Field Service in the West

WITH FIELD KITS READIED and all personal foot lockers packed in the stripped down barracks rooms, troops designated for campaign service fell in when "Assembly" sounded at the appointed time. If the post was a regimental headquarters, the departing men were played out, and sometimes escorted for a few miles, by a band, usually playing "The Girl I Left Behind Me." The infantry in a column swung out with "blanket rolls and haversacks slung over their shoulders, and their tin cups, which hung from the haversack, rattled and jingled as they marched . . . in column of fours. . . . The [military] glitter was all gone, nothing but reality remained."[1]

To concentrate troops for major Indian campaigns, the army

---

[1] Summerhayes, *Arizona,* 247.

sometimes had to transport regiments and companies over considerable distances. Twelfth Infantry companies, ordered into the field in 1878 for the Bannock Campaign in Idaho and southeastern Montana, traveled over the Southern Pacific Railroad from San Francisco to Carson, Nevada. "From Carson . . . we traveled in wagons. The infantry rode in these wagons thru Oregon and Washington," explained Emanuel Roque.

Whenever possible, the Army transported its campaign-bound soldiers over land grant railroads. Although they were faster than cavalry or foot troops, by modern standards the western railroads of the seventies and eighties were tedious transportation. Traveling from Plum Creek, Nebraska, to another Union Pacific station in Wyoming, Thirtieth Infantrymen spent four hot days and nights "on the cars" in July, 1868.[2] Companies of the Fifth Infantry dispatched from Fort Keogh to Fort Custer, during a threatened Crow outbreak in October, 1887, went via the Northern Pacific Railroad, from Miles City to Custer Junction, the closest rail point to Fort Custer. The ninety mile rail trip took a little over four hours, at an average speed of less than twenty-five miles an hour.

Railway accommodations for Regular soldiers were rarely comfortable, although First Cavalrymen, when rushed in 1882 to guard Arizona civilians and property from marauding Apaches, were furnished the best cars available. "On our return," wrote an officer of the command, "we entrained at Tucson, and the niggardly railway accommodations furnished . . . were in marked contrast with the luxurious train placed at our disposal on the way down, when nothing was too good for the troops, whose services were then badly needed."[3] Troops usually traveled in day coaches, with three men assigned to occupy two seats, so that all could not stretch out at the same time. They ate bread, dried fruit, sandwiches, canned goods, and coffee served from a

[2] Lester to Mrs. Stanley, MS, Aug. 3, 1868, FLNM.
[3] Hein, *Memories*, 135f.

baggage car. After several days of travel, the cars were generally littered and in sore need of cleaning. Some cars were furnished as crude sleeping cars, with wooden benches upon which travelers could relax. Primarily intended to accommodate the poorest class of westward-bound civilians, these "emigrant sleeping cars" were sometimes used by soldiers. Cavalry, when en route by rail, made frequent stops to feed and water the horses.

At the end of a rail journey, infantry customarily marched to their ultimate destination, but wagon transportation was not uncommon. Five companies of the Twelfth Infantry traveled hundreds of miles by wagons en route to the 1878 Bannock campaign. "There were four sleek mules to each wagon," said Emanuel Roque, "we rode forty miles a day, our seats were boards across the wagons." Lieutenant Frank D. Baldwin charged and captured an Indian village, near McClellan Creek, Texas, November 8, 1874, using his wagon-borne Fifth Infantrymen in a combination horse and wagon attack that won him his second Congressional Medal of Honor.

River steamers were used to carry Regular troops on the Colorado, Red, Yellowstone, Missouri, and other navigable western rivers. The slow and tedious upstream travel often compelled soldiers to spend a week or ten days crowded on the decks. "Marching on board [a chartered Missouri River boat in 1866], the long line filed up the stairs to the cabin and upper decks . . . where [the Eighteenth Infantrymen] . . . were allowed to break ranks and adjust themselves and their effects in the most comfortable manner possible."[4] Describing steamer transportation on the Yellowstone in July, 1876, Captain Simon Snyder wrote:

> The weather is very warm, it being now 98 in the shade. The officers occupy the cabin, which is very small, while the men, 350 in number [of the Fifth Infantry] are crowded on the upper deck in the broiling hot sun all day long, and at night to for that matter. The upper deck is 208 ft. long and 25 ft. wide. The lower

---

[4] Lockwood, *Drummer-Boy*, 125.

deck is [filled] . . . by 100 horses and mules . . . with army wagons, etc.[5]

Snyder noted that the steamer's boilers required about two cords of wood an hour, and that soldiers were detailed to disembark and cut the wood as needed. Boats were sometimes fired upon in hostile country, but such attacks produced few casualties. River steamers usually did not run at night, and soldier passengers were sometimes allowed to sleep ashore.

Troops sometimes passed through towns and settlements in the course of their campaigns. The citizens of Bismarck, Dakota Territory, turned out to greet and cheer enthusiastically companies of the Seventh Cavalry en route to campaign against the Sioux and Cheyenne in the spring of 1877. Thirteenth Infantrymen detraining at San Marival, New Mexico, while on their way to the Victorio campaign in 1880, were met by a host of end-of-track gamblers, saloon men, and other frontier parasites comprising the population of the town. "They [jeered and cat-called] . . . and told us many pleasant things as to what Old Vic would do to us when he caught us," wrote Private John G. Brown. Most civilians living on the Apache frontier, however, "were much relieved of anxiety and [mental] suffering when they saw us coming," said Sixth Cavalryman Edward Sauter.

The first day's march of a campaign column was generally less than fifteen miles, during which the troops adjusted themselves to marching, and arranged the details of routine ogranization for the days and weeks ahead. Position in column was usually rotated among the companies, but the favored leading position was first occupied by the senior captains. If the force included cavalry, infantry, and wheeled vehicles, the cavalry generally had the advance, followed by the main body of infantry "in columns of fours, with the artillery and supply trains in the rear."[6] When the column contained cavalry, some of them were

[5] To his mother, MS, July 30, 1876, S-R Coll.
[6] Lockwood, *Drummer-Boy*, 132.

INFANTRYMEN DIGGING TRENCHES
on maneuvers in northwestern Nebraska, 1889.

Courtesy Mrs. Howard Sutton

COLUMN OF TROOPS
on the march, 1889, in northwestern Nebraska.

Courtesy Mrs. Howard Sutton

sent out as flankers, paralleling the main command, and another detail acted as rear guard. Two pieces of light artillery were sent out about one-half mile on either flank of the First Infantry, when that regiment took the field in 1876, explained Sergeant James S. Hamilton, and the men assigned as gunners were the only ones who rode. This could be arduous duty, because the gun crews often had to "make their own road."

Pioneer details generally went in advance of the main column, to bridge ravines and smooth a passable route for wagons and other wheeled transportation. This strenuous duty was rotated among the units in the column. Leaving camp on the Rosebud, August 8, 1876, at five o'clock in the morning, General Miles's Fifth Infantry made a hard day's march of ten miles, up Rosebud River. The command "got into camp on Rosebud about 4 p.m." wrote Captain Simon Snyder.

> The day was very warm, all hands suffering from thirst. R [an officer] played out. Before F, H, and K Cos. had time to pitch their tents, we were ordered to build bridges, which kept us at work until dark.

> August 9. Up bright and early and at work on bridges for almost an hour before they were completed. Had a hard march of about 11 miles [in a drenching rain] . . . camped at 5 P.M.[7]

Sick, exhausted, or lame soldiers were generally transported in light Dogherty wagon ambulances at the rear of a column. Surgeon Holmes O. Paulding sent several of Gibbon's Seventh Infantrymen to the ambulance wagon in June, 1876. They were "faint from heat and lack of sleep . . . the men don't get over 5 hours of sleep a day, [wrote Paulding] reveille at 2 A.M."[8] Recounting his 1866 campaign service with the Eighteenth Infantry in Wyoming, Private William A. Murphy stated, "there was only one ambulance for sick soldiers, as the [officers'] women

[7] MS, S-R Coll.

[8] Diary, June 12, 1876, MS, Office of the Chief of Military History, U. S. Army, Washington, D.C.

and children had all the others in use, and you have an idea of what it meant for a soldier to be sick." When no wagons or ambulances were taken on campaign, disabled regulars had to be carried by their friends or transported in animal drawn litters and travois.

Troops on the march went in route step, swinging along pretty much as they pleased, provided they maintained a regular formation. Snatches of music occasionally rippled through the ranks in the morning, when a cheerful soldier whistled, sang, or perhaps played a harmonica. Blouses were taken off when it was warm, and soldiers often stripped to undershirts in very hot weather. Few natty uniforms were in evidence, for experienced soldiers wore their oldest clothing and used uniforms, purchased from discharged men, for field service. Members of the same unit might wear several varieties of head gear, including kepis, campaign hats, civilian felt hats, or straw hats in summer.

The army offered new campaigners specific advice, gleaned from long experience, on how best to avoid hardships and what to do when they were inevitable. *The Soldier's Handbook* cautioned infantrymen to wash their feet every night, to keep them soft, and to keep the toenails closely clipped. "Rub the feet well [with soap] before the march . . . ."[9] Loose fitting shoes and wool socks were recommended for marching, and soldiers who got a soaking were told to keep marching until they were dry, to avoid illness. Sound advice was the direction to boil and aerate all sluggish water used for drinking, and to keep the woolen canteen cover wet to cool its contents.

The length of a day's march varied according to terrain, time of year, and availability of wood and water. An average of many marches, by infantry and cavalry, indicates a usual daily distance of about twenty miles. Cavalry could move faster and farther than foot troops for a few successive days, but over a

[9] N. Hershler, *Handbook*, 53.

period of weeks, hardened infantry could usually outdistance horsemen on grain-fed army mounts. Marching records were logged by an officer detailed to the duty, and were commonly "measured by a meter connected with a wheel on an ambulance."

Columns while on a campaign usually went into camp in the afternoon, to allow enough daylight time to take care of setting up camp and performing many routine chores. Horse and mule picket lines had to be set up, camping areas assigned to the various companies, guards posted, and water and cooking fuel collected. Where wood was lacking, wrote Musician James D. Lockwood, "each soldier upon coming into camp after a day's march, was expected to take a sack and go around over the prairie and collect it full of Buffalo Chips."[10] A more pleasant camp arrival routine was described by Private William G. Wilkinson:

> Immediately on getting into camp, it was the custom, in the [Eighth Cavalry] troop of which I was a member, to have a couple of men take buckets and get some water, while others got some wood. A fire was started, and in a short time, each man was given a cup of good strong black coffee. It was surprising how quickly they recovered from the fatigue of a hard day's march after getting their coffee.

Camp organization was supervised by the officer of the day, who assigned unit camping areas and picket lines, designated locations for sinks, and posted guards. Soldiers set up their own two-man tents, or the large cone-shaped Sibley-tents, and erected accommodations for officers as well. Some men felt that officers took too much personal equipment with them on campaign. "Our [camp] work," wrote Trumpeter Ami Frank Mulford, "is increased by so many men being detailed to wait on the officers."[11] After camp was set up, and the evening meal eaten, soldiers detailed for guard duty assembled for guard mount in the evening instead of in the morning as in post.

[10] *Drummer-Boy,* 134.
[11] *Fighting Indians,* 62.

Columns moving through dangerous country generally corralled their wagons and made other preparations for defense. The soldiers camped outside the wagon circle, to defend it in case of attack. If hostiles raided the camp, the mules and horses were driven into the wagon corral, while the soldiers fought outside.[12] Camp life and routine was a new experience for most recruits. Several Sixth Cavalry companies were camped along the Gila River, in Arizona, during the 1885 Geronimo outbreak.

> It was the first time in my life that I had slept out of doors [wrote Terrence J. Clancy], and what with the stomping and snorting of the horses, and the rattling of the chains on the wagon tongues—where the mules were tied—sleep was out of the question. Besides, the ride had made me so stiff that all the bones in my body ached.

Regulars customarily carried only one wool blanket apiece, but cavalrymen frequently "used the saddle blanket too." When opportunity permitted, frontier regulars stuffed their cloth mattress sacks "with straw or grass or whatever was available," said Sergeant James S. Hamilton. Having only one blanket each, soldiers generally pooled their blankets and slept two and three together in cold weather. Rubber blankets were placed next to the ground, to keep out dampness. When occupying Sibley tents, ten to fifteen men arranged themselves like the spokes of a wheel, with feet toward the center pole. Cartridge belts, accouterments, and weapons were hung on or stacked around the pole. Soldiers generally slept with all or most of their clothing on.

The tired soldiers had to accustom themselves to nocturnal disturbances in camp. Mules and horses sometimes stampeded or otherwise aroused the camp. Pursuing Geronimo in 1885, a column of the Sixth Cavalry was camped in the Mogollon Mountains of Arizona. The command was tired, and the soldiers had relaxed for some badly needed rest, when "a string of men

[12] John F. McBlain, "With Gibbon on the Sioux Campaign of 1876," *Cavalry Journal*, (June, 1896), 140f.

[guards] on foot herded the animals right in camp—and, what a night *that* was! A fellow had to keep awake to prevent the mules and horses from walking on him." Hostile warriors frequently raided horse and mule herds, or set prairie fires to harass the soldiers.

Routines connected with making evening camp usually allowed some degree of relaxation, but preparations for resuming the march in the morning were a different matter. When forced marches were required, western regulars were on the move long before daybreak, and reveille sounded before sunrise. Usually less than an hour was allowed for breakfast, personal packing of equipment, and attending to the horses and mules.[13] The sounding of the "general" signaled the breaking of camp.

> At the first note of the trumpet, all canvas was dropped almost as one tent. Each man had an allotted task; each had already rolled his bedding, carried it to the wagon and laid it on the ground [or packed it on his horse or himself, when wagons were not used]; two men were in each of the troop's two six-mule wagons to pack the equipment, rations and forage as it was handed up. As the tents dropped, a man took the poles, two others folded and rolled the tent. . . . It was a nice job to pack the equipment of a 65 man troop, together with ten days' rations and forage for the horses and mules in two wagons and do it in 15 minutes.

The last call was sounded fifteen minutes after the packing was scheduled to be finished, continued Private (later Major) William G. Wilkinson, and the command resumed the line of march.

Under normal conditions, a column marched for four or five hours in the morning, and halted before noon for about two

[13] Wilkinson, "Four Months in the Saddle, The Cross Country March of the 8th Cavalry . . . ." 1888, MS, 3. Wilkinson was an enlisted man on this march, and listed the following morning schedule: 4:45, first call; 4:55, reveille and stable call; 5:00, mess call; 5:30, general (strike camp); 5:45, boots and saddles; 5:55, fall in (assembly); 6:00, forward march.

hours. Horses and mules were fed, watered, and rested during the "nooning" and the soldiers ate their midday meal. The monotonous basic field ration was salt pork, hardtack, sugar, and coffee. Pack mules or wagons carried rations on long marches, but each man usually carried his own food for at least one day. The pork was packed in the soldier's mess kit, or "meat can." "The greasy meat," explained Lieutenant W. B. Weir, ". . . is carried in the meat-ration can, whose two parts are only pressed together, and being carried on its end [in the haversack]. . . . the heat of the sun melts the grease, which very easily runs out."[14] Carrying hardtack crackers in the haversack was not very satisfactory either, as they generally broke up and crumbled. Each man had his own quart canteen, and a water wagon was sometimes included in the column, wrote Sergeant James S. Hamilton. When water was scarce, its use was strictly regulated and supervised.

The limited facilities for transportation sometimes restricted troops in the field to only two meals a day, commented Private Harvey J. Ciscel. Remarking on the adjustment to slender rations in 1876, Seventh Cavalryman Jacob Horner said, "It is surprising how little one can live on." Horner and his mates were issued twelve hardtack crackers and a piece of "sowbelly" every day. "I'd eat it all for breakfast and still be hungry," explained Horner.[15] The twelve crackers added up to about one pound of hard bread, the regulation issue, but shortages were common. Private William A. Murphy stated that Eighteenth Infantrymen, while on the march in 1866, were issued only seven of the four-inch square crackers every two days. "A hungry man," emphasized Murphy, "could have eaten the entire two day's rations at one meal and asked for more."

Weeks of subsisting on poor rations must have gradually

[14] "Infantry Equipments," Ordnance Notes No. LXVII, in *Ordnance Notes, Nos. 41–67*, 531.

[15] Roy P. Johnson, "Bismarck Man, Nearing 94, Recalls Custer Indian Wars," *Fargo Forum*, Sunday, Aug. 29, 1948, 20.

sapped the vitality of campaigning regulars. Trumpeter Mulford commented on the monotony of field rations in his 1877 diary: "We now have a change of diet: hardtack, bacon and coffee for breakfast; raw bacon and tack for dinner; fried bacon and hard bread for supper."[16] Unauthorized hunting was not allowed, which irritated Mulford because he knew the column's scouts kept the headquarters' mess well supplied with fresh meat. "At night," wrote Sergeant Perley S. Eaton, "we would make our supper of coffee, hard tack and bacon. The hard tack had bugs in it, and the bacon had worms too . . . anything was good enough for a soldier." Eighth Cavalryman Williamson wrote, on the quality of 1890 field rations, that "some of the hardtack . . . was packed in 1863, the labels and date of packing were still on the boxes. The hardtack had a green mould on it, but we just wiped it off and they were all right . . . most anything tasted good."

After prolonged consumption of the staple field rations, an occasional dish of baked beans or bean soup was extremely welcome. "Once in a great while we would get a cup of bean soup," recalled Seventh Infantryman Joseph Sinsel, "and it tasted as good to us as an ice cream cone to a child."[17]

Some improvements were made in the army field rations during the late eighties, although hardtack, bacon, and coffee staples continued to make up the bulk of the rations. Canned baked beans were added to issue supplies in the middle eighties, and quickly became a favorite campaign food. Living on the basic campaign staples for extended periods frequently caused scurvy and other nutritional diseases, until canned tomatoes were added to the field rations in the late eighties. The acids in the tomatoes were an effective antiscorbutic. Soldiers ate the tomatoes warm or cold, and drank the juice with relish. Canned corned beef, added to the campaign rations about 1890, was not warmly welcomed. "Sometimes," wrote Private Louis Ebert,

[16] *Fighting Indians*, 79.
[17] "Joseph Sinsel of Butte, Member of Gibbon's Command in 1876 . . . ," *Billings Times*, Apr. 30, 1925.

"we had canned beef, which in those days was not fit to eat."[18]

Methods of preparing and cooking staple rations in the field were limited by time, materials, and the abilities of the rank and file. The art of cooking was not taught to new men at the recruit depots. Army advice on preparing food was aimed chiefly at making rations safe to eat. "Disease and often death," warned *The Soldier's Handbook*, "is the result of bad and illy-prepared food; therefore it is of vital importance to every soldier to know this useful art."[19]

Over the years, regulars developed their own recipes for the issue field rations. The salt pork was first parboiled, if water was available, and then broiled on a stick or fried in the mess kit, although some considered it a delicacy when dipped in vinegar and eaten raw.[20] Old hardtack was generally too hard to chew without a preliminary soaking. When dampened, fried in salt pork grease, and sprinkled with brown sugar, the hardtack tasted very much like pastry, and was dessert for many meals. An example of soldier-improvised recipes was the "mess" of "pulverized hardtack, bacon, and raisins, boiled in condensed milk," cooked up in 1877 by Trumpeter Mulford and his Seventh Cavalry "bunkie."[21] Issue coffee was not ground, and was received in the bean. The green coffee was roasted in a Dutch oven or frying pan, then "ground" by placing the beans in a cloth and pounding them with stones or a gun butt.

Fresh meat sometimes was issued on campaign, when cattle were herded along with the column and butchered at the direction of the quartermaster, or when buffalo and other wild game helped to vary the issue rations. Indian scouts accompanying the Seventh Cavalry in 1876 sold venison to meat-hungry soldiers at

[18] A comparable statement about the canned meat of the Spanish-American War was: "Tinned beef killed more soldiers than Spanish bullets."

[19] Hershler, 49.

[20] Johnson, "Jacob Horner," in *North Dakota History*, Vol. XVI, No. 2 (1949), 80f.

[21] *Fighting Indians*, 76. The raisins and condensed milk were bought from a sutler on the steamboat *Far West*.

two dollars for a hindquarter and one dollar for a forequarter or saddle cut. Business was brisk, and the scouts earned more than one hundred dollars each in about one month.[22]

Soldiers sometimes hunted for themselves, adding antelope, venison, buffalo, and wild fowl to their menus in the field. A breakfast treat of sage hens, rabbits, and baked beans was savored by a detail of First Cavalrymen on campaign in 1890. An experienced campaign cook had three men dig a large hole in the ground, and three others gather a supply of fire wood. "The cook soon had a big fire blazing in the hole," said Jacob Markert, "before going to bed he stuck a big pot of beans in the hole, put the sage hens and rabbits on top of the beans, put on the airtight lid and covered the whole business with coals . . . then dirt."[23] For diversion, and in the hope of enjoying a change of diet, western regulars frequently fished streams and rivers near their camp sites. Trout and catfish were the usual catch.

Chance encounters with citizen wagon trains and stops at infrequent road ranches and settlements were seized upon by the rank and file as opportunities to obtain extra food. On patrol just after the Wounded Knee fight, in January, 1891, a detachment of Seventh Cavalry stopped at a lonely little store and post office in Dakota.

> There was a little woman there [wrote Private Clarence H. Allen], who came from the East, and she made pies and biscuits and sold them to the troops. We begged, borrowed and stole any dollar, paid two for one [against payday credit], if necessary, for those of us who had not saved our money, to get enough to buy a pie or biscuits.

Refreshments purchased by soldiers at way stations and settlements on the line of march were not limited to foods, when beer and liquor were available. During rests campaigning regulars

22 O. G. Libbey, *The Arickara Narrative of the Campaign Against the Hostile Dakotas, June, 1876,* 72.

23 "84-Year-Old Veteran," *Happy Harvester,* Vol. VII, No. 3 (1951), 1.

took full advantage of the diversions offered by the nearby communities. In camp at Fort Concho, Texas, in 1888, Eighth Cavalry enlisted men enjoyed themselves in the neighboring town of San Angelo, described by Private William G. Wilkinson as "wide open."

> The writer was lucky enough to make a small stake playing poker in the White Elephant . . . . A trumpeter had been in town all day borrowing the price of a drink, but could not make connections often enough to get drunk. Late that night, he was pestering one of the bartenders . . . until finally the bartender said, "Here, I'll give you a drink;" then he put a large tumbler on the bar and filled it with whiskey and said, "Now, damn you, drink that and get out of here!" The man looked at it, and it almost sobered him, but he finally drank it like so much water . . . it is a wonder that it didn't kill him. Sometime later, he was lying up against a building, completely unconscious, but he was alright the next day, and apparently suffered no ill effects.

Enterprising traders sometimes brought beer and whisky to soldiers out on campaign. Traders set up in business on a river steamer plying the Yellowstone in 1876, and sold liquor to soldiers at the base camp at the mouth of Powder River. When campaigning troops were paid at Fort Peck, Montana Territory, in the summer of 1879, "post traders from all over the country brought beer there in wagons, more came by boats . . . ."[24] Seventh Cavalry companies, camped briefly near Fort Buford, Dakota Territory, in the summer of 1877, secured copious supplies of whisky from the sutler at the fort.

In camp liquor raised disciplinary problems just as it did in the garrison. Some First Cavalryman, while in the field in 1890, appropriated a supply of medical whisky. The captain found out about it, and ". . . the entire detachment, the guilty and the innocent, were ordered to walk along-side of their horses for three days, carrying their saddles and blankets. At noon on the

[24] "How E. M. Locke Saved the Command of Captain Clark from Massacre," *Rocky Mountain Husbandman*, Vol. LXVI, No. 4, Great Falls, Mont., (1942).

second day he relented."[25] Discipline was generally relaxed in the field, but had to be maintained to some degree in order to keep the men pointed to the task at hand.

When we were on any campaign or line of march [wrote Sergeant Perley S. Eaton], the discipline wasent so strict, everybody looked out for himself, cooked his own meals, and done his own laundry—there wasent any roll calls and everybody done as he pleased [no spit and polish, and] no shaving, and if we were on a long campaign we came back with a full beard.

Infractions of discipline in the field were often of a different sort from those in garrison. Soldiers were tempted to shoot at wild game while on the march or in camp, and this was generally forbidden.[26] Two Seventh Cavalrymen, while on the march June 20, 1877, were caught firing at rabbits, and were punished by being ordered to walk during marches for one week. One day's walking on the march was ordered for an 1864 cavalryman, who carelessly allowed his horse to get away from him. This was one of the common field punishments among frontier cavalry.

The strictness of the discipline maintained in the field, depended on the commanding officer. Men might be "bucked and gagged," or "spread eagled" or forced to "carry the rail" on campaign, but guardhouse sentences were difficult to manage without a post lockup. Lieutenant Colonel George A. Custer overcame this problem by arranging for an improvised guardhouse in a deep Kansas dugout.[27]

[25] "Indian Fighter Recalls Times in the Badlands," in *Winners of the West*, Vol. XIV, No. 4 (1937), 6.

[26] "General Field Orders No. 2, Camp on Knife River, Dept. of Dakota, May 22, 1876, " MS, Bates Coll. "Firing in camp or on the march is strictly forbidden except [for men detailed to hunt]. . . . It should be remembered that the sound of firing is the signal for an alarm, and should not be heard under circumstances likely to mislead. Company commanders will be held responsible."

[27] Ryan to Mrs. Custer, MS, Mar. 17, 1908, Package No. 36, Custer Coll., CBNM. "Do you recollect the large hole that General Custer had dug in the ground [at Camp Sturgis, Kansas], on the side of the hill, where the guard house

The climate and geography of the western mountains and plains caused the most severe of the hardships endured by campaigning regulars.

> Human energy can stand a great deal [wrote Fifth Cavalry Sergeant Major C. R. Hauser], but service under extreme weather conditions, often without shelter, food, wood, or water . . . sapped their [soldiers'] strength and vitality. It made old men of young men, and carried away many a hardy soul, when he should have been in his prime.

An upsurge of Apache warfare occasioned the immediate transfer of Third Cavalry companies from Fort Washakie, Wyoming Territory, to Wilcox, Arizona Territory, in April, 1882. "We made our last camp in Wyoming in a snow storm," recalled Sergeant Perley S. Eaton, "in ten days we were in [Wilcox,] Arizona, where it was 120 in the shade and [we] had to buy water for the horses." Campaigning in the heat of the Southwest was hard on the soldiers, but the bitter cold of a high plains or mountain winter was harder and more often deadly. Sixth Cavalry troops stationed in New Mexico were ordered to the Sioux agencies in South Dakota, in October of 1890. These men detrained at Rapid City, South Dakota, in zero weather, and took up their line of march the following morning. "We did not get overcoats and [over] shoes for nearly two weeks," wrote Private Louis Ebert, "a few men died of pneumonia."

Bands of hostile Indians and reservation runaways could not move rapidly in winter, because their ponies were in poor condition after subsisting during the winter months on the bark of willow trees. Disciplined, determined, and well-led soldiers forced the Indians to stand and fight, or surrender and come in to the reservations. Without able leadership and iron discipline,

---

was, and where we used to put prisoners at night? I was sergeant of the guard there the day there came very nearly being a riot between the guards and the prisoners, and probably if Lt. McIntosh, who was officer of the guard . . . had not arrived on the scene as soon as he did, the 7th Cavalry would have been a couple of men short."

the Regular Army could not have campaigned successfully against the hostiles, in the snow and cold.

Harrying the hostile Sioux, near the upper Missouri River in Montana, Captain Simon Snyder's Company F of the Fifth Infantry pressed the Indians relentlessly, in temperatures ranging from ten below to seventeen degrees above zero. Captain Frank Baldwin's command of the same regiment carried out its assigned operations in the vicinity of Fort Keogh, Montana Territory, in the early winter of 1876, arriving back at the post December 23, in minus forty degree weather.[28] The Sioux and Cheyennes could not keep the field against an enemy that moved in all weather, but the army's gains were achieved by the suffering of its officers and enlisted men. "Sometimes," recalled Sixth Cavalryman Louis Ebert, "we did not even pitch a tent—sleeping on top of snow and on frozen ground." Even when tents were available, they were little protection from the bitter winds of the plains. Men equipped with Sibley tents cleared snow away to pitch their shelter, and luxuriated briefly in the feeble warmth of the conical sheet-iron stove. The heat of the stove generally thawed the ground a little. "Our blankets would stick down" wrote Private Clarence H. Allen, "and before morning they were frozen to the ground, and so was everything else that touched the ground." Soldiers did not remove their clothing in the intense cold. "I kept my rubber shoes on my feet for two months, and my socks kept my shoes company," wrote First Cavalryman John Larson, "if I pulled them off they would have frozen stiff."

Unprepared for winter campaigning in the West, the post-Civil War regulars found the necessity quickly thrust upon them. The annihilation of the Fetterman command outside Fort Phil Kearny, Dakota Territory, December 21, 1866, so sharply reduced the post's garrison that the remaining troops were insufficient to man the blockhouses and palisades, if the numerically superior Sioux decided to press home an attack. Snow drifted level with the top of the stockade, and determined war-

28 Snyder, Diary, Dec. 23, 1876, MS.

riors could have walked into the fort. The nearest troops were about ninety miles to the south, at Fort Reno on the Bozeman Trail. When the famous "Portugee" Phillips reached Fort Reno, troops set out as a relief party at once in temperatures ranging from twenty-five to forty degrees below zero. "They waded or dug their way through snows, knee deep, and often waist deep . . . [and on arrival at Fort Phil Kearny] many had both hands and feet frostbitten."[29]

In the plains country winter often covers the region suddenly and without warning. In the late fall of 1867 it struck companies of the Fourth Infantry, campaigning between Forts Laramie and Reno, on their return march to Fort Laramie. Corporal Cyrus Reed described the severe suffering of the troops:

> On our way back we forded the North Platte River, near Fort Fetterman. . . . The second snow [of the season] had already fallen. The ice across the Platte was not strong enough to hold us, so we broke the ice with the butts of our muskets and forded the river up to our arm pits in the icy water. A few days later, we staggered into Fort Laramie, that is what was left of us, our feet wrapped in our torn blankets, as our shoes were gone.

These men had not been issued special winter clothing, such as buffalo coats, overshoes, and other items that later became standard equipment.

Regulars soon learned to outfit themselves for winter campaigning on the plains. Detailing his November, 1876, cold weather apparel, Captain Simon Snyder wrote:

> I am now wearing two flannel and a buckskin shirt, one pair of drawers, trousers of buckskin and a pair of army trousers, two pairs woolen socks, a pair of buffalo overshoes and big boots, a heavy pair of blanket leggings, a thick blouse and heavy overcoat, a heavy woolen cap that completely covers my head, face and neck except nose and eyes and still I am not happy . . . when

---

[29] Carrington, *My Army Life*, 193.

I am all fixed out I am a sight to behold and have all I can do to mount my horse.[30]

Campaigning seven years earlier, in western Kansas, the same captain and his men, lacking the winter clothing they later obtained, spent ". . . two days in bed in order to keep warm."[31]

Even when troops were warmly clothed and prepared for winter field service, intense storms and knife-like arctic cold threatened death for units caught in the open. Elements of the Second Cavalry suffered excruciatingly when a tempestuous snowstorm in November, 1871, overtook them along the Yellowstone River, about one hundred and fifty miles east of Fort Ellis, Montana Territory. The temperature dropped rapidly to forty degrees below zero, and fierce winds drove snow into the men's eyes. Soon the command found itself moving in the familiar circle of those who are lost.

> Many troopers became numb, and a few threw themselves from their horses and had to be lifted back and forced to follow . . . . Some men wept and begged to be permitted to lie down and die; others wandered from the column and were forced to return . . . . Cries that hands and feet and parts of the face were freezing were heard on all sides . . . . There was great confusion; for a time it looked as if all discipline would be lost, and the command scattered on the prairie . . . the cooler heads fairly drove the others before them. After five hours . . . we stumbled on the timber we had been seeking. Trumpeter Page, brave fellow that he was, seized his trumpet and sounded the "Rally" . . . it meant life [to the snow-blinded men still outside the timber].[32]

Fifty-three of the 150 men had their hands and feet frozen. In late December, 1890, companies of the Eighth Cavalry, in the field against the Sioux in South Dakota, were caught by a severe storm, while on the march near Slim Buttes. Private William G.

[30] To his mother, MS, Nov. 5, 1876, S-R Coll.

[31] Snyder, Diary, Feb. 2, 1869, MS.

[32] Brigadier General Edward J. McClernand, "With the Indians and the Buffalo in Montana," *Cavalry Journal*, Vol. XXXV, No. 145, 507.

Wilkinson explained, "We took the horses' feed bags and pulled them over our heads and faces to protect us against the storm and allowed the horses to pick their own way."

Winter campaigning levied heavy tolls on the rank and file of the western regulars. Some men deserted rather than brave the frontier winters, but, wrote Sergeant James S. Hamilton, most "were an uncomplaining lot and remained loyal and faithful to their line of duty at all times." Severely frostbitten men often suffered the loss of fingers, toes, hands, and feet when gangrene set in after freezing.[33] Amputation was the only recourse. A Third Cavalryman, nearly frozen on campaign against the Utes in Colorado in 1879, was found and treated by his comrades before his useless legs became completely frozen. Suffering intensely, while his friends worked to restore circulation, the soldier grimly quipped, "I am going to sell needles and thread and pins [if the legs had to be amputated] . . . I'm going to make more money than you fellows."[34] Fortunately, the man's legs were saved.

In addition to the hundreds who suffered illness, severe frostbite, and even loss of limbs, in the course of winter service, many regular deaths were directly caused by exposure and freezing. Third Infantrymen campaigning in the northern Rocky Mountains in 1878 suffered greatly, said George App, when

> . . . a blizzard suddenly set in and they were snow bound for five days. They had tents for shelter, but the cold was intense, and there was a careful check each morning to see if any succumbed to the cold over night. Several of the soldiers died in their sleep and were found frozen stiff in the morning.[35]

[33] Otis, *Surgical Cases,* 191f. Sample Case: A Second Cavalryman had both feet frozen and amputated, at Fort Reno, Dakota Territory, in Jan., 1867. His wounds did not heal correctly, and a reamputation was necessary in July, 1867. He was finally discharged, with a $20.00 a month pension for loss of both feet, in Sept.

[34] William Damn, Third Cavalry, 1879– , "The Meeker Massacre and Ute Jack's Death," *Winners of the West,* Vol. XIII, No. 9 (1936), 3.

Sergeant James S. Hamilton, First Infantry, recalled at least one man who was so badly frozen that he "was given a merciful drug to give him his last final sleep."

The piercing, wind-driven cold of the plains maimed scores of western regulars for life. After General Nelson A. Miles's 1874 winter campaign on the south-central plains, about twenty men with frozen hands and feet were sent to the post hospital at Fort Dodge, Kansas, in January, 1875. An eastern reporter, assigned to relay frontier news to his paper, interviewed several of the sufferers in the hospital. One of the men who had read some of the journalist's material, recalled Sixth Cavalryman A. E. Weed, hailed him to his bedside and said, "Cully, the man who wrote that piece about the beautiful [Kansas] snow never camped on Bear Creek in the middle of winter!"

Winter weather inflicted the worst of the western regulars' campaign hardships, but the parching heat of summer and the sometimes torrential rains added their quota of discomfort and suffering. Usually dry, the heavens sometimes opened and deposited what is normally a year's precipitation in the course of two weeks or so of heavy rains. The generally hard-baked ground then turned into a semiliquid gumbo quagmire, bogging down horses and foot men alike. During a two-day deluge, in camp at the mouth of Powder River, on the Yellowstone in 1876, Fourth Infantryman W. E. Helvie said, the men had no tents, and had no way of keeping themselves or any of their equipment from becoming thoroughly waterlogged. "You could stand up like a pelican and let the water run off your back," wrote Helvie, "and it would not scald you either!" General Crook's shelterless regulars endured twenty-six days of rain in the course of their fifty-two-day "starvation march" campaign through Montana and South Dakota in the late summer and fall of 1876. A young officer explained to his father that this was especially hard on

35 "Interview with Indian Wars Veteran George App [Third Infantry, 1873–78]," *Bridgeport* [Conn.] *Post,* July 27, 1933.

the older men, because the rain and exposure "caused many to suffer with rheumatism and kindred ails."[36]

Although torrential rains and high water caused great hardships, the lack of water in the desert and arid regions of the West was even worse to endure. Water is rarely plentiful on the plains; many of the rivers and streams flow only intermittently in the spring and fall. In many of the army's western campaigns the governing factor was the availability of water, which often had to be carefully rationed to soldiers and their animals alike. It could at times be obtained by digging in apparently dry stream beds and water holes, but such sources of supply did not yield copious amounts of the vial liquid.[37] Small water holes and streams near camp were often placed under guard to make sure that the slender resources were carefully used.

On dry marches, western regulars used even the water found in old buffalo wallows or other stagnant pools. Private William G. Wilkinson explained that "in many cases this water was covered with a green scum, which we skimmed off, and then scooped up [water] with a spoon, then put vinegar in it to kill the taste: after all, it was water, and many days we went without it." Vinegar was an ineffectual disinfectant, and before chlorine tablets were developed, regulars sometimes died from drinking bad water. Water from many western streams and pools, impregnated with alkali and other minerals, is unfit for human use, and may be actually poisonous.

Troops campaigning in the Southwest suffered water short-

[36] W. S. Schuyler, to his father, in *General George Crook, His Autobiography*, ed. by Martin F. Schmitt, 211.

[37] Captain H. E. Palmer, "History of the Powder River Expedition of 1865," *Transactions and Reports of the Nebraska State Historical Society*, Vol. II (Lincoln, Neb., State Journal Company, Printers, 1877), 206. On Cheyenne River, Dakota Terr.: "We found water by sinking iron-bound casks and empty cracker boxes in the apparently dry sand beds of the main streams and tributaries of the south middle, and north forks of the Cheyenne River—not a drop of water visible in the main branch."

ages more often than did men serving in other areas of the West. Thirteenth Infantryman John G. Brown wrote that he had twice suffered extreme thirst in New Mexico in the early eighties. "Both times for 4 and 5 [*sic*] days, except for a cup of coffee each day, and the water to make our coffee was well guarded. We were tenderfeet and did not know the water holes in New Mexico." The hostiles, of course, were not handicapped to the same degree, and their ability to elude soldiers in cross-country pursuits was based to a large degree on their knowledge of where and how to obtain water. Three companies of the Fourth Cavalry, in the spring of 1882, were sent on a scout in Arizona, looking for hostile Apaches. The command expected to replenish their water supply at the end of a forty mile march, but found none available for seventy-six miles.

> Each man had two canteens, nearly half a gallon of water, which with ordinary economy was enough for three days, yet the inexperienced recruits were almost without exception out of water the first night [of the three-day march]. . . . I [Lieutenant George H. G. Gale] went back on the trail to pick up stragglers . . . . The suffering among the men was confined mostly to recruits . . . who up to that time had thought that being thirsty meant roughly to make it convenient to go into the next room for a drink of it.[38]

Parched regulars soon learned to follow Indian examples in making use of even the most meager and unpalatable emergency sources of water. "Once we were lost in San Simon canyon," wrote Sixth Cavalryman Terrence J. Clancy of his 1885 campaign experiences in the Southwest, "we made a dry camp and ate mescal poles and roots [for three days]." Once Fourth Cavalry troopers pursued some Apache hostiles for seven miles on foot in Arizona "in great want of water. Some of the soldiers cut

---

[38] Lieutenant George H. G. Gale, Fifth Cavalry, to his sister "Susie," MS, May 19, 1882, lent by Mrs. Mary Barr, San Antonio, Tex.

the pulp out of the cactus and chewed it, but this gave little relief."[39]

Like most military operations, Indian campaigns required a large measure of calculated risk. Troops encumbered with slow-moving supply trains could not hope to overtake the elusive hostiles, but men without supplies of food and clothing could not keep the field at all. Planning a strike against the enemy involved careful weighing of supply factors, and when a commander seriously miscalculated his need for supplies his men suffered accordingly. Fifth Infantrymen pursuing the Sioux in Montana in the fall of 1876 expected to endure supply shortages, when ordered to proceed with only a limited number of pack animals and no wheeled vehicles. "During the greater part of the time [we] had nothing to eat but bacon and hardbread with a little coffee, sometimes on half rations for days at a time," wrote Captain Simon Snyder.[40]

Perhaps the most striking example of troops suffering for lack of supplies is that of General George Crook's "starvation march" of 1876. Crook was intent on catching the hostile Sioux and Northern Cheyennes in southern Montana, or South Dakota. The General was determined not to hamper his column's mobility with a supply train, and fully expected that he and his men would be on short rations before the end of their march. Heavy rains, however, impeded the advance, and the men were in a dangerous condition from lack of food and clothing fully three weeks before they reached their objective: the Black Hills. Suffering among the men reached and often surpassed the limits of endurance. Staff Officer Walter S. Schuyler related his part in the campaign to his father, trying to convey to him an understanding of what the rank and file had endured.

I have told you of what I experienced on this march, but you can gather from that no realization of the suffering of the men,

[39] Brigadier General James Parker, "The Geronimo Campaign," *Proceedings, Order of Indian Wars, January 26, 1929,* 34.

[40] To his mother, MS, Oct. 15, 1876, S-R Coll.

particularly the infantry. I have seen men become so exhausted they were actually insane . . . . I saw men who were very plucky sit down and cry like children because they could not hold out.[41]

This officer stated that the men suffered more than the officers because they were improvident and did not budget their rations. Supplies of pork, hardtack, and coffee were exhausted the evening of September 7, when each man was issued a quarter ration of each. The next day, one of the campaigners wrote in his diary:

> The men reduced to a state of starvation clamored loudly for meat of some kind . . . . They were glad to get mule flesh. Orders were given to the Commanding Officers to select some of the fatest horses among the cavalry . . . and issue them the same. Broiling and roasting kept up all night.[42]

During the night, a detachment of cavalry, sent ahead to scout for sources of food and for the hostiles, discovered the Sioux village of American Horse at Slim Buttes, Dakota Territory. In the early morning of September 9, Crook's emaciated regulars attacked and captured the village, and drove off a large band of warriors who attempted to retake it. The village contained some dried buffalo meat, much of which was wolfed by the hungry soldiers. After burning the hostile camp, the column resumed its line of march toward the Black Hills settlements. On September 12, the troops made thirty-six miles on rations of horse meat, dried buffalo meat, and one and one-half tablespoons of beans per man. No rations were issued that night. "Men very weak and despondent," wrote a campaign diarist, "Many of them unable to stand on their feet, and some droping to sleep on the ground where they had been halted . . . [lying unconscious on the] wet ground without any covering of any kind."[43] A cold rain set in again about ten o'clock that night, and

---

[41] In *General Crook*, ed. by Schmitt, 206.

[42] Diary, Aug., 1876–Aug., 1877, MS, Internal evidence does not reveal the diarist's name, only that he was with Crook in 1876, and that he was probably an enlisted man. The diary is in the possession of Mr. Richard Flynn, Blair, Neb.

[43] *Ibid.*

continued until well past sunrise. If the cavalry detachment sent ahead to the Black Hills had not reached Deadwood and started a relief train to the command when they did, Crook's determined strike at the hostiles would have ended in disaster.

Campaigning regulars managed somehow to get by on the staple rations carried with them in the field, but General Crook's was not the only command to subsist occasionally on horse and mule meat. Most of the Seventh Cavalry made a series of forced marches in the late summer of 1877, trying to intercept Joseph's Nez Percés before they crossed north of the Yellowstone River. The grain-fed cavalry horses became unable to continue the pursuit, rations gave out, and as of September 16, "the soldiers had been five days on mule meat straight . . . pursuing the Indians on foot."[44] Though the Nez Percés were forced to make a brief fight on Canyon Creek just north of the Yellowstone, the worn-out command could not hold them, and the Indians continued their flight toward the Canadian line. Another body of troops in the field pursuing elusive Nez Percés was also reduced to a diet of horse flesh. Gibbon's Seventh Infantry toiled over the mountains of southwestern Montana to halt the hostiles at the Big Hole, in the Bitteroot country. From July 29 to August 9, the command averaged twenty-two miles a day, and unsuccessfully attacked the Indian camp just at dawn, August 9. Supplies ran out, and the day following the indecisive battle the exhausted soldiers "ate horse."[45]

Routine discomforts and minor hardships were expected as a matter of course on Indian campaigns. Frontier regulars were as addicted to tobacco as more modern soldiers, and when supplies ran out in the field, smokers and chewers experienced an intense craving.[46]

[44] *Bozeman* [Mont. Terr.] *Avant-Courier*, Sept. 27, 1877, 2.

[45] E. E. Hardin, Diary, Aug. 10, MS.

[46] Mulford, *Fighting Indians*, 89. After most of the men had been three days without tobacco, one of them asked the Colonel for a chew, and got it. He then blurted out that he would desert unless he got more, and was subsequently placed

Personal cleanliness was almost impossible to maintain in the field, and lice frequently infested the dirty, unshaven soldiers. "We had cooties then, just as the army of today," said Seventh Cavalryman Jacob Horner, "on our return to Fort Lincoln [fall, 1876], we burned our clothes."[47]

Subsistence living on campaign posed several types of health problems in addition to that of lice. In hot weather, heat prostration and sunstroke felled weakened soldiers. Typhoid and other contagious diseases occasionally broke out, sometimes with fatal results. Medical science had not yet identified and isolated many diseases, viruses were as yet unknown, and maladies such as "camp fever" are noted in the diaries and notebooks of army surgeons on campaign. Before the late eighties, scurvy frequently afflicted regulars who had lived too long on the field-ration staples. Some of Colonel Gibbon's men fell ill with scurvy during a Sioux Campaign, in August 1876. No antiscorbutics were issued to the sick men, but those with money were permitted to purchase small amounts of vegetables and canned goods from the commissary, a situation that disgusted and appalled the surgeon.[48] Wild berries, plums, onions, and edible legumes were eaten in season and probably saved many a regular from the ravages of scurvy.

A commonplace hardship, and often a dangerous one, was the prairie fire of the plains. Hostile raiders sometimes set fires to harass the troops, and the carelessness of the soldiers themselves caused more than one prairie fire. Fire call sounded through camp at the first sign of fire, and soldiers whipped and beat the flames with shelter halves, coats, and all kinds of other makeshift implements.

Through almost every campaign hardship, the rank and file

under guard. Soldiers who had hoarded tobacco sometimes retailed it to their fellows at ten dollars per pound—payday credit.

[47] Johnson, "Jacob Horner," 81.

[48] Paulding, Diary, Aug. 4, 1876, MS. ". . . camp fever among the men." (Scurvy breaking out.)

regulars maintained something of their sense of humor. Ragged, gaunt enlisted men could usually laugh at each other's appearance and joke about "hobo brigades" and a diet of "angle cake" (hardtack) and "Cincinnati chicken" (salt pork); the quips of the jokesters cheered their comrades in unpleasant situations. March, 1876, was bitter cold, and snow lay deep in northern Wyoming. General Crook's troops were camped over night on Crazy Woman Creek, while searching for the Sioux and Cheyennes. Soldiers grumbled and muttered, hugging tiny fires, when "a soldier got out of his [pup] tent, and in the frosty air of midnight shouted loudly enough for all the command to hear him, 'I want to go ho-O-o-ome!' "[49]

Frontier soldiers often endured extreme hardships for weeks and months of campaigning without even catching sight of the will-o'-the-wisp Indians. Evidences of their passage, burned wagons, desolated ranches and stage stations, and the bodies of dead soldiers or citizens, made deep and lasting impressions on the soldiers. Trailing a band of Apaches, in May, 1882, companies of Third Cavalrymen were camped one night when a wounded civilian lurched into camp crying that his brother and another man were missing after the three had been surprised by Indians. "The Captain sent out a detail of men, and sure enough," wrote Sergeant Perley S. Eaton, "we found the two men dead—shot a dozen times and horribly mutilated." In 1885, Sixth Cavalryman Edward Sauter was one of a detail of soldiers who found two more dead civilians in New Mexico. One of the men had made a stout resistance, as was shown by the empty cartridge cases near his mutilated corpse; his face had been crushed to a pulp with rocks. Such discoveries drove home to the rank and file the realization that they were pitted against capable, ruthless, and deadly enemies.

Whether a campaign had been successful or not, enlisted regulars universally welcomed the end of prolonged field service and a return to the comparative comfort of their quarters. Spirits

[49] Finerty, *War-path and Bivouac*, 58.

rose, and the tired men looked forward to a temporary rest, at least. Troops coming in after intensive campaigns were welcomed with as much of a celebration as circumstances permitted. Coming in to a regimental headquarters post, the weary regulars were generally met by a band, playing lively, rousing marches, and, almost always, "When Johnny Comes Marching Home." Companies of the Thirteenth Infantry left Fort Wingate, New Mexico, to take the field against Apaches, September 22, 1885. "We returned to Fort Wingate, September 16, 1886," wrote Corporal F. J. Gehringer, ". . . the band met us at the foot of the Mountains, and played us in . . . . We were a sight to behold, hardly a [complete] uniform on a man—many had just overalls." These regulars had made seventy-one camps and marched 1,120 miles during their year in the field. Replacement recruits waiting for the Seventh Cavalry at Fort Abraham Lincoln, Dakota Territory, in the fall of 1876, were struck with the unkempt, worn appearance of the regiment's rank and file when the outfit finally came in from the field. The campaign veterans were "unshaven, uniforms flayed [sic] and dirty, and many with their hair nearly down to their shoulders; gaunt and hungry-looking, yet [they were] . . . cheerful."[50]

Men returning from winter campaigns were often in very poor condition. Marching into Camp Supply, Indian Territory, after their successful winter attack on the Southern Cheyennes in 1868, the Seventh Cavalry was

> . . . almost destitute of clothing, [wrote Sergeant John Ryan] our trousers being patched with seamless meal bags. A large number of the hats belonging to the men were made of the same material. The legs of our cavalry boots were pretty scorched and burned from standing around camp fires, and as substitutes we used leggings made from pieces of tents. A number of men had to use woolen blankets in place of overcoats [lost at the Battle of the Washita] . . . . You can talk about ragamuffins in this part of the country on the 4th of July, but they could not begin to com-

[50] Mulford, *Fighting Indians*, 27.

pare with the Seventh Cavalry when coming off that winter campaign.[51]

Sergeant James E. Wilson commented that he and the rest of the Twentieth Infantrymen who returned to Fort Keogh, Montana, after the Sioux Campaign of 1890 and 1891 had to draw entirely new issues of clothing.

Regardless of their appearances and condition, soldiers returning from campaign were ready to celebrate vigorously. Companies of the Twenty-first Infantry, ordered back to their station after the turmoil subsided on the Sioux reservations early in 1891, marched to entrain at Valentine, Nebraska. They had just received their pay, explained Private Walter C. Harrington, and were eager to spend it. A few of the soldiers discovered a "hog ranch" located about one mile from town. "All the men had plenty of money . . . and made a hike en masse to the joint referred to; they held up the train we were to take about 30 hours before they could be rounded up."[52] Eighth Infantry soldiers, returning from the same campaign, marched to Chadron, Nebraska, to reach the railroad. With four months' pay burning holes in their pockets, the soldiers virtually took over the town.

> The peaceable population that night took to the hills or barricaded their homes, and the boys proceeded to decorate the town a bright red . . . . [During the night an eighteen inch snow fell, covering the packs and other equipment the soldiers had hastily left by the railroad tracks.] There was enough equipment left under the snow to equip a company of militia. I myself lost a cartridge belt and trench knife [wrote August Hettinger].

Perhaps the townsfolk of overwhelmed Chadron overlooked

[51] Ryan, "Custer's Last Fight," *Billings Times*, July 5, 1923.

[52] He wrote that while his comrades were whooping it up he proceeded to board the train. "I was the only enlisted man who stayed on the train, and I remember distinctly while sitting alone in the coach, Lieutenant Monroe McFarlane came through the car, and as I rose to salute him, he smiled and said, 'Harrington, you and I are the only decent men in the command.'"

boisterous minor transgressions on the part of the soldiers whom they had so recently viewed as deliverers.

Rarely have American soldiers sustained the persistent and eroding hardships experienced by the rank and file regulars during the western Indian campaigns. Weeks and months of subsisting on substandard field rations, often without adequate equipment and clothing, resulted in a high incidence of rheumatism and similar ailments, permanent physical impairment due to improper diet and exposure, and probable shortening of the average regular's life span by several years. These were the men whose ruefully proud campaign boast was "forty miles a day, on beans and hay, in the Regular Army, O!"

13.

Combat

IN THE COURSE OF ITS MISSION to protect the frontier and pacify the mountain and plains tribes the Regular Army chalked up thousands upon thousands of miles. Many of the footsore infantry and weary cavalry soldiers never heard a shot fired in combat. Sometimes their mere presence was enough to restrain potentially hostile Indians, but during the campaigns innumerable skirmishes and a moderate number of small-scale but bitter pitched battles were fought. The enlisted regulars had ample reasons to remember their combat with the as yet unconquered warriors of the Trans-Mississippi West.

Scouting, to keep possibly hostile Indians under surveillance, to provide a measure of police protection to scattered citizens, and to locate warring bands, was a constant and necessary duty. The usual scouting detail, explained Sergeant James S. Hamilton, was composed of ten soldiers, an officer, and generally some

Indian scouts or allies. Soldiers differed on the importance and value of their Indian scouts. Seventh Infantryman Homer Coon commented that during the 1876 summer campaign against the Sioux along the Yellowstone, "General Terry sent out [Indian] scouts, but they would return, they were a poor lot. It seemed to us that they had a yellow streak and would not venture very far as they would be gone a day or two and then return."[1] During the 1877 operations in pursuit of Sitting Bull's band, Trumpeter Ami Frank Mulford wrote: "It begins to look as though these Indian scouts come in and report the first thing they think of, in order to make the Commanding Officer believe they are doing good work."[2] Private Charles Goodenberger stated that the Apache scouts serving with the Ninth Infantry in the late 1880's were of little value, because they could not be trusted.

Others of the rank and file believed Indian scouts were useful, if carefully supervised and controlled. "When not allowed liquor they were faithful and excellent soldiers," wrote First Cavalryman Thomas E. Gutch of the Apache scouts he served with, "when they were drinking they were treacherous—unreliable and liable to go bad." Second Cavalryman James B. Wilkinson had a high regard for the services of the Indian scouts recruited at Fort Assiniboine, Montana Territory, in the early eighties. "They saved the whole troop once," wrote Wilkinson, "we couldn't have gotten along without them in the far north."

Locating war parties could be a dangerous assignment. Men scouting for hostiles realized that they might be ambushed themselves, or meet an overwhelming body of the enemy. In hostile territory, soldiers on scout were understandably edgy and generally were healthily apprehensive. Ten Sixth Cavalrymen, commanded by Lieutenant John J. Pershing, were on a night scout in the tension-charged Sioux country, just before the Battle of Wounded Knee, in December, 1890. "About mid-

[1] Coon, "Recollections of the Sioux Campaign," MS, Coe Coll., Yale Univ. Lib., 4.

[2] Mulford, *Fighting Indians,* 79.

night," wrote Private Louis Ebert, "as we came out on a flat, we ran into some Indians skinning a beef—we did not expect to see them, nor they us, we got away as fast as possible. A few minutes later, I looked back and the whole flat seemed alive with Indians." No fighting had broken out yet, but the future commander of the American Expeditionary Force of World War I was not taking any unnecessary chances.

Soldiers sometimes felt that their commanders were a little too cautious. A detachment of First Cavalry, searching for the Apache Kid in 1892, followed what they were sure was a hot trail into a canyon just at dark. The officer in charge, stated Clarence Gould, posted ". . . a sentry at each end of his tent . . ." During the night, a prowler dropped bundles of burning grass from the canyon rim, but was not glimpsed. "The report of the detachment upon returning to the post," said Gould, "was no sign of the Kid."

Most of the encounters with hostiles, of the scouts and other troops campaigning in the field, came in the form of hit-and-run brushes and skirmishes. Casualties were usually light, and short-range firing was limited. Indian warriors were essentially raiders, sparring with their enemies rather than engaging in toe-to-toe combat. Private Charles Lester described the results of such a skirmish, near Fort D. A. Russell, Wyoming Territory, in a letter to his sister. "There was about twenty of us [Fourth Infantrymen]," wrote Lester, "had a little sqirmish with the red skins the other day. There was about 25 of them—as near as I could judge—we killed three of them and the rest excaped."[3]

Troops traveling in country where hostile contact was imminent almost always were preceded by skirmishers and flanked by other parties ready to go into skirmish formation at first sight of the enemy. The South Dakota Sioux reservations were in an uproar when the Seventh Cavalry marched toward Pine Ridge Agency in the early winter of 1890. Private Jesse G. Harris was

[3] To Mrs. Stanley, MS, June 16, 1869, FLNM.

assigned as an advance guard as the column neared the agency. "My name came up for advance guard," wrote Harris, "I was put about one quarter mile in front and about one half mile to the right of the main command, with orders if I met any hostile Indians to shoot and fall back—and I was ready to do just that, anytime." "It wouldn't have taken me long to fall back, I was scared," said Harris. Men in a thin, extended line of advance skirmishers well knew what would happen to them should the troops suddenly be confronted by warriors, and they also knew that they were the most likely targets for any unseen Indian snipers, who might try to discourage the column's advance.

Skirmishers were sent ahead by the commanding officer of the two Eighth Cavalry troop units awaiting developments just outside Sitting Bull's village, on Grand River, the morning of December 15, 1890. The Indian police sent in to arrest Sitting Bull became embroiled in a deadly fight with with the old chief's supporters, and the waiting soldiers could plainly hear sounds of staccato gunfire coming from the village. Private William G. Wilkinson and seven of his fellow troopers were sent forward as skirmishers.

> That meant we were to draw fire first [wrote Wilkinson], it gave us a peculiar feeling, to go forward like that, in the dark not being able to see what is in front of you, not knowing what minute a bullet with your number on it is coming your way. It is not so bad if you can see where you are going.

Wilkinson was not the only skirmisher who felt apprehensive about the maneuver. Sergeant George B. DuBois, F Troop, Eighth Cavalry, wrote to a friend that the commanding officer had not favored going to the aid of the besieged policemen at all, and that when the skirmishers were ordered ahead, ". . . none of the officers dared come up."[4] When other Eighth Cavalry

---

[4] To George Thomas, Dec. 18, 1890, *Winners of the West,* Vol. XII, No. 4 (1935), 4.

troops later blocked the flight of a band of reservation runaways, in December, 1890, the colonel sent out a skirmish line to face the heavily armed warriors lined up in front of the rest of the band. One of the skirmishers, Private Harvey J. Ciscel, said, "I felt like every one of them painted devils was looking at me as their first target." Ciscel added that he and the other soldiers believed that the colonel had sent out the few skirmishers to provoke the Indians into firing, so that he could fall on them with the rest of the command. Fortunately, the Indians surrendered quietly, and no shots were fired.

Bungling of relations with chance-met Indian bands sometimes resulted in unnecessary combats, and on the other hand, astute handling of some potentially explosive situations at times prevented bloodshed. A detail of twenty Second Cavalrymen, commanded by a lieutenant, was dispatched from Fort Assiniboine in 1882 to overtake a reported party of Indian horse thieves. Private James B. Wilkinson explained that the detachment suddenly encountered a large band of Sioux, who, believing themselves to be the object of the soldiers' pursuit, opened fire from well-chosen positions. The officer and his men knew they were greatly outnumbered. While the lieutenant parleyed with the leader of the warriors, "we were not allowed to fire back, we were ordered to sit still and take it," wrote Wilkinson. "We soldiers had wanted to fire back at the Indians, but they could have wiped us out very easily, our officers knew best," and the lieutenant's cool judgment averted a potential tragedy. Sergeant Armand Unger, Fifth Cavalry, remarked that he had often been present on occasions when hasty resort to force would have precipitated needless fighting, and that he believed it was harder to prevent combat than to begin it.

Troops shot at by Indians were not always so cool when ordered to hold their fire. A detachment of the Eighth Infantry was guarding Pine Ridge Agency, South Dakota, December 29, 1890, when a body of overwrought Sioux commenced long-range sniping at the Agency. The soldiers took cover and were

First Cavalrymen playing poker

near Fort Grant, Arizona, about 1890. John Stokes, third from left, standing, and Nathan Bell, seated, leaning on table, gave firsthand information on their army life for this book.

Courtesy Nathan C. Bell

First Cavalrymen grooming horses
on picket line, Fort Grant, Arizona, 1890. Their white canvas stable
clothes gave rise to the nickname "government ghosts"
for the men on stable detail.

Courtesy Nathan C. Bell

sent out as skirmishers, but were actually in no danger of being dislodged, though most were eager to reply to the Sioux bullets. "We had a general . . . Brooks," wrote Sergeant Washington McCardle, "we stood in line 500 yds away from the Indians who was firing on us and General Brooks wanted us to wait for orders from Washington. We did not wait!"

Soldiers deployed as skirmishers took what natural cover was available, in a line, with intervals of about three yards between men. Cavalry usually did its actual fighting dismounted, with every fourth man detailed to hold the horses. Few men could hit a target shooting from the back of a horse, while mounted men were easy marks for the enemy. The men were generally allowed to fire at will, and cautioned to select good targets before shooting. "Fire low," advised the officers and the *Soldier's Handbook,* because bullets often glanced off the bones of the head and upper body, but abdominal wounds were usually fatal.[5] "After lying down and taking sights," wrote Private Clarence H. Allen, the "soldiers would take sighting shots at a certain spot . . . to give them the range and the distance . . . ." Because estimating the correct distance was vitally important in obtaining any degree of accuracy with the high trajectory, forty-five caliber Springfields, officers usually told their men the distances for which to set their sights.

Skirmishing demanded more skill in marksmanship than did mass volley firing in a line of battle. Veteran soldiers known to be capable riflemen were commonly assigned to skirmish duty. Seasoned men, explained Green A. Settle, were customarily in the first "set of fours" in column, because their captain had confidence in their abilities, and knew that he could call on one of them to try a long, sharpshooter's shot when needed. A Private Tuttle, of E Company, Seventh Cavalry, known as one of the best marksmen in the regiment, was killed by a Sioux bullet in 1873. He had provided himself with a "sporting Springfield rifle" at personal expense, and shot several warriors with it when a war

[5] Hershler, 53.

party opened fire on part of the Seventh, near Pompey's Pillar, in August, 1873, on the Yellowstone River in Montana.[6] A hostile bullet ended his career, when he tried to get closer to the Sioux. "He was one of the most useful and daring soldiers who ever served under my command," wrote Lieutenant Colonel George A. Custer.

Skirmish casualties were usually light on both sides, but occasionally an Indian sharpshooter scored a hit on a regular. Exchanging shots with a party of hostiles along Milk River, Montana Territory, in 1882, a detail of dismounted Second Cavalrymen were using their carbines to good advantage, when Private Lawrence Lea cried out, "Oh. I am hit!" A heavy bullet had shattered his right thigh, just above the knee. Two friends carried the badly injured man to the ambulance wagon, where the detachment's surgeon cleaned and dressed the wound and prepared the soldier as best he could for the jolting, one-hundred-and-twenty-mile ride to Fort Assiniboine.[7] The Indians managed to escape, and the soldiers returned to post with their wounded.

Ambush, either totally concealed or through use of a few decoy warriors, was the western Indians' main strategic reliance. In this manner a surprised, and, if possible, a tremendously outnumbered enemy could most easily be routed, with the least likelihood of casualties for the attackers. Western regulars soon understood this, and for this reason almost invariably sought open ground when preparing for combat with hostiles, and in traveling through hostile territory kept to the open as much as possible. Sometimes they could not avoid dangerous terrain. A sergeant and four Sixth Cavalry troopers, ordered to carry dispatches to another unit just after the Battle of Wounded Knee,

[6] Custer to Acting Assistant Adjutant General, Yellowstone Expedition, MS, Research Files, CBNM.

[7] Private Lea's leg had to be amputated at Fort Assiniboine. He subsequently spent a year in the Soldiers' Home, Washington, D.C., and, when granted a disability pension, returned to his native Norway, where he was still alive in the late 1930's.

had to take the most direct route to their goal. One of the couriers, Private Louis Ebert, explained that

> On the way, a sniper we could not see shot me in the fleshy part of my leg. The Sergeant told me we would have to disinfect the wound. When I asked him what with, he took a big chew of tobacco, he then pulled the wound wide open and spit the nicotine into it, then kept working it until blood and chew ran out below. He then took part of my shirt for a bandage and helped me in the saddle. We road about ten miles to an infantry camp, where a nurse dressed the wound right. I never went to a doctor . . . .

The mountain and plains warriors were masters of sneak-attack techniques. The mountainous areas of the Southwest were especially well suited to ambush and surprise raids, and the Apaches took full advantage of their opportunities. Men campaigning against Apaches were continuously reminded, by the frequency of such attacks, of the need for vigilance on the march and in camp. Pursuing Geronimo's band, in the rugged Mogollon Mountains in 1885, a detachment of the Sixth Cavalry was camped along a flowing stream. The water was very welcome, explained Terrence J. Clancy, and many of the men were enjoying a rare bath, when ". . . the Rawhides opened fire on them from a point over the camp . . . . the troop had quite a time for a while, even the bathers took part in the skirmish—just as they were." The raiders were routed by a flanking movement, but several soldiers were set afoot for the remainder of the scout, because the Apaches had deliberately shot their horses.

Thirteenth Infantryman John G. Brown, commenting that army leadership was not always equal to the guerrilla warfare skill of the Apaches, pointed out that one troop of Ninth Cavalrymen in New Mexico in the early eighties, was ambushed twice by Victorio in a three-month period. "That troop," wrote Brown, "was under the same West Point Officers and same Indian Scouts and maybe we didn't razz . . . [them] when we met them at [Fort] Wingate." On the other hand, some officers fully realized and respected the Apaches' abilities, and handled their commands with considerable caution. Pursuing Apaches in the Mogollon Mountains in 1885, Sixth Cavalryman Edward Sauter's command was very close to its quarry at sundown. "We could see the Indians ahead, going into a place called Horseshoe Canyon," wrote Sauter. The canyon could easily have proved to be a death trap for troops entering it after the hostiles. "The ranking officer was Captain Overton (Cocky Overton) . . . he decided it would be unwise to follow the Indians any further that night . . . we never did get sight of those Indians again."

The plains Indians were adept at surprise raids and lightning attacks, especially when Army mules and horses might be stampeded and stolen. Soldiers knew that lurking warriors commonly lay in wait in the vicinity of camp, hoping that a sentry would become careless, or a forgetful soldier stray away from safety. "We were not allowed to venture out of camp [on Trout Creek, Judith Basin, Montana, in 1875]," wrote Seventh Infantryman Homer Coon. Explaining the need for extreme caution, Coon told of a party of Sioux who approached camp masquerading as friendly Crows. "As they approached . . . they headed for our herd. Corporal Abbott was seen coming toward camp at great speed. He reported they were Sioux. We were at dinner at the time and before we knew what all the fuss was about they had passed close by our camp and killed three soldiers. They got the herd going fast and were out of sight in short order."[8] Crow allies later tracked the raiders, killing eight of them and retaking some of the stolen horses and mules. The infantrymen were capable fighters and campaigners, but without the aid of their Crow scouts and allies they would have been sadly handicapped.

Some commanders refused to heed warnings of the Indians' skill in preparing ambushes. The annihilation of the Fetterman command, outside Fort Phil Kearny, Dakota Territory, December 21, 1866, is probably the outstanding example of this, but it is not the only one. Men guarding the outer limits of a Fourth

[8] "Sioux Campaign," MS, 5.

Infantry camp near Fort Laramie, in 1867, were attacked by a party of hostiles. Colonel C. H. Carlton ordered Corporal Cyrus Reed to take a detail of twelve men and go to the relief of the pickets, about half a mile from camp. Reed respectfully informed the Colonel that he was certain that a willow thicket between the camp and the outposts was an Indian ambush, but the officer told him to carry out his orders anyway. "I took the 12 men and went," wrote the Corporal, "we charged the thicket of willows, fired our guns and made a rush through, but when we got through, there were only 2 of us, the rest laid dead in the ambush of the willows."

Surprise has always been an important element in warfare. A confused enemy is an ineffectual opponent. Some soldiers, when suddenly and unexpectedly fired upon by hostile warriors, became excited and unable to function effectively. "I was in an engagement with Apache Indians two days before Christmas, 1870," wrote E. Hoffner, "and one of our troopers stood stock still and fired straight up in the air." When Apaches staged a surprise attack on a camp of eight Fourth Cavalrymen, in Guadeloupe Canyon in 1884, the soldiers were eating their noon meal. The ranking sergeant was hit at the first fire. "He fell with a biscuit and a piece of meat in his mouth and did not move again," wrote W. B. Jett. A recruit sentry, who had talked of wanting to come to grips with the Apaches, ". . . immediately ran but was shot down . . . ," and one man ran into his tent and began to pray on his knees, but another soldier started him to cover in the rocks. "I was scared . . ." admitted Jett, and added that for the first time he was "afraid of going to hell." A few men managed to escape.

The demoralizing effect of surprise was increased when the troops had not been well drilled, trained, and disciplined. A scout in force was sent into the Lava Beds stronghold of the tenacious Modocs in April, 1873. Major Evan Thomas led the combined force of infantrymen and artillerymen acting as infantry. The detachment penetrated some distance into the weird rock formations, when sharpshooting Modocs suddenly opened fire from hidden positions.

> At the first fire [wrote observer Lieutenant Harry D. Moore], the troops were so demoralized that officers could do nothing with them. Capt. Wright was ordered with his company to take possession of a bluff, which would effectively secure their retreat, but Captain Wright was severely wounded on the way to the heights, and his company, with one or two exceptions, deserted him and fled like a pack of sheep; then the slaughter began.[9]

The ill-starred reconnaissance turned into a bloody fiasco, with four out of the five officers and twenty-four soldiers killed, and twenty-one men wounded or missing from a total strength of sixty-five men. When a strong detachment was finally able to fight its way through to the trapped soldiers, it found "dead and wounded, officers and men, in one confused heap. Almost all were shot several times—Major Thomas four times, Captain Wright three, . . . many of the bodies were stripped of their clothing."[10] Soldiers trained only for the parade ground were no match for the western warriors in guerrilla warfare.

The army's emphasis in the late 1870's and the 1880's on training soldiers for field service was inspired in large part from painful experiences in hard-fought Indian skirmishes and battles. Untrained regulars suffered heavily because they were not proficient riflemen and had not been schooled and conditioned to think for themselves in unexpected combat situations. Only men trained to withstand surprise attacks, and if necessary display a high degree of individual initiative in repelling lightning assaults, could stand firm and press home telling counter-attacks. Ambushed by a superior force of Apaches in 1885, well-trained

[9] To his family, from Camp in the Lava Beds . . . South Shore of Tule Lake, California, MS, Apr. 29, 1873, Order of the Indian Wars File No. 28, Washington, D.C.

[10] *Ibid.*

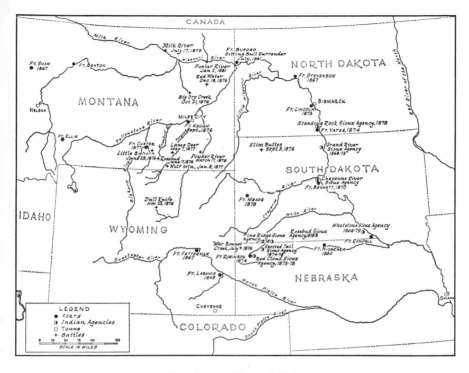

THE SIOUX WAR, 1876–81
The Soldier's Frontier

Eighth Cavalrymen reacted instantly, took cover and advanced against the war party, which was successfully driven off. "They proved their training," said Lieutenant S. W. Fountain.[11] Major E. V. Sumner, emphasizing the necessity for regulars to stand firm under surprise attack, stated that they must hold their ground, because the warriors would certainly torture and mutilate any dead or wounded soldiers abandoned in retreat.[12]

The vast majority of disciplined enlisted men displayed considerable steadfastness under attack, and not a few qualified as heroes. A detachment of about forty Fourth Infantrymen was attacked by a large war party, while on a reconnaissance out of Fort Laramie, in 1867. Corporal Cyrus Reed was hit in the wrist with an arrow, which severed the cords and main arteries.

> I was fast bleeding to death [stated Reed], when a little Irish boy . . . [Steven Murphy] came running to me . . . . "Be God Reed, you're entirely kilt, so ye are, I'll stay by you till Hell freezes over," and so he did. He loaded my gun for me alternately with his own, and I had to fire from a reclining position, as I was too weak to stand. I would have bled to death, but . . . Murphy corded my wrist with buckskin thongs. When the fight was over, they put me on a horse in front of my friend Murphy and got me to Fort Laramie . . . .

The detachment finally repelled the attack, and Reed fully recovered from his wound. He later slipped out of the post hospital to rejoin his company, when an expedition left the post for the Powder River country a few weeks later.

By Indian choice, pitched battles and toe-to-toe combat were the exception rather than the rule. Warriors were seldom so well armed as the regulars, nor well enough disciplined to fight troops successfully in large-scale, prolonged battles. The Indians were raiders, expert in the maneuvers of surprise, fast attack, and withdrawal before the enemy could retaliate effec-

[11] "Lieutenant Fountain's Fight With Apache Indians, Dec. 19, 1885," in *Proceedings, Order of Indian Wars, January 19, 1928*, 41.
[12] *Ibid.*

tively. War honors, or coups, were earned through skill. Bravery was essential, but not the tenacious courage required for hours and days of line-of-battle fighting or the defense of a position against persistent and repeated attacks. In such fighting horses, guns, and other loot were not easily obtained, and casualties were bound to be heavy. The loss of even a few warriors from a large band was a serious matter, and, whenever possible, casualties were avoided. A dozen men lost from a company of soldiers could easily be replaced with recruits, but a generation was required to replace Indian warriors killed in battle. Some soldiers misread the Indians' reluctance to stand and fight as a form of cowardice, an error in judgment that cost the lives of some who were so deceived. When the village and family of a hostile were threatened, he could stand and fight to the death rather than surrender, and when he thought success was sure he sometimes elected a fight to the finish.

Trained and disciplined to fight their enemies in nineteenth century, set-piece battles, many western regulars felt frustrated by the Indians' apparent unwillingness to stand up and fight. The men who did come to grips with the elusive enemy, however, in such battles as the Washita in 1868, the Lava Beds in 1873, the Little Bighorn and Rosebud in 1876, Clearwater, Big Hole, and Bear's Paw Mountain in 1877, the Apache fights in the 1880's, and Wounded Knee in 1890, soon learned that, although disinclined to engage in pitched battles, the western Indians could be fierce, brave, and deadly enemies in close combat.

When a big fight seemed to be imminent, rank and file regulars were eager to know their commanders' plans and what parts they might individually be expected to play. Scouts from Colonel John Gibbon's column returned to camp the night of August 8, 1877, reporting that Joseph's Nez Percés were camped only five miles away, on a small creek in the Big Hole basin of southwestern Montana. The Colonel held a council of war with his company officers, who returned to relate the plans to their men, explained Private Homer Coon. "Our command went to work getting ready," wrote Coon, ". . . our train was corralled, all of us left behind anything that would hinder us in a fight, such as overcoats, blankets, etc. . . . Every man was issued 100 rounds of ammunition. Most of the men left their blouses behind."[13] Under cover of night, the Seventh Infantrymen and their citizen allies moved to attack the hostiles at dawn the following morning. Realizing that the Nez Percés had already proved themselves formidable enemies, the men were keyed to a high pitch, and perhaps were more than a little apprehensive and nervous. Second Infantrymen approaching Pine Ridge Agency at night during the 1890 Sioux outbreak were cautioned not to light matches and to talk only in whispers. Even the Civil War veterans and other seasoned enlisted campaigners in the ranks, wrote Richard T. Burns, ". . . were getting pretty nervous before daybreak and began slipping cartridges into their rifles, and the officers warning them not to do so."

Preparing for what was expected to be heavy fighting, soldiers naturally were apprehensive. Two companies of Eighth Cavalrymen were waiting outside Sitting Bull's village, December 15, 1890, when gunfire signalled that the Indian police sent in to arrest the chief had met stiff resistance. Sitting Bull's warriors were known to be numerous and well armed. Word was passed for the soldiers to limber up their numbed trigger fingers and remove their overcoats, preparatory to advancing on the village.

> We were getting pretty low spirited and that didn't help us any, [wrote Private William G. Wilkinson]. Lieutenant Brooks said, "Captain, I think we could die just as well with our coats on." The Captain, who was inclined to profanity, said, "Well, God Damn it, keep them on!" This created a laugh, and raised our spirits.

[13] "The Outbreak of Chief Joseph," MS, Coe Coll., 2.

In this case, the Sioux chose to retreat from the village, and only a minor skirmish resulted.

By the middle seventies most experienced regulars had come to view the western warriors as worthy and capable foes, not to be underrated. Assembled to offer battle they were an awe-inspiring sight. General George Crook's men, camped at the bend of the Rosebud, June 17, 1876, were confronted by about fifteen hundred Sioux and Cheyenne braves, who had come out to fight the soldiers on ground of their own choosing, rather than allowing the troops to get close to their village. Viewed from the soldiers' camp along the stream, the north side of the valley fairly swarmed with painted and feathered hostiles. "All the Indians in the world seemed gathered right there in front of our troops and the hospital tent, where I was stationed," wrote Major H. S. Bryan, an enlisted man in 1876, "I saw enough Indians to last me the rest of my life."

Campaign-weary soldiers were often anxious to close with the enemy in a pitched battle, and had more esteem for commanders noted as successful attackers than for those they believed to be overcautious. In the summer of 1877 Trumpeter Ami Frank Mulford commented that he and his comrades "did not have much faith in our present commanders as being eager to lead us on a charge against any considerable body of hostile reds."[14] Soldiers ordered to the attack quite naturally were more likely to perform efficiently when led by competent officers who had the respect and confidence of their men. A confused, rattled officer could not very well lead his men in a successful assault. In April, 1873, First Cavalryman Charles B. Hardin, who retired as a major, witnessed an incident in which a noncommissioned man took the initiative in a successful counterattack and the rescue of two wounded officers, in spite of another officer's bungling. The two officers had gone out from their own lines to parley with the Modoc hostiles in the Lava Beds of northern California. The

[14] *Fighting Indians*, 64.

Modocs allowed them to approach close to the Indian positions, and then opened fire. The officers turned to escape, and disappeared from view in the rock labyrinth. Private Hardin and a sergeant saw where the officers had taken refuge, and told a third officer, who, apparently rattled and uncertain what to do, ordered the soldiers to counterattack in a different direction.

> The Sergeant was compelled to obey [wrote Hardin], but at the same time was determined to protect the attacked officers. Turning to me, he said, "You know where they are. I can not get away from this lunatic. You drop back and when clear run up this draw and hurry to that hog-back. The officers are down behind that."

Hardin followed directions, found one of the officers badly wounded, and was instrumental in having both taken back to safety. Many of the other soldiers in the unit left the confused officer and joined Hardin, when he cried out that he had found the injured men.

A soldier's account of one of the most publicized yet controversial attacks in Indian Wars history reveals an enlisted man's reactions. About to open the Battle of the Little Bighorn, Major Marcus A. Reno's three-company battalion rode toward the southern edge of the gigantic Indian encampment the afternoon of June 25, 1876. "Lieutenant Varnum, a very brave officer in command of the scouts, rode ahead of . . . [the] battalion," wrote Sergeant John Ryan, "he swung his hat around in the air and sung out to the men; 'Thirty days' furlough to the man who gets the first scalp,' We were very anxious for the furlough, but not so particular about the scalp."[15]

Reno's attack on the Sioux and Cheyenne village was ordered by the regiment's commander, Lieutenant Colonel George A. Custer, and the men in Reno's command expected to go into immediate action. Other offensive actions were not planned, however, but came as reactions to hostile initiative. Taken unaware

[15] "Custer's Last Fight," *Billings Times*, July 5, 1923.

by a strong party of Modocs, May 10, 1873, three companies of First Cavalrymen were fired on while in camp, from a range of only about one hundred yards.

> I saw a line of Modocs pop up their heads and fire a volley [wrote Charles B. Hardin], This at first caused some confusion. Men rolled over behind saddles and bundles of blankets—no covering however small being ignored, fastening on belts and pulling on boots under a hail of bullets . . . . There was a possibility of a panic, but this was happily averted by Sergeant Thomas Kelly of our troop, who sprang up and shouted, "God damn it, let's charge . . . .[16]

Responding with a will, the regulars drove off the Indians, killing five of them. The sergeant's prompt initiative led the men to an attack in the face of what could have been disaster. One almost hears the echo of another famous and profane battle cry in Hardin's account, that of Marine Sergeant Dan Dailey in Belleau Wood, forty-five years later, who rallied his men with the shout of "Come on you Sons of Bitches, do you want to live forever!"

A certain amount of confusion is always present in combat situations. Regulars attacking enemy Indians were sometimes jittery and personally unsure, since they were individually no more eager to stop a bullet than soldiers have ever been. Discipline, training, and *espirit de corps* were important in pressing home an attack in the face of Indian gunfire, and sometimes, the individual strength and determination of one or two enlisted men were vital factors. Advancing on a group of hostile Sioux during the Battle of Wounded Knee, Seventh Cavalryman Green A. Settle found himself beside a Sergeant Burnett. Settle was a second enlistment regular, and Wounded Knee was not the first place he had been under fire.

> We saw two [mounted] Indians coming after us [wrote

[16] "The Modoc War," *Proceedings, Order of Indian Wars, January 24, 1931*, 45f.

Settle], as we were alone, Burnett started to run, and I told him I wouldn't run, he says, "If you don't, I won't", so on they came . . . I dropped flat on the ground, raised my carbine, when I thought he [one of the braves] was at the proper range [I fired] . . . he threw up his hands and pitched forward and fell on the left side of his pony.[17]

Most regulars realized that to run from a fight was virtually suicide, and the bravery of even a single man may have turned the balance on more than one occasion.

It was in line-of-battle fighting that the regular rank and file proved their worth and showed to best advantage. Although they were usually less mobile than their Indian adversaries, their steadiness in pitched battles could seldom be matched by the savage warriors. "The group formations of the army made a bigger target," said Pawnee Scout Rush Roberts, "but army marksmanship was better and steadier." Formed in battle lines, infantry and dismounted cavalry deployed in single and sometimes double firing lines, with about three yards between individuals. Firing was sometimes directed by volleys, but was usually left up to the men doing the shooting. Rifles and carbines belched smoke, while Indian bullets hummed and splattered, and arrows zinged through the air if the hostiles were close enough. Company officers generally moved around among their men, advising them on their shooting and seeing that the unit maintained its assigned position. Describing the firing line established by Major Reno when he attacked the edge of the Indian camp in the valley of the Little Bighorn, Sergeant John Ryan explained how the men were deployed, and that "Lt. Hodgson walked up and down the line, encouraging the men to keep cool and fire low."[18]

Company officers were not always in firm control of their men in close combat situations, even when troops had been formed

[17] To Commander Ralph Donath, MS, Feb. 28, 1936, United Indian War Veterans, San Francisco, Calif.
[18] "Custer's Last Fight."

according to plan. When gunfire suddenly erupted from Big Foot's surrounded Sioux camp at Wounded Knee, officers and men alike were taken by surprise. "We were not expecting any trouble [in disarming the Indians] until it really started," wrote Private Jesse G. Harris.

> The only command I heard (and we were mounted) was "Prepare to dismount," [stated Private Clarence H. Allen]. We went off our horses—some on one side, some on the other. Every fourth man was supposed to take the horses back, but a lot of them didn't. The horses were simply turned loose and ran wherever they wanted to. As soon as we got off, we immediately laid down as quickly as we could and got a shot in. In the meantime, the two troops that had formed the hollow, dismounted, square [around the Indians] dropped, ran—did anything they could to get away.

Private Harris added that ". . . Captain Godfrey was telling us not to shoot the women and kids . . . things were getting pretty hot, and our 1st Sergeant said—'to hell with the women,' and Captain Godfrey gave the command to open fire."[19] In such combats, commented Private Robert C. O. Norman, "everyone was trying to look out for himself."

Although generally formed into battle lines for combat, the enlisted men were often ordered to advance as individual skirmishers, using whatever cover was available and firing at will. This was essentially the Indian method of fighting, except that company officers and noncommissioned men usually retained some measure of control over the soldiers. A strong band of Apaches was pursued for weeks by companies of the Third Cavalry in May and June, 1882, and was finally brought to bay in Big Dry Wash Canyon, Arizona, where the hostiles occupied very strong natural positions, July 17.

---

[19] Harris added that the sergeant was an old soldier named Gunther, who "had almost thirty years service, and I understood he had seen lots of Indian service."

We got there about daylight [related Sergeant Perley S. Eaton], and the battle started—it lasted all day until [a storm came up] about 6 o'clock at night . . . . the Indians firing from their fortifications and the soldiers shooting from the rim of the canyon, using what shelter they could from large trees, rocks, stumps and fallen trees . . . . we could usually draw their fire by sticking a hat out from behind a large tree, on a stick—that showed you where they were.

Some enlisted men displayed considerable initiative while fighting as individuals in extended skirmish lines. An incident of the Battle of Bear's Paw Mountain, described by Seventh Cavalryman Albert J. Davis, illustrates this aspect of combat. Joseph's Nez Percés had finally been brought to bay by General Nelson A. Miles's column, and were attacked by the troops September 30, 1877. The assault cost many army casualties, and fighting soon settled into a siege of the Indian position, with troops assigned to hold particular segments of the battle line surrounding the Nez Percés. One of Davis' comrades engaged in a duel with an Indian sharpshooter. "I saw him [the Indian] later, when a white flag went up," wrote Davis, "he was well punctured, the corporal had wormed over to him, scalped him and dragged back his fixings, also his gun, and this during hot action."[20]

The corporal mentioned in the previous incident must have been a good marksman himself, and also must have been endowed with considerable coolness and bravery under fire. Remaining in position on the firing line in combat was often a harrowing experience, especially for neophytes unaccustomed to the whine of bullets. Private John R. Nixon emphasized that few western regulars would ever forget "the first time on the firing line [when they] . . . heard the bullets buzzing like bees . . . [and] rubbed skin of the nose trying to duck in to the ground . . . ." Sixth Cavalryman Henry F. Ofdenkamp recalled that at the Battle of Cibicue Creek, Arizona, August 30, 1881,

[20] "Letter," *Winners of the West*, Vol. VI, No. 9 (1929), 3.

"... there were so many Indians [hostiles and mutinied Apache scouts] that the bullets put one in mind of a hail storm." At Major Reno's defense position in the Battle of the Little Bighorn, five miles south of where the Custer battalion was annihilated, the remaining seven companies of the Seventh Cavalry were pinned down by at least fifteen hundred hostile Sioux and Cheyennes who surrounded them. Most of the warriors remained at ranges of several hundred yards from the troops, but the concentration of bullets aimed at the soldiers was terrific, and most of the men sought whatever cover they could find. "Dan Neally ... ," said Private John Burkman, was "known [ever after] as Cracker Box Dan. He kept behind a cracker box at Reno Hill . . . . Captain Miles Moylan . . . was called Aparoho Michie, because he was laying behind an Aparoho [pack mule aparejo] all the time."[21]

The rank and file knew as well as their officers that to panic and run from a fight invited disaster. Disciplined, and, after 1880, battle-trained to some degree, western regulars as a rule stood firm in combat, but men inadequately supplied with ammunition or poorly armed lacked confidence in their ability to fight. When Captain Benteen's three fresh companies of Seventh Cavalry joined Reno's routed troopers on the bluffs just east of the Little Bighorn River, the afternoon of June 25, 1876, the newly arrived companies were ordered to divide their ammunition with Reno's men. The soldiers all knew they were involved in one of the biggest Indian battles in western history, and, wrote Lieutenant (later Major) Edward S. Godfrey, "I noticed that the [Benteen] men gave up their ammunition ungraciously."[22] Writing of his enlisted participation in actions against the Modocs in 1873, Major Charles B. Hardin related an excellent example of soldier reaction to being armed with inferior weapons. Advancing against the well-entrenched hostiles, wrote Hardin,

[21] O'Donnell, Statements by Burkman, MS, O'Donnell Coll., MSS 4–2.
[22] "Cavalry Fire Discipline," *Journal of the Military Service Institution,* Vol. XIX, No. 83 (1896), 256.

. . . all was going well with me until a shell stuck in my Sharp's carbine. I was almost in a panic until that shell was removed . . . . In another engagement . . . a certain troop, 1st Cavalry, armed with Spencer carbines, went into action with a bad lot of rim-fire cartridges. Several men of that troop told me that the failure of so many cartridges almost caused a panic, and would have caused a panic had it not been for the fact that other troops with them had Sharp's carbines that never missed fire.[23]

The heavy casualties of pitched battles sobered and shocked many regulars, especially when the dead and wounded were members of the same tightly-knit company, and many were sickened at the sight of blood and wounds. Though the vast majority of enemy bullets whistled harmlessly overhead, or kicked up dirt and rocks, some found billets in the bodies of soldiers. Arrows and the soft lead bullets used in the late nineteenth century made ghastly wounds. Their victims sagged in agony or lurched out of line to the ground. Holding an exposed position on the Seventh Cavalry defense perimenter in the Reno-Benteen portion of the Battle of the Little Bighorn, Jacob Adams was firing next to Corporal George Lell, when a hostile bullet crumpled the Corporal. "Poor George," said Adams, "was shot through the stomach and begged piteously for water . . . ." before he died the afternoon of June 26, 1876.[24] A few yards away, continued Adams, "A German recruit was lying down on the firing line when a heavy . . . ball struck him in the breast, passed entirely through his body, and came out of his back just above the hip."

A trumpeter shielded his captain with his own body at the Battle of Bear's Paw Mountain, wrote Seventh Cavalryman Ami Frank Mulford, and took a bullet in his side. He was quickly examined after dark by the surgeon and left for dead when his comrades withdrew to better positions. Early the next morning, he was seen to be still alive, and was brought in by his friends.

[23] C. B. Hardin to Godfrey, MS, Aug. 31, 1922, Bates Coll.
[24] McCormack, "Man Who Fought With Custer," *National Republic*, Vol. XXI, No. 11 (1934), 14.

"I'm the man you left on the ridge . . . ," he told the surgeon, "if you are going to probe my wound with a finger, as you did last night, please cut the nail off!"[25] Even combat wounds occasionally served as topics for grim humor. A Fifth Cavalryman, who had repeatedly boasted that no Indian could hit him, recklessly exposed himself to Cheyenne gunfire at the Dull Knife Fight, November 25, 1876, and was hit by a bullet. "Yes they can too, Captain—give 'em hell," cried the soldier as he fell.[26] The wound proved to be a slight one though, and the man was soon firing along with his comrades, whose cries of "Yes they can too," injected an element of humor in the hard-fought battle.

Few battles of the Indian Wars lasted longer than one day, but there were some notable exceptions, when troops were pinned down for longer periods, or when hostile warriors, unable to retreat, made an unusually stubborn resistance. The seven surviving companies of the Seventh Cavalry were besieged for twenty-four hours after the Custer battalion was annihilated at the Battle of the Little Bighorn. Colonel John Gibbon's men were kept under attack by the Nez Percés for two days at the Battle of the Big Hole, August 9 and 10, 1877. Gibbon's men were hastily dug in for defense against superior numbers of Nez Percés, when the hostiles fired the dry grass in an attempt to force the soldiers into the open. "Officers were praying the Lord for the wind to change," wrote Seventh Infantryman Homer Coon, "and some of us were praying also."[27] The fire failed to burn over the soldiers' positions, but the men were compelled to sustain repeated fusillades from the capable Nez Percé riflemen, who probably understood the manipulation and value of long-range leaf sights better than any other western Indians. The evening of the second day of the battle, the troops were nervous and jumpy lying in their rifle pits and trenches after two days of effective Nez Percé gunfire. "Sergeant Mautz . . . ," wrote

[25] *Fighting Indians*, 122.
[26] Wheeler, *Buffalo Days*, 142.
[27] "The Outbreak of Chief Joseph," MS, 5.

Homer Coon, "took out his mouth organ and commenced to play when someone recognized him and shouted, 'Shoot that German, do you want the Indians to get you next?' . . . . Poor Mautz, in going out of his hole to see someone, was shot and killed."[28]

General Miles's troops besieging the Nez Percés at Bear's Paw Mountain, Montana Territory, remained on the firing line for even longer periods than had Gibbon's men. After failing to capture the hostile camp in the initial attack, September 30, 1877, the troops took up positions around the Indians and dug in for prolonged combat. Company F. Fifth Infantry, was one of the units comprising Miles's force. Its commander, Captain Simon Snyder, in his diary entry of October 2 noted that his company was still in the line, "last night and today very disagreeable snow and sleet . . . with no covering at all, we all suffered." Firing continued sporadically until October 4, when Snyder's company was "relieved from the skirmish and picket line . . . . [after having been] continuously on duty since the morning of the 30th."[29]

Frontier regulars were rarely put to the test of extended combat, covering several days or weeks in relatively stable positions, but in the 1873 campaign of attrition against the tenacious Modocs the troops experienced a type of trench warfare similar to that of World War I. All through the spring of 1873, regulars inched their way forward, through the tortuous Lava Beds of northern California, constricting their lines around the Modocs. With inadequate manpower and supplies, units were compelled to hold portions of the line for extensive periods. Describing the effects of such warfare on the rank and file of the Twenty-first Infantry, Lieutenant Harry D. Moore wrote on April 29, 1873, that it had been ". . . just exactly two weeks, as shown by the *Farmers' and Mechanics' Almanac*, and a year and a half as indicated by the appearance of my regiment," since the Twenty-first had gone into the lines.[30] As in stand-up, pitched battles, the

28 *Ibid.*
29 Snyder, Diary, Oct. 4, 1877, MS.
30 To his family, MS, Apr. 29, 1873.

regulars' qualities of steadiness and endurance showed to good advantage in the ultimate defeat and dislodging of the Modocs.

Although often unskilled in the guerrilla type warfare waged by the western Indians, and usually no match for the hostiles in mobility, disciplined regulars proved themselves to be valiant defenders of the many small forts, Indian agencies, and isolated stations they garrisoned. The western warriors' distaste for making frontal assaults on even a small number of well-prepared enemies had a great deal to do with the soldiers' successes. Only disciplined fighters can be brought to launch repeated, steady attacks, with the certainty of sustaining some casualties, against a foe they know will remain firm and deadly to the last. The hostiles of the western mountains and plains did not have the regimented discipline required for this kind of fighting.

Only thirty men and a sergeant garrisoned the Ponca agency, thirty miles south of Fort Randall, Dakota Territory, in 1875. The soldiers prepared breastworks of piled cordwood, and mounted an old muzzle-loading cannon, filled with stones and scrap iron, in anticipation of attacks by the powerful Sioux. When the hostiles attacked in large numbers, the awesome boom of the cannon and their realization that well-armed and supplied soldiers were defending the government-assigned headquarters of their Ponca enemies deterred the Sioux from pressing home a mass assault. Contenting themselves with long-range firing and harmless individual forays and feats of daring, the Indians refrained from committing themselves to close-range action and probably suffered few if any losses. Only two of the soldiers were slightly wounded. Hundreds of shots were fired by both sides, wrote John E. Cox. "Many people," explained Cox, "then and since, did not understand the slight casualties that usually accompanied Indian fighting," because they did not understand the Indians' concepts and methods of warfare.[31]

The swarms of Sioux, Cheyennes, and Arapahos, lurking around Fort Phil Kearny, Dakota Territory, during its occu-

[31] "Soldiering," *North Dakota History*, Vol. VI, No. 1 (1931), 64.

pancy from 1866 to the summer of 1868, never actually attacked the palisaded fort. Well built for defense, the loopholed block-houses and walls were too formidable for the hostiles, although they vastly outnumbered the garrison. To keep the Sioux and their allies at a distance, and to facilitate marksmanship, Colonel Henry B. Carrington ordered the placing of slender poles, tipped with white cloth, in the immediate vicinity of the fort at meas-ured ranges, ". . . so that soldiers on the parade ground, in the block-houses, or on the stockade sentry platform would know exactly when an Indian would come within accurate firing dis-tances . . . ."[32] Eighteenth Infantryman S. S. Peters said that these preparations instilled self-confidence in the soldiers.

Readiness, on the part of a small unit of regulars, to defend a position against hostiles many times their own number was the responsibility of the senior officer or noncommissioned man present. A competent and experienced officer knew that setting up defenses not only strengthened the troops' position, but added greatly to the soldiers' psychological well-being and de-termination to fight. On campaign in the Ute country of Colo-rado, in the fall of 1880, Private Wallace E. Bingham's nineteen-man company of the Twenty-third Infantry was faced with the imminent possibility of attack by a force of Utes estimated to number about five hundred warriors. A reckless white drunkard had wantonly shot a Ute, and the Indians took up positions to attack the ranch where the soldiers were camped with the bull train they were escorting. Many of the enlisted men were despondent over the prospects, related Bingham, so "our Cap-tain had all the extra rifles gotten out, cleaned, and inspected. We had with us 10,000 rounds of ammunition. It was opened . . . ."[33] "It sure looked like war," said Bingham, but the men were prepared for it and keyed up to fight. When a cavalry column, commanded by General Ranald S. Mackenzie, arrived late that night, a fight was averted.

[32] "Service Account," in Carrington, *My Army Life*, 110.
[33] "Early Days on the Frontier," MS, 100.

Defense preparations often proved to be significant factors in repelling forays of warriors. Third Infantrymen garrisoning Camp Supply, Indian Territory, from 1872 to 1874, sustained repeated raids, and the men became accustomed to maintaining a state of readiness. "Contact with the Indians," wrote Private H. Harbers, "was frequent, and we would lie down behind the windows with cartridges strewn over the floor," ready to hand at all times. Sentries, continued Harbers, were subject to persistent sneak attacks by prowling enemies. Describing one instance, when a wounded sentry dislpayed remarkable coolness and determination, Harbers wrote:

> At 8:20 I went to the farthest end of my beat to exchange the situation [with the adjoining guard]. . . . When I got at No. 3 Post, Humpy Brown did not report [and I hurried to rouse the corporal of the guard]. . . . When the grand round came, the officer in charge asked me what was the matter. They hunted in the haystack and found Brown with two arrows in his neck. They asked him why he did not call out, and he said, "Oh, I was waiting for the man [Indian] to show himself before seeing me— I was going to get him!"[34]

"Humpy" Brown symbolized the toughest type of western Regular. He recovered from his wounds, and, except for his brief mention in a comrade's obscure relation of frontier service, disappeared into the anonymity of the Regular Army.

The ability of troops to suffer reverses in combat and still retain their discipline and fighting qualities is one of the severest tests to which a military unit can be subjected. Regulars who were ambushed or surrounded by superior numbers depended as much on their mettle as soldiers as they did on their weapons. A unit fighting for its life had to maintain discipline, sometimes at the forceful insistence of its officers. Faced by large numbers of Sioux riflemen, posted on high ground surrounding them on three sides, companies of the Seventh Cavalry deployed near

[34] "Service Account," in Ashburn, *Medical Department*, 102.

Drexel Mission, White Clay Creek, South Dakota, on December 30, 1890, were engaged in a fierce fire fight. Private Jesse G. Harris and a few other D Troop men were sent back to the pack train to bring up reserve ammunition. Returning with the heavy, thousand-round boxes, wrote Harris, "I troop Captain Nowland [Nowlan] asked me where we were going, and the men carrying the boxes told him [that] Captain Moylan [had] ordered them to take it to A Troop—he [Nowlan] ordered us to deliver it to him—the men hesitated—the Captain pointed his .45 Colt at them, and they left the boxes . . . . we found out afterwards that half his men had only one round of ammunition."

When regulars were pinned down by superior opposing forces, most of the rank and file held fast and fought as ordered, but the possibilities of defeat sometimes unnerved inexperienced men or soldiers who had been injured or had succumbed to exhaustion. In a desperate situation after their repulse from the Nez Percé village at the Battle of the Big Hole, officers and men alike realized that they could not stand against a determined assault. "Some of the wounded covered up their heads and expected to be killed," wrote Lieutenant Charles A. Woodruff the day after the battle, "I got my two revolvers, said my prayers, . . . and determined to kill a few Indians before I died . . . ."[35]

An even more crucial situation faced Major Reno's three Seventh Cavalry companies driven in retreat back across the Little Bighorn after their abortive attack on the Indian encampment. All semblance of order was lost, as the soldiers rode headlong for the river, jumped their mounts into the stream and urged them up the east bank. Warriors mixed in with the troopers, and the scene was one of almost complete chaos. Trying to relate his part in the retreat, Private William F. Morris said,

[35] Edgar I. Stewart, editor, "Letters from the Big Hole [by Lieutenant Charles A. Woodruff, Seventh Infantry]," *Montana Magazine of History*, Vol. II, No. 4 (1952), 55. Of a total command of 182 men, Colonel John Gibbon's troops and citizen volunteers sustained casualities of 61 killed and wounded, Aug. 9 and 10, 1877.

I remember saying to Tom Gordon [as they struggled up the east bank bluffs], "It was pretty hot down there!" He answered, "You'll get used to it shavetail [recruit]." As he spoke, there came a rain of bullets . . . Gordon fell dead with a bullet in the brain, Bill the Tinker was shot through the throat and fell from his horse. I was shot through the left breast, by a big Indian close to me, but managed to stay on my horse and reached the top of the bluff . . . .[36]

Halted at the summit of the bluffs, Reno's exhausted men were formed into ragged defense lines and commenced firing on the enemy. Most of Reno's casualties in the opening phase of the battle fell during the disorganized, undisciplined retreat.

The retreat from the advance position at Wier Point, also during the Battle of the Little Bighorn, could have occasioned further heavy losses. Actually more of a withdrawal to better positions, the move could have been disastrous had not discipline been maintained. The appearance of rapidly increasing numbers of hostiles, concentrating gunfire on the soldier flank and rear, could have resulted in panic. Major Edward S. Godfrey, a lieutenant in 1876, stated that he kept control over some of his men only by threatening to shoot them, and that when the order was passed allowing every man to get back as best he could, ". . . some of the men started off like sprinters."[37] However, many troopers were not stampeded, and most held their assigned places in line during the retreat. Some exhibited the cool steadiness that was the hallmark of the western regular. Describing his part in the retreat, Captain Winfield Scott Edgerly commented on the conduct of a Private Saunders.

When I handed my carbine to Private Saunders, I noticed that he had a broad grin on his face, altho' he was sitting in a perfect shower of bullets. I didn't have time to question him then, but

[36] Clipping, no source indicated, but with a pencil inscription, "1913," Package No. 35, Custer Coll.

[37] "Cavalry Fire Discipline," 258.

the next day after the firing ceased I asked him what he was laughing at at such a time. He replied, "I was laughing to see what poor shots those Indians were; they were shooting too low and their bullets were spattering dust like drops of rain." I never saw a cooler man under fire than Saunders.[38]

Edgerly made no mention of having to threaten his men with a gun to retain discipline, and even saw humor in the fact that a fat veteran soldier lost control of his horse during the retreat.[39]

The difficulty of, and necessity for maintaining order, when carrying out a withdrawal under enemy fire, was understood by most of the regular rank and file. To turn tail and run from an Indian fight often meant irretrievable defeat. Plains Indians, emboldened by the sight of an enemy leaving the field in panic, would usually take full advantage of the situation. Describing a withdrawal from exposed positions during the Drexel Mission fight, December 30, 1890, Private Clarence H. Allen explained that

> The troops were formed into line. I was on the right of our squad and the guide was in the center. I reversed my carbine, holding the butt in the air to march. Some of the boys were inclined to walk fast enough to get out of line, and when one would, you could hear some of the good ones give him a good cussing out, to stay in line.

The essence of the regular's discipline, training, and combat value is capsuled in Private Allen's last phrase, "to stay in line."

[38] "A Narrative of the Battle of the Little Big Horn," MS, Package No. 11, Custer Coll., 8.

[39] *Ibid.*, 9. "We had in our troop a corpulent old tailor known throughout the regiment as Jimmy Wynn, who was riding an old horse, blind of one eye, and ordinarily very quiet. The instant he mounted [when ordered to withdraw], his horse started for the rear at full speed and one of the most laughable sights I ever saw was Jimmy pulling at the reins with both hands, his carbine dangling [from his shoulder sling] by his side, a veritable fat John Gilpin. He wasn't able to stop until he reached the horses of the rest of the command."

14.

Cowardice, Heroism, and the Aftermath of Combat

IN RECENT YEARS the fact has been recognized that some men in almost every military unit are psychologically and emotionally unfit for combat, or become so after prolonged stress. More than a generation after the Indian Wars, men who broke under the strain of action were described as "shell-shocked," and in modern times the personality disintegration occurring among soldiers is called "combat fatigue." Such terms had no place in the army's lexicon in the time of the Indian Wars, when men still conceived of personal combat conduct in such terms as "bravery," "gallantry," and "heroism." Any unacceptable conduct in action was likewise lumped under the heading of "cowardice," regardless of circumstances. Regular officers and soldiers were expected to fight hard and well, in spite of overwhelming odds, hunger, thirst, fear, or exhaustion. Late nineteenth-century regular army men understood this, and the vast majority of them did their best to perform as required. The term "coward" was probably applied to some men, who under present conditions, would be sent to rest camps or hospitals rather than stigmatized.

The percentage of combat failures was smaller among western regulars, all of whom were volunteers, than is usually the case in mass armies composed mainly of conscripts. A few rank and file regulars, however, proved to lack the qualities required in combat with hostile Indians. Company B, Second Cavalry, and a party of Indian scouts attacked a strong Arapaho and Cheyenne band, at Snake Mountain in north-central Wyoming, July 4, 1874. The hostiles fought stubbornly to hold their village, and only "two or three" soldiers failed to conduct themselves acceptably.[1] Writing of General George Crook's 1876 infantry and cavalry column, correspondent John F. Finerty stated that although the men expected to face the most powerful array of Indians they had ever confronted, they seemed prepared to do so, and that he had encountered only one enlisted man who could be classified as a "constitutional coward."[2] This soldier's superiors apparently recognized the fact, for he was one of a small number of men detailed to remain as camp guards when the command pushed north into hostile territory, just before the Battle of the Rosebud. Finerty described the man as delighted and greatly relieved to be left behind, stating unashamedly, "They'll never catch me in this fix again, if I have to desert when I get back to the railroad, if I ever do."[3] He was not the only regular to admit a reluctance to fight the western warriors. In 1867 a number of Third Cavalrymen, expecting to be posted for night guard while in camp at the Cimarron Crossing of the Santa Fe Trail, reported themselves on the sick list to escape the dangerous duty, to which W. T. Parker was assigned.

Even trained and disciplined soldiers sometimes became

[1] Brigadier General F. U. Robinson, "The Battle of Snake Mountain," *Military Affairs*, Vol. XIV, No. 2 (1950), 98.
[2] *War-path and Bivouac*, 113.
[3] *Ibid.*

frightened and "stampeded" when surprised. While on campaign in southern Colorado in 1880, a Twenty-third Infantry corporal abandoned his wood-cutting detail and ran to the main command shouting that Indians had attacked and despoiled the wood camp. A detachment was ordered to relieve the woodcutters, explained Wallace E. Bingham, and ascertained that only two Indians had surprised a single soldier and robbed him of his cartridges. The corporal was placed under arrest and later reduced to the ranks for deserting his men.

In pitched battle against heavy odds, a few regular enlisted men "skedaddled" when overcome with fear, though if detected by their comrades, their lives were made miserable in consequence. Private John Burkman in his account of the desperate defense by the seven surviving companies of the Seventh Cavalry, after Custer and the other five companies had been wiped out, related that "Billy Blake, a private, made believe he was hurt and lay with the wounded at Reno Hill. Fact was he was not hurt. He was very much ashamed of it afterward and could not stand the scorn of his comrades and joined another company."[4] On the other hand, continued Burkman, both he and Trumpeter Penwell, who had been close to Lt. Edward S. Godfrey on the defense lines at Reno Hill, refuted that officer's statement, in a speech to the officers at Fort Custer in 1886, that he had been compelled to threaten troopers with his revolver to keep them from leaving their positions. Frontier regulars were as proud of their honor as their commissioned superiors were of theirs.

Cowardice on the part of a soldier was considered by his comrades to be on the same repugnant and loathsome level as stealing from his mates in the company. But, if the rank and file believed an officer was a coward the results were serious and could even be disastrous. An officer who lost the respect and confidence of his men, because of conduct they interpreted as evidence of cowardice, could not be an effective combat leader. Explaining

[4] O'Donnell, Statements of Burkman, MS, O'Donnell Collection, Custer Battlefield National Monument.

his reasons for having had ". . . no use for [Lieutenant William W. Cooke] . . . as an officer or a man," veteran Anthony C. Rallya, Seventh Cavalry, 1866–71, stated that he had been assigned as one of Cooke's sharpshooters, just prior to the Battle of the Washita, November 27, 1868. "When the battle . . . farely began," wrote Rallya, "we did not see anything more of Cooke until the fight was over."[5] Commenting on the quality of the Second Cavalry officers he served under in the early eighties, Private James B. Wilkinson stated that his captain was a drunkard, but was still well thought of by his men. However, a Captain Norwood of L Company, stated Wilkinson, was known among his men as a coward, and that ". . . he asked his men to build a wall of stones around him during a skirmish!"

A story current in the early eighties among the rank and file of the Third Cavalry, was of a more serious incident in which the cowardice of an officer cost the life of one of his men. Several companies of Third Cavalry were hotly engaged with a strong force of Apaches, at the Big Dry Wash, Arizona, in July, 1882. The hostiles were replying accurately to the soldiers' fire, and every trooper sought some form of cover from which to fire. Sergeant Perley S. Eaton wrote that

> . . . at the height of the battle, a soldier from one of the companies was shooting from a large tree, when the captain of his troop came along to where the soldier was and pushed him from the tree and took shelter there himself—the soldier was shot dead.

Whether the story was entirely true or not, the soldiers' attitude toward the officer in question must have been heavily influenced by what they believed to have been his display of funk.

Barracks room tales accusing officers of cowardice were frequently erroneous, and can be attributed in part to enlisted malice, or hatred of an unpopular superior. Not all such tales, however, were groundless. General George Crook's autobiography tells of one officer, who, Crook said, allowed a band of hostile

5 To Dustin, MS, Oct. 13, 1930, Correspondence Files, Dustin Coll.

Apaches to escape in 1871, and was later court-martialed in 1876 for ". . . misbehavior before the enemy in an engagement with a band of Sioux and Cheyennes," March 17, 1876.[6] A detailed account of an inexperienced officer's failure was given by Captain R. G. Carter.

> Once a detail was sent out scouting under Lt. ———. They were attacked by Indians outnumbering the men two to one. This officer *ran—unqualifiedly ran*, begging his men to follow and "not fire a shot for fear of angering the Indians." [Sergeant] Charlton rode beside him and said: Lt., if we stop and make a stand they will run." "No! no! we can do nothing but try to outrun them," ——— said. Charlton then *took* command and also chances of being tried for disobedience of orders, made a stand with the men, who were more experienced in such warfare than this young untried officer, and drove the Indians off. This officer came to him afterwards and asked him not to say anything about this at the post, and Charlton told me that he never did.[7]

For every authenticated instance of an enlisted or commissioned man's cowardice in the face of the enemy, there are dozens of documented accounts of exceptionally courageous conduct. Bravery, however, is an abstract and relative quality, defying any single, all-embracing definition. What some might term bravery in a given situation others might very possibly, and honestly, not extol as noteworthy courage. Steadfastness in combat, regardless of circumstances, was expected as a matter of course from United States regulars in the late nineteenth century, but outstandingly firm devotion to duty, as exemplified in the fight to the death by Lieutenant Colonel George A. Custer's five companies of the Seventh Cavalry, June 25, 1876, was universally recognized and lauded. Requested to write a short biographical sketch of her dead husband, for a publication sponsored by his Civil War unit at reunions in the late nineties, Mrs. George W. Smith readily complied, and highly praised the in-

[6] *Crook, Autobiography,* 164f.
[7] *Old Sergeant's Story,* 92.

itiative and bravery of her late husband's colored Ninth Cavalry regulars. Lieutenant Smith's twenty-five man detachment was ambushed in Guerillo Canyon, New Mexico, by a war party of sixty to eighty Apaches. The Lieutenant was killed shortly after the fight began, about ten o'clock in the morning, but, wrote Mrs. Smith, "his command continued to fight, and by their bravery without a commander (God bless them) saved the body . . . a braver set of men never lived."[8] By the time the Apaches withdrew, about half-past two in the afternoon, the soldiers had lost three killed and three wounded, a casualty rate amounting to twenty-five per cent of the detachment.

Another kind of courage was highly commended by General Alfred Terry, in Field Orders No. 5, Department of Dakota, July 26, 1876. After Indian scouts had returned to the General's camp with dispatches he had ordered sent to General Crook, three enlisted Seventh Infantrymen volunteered to undertake the hazardous hundred-mile journey, through country known to be occupied by bands of Sioux and Cheyennes numbering at least two thousand warriors. Privates William Evans, Benjamin F. Stewart, and James Bell not only accomplished their mission, but made the return trip with Crook's reply as well.[9]

Many instances of initiative and bravery in combat were singled out for commendation. The leadership and courage of Sergeant Conrad at the Battle of the Washita were vividly recalled by Major Edward S. Godfrey in his essay on "Cavalry Fire Discipline" written almost thirty years later in 1896. The May 14, 1880, defense of Tularosa, New Mexico, against about one hundred of Victorio's Apaches, was organized and led by Sergeant George Jordan, whose leadership of a twenty-four-man detachment of Ninth Cavalry troopers won him the Congressional Medal of Honor.[10] Major General Philip H. Sheridan gave official recog-

[8] "Captain Geo. W. Smith," in *Proceedings of the Army of the Cumberland, 14th Corps,* [1894–97], 125.

[9] General Field Orders No. 5, Dept. of Dakota, Camp at Mouth of Big Horn River, July 26, 1876, MS, Nat. Arch.

Four Twelfth Infantrymen rehearsing
for a variety show, with Indian policemen and civilians,
at Fort Yates, North Dakota, about 1890.

PRIVATE JOHN R. NIXON
of the Seventh Cavalry, in the field service dress of the late 1880's and
early 1890's, at Fort Riley, Kansas. Private Nixon had recently returned from the Sioux War of 1890–91, where he participated in the
tragic fight at Wounded Knee.

nition to another sergeant's combat performance in 1868. Announcing the noncommissioned officer's exploit, Sheridan said:

> The Major General . . . is pleased to notice the gallant and meritorious conduct displayed by Sergeant Edward Glass, 3rd U. S. Cavalry, and four enlisted men of Co. H, 3rd U. S. Cavalry, while patrolling the Rio Tularosa, New Mexico, in resisting and finally repelling an attack made upon them by a body of Indians numbering about two hundred. The persistent energy of Sergeant Glass in returning and renewing the fight, after having twice been driven from his position . . . resulting in the defeat of the Indians . . . was very creditable, and is warmly commended.[11]

One of the most outstanding feats of perseverance and brave tenacity in combat was that credited to Sergeant T. B. Glover, Second Cavalry. Early in February, 1880, the sergeant took a fifteen man detachment from Fort Keogh to pursue a band of marauding Sioux. Temperatures lower than fifty degrees below zero were recorded at the fort during the time the detail was out, and the sergeant's men were further hampered by earlier heavy snowfalls. Pushing ahead, Glover found the hostiles in camp and promptly attacked and surrounded them, February 7. Unable to press home a frontal assault, the sergeant sent one of his men back forty miles to the fort for help, while he and his twelve remaining men laid siege to the Indian camp. Captain Simon Snyder's Company F, Fifth Infantry left Fort Keogh, mounted, at ten o'clock the night of the seventh and arrived at Glover's position by eight o'clock the morning of February 8, to find the sergeant grimly maintaining his line around the hostiles.[12] The captain was so impressed with Glover's achievement

[10] *Deeds of Valor,* II, 273–76.

[11] General Orders No. 16, Fort Leavenworth, Kansas, May 20, 1868, *Index of General Orders, Dept. of the Missouri, 1868.*

[12] Snyder, Diary, Feb. 7 and 8, 1880, MS. *Army Registers* record that Sergeant Glover was an officer during the Spanish-American War and during World War I.

that he ordered the sergeant to accept the Indian's surrender, rather than taking the credit himself as senior officer present. General Nelson A. Miles rewarded Glover and his detail by relieving them of all post duty for a month, and the sergeant later received the Congressional Medal of Honor.

In an almost hopeless situation, the bravery of a wounded enlisted man was credited with saving the lives of the other wounded, after a disastrous Modoc ambush in the spring of 1873. An officer who was a member of the rescue force that found the heaps of dead and wounded twenty-four hours later, wrote:

> One wounded man—wounded in the arms, both forearms broken—in the back and the heel, kept all the Indians from the wounded men, and prevented them from mutilating the bodies of the officers. A brave man! and deserving of substantial notice by the government.[13]

Courageous actions were not always motivated by purely selfless drives, and men involved in them were at times extremely keyed up. The wounded were suffering terribly for lack of water the second day of Colonel John Gibbon's defense against the victorious Nez Percés at the Battle of the Big Hole, August 9, 1877. Colonel Gibbon called for volunteers, to make their way over the one hundred yards between the trenches and the sparkling mountain stream below them.

> Charlie Hines, Ed Welsh and myself [Private Homer Coon] finally undertook it. I want to say it was not entirely on account of the wounded that we volunteered—we were so nearly famished ourselves for a drink that we were thinking of ourselves too and the beautiful stream we could see glistening down below. . . . I never realized before how much those [four] canteens held; it seemed as though they never would fill up. . . . as thirsty as I was . . . I actually forgot in my excitement to get a drink for myself.[14]

[13] Moore, to his family, MS, Apr. 29, 1873, Order of Indian Wars File No. 29.
[14] "The Outbreak of Chief Joseph," MS, Coe Coll.

All the water was given to the wounded back in the trenches, and Private Coon never got any of the water for which he had risked his life.

A similar act, on the part of Ninth Cavalry First Sergeant Henry Johnson brought him the Congressional Medal of Honor for his conduct at the fiercely fought Battle of Milk River, against the Utes in Colorado, October 1, 2, and 3, 1879. The twenty-nine-year-old, Virginia-born Negro ". . . voluntarily left a sheltered position [the night of October 2] and under heavy fire at close range made the rounds of the pits to instruct the guards, and also on the next night fought his way to the river and back to bring water to the wounded."[15]

No well-developed and graded system for officially recognizing enlisted men's heroism existed during the late nineteenth century. Within the company and regiment, a soldier's courage and gallantry were frequently rewarded by promotion to or within the noncommissioned ranks. Until long after the last Indian War, the only medal authorized for heroism was the Congressional Medal of Honor, established during the Civil War. Medals of Honor were not awarded frequently, but, because there were no other decorations, some were conferred on enlisted regulars for heroism in action against hostile Indians that today would probably be withheld in favor of lesser medals. From 1865 through the early 1890's, a wide variety of courageous acts were rewarded with the Medal of Honor.[16] The record of heroism in offensive and defensive action, rescuing of wounded

---

[15] *Deeds of Valor*, II, 258.

[16] Adjutant General, *Decorations*. The Medal of Honor was awarded during the Indian Wars for such combat heroism as: showing combat initiative and rescuing wounded men under intense close-range fire; securing water for the wounded, outside the lines; showing conspicuous gallantry as a sharpshooter; bringing body through hostile lines, bringing up reserve ammunition, and rallying soldiers in exposed positions; declining to leave the line after being wounded, and continuing to fight bravely; capturing war parties, of Sioux, larger than the capturing detachment; carrying dispatches alone for long distance through hostile territory.

comrades, and other displays of exceptional courage by enlisted regulars have significantly enriched the American military tradition.

Recognizing the need for some method of rewarding combat bravery that deserved high commendation but was not quite up to the standards of the Medal of Honor, Congress authorized the awarding of Certificates of Merit by the Act of March 3, 1874. These certificates were issued only for heroism in action, sworn to by a soldier's commanding officer, on the part of an enlisted regular "in good standing." Unlike the Medal of Honor, Certificates of Merit entitled their holders to two dollars extra pay per month. Only fifty-nine of the elaborate parchment certificates were awarded from 1874 to 1891. Their holders seem to have possessed qualities that make good, long-term regular soldiers, for twenty-three of the fifty-nine men were still in the Army in 1891. The significance of the Certificate of Merit can best be measured by the fact that by the Act of March 5, 1934, men who had received them years before were to be issued the Distinguished Service Cross, upon application to the War Department.

Many soldiers who deserved them were not rewarded with a Certificate of Merit or the Medal of Honor for lack of firsthand corroboration by a commissioned officer, and the inevitable variance of opinion as to what constituted outstanding bravery. Moreover, some deeds for which the medal was recommended were not fully and exactly reported, and, in some cases, men who believed they should have been recommended, but were not, felt that they had been cheated. Following the annual dinner of the Order of Indian Wars, February 23, 1935, the toastmaster called on General David L. Brainerd, who had participated in several Indian fights as a Second Cavalry enlisted man, from 1876 to 1884, to regale the members with an anecdote or two from his personal experiences. The old General cordially complied, and told the story of an unnamed private, during an attack on a hostile village. The soldier, a comrade of General Brainerd's,

. . . was riding an outlaw horse which appeared to be running away, dashed through the village firing his revolver left and right. On reaching the other side of the village, the horse, apparently sensing the absence of other horses of the troop, turned back and dashed through the village again. In the meantime, the soldier had . . . reloaded his revolver, and on the return dash through the village repeated the random firing. For his apparent display of bravery the soldier was recommended for the Medal of Honor.[17]

Though this Second Cavalryman was unwillingly thrust into the midst of the hostiles, his presence of mind and pluck cannot be denied. A soldier who was not recommended, but who believed he merited the Medal of Honor or a Certificate of Merit, was Seventh Cavalry Sergeant John Ryan. By his own statements, which are substantially corroborated by other accounts, Ryan played a conspicuous part in the defense of Reno Hill at the Battle of the Little Bighorn. He took his discharge shortly after the battle, in 1876, after ten years in the regiment, because he believed he had been purposely slighted by the Seventh's surviving senior officers, Major Marcus A. Reno and Captain Frederick W. Benteen. Sergeant Ryan had been court-martialed and reduced to the ranks by Benteen several months before the Battle. Because Custer reinstated him, Ryan felt certain that Benteen had developed a grudge against him that kept the captain from recommending him for the Medal of Honor.[18] In an army composed of average men, personalities no doubt have always to some extent influenced recommendations for honors and decorations.

Sergeant Ryan later developed animosities toward the two officers he believed had cheated him of his medal after the Little Bighorn, but it is safe to assume that his first reaction to the withdrawal of the hostiles was one of intense relief, followed by emotional letdown. The Sioux and Cheyennes abandoned their attack the afternoon of June 26, 1876, when they learned of the

[17] *Proceeding, Order of Indian Wars, February 23, 1935,* 16.
[18] To Mrs. Custer, MS, Sept. 6, 1909, Package No. 35, Custer Coll.

proximity of the Terry-Gibbon column. General Terry arrived at the Reno Hill defense site early the following morning, bringing the news that Custer and the other five companies of the Seventh Cavalry had been annihilated, five miles down stream. In a letter to his mother, Dr. Holmes O. Paulding, Colonel Gibbon's surgeon, described the survivors:

> All the men were—when I got there [to the defense area]—in spite of their hardships and sufferings, cheerful and apparently as cool and nonchalant as though nothing much had happened and though the announcement of Custer's fate fell on them like an unexpected shock, they soon rallied. The fact is that now we are lying quietly in camp. They appear to be just beginning to realize what it all means.[19]

One of Gibbon's Seventh Infantrymen commented that after the relief troops and the rescued Seventh Cavalry troopers had set up camp, along the west bank of the Little Bighorn, "the remainder of the 7th Cavalry . . . were about all in, most of the officers and men I saw would sit in front of their dog tents with drawn faces thinking of their loved ones at home."[20] Private John Burkman, himself a Little Bighorn survivor, later remarked that the men were extremely nervous, and that when they rendezvoused with the steamer *Far West*, on the Big Horn River, June 29 and 30, many of the men sought emotional release and equilibrium in drinking what whisky and Jamaica ginger they could obtain on the boat.[21]

Nine years before the Little Bighorn disaster and the subsequent relief of the Reno-Benteen survivors, a detachment of Twenty-seventh Infantrymen experienced a similar but more spectacular rescue. About ninety miles south of what would later be the Little Bighorn battlefield, on August 2, 1867, fewer than forty men defended themselves, in a corral of dismounted wagon

[19] Hudnutt, editor, "New Light on the Little Big Horn," *Field Artillery Journal*, Vol. XXVI, No. 4 (1936), 353.

[20] Coon, "Sioux Campaign," MS, Coe Coll.

[21] O'Donnell, Statements of Burkman, MS, O'Donnell Coll.

boxes, against a horde of at least one thousand Sioux, Cheyennes, and Arapahos. Detailed to guard a wood camp, five miles from beleaguered Fort Phil Kearny, the small detachment was well prepared for action when it began in the morning, but the loss of a lieutenant and five soldiers killed and two more men wounded had reduced the defenders to fewer than thirty men by mid-afternoon, and the strain of prolonged combat was beginning to tell on the survivors.

> Suddenly the Indians on the Big Hill moved swiftly down into the valley of Big Piney [Creek]. The boom of the big gun [field howitzer] was heard, and again, and again, and towards the east we could see the glorious caps on the heads of our comrades in the long skirmish line. We jumped to our feet; we yelled; we threw our caps in the air and hugged each other and some of us cried. The strain was over![22]

A member of the relief force sent out from the fort, Private William A. Murphy, wrote that the men inside the wagon box corral ". . . were a hard lot to look at. The day was hot and the sun was beating down on them. The smoke from their guns had colored their faces and they looked as though they had used burnt cork on their faces."[23] Virtually beyond hope, these men had the emotional experience of condemned men reprieved while standing on the gallows waiting for the trap to drop.

After the last shot was fired, and the weary soldiers were allowed a short interval of rest, regular survivors of an Indian fight often had duties as grim and gruesome as those facing combat troops of earlier and more recent times. Like other soldiers they were painfully impressed by the sight of badly wounded friends and comrades collapsed awkwardly in death and sometimes grotesquely mutilated. Recalling his reactions to the carnage resulting from the Battle of Wounded Knee, Eighth Infantryman

[22] "Sergeant Gibson's Address [Wagon Box Fight location, Aug. 3, 1908]," in Carrington, *My Army Life*, 273.

[23] Eighteenth and Twenty-seventh Infantry, 1866–69, "Winning of the West for the Nation," MS, United Indian War Veterans, San Francisco, Calif., 12.

August Hettinger wrote that when he was on the field, December 30, 1890, a day after the fight, ". . . the first sight of the mutilated bodies and the expressionless faces of the dead had the effect of turning one sick . . . but," added Hettinger, ". . . you get used to it." The discovery of stripped, scalped, and mutilated soldiers marking Reno's retreat route, from the valley of the Little Bighorn to the east bank bluffs, shocked and sobered Gibbon's Second Cavalrymen and Seventh Infantrymen as they approached the Reno-Benteen defense site, June 27, 1876. "General Terry," said Private Homer Coon, ". . . saw the slaughter and cried. We all saw it."[24]

Men repeatedly exposed to sights of ghastly wounds and revolting mutilations, frequently became calloused. After observing hostile savagery in mutilating and scalping white citizens and soldiers, not a few frontier soldiers repaid the Indians in their own coin by taking scalps themselves. Regulars were forbidden to scalp Indians, but, as Seventh Infantryman Joseph Sinsel remarked, when asked in 1925 about the Nez Percé scalp he kept in a buckskin pouch, "soldiers were not supposed to scalp Indians . . . but more than one Indian lost his scalp-lock which afterward appeared in the possession of a soldier."[25] Men detailed to search for dead and wounded soldiers and gather up prisoners after combat frequently scalped their dead enemies. Informing his sister that his Fourth Infantry detachment had killed three Indians in a June, 1869, skirmish near Fort D. A. Russell, Wyoming Territory, Private Charles Lester, Company H, commented, "we took the scalps of the ones we killed and let them lay . . . ."[26] In a 1936 letter Private George App told of a Third Infantry comrade of the middle seventies who had recently visited him, and said that the last time he had seen the man, prior to late 1877, he had exhibited the ". . . braid of some Indian buck that had been killed." After the epic August 1, 1867, defense of

[24] "Sioux Campaign," MS, 3.
[25] "Joseph Sinsel of Butte," *Billings Times*, Apr. 30, 1925.
[26] To Mrs. Stanley, MS, June 16, 1869, FLNM.

the hay corral two miles from Fort C. F. Smith, Twenty-seventh Infantry Musician James D. Lockwood wrote that "before leaving the ground they [soldiers] scalped the dead Indian [who fell so close to the corral that his friends could not recover the body] in the latest and most artistic western style, then beheaded him, placing his head upon a high pole, leaving his carcass to his friends or the wolves."[27] Twelfth Infantryman Emanuel Roque stated that while in the field during the 1878 Bannock outbreak he and his comrades were shown further grisly evidence of white savagery repaying Indian barbarities. "One day a white scout brought in the head of an Indian in a gunny sack," said Roque, "he claimed it was the head of Buffalo Horn, the Indian chief."

When the Reno-Benteen Seventh Cavalry survivors saw the gashed and desecrated bodies of their comrades, killed in the opening phase of the Battle of the Little Bighorn, the bodies of several Sioux warriors found cached in nearby trees and in a burial tipi were subjected to even more thorough destruction. As a member of Gibbon's relief column, Private Homer Coon saw the Indian bodies dismembered and thrown on a brush fire by the infuriated Seventh Cavalrymen.[28] When Sitting Bull, most influential hostile leader at the Little Bighorn holocaust in 1876, was killed by Indian policemen, in his village on Grand River, South Dakota, December 15, 1890, eyewitness Sergeant George B. DuBois stated that the elderly leader's body was mutilated. In a letter written to a friend three days later, DuBois wrote:

> The scenes around the camp were awful. I saw one [policeman] go up to old Bull and cut him across the face with an axe. One cut him with a knife till his own squaw wouldn't know him. The dead looked horribly cut and shot.[29]

[27] *Drummer-Boy,* 189.

[28] "Sioux Campaign," MS, 4.

[29] F Troop, Eighth Cavalry, to George Thomas, Dec. 18, 1890, *Winners of the West,* Vol. XII, No. 4 (1935), 4.

Though Sergeant DuBois explained that Sitting Bull was muti-lated by Sioux policemen, he made no mention of any attempt to stop it on the part of the Eighth Cavalry commissioned officers who were present.

Unless a village was attacked, or a band of hostiles surrounded, very few combatant Indians fell into the hands of the army, and the warriors went to great lengths to recover their dead and wounded friends, often suffering additional casualties in the process. The mountain and plains Indians, with a few notable exceptions, took no combatant, and very few noncombatant, prisoners; no quarter was the rule rather than the exception. Rank and file regulars, and their officers, accepted this as a condition of Indian campaigning, and in more than a few instances, when Indian prisoners could have been taken, retaliated by observing the same barbaric rule. After the Battle of Wounded Knee, wrote Seventh Cavalryman Andrew M. Flynn, soldiers nervously scoured the battlefield for their dead and wounded, harassed by intermittent Sioux sniper fire. Searching was temporarily halted while a squad of sharpshooters was brought up to ferret out the tenacious hostiles. Passed over at first glance, a group of five warriors was discovered to be only feigning death and taking shots at soldiers when they could. When the sharpshooters opened a concentrated fire on them, wrote Flynn, ". . . they let out a great yell and threw their blankets and guns away, but it was no good, they were all killed."

Although combat sometimes reveals high qualities of latent bravery and self-sacrifice, it also often lays bare a basic savagery in the personalities of otherwise civilized men. Indian campaign-ing regulars were no exception, and, explained one of Crook's 1876 "starvation march" infantrymen, some soldiers did lots of things that were never included in any official reports. This sol-dier stated that a few prisoners, besides women and children, were taken when Crook's men captured American Horse's Sioux village, September 9, 1876, at Slim Buttes, but that the captives had been put out of the way by the time the column resumed its line of march the following morning.[30] "When at war, it was kill them all," emphasized Sixth Cavalryman George Whittaker, and some soldiers followed this policy to the hilt. They had heard stories from veteran comrades, detailing Indian brutality and ruthlessness, many had seen evidence of it, and their treatment of dead and disabled warriors and hostile captives was heavily influenced by such examples. "Around the post [Fort Riley, Kansas, 1890] I didn't here much about Custer [and the Little Bighorn]," wrote Seventh Cavalryman Jesse G. Harris, "but after we started for Pine Ridge, S. D., I heard lots of remarks from the older soldiers. This [Wounded Knee, December 29, 1890] is where we got even." A number of Sioux prisoners were rounded up and brought in after the battle, but few were taken during or immediately after combat.

After the dead Sitting Bull's followers fled from their village, December 15, 1890, upon the approach of two companies of the Eighth Cavalry, "we went down to the creek on a skirmish line and hunted all around," wrote Sergeant George B. DuBois, "we found only one buck in the brush and made short work of him"; the Sergeant added that he had personally restrained a Sioux policeman from shooting a six-year-old child.[31] In some cases, Indian children were not spared. "I heard from other [Fourth Cavalry] soldiers that sometimes no [Indian, mainly Apache,] prisoners were taken but all were shot regardless of sex or age," wrote Sergeant Reginald A. Bradley. Seventh Cavalryman Andrew M. Flynn corroborated this statement, and said that while he was serving as a litter bearer after the Battle of Wounded Knee, he found two Sioux babies lying with the bodies of their dead mothers and brought them in to the aid station, where a Sergeant seriously told him he should have "bashed them against a tree." The morning after the Battle of the Big Dry Wash, Arizona, in July, 1882, the hostile Apaches were found to have escaped during the night, and only one badly wounded squaw fell into the

[30] Letter to Brininstool, MS, June, 1935, Dustin Coll. No. 316.
[31] To Thomas, Dec. 18, 1890.

317

hands of the soldiers. A surgeon amputated the woman's bullet shattered leg, but "some of the men thought the best thing to do was throw her into a canyon," wrote Sergeant Perley S. Eaton. The Sergeant added that he heard that the enlisted Apache scouts ". . . killed the [other] wounded after the battle, but I don't know how it was."

An important medicine man was taken prisoner at the beginning of the Battle of Cibicue Creek, Arizona, August 30, 1881, and the trouble-making Apache was held as a hostage. The shaman was one of the first casualties, when his followers and mutinous enlisted scouts opened fire.

> Colonel Carr [wrote Sixth Cavalryman Henry F. Ofdenkamp] ordered that if trouble started someone should shoot the medicine man, which was done by our young bugler, Miller—he put .45 pistol bullets thru [sic] the medicine man's head but that didn't finish him, but he was finished before we left, and not by bullets either!

Withdrawing quietly with their wounded that night, the troops slipped away from the Apaches. To maintain silence the wounded medicine man was killed with an ax.

Not all frontier regulars condoned the killing of wounded hostiles and captives, and conscientious officers often saved the lives of Indian prisoners. When a calloused sentry told a small mixed lot of 1876 Sioux captives that they would all be hung, Major Andrew S. Burt reprimanded the soldier and "signed" to the Indians that their lives would be spared.[32] The rules of war observed by the western Indians and the majority of civilian frontiersmen, however, were significant conditioning influences on enlisted regulars. Thirteenth Infantryman Joseph Parker wrote that most of the soldiers he served with during the early 1870's in Montana, took their cue from the enemy and the citizen Indian fighters, and rarely spared captives. Assessing his company's combat behavior, from the perspective of sixty-eight years, Ser-

[32] Burt, "Forty Years," MS.

gcant Parker said, "we were bewhiskered savages living under canvas."

Even though regulars sometimes violated codes of civilized warfare, which forbade the scalping and killing of wounded enemies, and the murdering of helpless prisoners, regular training and discipline saved the lives of some hostile captives taken by men whose comrades had been butchered by the same Indians. Sergeant John Ryan was in charge of the guard ordered to disarm four hostage leaders of the Southern Cheyennes, Bull Head, Dull Knife, Cut-em-up, and One Stab, several months after the Seventh Cavalry had fought them at the Battle of the Washita, November 27, 1868. Ryan said that he and his men were hoping for an excuse to shoot the captives, on the slightest provocation or smallest evidence of treachery, because the soldiers knew that these Indians had killed and indescribably mutilated Major Joel Elliott and his detachment when they were cut off from the main command at the Washita fight.[33] Only rigid discipline and adherence to orders kept the soldiers from shooting the Cheynnes in cold blood.

Some Indian prisoners had no faith in the promises of their army captors, and many viewed close confinement in a guardhouse as hardly preferable to death. Crazy Horse's desperate break for freedom, from the guardroom at Fort Robinson, Nebraska, in 1877, was very likely prompted by the famous warrior's sudden realization that he was being taken to a cell. As he lunged toward the guardhouse door he was mortally stabbed by a sentry's bayonet and died the following morning. His case was not unique.

> Su-ala-lee, an Apache Mojave chief [who came in and surrendered at Camp Verde, Arizona] . . . . While on his way to the blacksmith's shop under guard, to be ironed as a necessary precaution, he suddenly became terror stricken and breaking away from his guard fled into the open country.[34]

33 "Custer's Last Fight," *Billings Times,* July 5, 1923.
34 Hein, *Memories,* 86.

His freedom was abruptly ended, said Colonel Hein, when an officer shot and killed him. Indian emissaries came in to parley with General Miles, at Cantonment Tongue River (Fort Keogh), Montana Territory February 24, 1877, for the release of several captive women and children. The hostile delegates " . . . begged hard for the squaws and children we have here," wrote Captain Simon Snyder, "but Genl Miles would not give them up."[35] When the Indians departed under a flag of truce, "one of the Indian captives killed herself by a shot through the heart [with a hidden pistol]."[36] Learning that Miles had refused to treat for her freedom, this woman destroyed herself rather than remain a prisoner of the soldiers.

Many acts of kindness and humanity shown to wounded and captured Indians by enlisted regulars, partly offset the savage lapses from civilized conduct of some of their comrades. Seventh Cavalry litter bearers brought in some wounded Sioux, along with their own casualties, following the Battle of Wounded Knee. Private Clarence J. Allen, who had received training in "first aid to the injured," was one of the men assignd to assist the surgeon in preparing the wounded for transportation back to Pine Ridge Agency.

> I myself had to bandage up several bad cases [wrote Private Allen] . . . one big brave was shot through the stomach by a ricochet bullet and the intestines were protruding, which had to be pushed back and bandaged the best we could, until we could get him into the agency.

Allen also said that he gave first aid to an Indian boy, bandaging the youth's bullet-pierced thigh. The day after the battle, Eighth Infantryman August Hettinger stated that five wounded but still living Sioux were found on the snow-covered battlefield. The helpless Indians were placed in a nearby deserted cabin and

[35] To his mother, MS, Feb. 24, 1877, S-R Coll.
[36] Snyder, Diary, Feb. 24, 1877, MS.

given the water they craved, but all were dead when visited the next morning.

After the Wounded Knee tragedy, hundreds of starving and freezing Sioux were brought in to Pine Ridge Agency. Most of them had fled into the badlands, believing the soldiers had come to kill them all. Some were the remnants of Big Foot's shattered band. Herded back to the Agency by flanking soldiers, the abject Sioux presented a spectacle of pitifully miserable humanity.

> My memory is keen as I see them coming down a high hill, just back of our camp [wrote Private Walter C. Harrington], after a hard march in charge of Captain Lee . . . a sorrowful, bereaved, dejected, hungry looking lot of bucks, squaws and papooses . . . I remember how the squaws cried as they saw the soldiers "drawn up" under arms at the bottom of the hill . . . . I remember how the soldiers spent their money at the Agency Trader's [store] for whatever comforts he had [to give to the Indian women and children], and how quickly the Indians responded, and all tension died down.

Hardtack, salt pork, and coffee were shared with the captives by many compassionate soldiers.

Joseph's Nez Percés were in similarly poor condition when they finally surrendered to General Miles on October 6, 1877. The ragged Indians were given coats and blankets, and on the march to Fort Keogh, October 7, Miles arranged for the captives to ride their own or extra army mounts, and had their belongings carried in wagons and on pack animals. Out of consideration for the comfort of his prisoners, as well as for that of his own better-prepared soldiers, Miles ordered the column to remain in camp October 8, because of the cold and stormy weather. When the column reached the Missouri River, the Nez Percé sick and wounded, as well as the disabled soldiers, were placed on board a waiting steamboat for faster and more comfortable transportation to post hospitals.[37]

[37] *Ibid.*, Oct. 14.

Although a few brutal enlisted men may have killed Indian women and children in cold blood, most such deaths probably were accidental accompaniments of attacks on hostile villages. Indian women sometimes took an active part in such fighting themselves, and a bullet directed at a soldier could be just as deadly when fired by a woman as it could if shot by a warrior. "Still," said Major Mauck, "soldiers dislike to kill squaws. I have known them to take care of Indian babies whose mothers were killed, for days together, and keep them alive on sugar and water until they got into camp."[38] A modern psychologist might aver that guilt complexes motivated such soldiers to attempt atonement by saving the helpless children. In any case, there is evidence that many captive children were kindly cared for by rank and file regulars. In 1882, Signal Corps Sergeant Will C. Barnes adopted the two orphaned sons of the mutinous Apache scout Deadshot, after their father was executed for his treachery at the Battle of Cibicue Creek, and was their foster father until they reached the age of self-reliance.

The bodies of defeated hostiles were usually looted by the soldiers after a fight. This was also the practice of the Indians, who rarely left anything of value on the body of an enemy. The articles taken by the regulars were generally in the nature of trophies. Soldiers have always been avid souvenir seekers, and none more so than American service men. But to the Indians, the arms, clothing, horses, and other loot taken in combat had very real utility value as well as trophy significance. Like scalping and killing captives, seizure of material wealth from the enemy was basic to the western warrior's concept and practice of war.

Western soldiers collected all manner of beaded and quill-worked articles, ornaments, pipes, war bonnets, weapons, and other loot. After the Battle of Wounded Knee, said Seventh Cav-

[38] "The Experience of Major Mauck in Disarming a Band of Cheyennes on the North Fork of the Canadian in 1876," in *Proceedings, Order of Indian Wars, January 19, 1928*, 46.

alryman Jesse G. Harris, "I wanted to go out and get one of them ghost shirts [from a dead Sioux], but my officers wouldn't let me." Eighth Infantry Sergeant William N. Taylor's assignment to search the Wounded Knee field the day after the fight gave him a better opportunity to obtain a souvenir than Private Harris had back at Pine Ridge Agency. Taylor did not find a ghost shirt, but he did take a pair of beaded mocassins from the feet of a dead brave. Many frightened Sioux had hastily abandoned their cabins and tipis on the Rosebud and Pine Ridge Reservations immediately before and after the Wounded Knee fighting. First Cavalrymen scouting on the reservations stopped at several such places looking for "Indian stuff," said Sergeant Theodore E. Guy. In one cabin, Guy found a sewing machine, tin plates, and a horn spoon, "just like we had in Poland," but none of the exotic, savage trappings he was anticipating.

As soon as a skirmish or battle ended, and sometimes while bullets and arrows were still flying, soldiers did what little they could for their wounded. Often without the direction of a surgeon, and untrained in first aid until the late eighties, soldiers gave the wounded such makeshift care as limited time, materials, and skill afforded. No individual first-aid packets were issued during the Indian campaigns. Few rank and file regulars knew anything about such vital matters as staunching dangerous bleeding, and soldier lore ran to such measures as spitting tobacco juice into wounds to prevent infection. First-aid advice in *The Soldier's Handbook* was limited to an explanation that cuts healed more rapidly than bullet wounds, that a wounded soldier should be placed on his back, and given a drink of water, and that there were two types of bleeding, veinous and arterial, the latter requiring a tourniquet.[39] "I don't think we knew much about first aid . . . ," commented Sergeant Perley S. Eaton. In the late eighties some emphasis was given to training two to four men in each company as litter bearers, mainly through a series

[39] Hershler, 52, 54.

of lectures delivered by post surgeons.[40] Clarence H. Allen, who served from 1887 to 1891 in the Seventh Cavalry, remarked that he was the number one litter bearer in his troop, and that they had been partially "trained to take care of people hurt in engagements, etc., we had learned bandaging and other things necessary."

Medical knowledge and techniques had not yet been developed that could possibly have saved some of the regular wounded, even when a surgeon was available. Friends and officers administered what comfort they could, while the mortally wounded lay waiting for death. An Eighth Cavalry blacksmith named Collins was fatally shot in a fight with Apaches, at Dry Creek, New Mexico, December 19, 1885. The Apaches were driven off, recounted Lieutenant S. W. Fountain, and "as soon as I could I went to Collins. He asked me to pray for him. I had my little prayer book with me and read to him the prayers for the dying. He realized his condition, was calm and followed the prayers with appreciation. He died soon after."[41] During the 1879 Sheepeater Campaign in Idaho, wrote Colonel W. C. Brown, ". . . Private Harry Eagan, Company C, 2nd Cavalry, was shot through both hips [by a hostile at Soldier Bar], necessitating amputation [in the opinion of the detachment's Surgeon]. He died under the operation, and was buried on the spot." An Eighteenth Infantry private was scalped and pierced by an arrow, near Fort Phil Kearny, August 27, 1866, but managed to crawl half a mile to a blockhouse, and lived for another twenty-four hours with the arrow in his chest.[42] The surgeon did his best for the man, but the soldier died shortly after the arrow was pulled out.

By 1865 nearly all the western Indians used arrowheads cut

[40] Med. Hist., Fort Laramie, 1885–90, MS, Nat. Arch., *passim*. The first-aid program was begun in 1887, with a series of weekly lessons and lectures for the newly-designated hospital corpsmen and litter bearers.

[41] "Lieutenant Fountain's Fight, December 19, 1885," *Proceedings, Order of Indian Wars, 1928*, 41.

[42] Bisbee, "Indian Service," *Proceedings, Order of Indian Wars, 1928*, 28.

from sheet or strap iron, and these missiles produced wounds that were dangerous and difficult to treat. "When they struck a bone they almost always bent over and clinched, making it a very painful and difficult task to extract them."[43] Army doctors adopted a special device for removing arrows developed by a Dr. Bill. Because the sinew-wrapped iron heads quickly loosened from their shafts, Bill invented a technique for withdrawing the head and the shaft together by inserting a thin wire, looped at the far end, into the wound along the arrow shaft. The wire was manipulated into place, so that the loop engaged the arrowhead, and was then carefully withdrawn to bring the arrow with it.[44] The shock of such an operation could easily have been as serious as the original wound.

In any case, deep penetrating arrow wounds of the trunk were commonly fatal, as were bullet and arrow wounds of the abdomen. Peritonitis usually set in, and the wounded died before reaching a hospital. *The Soldier's Handbook* stated that bullet wounds of the stomach and digestive organs were almost always fatal, but that death was rarely instantaneous. "Generally," explained the *Handbook*, "the person lives a day or two, with perfect clearness of intellect, and often not suffering greatly."[45] Seventh Cavalryman William F. Morris gave a different report, after he saw one of his comrades shot through the abdomen in the opening phase of the Battle of the Little Bighorn. "I dismounted to help him mount behind me, but he was in such agony that he shrieked, 'Leave me alone, for God's sake.' He refused to try to stand, and I dragged him to a tree, where I propped him up with his back against a trunk."[46]

Transportation of wounded soldiers to a post hospital was difficult. In so-called civilized warfare, wounded soldiers cap-

---

[43] R. B. David, *Finn Burnett, Frontiersman*, 88.

[44] Otis, *Surgical Cases, 1865–1871, Circular No. 3*, 162.

[45] Hershler, 53.

[46] Clipping, no source indicated, but with the pencil inscription "1913," Package No. 35, Custer Coll.

tured by the enemy were supposed to be accorded the same attentions as the captor's own injured received. But wounded regulars who fell into Indian hands could expect a quick death at best, and possibly be subjected to agonizing tortures and mutilations. For this reason, army combat casualties, if it was possible, were carried away by the rest of the command.

Facilities for moving disabled men were miserably inadequate. Many detachments and campaign forces had no wheeled vehicles in which the sick and wounded could ride, and portable stretchers were not included in field equipment, unless an ambulance wagon carried them. Wounded men were often carried on hand litters made by their comrades from poles and blankets. Several wounded Seventh Cavalrymen were borne on such crude contrivances for a distance of fifteen miles, after the Battle of the Little Bighorn. Second Cavalryman John F. McBlain reported that

> One poor fellow was shot through the body, and the agony he endured was terrible; he was carried in a hand litter, so that he should be jolted as little as possible [some were in horse litters and travois], and it required four strong men to carry him. Even now I see the care displayed by Lieutenants Jacobs, Hamilton, and Roe and Matt Carroll [civilian quartermaster employee], four large men, as they gingerly picked their steps and carefully handed the litter over to four stout enlisted men.[47]

After the repulse of the regulars' attack against the Modocs in the Lava Beds on January 18, 1873, First Cavalrymen carried their wounded back with them in a nightmare, thirteen-hour retreat to their base camp. Colonel William H. Miller, then a newly-joined lieutenant, wrote that one of the wounded men,

> . . . shot through the left arm where the artery was cut, and who had lost so much blood (an immense amount) that he was barely alive, was carried the whole distance in a blanket by four men

[47] "With Gibbon on the Sioux Campaign of 1876," *Cavalry Journal*, Vol. IX (1896), 147.

with the corners of the blanket thrown over their shoulders. He fainted almost every time he was lowered to the ground in order to change the men who were carrying him . . . . Arriving at the camp [on the shore of Tule Lake] . . . it was necessary to send the wounded in jolting army wagons to the nearest hospital at Fort Klamath, Oregon.[48]

Eighteenth Infantryman William A. Murphy wrote that during his campaign service in the late sixties, wounded men were "usually . . . put on top of a freight wagon [load], next to [the] wagon sheet (where they could burn up or freeze, depending on the season). Often it would be several days before a wounded man could see a doctor." One of the soldiers who was badly shot at Wounded Knee, Private Hugh McGuinness, wrote that transportation of the disabled men was very slow and crude, and "some cases were lost because of our being so far from civilization." Commenting on the transportation of sick and wounded soldiers in wagons, newspaper correspondent John F. Finerty wrote in 1876 that they ". . . might as well be stretched on the rack as in an army wagon."[49]

For lack of ambulances, wounded soldiers sometimes had to be carried back to post on horseback, or on Indian-style travois. After the Snake Mountain fight in north-central Wyoming, July 4, 1874, the wounded were placed on horses, with other men detailed to ride beside them to help them stay mounted. "The wounded men suffered terribly, but we marched steadily all day, halting often to give them a drink of water. . . . [they] were all doing well, except one man named French, who had his left eye shot out."[50] The horse- or mule-drawn travois were simply constructed of two long poles tied to the animal's shoulders, with the opposite ends left to drag along the ground. A skin, blanket, or piece of canvas was stretched between the poles for an injured man to ride in. Lieutenant Homer W. Wheeler remarked that

[48] "Incidents of the Modoc War." MS, 10.
[49] *War-path and Bivouac*, 88.
[50] Robinson, "Snake Mountain," 25.

travois were more comfortable riding than an army ambulance. In November, 1876, travois were used to convey the wounded back from the Dull Knife Fight in Wyoming. The mule pulling one of the travois became fractious and began to run, whereupon Lieutenant Wheeler reprimanded the corporal who was in charge of the travois, and the wounded man cried out, "Let 'er go, Lieutenant, If I had sleigh bells I'd think I was taking a sleigh ride."[51] This soldier was seriously wounded in the hip, but seems to have ridden comfortably. Sergeant James B. Kincaid's diary entries mentioning travois transportation of the wounded after the Dull Knife fight indicate that some of the wounded riding in them were suffering from the rigors of the journey. "Make this [travois] easier for me or kill me to get me out of my misery," begged one of the disabled regulars.

Whether carried in hand litters, wagons, or travois, combat casualties often traveled several days before reaching a post hospital or other location where proper medical facilities were available. With their wounds dressed only with bandages, and without adequate antiseptics and pain-relieving drugs, the sick and wounded suffered greatly.

On their arrival at a post hospital, the injured and disabled were examined by a surgeon, who dressed their wounds, ordered medications, and saw that they were bathed and given clean underwear. Bullets were probed for and extracted when possible, cuts were sewn up, and bullet-shattered arms and legs were frequently amputated. Some operations were carried out under anesthesia induced by compelling the patient to breathe a vapor composed of equal parts of ether and chloroform. Gangrene and other infections all too commonly set in after amputations and surgical treatment of wounds, although Sir Joseph Lister's recently developed antiseptic techniques, employing carbolic acid, were in use to some extent as early as 1868. Gangrenous and otherwise infected wounds were customarily cauterized, an extremely painful and not oversuccessful technique. The surgeon

[51] *Buffalo Days,* 140.

came through regularly to check the progress of healing and to re-dress wounds. "It was not fun to see the serious wounds dressed, and to hear men groan as pieces of bone were removed or a bad spot was burned out with caustic," wrote Trumpeter Mulford, in describing his hospitalization at Fort Abraham Lincoln in the fall of 1877.[52]

Badly injured men were often anxious about their prospects for full recovery. A soldier, who had been shot in the head and in the shoulder by Nez Percé bullets at the Battle of Bear's Paw Mountain, was experiencing a great deal of pain and some paralysis in his arm.

> He would tell the Surgeon how he felt, and say he was not able to raise his arm, and asking the Surgeon if he thought its use would ever be restored, he would work the arm as much as he could, the while wincing with pain. He was not working for a discharge, he wanted to recover from the injury.[53]

Psychoneurotic battle casualties were apparently lumped in with other post hospital patients. A soldier whose mental equilibrium was violently disturbed as a result of the Battle of Bear's Paw Mountain was placed with other wounded and injured men in the Fort Abraham Lincoln post hospital.

> He almost constantly talked about Indians, and after he had tried to insert the tines of a fork in an ear to dig Indians out, he was placed in a straight jacket. . . . [but] before that was done, fearing that the galvanic battery would be used on him he sneaked into the dispensary and destroyed the machine.[54]

Although rare, such an account of what would more recently have been termed "battle fatigue" is not unique. Second Cavalryman George S. Howard's story of the Sibley scout, wherein a detachment of soldiers barely escaped from a large party of

[52] *Fighting Indians,* 133.
[53] *Ibid.,* 132f.
[54] *Ibid.,* 133.

Sioux, in July, 1876, mentions another such instance: "Cornwall, of Co. D. became insane from fright and suffering."[55]

Ambulatory and convalescent post-hospital patients were generally allowed more freedom than soldiers in garrison. "Eight of us were able to get about on crutches and were permitted to take exercise out of doors," explained Trumpeter Mulford, "we would line up and race for the sutler's store, the last man in to pay for the cigars." Tedium and boredom weighed heavily on the bedfast wounded. As in other situations, soldier jokesters were important in easing the tensions and discomforts of their comrades. A wounded trumpeter, nicknamed "Doctor" Scroggs, was especially adroit. Scroggs hobbled about the Fort Lincoln post hospital enlisted ward, clowning and pompously prescribing such treatments as a quart of whisky, or "perpetual furlough with pay." "He could get men to laughing whom he had found despondent," explained Trumpeter Mulford.[56]

Hospital life was materially better and less restrictive than rank and file regulars were used to in their companies, but the improved diet, better beds, and relaxations of discipline did not compensate for tedious inactivity, the sense of being out of normal company routines, and the pain and discomfort of injuries. "The hardest feature of military life is to be a patient in a military hospital," wrote Trumpeter Mulford.

Many wounded soldiers endured several weary months of slow convalescence. Dangerously shot in the thigh at Wounded Knee, December 30, 1890, Private Hugh McGuinness did not receive his medical disability discharge until almost eleven months later, in November, 1891. Many modern drugs and healing techniques were then unknown, and after the surgeons had done what they could, the rest was left to time and nature.

Permanently disabled soldiers were pensioned according to the losses they had suffered. Loss of an arm in the late sixties carried a pension of only fifteen dollars per month, and other pensions

[55] Diary, *Winners of the West*, Vol. XIV, No. 3 (1937), 3.
[56] Mulford, *Fighting Indians*, 132.

were proportionately small. Amputees were customarily fitted with artificial limbs, and, like the chronically ill and the mentally deranged, they could elect to enter the Soldiers' Home, in Washington, D. C. Medical discharges were usually received with mixed feelings. Although the dischargees experienced a sense of loss in being separated from friends and the shelter of the Army, they were at least free agents once more and were often envied by their comrades.

Recovery of soldiers killed in combat was given a priority, during and immediately following action, only slightly below that accorded to saving the wounded. A corporal, killed by Cheyenne bullets near Fort Robinson, Nebraska, in 1879, fell very close to the Indians, on thickly crusted snow. Private John Hauck volunteered to retrieve the body after dark, and, tunneling through the loose snow to where the corporal lay, he broke through the crust and dragged the corpse back with him. In his account of the skirmish in Sitting Bull's village, when the chief was killed, December 15, 1890, Private William G. Wilkinson described the collecting of the dead and the immediate aftermath of combat. The surgeon attended the wounded Indian policemen, and a

> . . . few of us [Eighth Cavalrymen] were detailed to gather up the dead and lay them in a row. Sitting Bull's body and those of the police we brought back to the post with us. The other [Sioux] bodies were left for the squaws to take care of. . . . cooks had gotten some coffee, bacon, and hardtack ready . . . we took the bridles off our horses, put their feed bags on, left our carbines in the saddle boots, and sat down in the snow to eat our breakfast.

Gathering the dead was a gruesome and unpleasant detail, especially if hostiles had reached them first. In 1874, wrote Nineteenth Infantryman W. E. Harvey, ". . . I saw my first men killed by hostile Indians. They were badly cut up and scalped, and it certainly made me feel creepy!" Relating his part in the recovery

331

and burial of three of Gibbon's men, killed and mutilated by the Sioux in 1876, John F. McBlain described the sight as ". . . one not soon to be forgotten."[57] Sometimes, the condition of the dead was too much for the men detailed to bring them back. Seventh Cavalryman Jacob Adams was one of the men sent to search for the dead after the Battle of the Little Bighorn. "Lieut. McIntosh was killed down in the [valley] bottom and Lieut. Gibson wanted me to get him on a pack mule," wrote Private Adams, "we went down and looked at him, but he looked so bad we left him there."[58] Deciding not to move the corpse, the men sent to retrieve it dug a shallow grave and buried the officer where they found him.

When there were too many killed, or it was otherwise impractical to transport them back to post, the army dead were generally buried where they fell. Customarily wrapped in a blanket, overcoat, or piece of canvas, the dead were placed in shallow graves. An officer read a short burial service, and the interment was concluded with the firing of three carbine or rifle volleys over the grave. Gravesites were generally obliterated, so that Indians could not disinter and desecrate the bodies.

If wagons or pack animals were available, dead regulars were usually brought back to post for burial. The five soldiers killed in the attack on Dull Knife's village of hostile Cheyennes, November 25 and 26, 1876, were strapped across pack mules for the return journey. While the last scattering shots were fired, ". . . the dead were being prepared for transportation on the pack animals by wrapping them in canvas to be laid across the animals."[59] Describing the return of the same dead and wounded, Colonel Homer W. Wheeler related a pathetic incident in connection with a dead soldier.

Private McFarland was just at the point of death, I stopped the

[57] "With Gibbon on the Sioux Campaign of 1876," 140.
[58] To General E. S. Godfrey, MS, Jan. 2, 1927, Bates Coll.
[59] William Garnett [part-blood scout], 1907 Interview, MS, Tablet No. 2, Ricker Collection, Neb. State Historical Society, 14.

travois until he ceased to breathe [then strapped the corpse on a mule and placed a wounded Indian scout in the empty travois]. One of McFarland's friends, who had been taking care of him, pleaded with me not to put his dead bunkie on a mule.[60]

The bodies of dead regulars frequently received considerable care and attention from their comrades at the post. Ties of friendship and unit self-sufficiency often followed fallen regulars even to the grave, when their comrades used their own best uniforms to dress the bodies for burial. For a favorite sergeant the men of Company D, Third Cavalry, pooled their money to ship Sergeant Casey's body to his home in Massachusetts, after he was shot by Ute Jack, at Fort Washakie, Wyoming Territory, in April, 1882. "He was greatly missed by the boys," said Sergeant Perley S. Eaton.

Late nineteenth-century enlisted regulars often made a point of memorializing their company and regimental dead. Subscriptions to collect money for special memorial monuments were common. First Cavalrymen killed at the Battle of Whitebird Canyon, Idaho, against the Nez Percés in 1877, were brought to Fort Walla Walla, Washington, for burial. Their comrades later collectively purchased a modest but impressive granite monument in their honor:

> In memory of 33 enlisted men of Cos. H and E, 1st U. S. Cavalry, killed in battle with Indians at Whitebird Canyon, Idaho, June 17, 1877.[61]

Similar monuments were raised by Seventh Cavalry enlisted men in honor of their comrades killed at the Battle of Bear's Paw Mountain and at Canyon Creek, both in 1877.[62] There is a fine

[60] *Buffalo Days*, 140f.

[61] Fort Walla Walla National Cemetery, Walla Walla, Wash.

[62] These two stone markers were moved to their present location in Custer Battlefield National Cemetery when the remains of soldiers buried in many abandoned post cemeteries were reinterred in Custer Battlefield National Cemetery, from 1888 through the 1940's. Both markers specifically memorialize enlisted soldiers.

plaque in the post chapel at Fort Riley, Kansas, in memory of the Seventh Cavalrymen who fell at Wounded Knee. Before a battalion of the Twenty-seventh Infantry marched away from Fort C. F. Smith, in the summer of 1868, the men of Companies D and H quarried out an eight-foot obelisk of native limestone, dressed its four faces, and inscribed on them the names of their dead. The shaft was raised between the rows of wooden headboards in the little post cemetery, where it remained, scarred by the marks of Sioux hatchets and bullets, for twenty-four years after the abandoned fort was burned by the hostiles.[63]

After the wounded had been brought in and the dead were given their last military honors, the final task was the disposition of property belonging to the dead. Clothing and personal effects were inventoried by the company commanders, in the presence of at least two other commissioned officers. By law, a dead soldier's personal property was to be delivered to his heirs, or it could be auctioned off and the sale proceeds sent. Pay and allowances due at the time of death were computed and forwarded with any money derived from auctioning the dead man's belongings. This was the responsibility of the company commander, who usually included a short, personal note of condolence to the closest relatives and next of kin.

The service records of deceased enlisted men were transferred to a special file in the adjutant general's office. Reading through the list of names, now housed in the National Archives, one is moved as by the sound of distant fife, drum, and bugle. It is a silent roll call, including a few cowards, more than a moderate number of heroes, and hundreds of steady frontier regulars. Now long since vanished as men, the qualities they exemplified are still honored in the arrows and other Indian Wars symbols included in the regimental coats of arms of the Army's older units. The red and blue-black striped campaign streamers, "Coman-

[63] The Twenty-seventh Infantry monument was moved from the Fort C. F. Smith site to Custer Battlefield National Cemetery in 1892, with the remains from the long deserted post cemetery.

ches, 1874," "Little Bighorn," "Arizona," and others, proclaiming obscure but historically significant service, can be seen fluttering from regimental flag staves on parade occasions, beside those indicating service in World Wars I and II and the Korean conflict.

15.

Enlistment's End, Discharges, and Re-enlistment Regulars

A LARGE MAJORITY of late nineteenth-century regulars left the army at the end of their first enlistment. Most of the younger men, who had joined the army for adventure in the West, had experienced their fill of western service by the end of the customary five-year enlistment period. The remembered comforts of home exerted a powerful appeal, after five years of austere and restrictive enlisted life.

The harsh realities of western campaigning determined some men to take their discharge as soon as possible. "Three months sleeping in snow and slush," was the deciding factor for Seventh Infantryman John Crump. After ten years in the Twenty-fifth Infantry, Sergeant Samuel Harris took his discharge in 1890, because he felt that since Indian troubles had decreased, regulars were spending more time as laborers than as soldiers. Some men remained comfortable in the ranks longer than others. Corporal Herbert Martin explained that he signed up again when his first enlistment expired in 1891, but that by 1895, "I was fed up with it, I wanted to get married, and get a good job." Like many army men, he wanted to enjoy a normal civilian life. The constant subordination and compulsions of enlisted service irritated many soldiers, and by the time their discharges were due, most had simply had enough of the army.

The Regular Army provided little incentive for ambitious soldiers, offering only the prospect of retirement after thirty years of service. Believing themselves to be at a dead end, isolated from the main stream of life, many energetic, restless soldiers left the army to pursue personal ambitions. Private John Johnson explained that he "had a chance to become a stationary engineer [in Omaha, Nebraska] by leaving the Army [in 1892]." Sergeant Reginald A. Bradley had received a good education in England, before joining the Fourth Cavalry in 1889, and when he became convinced that there was almost no possibility of obtaining a commission he left the army in 1894. Many soldiers were probably influenced toward discharge by western boom conditions and popular beliefs in get-rich-quick opportunities in the newly-opened regions. Third Cavalryman John L. Hubbard left the ranks in 1889 to search for gold in Alaska. Since army pay was very low by western standards, almost any kind of civilian employment was better paid; a factor deciding many soldiers against re-enlisting. As Sergeant Perley S. Eaton explained, "I just couldn't afford to stay in . . . any longer for the pay they were giving [in 1886]."

A few enlisted regulars left the army in order to further their formal education. Eager to make his way in business, Private Walter C. Harrington entered business college after discharge in 1896. Charles S. Winans, a veteran of the Geronimo campaign, went to college, after five years in the Southwest, and earned his law degree. Private Thomas E. Gutch entered medical school at the end of his enlistment, and Sergeant Charles Johnson and Private William G. Wilkinson both left the Army to go to college.

Campus life must have required a considerable adjustment on the part of young men who had spent several years in the ranks of the Regular Army.

The life of a bachelor in a regular army company on the frontier quickly lost its attraction for many men when they met a girl. Good fellowship with one's comrades was fine, but often could not compete with female blandishments. "I had a girl," explained Sergeant James S. Hamilton, "so I wished to marry and resume civilian life [in 1881]. The Army of those days was too rugged for a woman—I was offered promotion if I would stay, but I refused." Other matrimonially-inclined soldiers agreed with Sergeant Hamilton, and left the army rather than bring their brides to live on "suds row" in a western post. Women's influence played an important part in the decisions of the men. Seventh Cavalryman Jacob Horner wanted to re-enlist for another five years in 1881, "but my wife objected," said Horner, "she wanted a permanent home of her own and children."[1]

Until 1890, honorable discharges were issued only at the expiration of enlistment, or for medically determined disability incurred in line of duty. Because it was believed that the length of enlistments drove many dissatisfied soldiers to desert, two measures were adopted in 1890 to permit soldiers desiring to leave the army to do so legally before the expiration of their contracts. By authority of General Orders No. 80, Headquarters of the Army, soldiers who had completed three years of their five-year terms of service could apply for a three-month furlough, and, at the end of the three months, could either return to duty and finish their enlistment or receive an honorable discharge. A great many soldiers took advantage of this opportunity. Less commonly applied for were discharges authorized under the Act of June 16, 1890, whereby a soldier could purchase his discharge at the end of his first year of service. Applicants for purchase discharges paid a lump sum of $120.00, if in the first month of their second year of service, and five dollars less per month to the

[1] Johnson, "Jacob Horner," *North Dakota History*, Vol. 16, No. 2 (1949), 77.

DECORATING THE GRAVES
on the Custer Battlefield, Little Bighorn

Division of Manuscripts, University of Oklahoma Library

REGULAR MEMBERS OF A WESTERN "POST"
of the Army and Navy Union, their veterans' organization.

Division of Manuscripts, University of Oklahoma Library

end of their third year. Private Christ F. Feil obtained his purchase discharge in 1891, during his second year of service.

> I spoke to the First Sergeant about the Purchase Act. He told
> me to see the Captain, so I went to the Captain and explained
> things to him and asked him to put in an application asking for
> my discharge. He did not want me to quit soldiering, but I was
> determined to get my discharge . . . . My application was ap-
> proved of, and in two weeks time I was a citizen again.

Before applying for a purchase discharge, Feil had requested a
medical release after he was partly deafened in an accident. Disability discharges, however, were not readily secured, especially
if they might be pensionable. Private Harvey J. Ciscel spent five
months in the hospital, suffering from acute rheumatism after
the Sioux Campaign in the winter of 1890 and 1891. At the end
of a long convalescence, Ciscel was still unable to perform regular duty, and was assigned only to light tasks for the remainder
of his service. When discharged in 1893, no mention of his disability was made on the certificate. Some regulars were medically discharged, though, for disabilities less serious than amputations or other crippling injuries. After a few months of exposure,
substandard field rations, and recurring excessive physical demands incidental to infantry campaign service, recruit Joel
Shomaker's health broke and he was given a medical discharge.
A few regulars shammed sickness or injury, in the hope of obtaining a disability discharge, and although such attempts were
occasionally successful, the deceit was usually quickly detected
and punished.[2]

Regulations stipulated that all recruits had to be twenty-one,
unless the parents of a boy between the ages of eighteen and
twenty-one gave their written consent to his enlistment. If discovered the youths who had falsified their ages in order to enlist
were supposed to be discharged at once and returned home. Such
soldiers were not dishonorably released, but the class of dis-

---

[2] Mulford, *Fighting Indians*, 132.

charge issued in such cases was not usually honorable either. After J. H. D. Wherland had served three years in the Fifth Cavalry as "Henry Lowell," his parents secured his discharge in 1876, because he was still underage. When Private Martin Andersen's parents learned in 1891 that he had enlisted a year before at the age of seventeen, they got in touch with the War Department, from their home in Denmark, and had him released.

Some western regulars left the army with dishonorable discharges, via courts-martial. Shirkers, criminals, drunkards, and other worthless and troublesome enlisted men were consistently purged from the ranks.

A frequent topic of the soldiers' conversation was what they planned to do when their enlistments expired. Only rarely did one announce that he planned to make the army his career, and most were quite emphatic in stating their intention never to sign up again. Writing home to his sister, in September, 1869, Private Charles Lester expressed the attitude shared by many enlisted soldiers.

> I have just one year from tomorrow to serve [joined in 1867, when enlistments were still for three years], and thank God, then I am done Soldiering in the regular army. I don't believe there is a thing worse than being in the regular army and out of civilization, but I have got use to it and don't mind it so much as I use to—[3]

When the time came, and the soldier returned to civilian surroundings, he sometimes found himself ill at ease and uncomfortable. Thirteenth Infantryman John G. Brown was discharged July 24, 1884, after five years of service in the West. "I went back east," wrote Brown, but "the years I spent in the Regular Army unfitted me for contact with civilians of the East." However, most dischargees became adjusted to civilian life, and merged rapidly into the general population. Some went back to the army, and provided the professional enlisted cadre that added strength,

[3] To Mrs. Stanley, MS, Sept. 6, 1869, FLNM.

stability, and continuity to the composition of the late nineteenth-century Regular Army.

Although the army professed an official interest in promoting the re-enlistment of reliable veteran soldiers, the only inducement offered was a three-dollar monthly pay increase for five year men who re-enlisted within thirty days of discharge. Longevity pay, of one additional dollar per month for each subsequent five years of service, was also authorized for men who had completed more than one enlistment. Thus, financial gain could not have been a significant motivation for the men who re-enlisted.

Few of those who ultimately completed several terms of service seem to have intended to do so when they had first joined the army. It is more likely that many re-enlisted because they felt they had no alternative, did not feel comfortable as civilians, and had become well adjusted to the circumstances of regular army living. Thirteenth Infantryman Samuel D. Gilpin related the story of one such re-enlistee. A popular comrade of Gilpin's had talked about and planned for his discharge, at Fort Bayard, New Mexico, in 1881, declaring his intention to take the railroad to Chicago, find a good job, and never put on a uniform again. The day finally came, and, dressed in a suit of second hand "civies," with his "finals" pay and allowance money in his pocket, he bade farewell to his friends and left the post. However, said Gilpin, he was ". . . discharged one day and back in the company barracks dead broke the next." A third-enlistment soldier himself, Gilpin said that this was a common pattern of behavior.

In 1891, Secretary of War Elkins recommended a reduction of the time required for enlisted retirement, from thirty to twenty or twenty-five years. His report concisely described the majority of multiple-enlistment regulars.

> They are neither saints nor demi-gods. They are men, often rough in body, ignorant of books, and somtimes deficient in the minor morals, but strong in the sturdy virtues of obedience, truthfulness, fidelity. Prevented from forming family ties, they

are friendless in the social world . . . as guiless and as helpless as children in the sharp competition of civil life.[4]

Reporting that only one out of a hundred privates were retired after thirty years service, the Secretary explained that "few privates can endure 30 years' military service," and that continuous duty in the West sapped the strongest within ten to fifteen years.[5]

Some of the men who repeatedly enlisted, went into civilian life, and then enlisted again, were erratic, displaced persons who periodically returned to the army as a haven. After enlisted service in the Civil War, John D. Geoghegan was a sergeant when he was commissioned second lieutenant in the Tenth Infantry in 1866. He resigned during the 1869 reduction of the army, but enlisted in 1872 as "Oliver Sutherland," subsequently serving as private and sergeant of Company B, First Cavalry, until he was discharged on December 26, 1877. Nine years later, he again joined the army, April 1, 1886, but for some unexplained reason was discharged twenty-six days later.[6]

Many of the long-service regulars of the Indian Wars years had begun their military life during the Rebellion. When he retired on May 29, 1898, First Sergeant William A. Magee had completed thirty-five years of service. He had first enlisted in an Ohio volunteer regiment in 1863. Discharged in November, 1865, he joined the Regular Army eleven months later, and again took a discharge in October, 1869. Four months later, in February, 1870, he returned to his regiment, and remained with it until he was retired. The long service of some men, who had enlisted between 1865 and 1890, spanned periods during which the Regular Army underwent important modifications and rapid changes, as was the case in the early 1880's, the Spanish-American War, and World War I. These men were "old Army," and while some probably failed to adjust to changed conditions, the best of them

[4] *Ann. Report, Sec. of War, 1891,* I, 84.
[5] *Ibid.*
[6] Heitman, *Historical Register,* I, 451.

provided vital continuity to enlisted regular army traditions of steady loyalty and devotion to duty.

A very few enlisted men, mostly sergeants, remained in the army for more than one enlistment in hopes of achieving commissioned rank. The guidelines by which ambitious regulars could theoretically apply for a commission were set forth in Army General Orders No. 93, October 31, 1867. An applicant was first required to obtain a letter from the War Department authorizing him to apply, between the ages of twenty and twenty-eight, after serving meritoriously at least two years in the Regular Army. A board of four officers from the applicant's regiment passed on the merits of his application and the results of his academic examinations, and the regiment's colonel reviewed the board's recommendations before passing them on to the adjutant general's office, where the final decision was made. In practice, the commissions were rarely granted. Some of the men who applied resented the fact that many of the newly-commissioned officers in the late sixties and early seventies were appointed directly from civil life, chiefly for political considerations.[7] Finding that they really had no chance for a commission, some of the best noncommissioned men left the army.[8] First Sergeant Henry Hale, Sixteenth Infantry, took his discharge in 1882, after fifteen years in the Regular Army. Denied the commission he hoped for, Hale left the army to enter college, remarking, ". . . I should have left ten years before." A handful of sergeants who applied for commissions did receive them, and continued on as career army men. The possibilities were so slight, though, explained Sergeant Armand Unger, that sergeants seldom went to the trouble of making application.

The popular conception of Indian Wars regulars as ruthless, whisky-guzzling swashbucklers, with a "legion-of-the-lost" aura of romance, is not supported by the record of their civilian

---

[7] Sergeant Major John Burke, letter of February 17, 1876, *Reorganization of the Army*, 44 Cong., 1 sess., *House Report No. 354*, 123.

[8] James Larson, *Sergeant Larson, 4th Cavalry*, 325.

activities after discharge. No doubt some ex-regulars became criminals and social parasites, but the majority were quickly assimilated into the civil population, where a significant number made respectable contributions to society and held positions of trust and responsibility. First Cavalry Sergeant Theodore E. Guy worked as a clerk and studied law in his free time, following his discharge in 1892. He achieved his long-time ambition to become a lawyer, and was still actively practicing in 1954. By 1913, Seventh Cavalry, Little Bighorn veteran William F. Morris had risen to the position of Justice of the New York City Municipal Court. Commenting on the civilian careers of men he had served with in the Eighth Cavalry, Harvey J. Ciscel told of a meeting in the jail in Milwaukee, Wisconsin, many years after discharge, with a former comrade who had become a noted jewel thief. On the other hand, continued Ciscel, "Jack McLamore was a Sergeant in my company, and later a U. S. Senator from Miss."[9] George Ford, a nineteen-year-old Negro, enlisted in the Tenth Cavalry in 1867, serving two enlistments. In 1878, he was appointed Superintendent of the Negro section of Chattanooga National Cemetery. He served as supervisor of several national cemeteries, retiring in 1930. In 1898, he was granted a leave of absence in order that he might serve as a major in the Twenty-third Kansas Volunteers.

Ex-regulars entered varied professions after leaving the army. First Cavalryman Thomas E. Gutch earned a degree in medicine, and practiced as a physician for many years. After five years of soldiering on the frontier, in the First Infantry, 1872–77, Sergeant John E. Cox became a Baptist minister.[10] Reverend Charles S. Winans served five years in the Apache campaigns of the eighties before earning a law degree in college, after which he graduated in theology and spent the ensuing forty years as a Protestant minister. Reverend Joel Shomaker, who retired from

[9] No United States Senator can be identified as "McLamore"; the man, however, could very well have been in the army under an assumed name.

[10] "Soldiering," *North Dakota History*, Vol. VI, No. 1 (1931), 63.

thc active ministry in the late 1920's, had likewise served in the Southwest before his discharge in the 1880's. It is not likely that such men ever fitted the popular contemporary stereotype of the enlisted regulars as amoral, shiftless parasites and degenerates.

Some former regulars became successful businessmen. After thirty-five years of service, Sergeant James A. Richardson left the army and became a contractor for the New England Telephone Company.[11] Private Walter C. Harrington left the army in the mid-nineties, acquired a business education, later managed a brick plant, and finally owned and managed his own building supply firm.

For many discharged regulars, their contribution to the development of the West did not end with their army service. Some, who had originally joined the army in order to travel and become acquainted with the West, remained there when their terms of service expired.[12] The West was publicized as the land of immediate opportunity, and venturesome and observant soldiers often recognized possibilities to settle and grow up with the country. Land was relatively cheap, labor was well paid, unexploited natural resources awaited development, and all kinds of business activities were rapidly expanding. Stationed at Fort D. A. Russell, Wyoming Territory, Private Charles Lester explained to his sister in 1869 that he ". . . would like to be in this country, but not [as] a soldier—it is a good place for work, wages is from 60 to $75. a month here, but you have to run the risk of getting your hair lifted."[13] Seventh Cavalryman John Duke was of the same opinion, and when his enlistment ended in 1869, he traveled to Arizona as the employee of Army Surgeon David L. Magruder, remaining there as a miner, cattleman, dairyman, and hotel owner until his death in 1935.

11 "Sergeant James A. Richardson," *Portland* [Me.] *Sunday Times,* June 27, 1909, 11.

12 *Reorganization of the Army,* 45 Cong., 2 sess., *House Misc. Doc. No. 56,* 250.

13 To Mrs. Stanley, MS, June 16, 1869, FLNM.

Discharged soldiers participated in all the major civilian economic activities of the late nineteenth-century frontier West. Just as many civilians were smitten with the gold and silver fever, so were some of the western regulars. The West was a stockman's paradise in many areas, and some ex-regulars entered the cattle industry and were ultimately able to establish themselves as successful ranchers.[14]

Labor of all kinds was almost always scarce and in demand in the frontier West; many discharged soldiers remained to take jobs in the mines, on the railroads, and in other activities of the rapidly developing economy. Sixth Cavalryman Frank Heidelberger went to the Black Hills, after his discharge in 1893 at Fort Niobrara, Nebraska, where he worked as a tool sharpener and blacksmith in the mines. Sergeant Washington McCardle worked on ranches in Dakota, after leaving the Army in 1891, as did Twenty-fifth Infantry Sergeant Samuel Harris in 1890.

The lure of cheap land was as strong an influence on enlisted regulars as it was on civilians who came west, and some took up homesteads and otherwise acquired land for settlement. Sergeant William Diener left the Eighth Infantry in 1890. "After discharge I bought a little farm [near Sheridan, Wyoming]," wrote Diener, "one dollar down and one dollar a month. In twenty-four years I paid for the farm, raised seven children and sold out."

Men who as soldiers had become accustomed and toughened to life in the open found numerous opportunities for such living in several strenuous western occupations. Private George Whittaker became a guide and ranger in Yellowstone National Park when he quit the Army in 1894, as did Private James G. Morrison in the same year. Morrison became the chief scout in Yellow-

---

[14] Sergeant Will C. Barnes, "The Battle of Cibicue," *Arizona Highways* (March, 1936), 18f. Barnes began with a few head of cattle in 1882 and later became a noted and prosperous rancher. Private Harry L. Ertberg was discharged at Fort Custer, Mont., and settled near Rosebud, Mont., as a long-time cattleman. Sergeant Reginald A. Bradley was a cowboy when he enlisted in 1889, and after discharge he started a herd of his own in northern Calif.

stone, and later was appointed a Deputy United States Marshal. Private Richard F. Watson, after he left the army, took a job driving a stage coach from Farmington, New Mexico, to Durango, Colorado, and later was employed as a mail rider and as a station agent for the stagecoach company. Upon receiving his discharge at Fort Bayard, New Mexico, in April, 1888, Thirteenth Infantryman John M. Reichwein traveled back to his Cincinnati home. Within a month, he was back at Fort Bayard, employed as a teamster by the post quartermaster. He drove a stagecoach for awhile in 1889, was appointed a deputy sheriff in 1890, and in 1891 was elected constable of Central City, Colorado.

Because the West attracted thousands of restless and hopeful Americans and immigrants, there was a great demand for all manner of services and goods in the mushrooming communities. Expansion was the watchword, and some former regulars eagerly gambled as speculators on the ebb and flow of land prices, cattle markets, mineral possibilities and enthusiasms, as well as on other more stable forms of business. Enterprising dischargees displayed the same ingenuity exhibited by some civilian pioneers. Many ex-soldiers went into business for themselves with very little capital. Owning only a wagon, a Fourth Infantry dischargee moved his family to Laramie, Wyoming, in 1877, and, after acquiring a few empty barrels, launched a profitable water-hauling business.[15] Some of the new communities were eager to acquire the accepted cultural decorations of the times. Private Louis Ebert, Sixth Cavalry, had received some artistic training before joining the army in 1888. When he received a letter in 1893, offering high pay for painting and decorating the interiors of churches and theaters in western Nebraska, he took his discharge and subsequently made good money catering to the aesthetic tastes of his clients. Another ex-regular who successfully established his own business was Jacob Horner, a Seventh Cavalry

[15] Alice Mathews Shields, "Army Life on the Wyoming Frontier," *Winners of the West*, Vol. XXI, No. 5 (1944), 4f. The author married her husband while he was in the army, and accompanied him to Laramie after discharge.

trooper. He left the army in 1881, at Fort Totten, Dakota Territory, moved with his wife to Bismarck, and went into business as a butcher. The business throve, and Horner became one of the pillars of the town, serving six years as an alderman in the city government.[16]

Their familiarity with Indians led a few regulars to remain among the western tribes, at the expiration of their enlistments. After fifteen years as a Second Cavalryman, Joseph Kuhn decided not to re-enlist when his term expired in 1895. He first established himself as a baker and was soon able to purchase an Indian trading store in Arizona, where he carried on a moderately profitable business with the Indians until he sold the store and retired in 1942. Tenth Infantryman Henry Backes liked the Indians he knew in New Mexico, and when his time expired in 1893, he accepted a position teaching shoe- and harness-making at an Indian school in Santa Fe, New Mexico.

Services for the construction of all kinds of buildings and communications systems were in particularly heavy demand. Sergeant-Major W. H. Pickens, Fifth Cavalry, who had been a journeyman carpenter before he joined the army in 1873, elected to remain in the West rather than return to Chicago, when he was discharged in 1878. He settled in Plattsmouth, Nebraska, in 1879, and seeing ripe opportunities in the building trades, became a contractor and builder, "ranking among the first in Cass county [in 1889]."[17] When discharged from the First Infantry in Texas, Sergeant James S. Hamilton also established himself as a carpenter and builder. Seventh Cavalryman Jacob Sobl is a fine example of the regular army enlisted man who made a variety of contributions to the West after leaving the Army in 1882. Sobl homesteaded near Billings, Montana, and for a short time operated a business college in Billings. After disposing of the college, he was a rancher until 1890, when he entered the con-

---

[16] Johnson, "Jacob Horner," 77.

[17] "W. H. Pickens," *Portrait and Biographical Album of Otoe and Cass Counties, Nebraska*, 1069–71.

struction business, first as a labor foreman, and then as an independent contractor. Sobl built roads and bridges all over Montana and in Yellowstone National Park, finally retiring from business about 1920.[18] If Sobl had ever fitted the common civilian view of post-Civil War regulars as ambitionless ne'er-do-wells, he must have undergone a remarkable transformation in the army, for his activities after discharge marked him as a man of considerable energy and initiative.

Unlike their elder brothers of the Grand Army of the Republic, regular veterans of the Indian campaigns were not characterized primarily as "old soldiers" in the civilian society to which they returned. They did not even have a veterans' organization of their own until long after 1900. Americans did not think of the regulars, as they did of Civil War veterans, in terms of "our boys in blue," and the Regular Army was in a very real sense physically and psychologically isolated from the rest of American life in the late nineteenth century. It was seldom that the men who remained in the West, to participate in the economic and social development of the vast regions they had campaigned in, received popular recognition for their military service. The fact that the early settlers and builders of many western communities had come West as United States regulars was not usually publicized. However, inquiries into the antecedents of twentieth-century citizens of communities in the vicinity of abandoned army posts would reveal that a significant number of discharged regulars remained in the West and contributed to its growth.

[18] Elmo, "Livingston Resident With Reno at Time of Custer Massacre," *Rocky Mountain Husbandman*, May 12, 1938.

Tattoo

Soldiers of the Regular Army were the cutting edge and holding power of white government and civilization in the frontier West. Traders, surveyors, explorers, prospectors and other adventurers usually made the first contacts with the western Indians, but regulars were often the Indians' first continuing contact with the white culture and government. The ill-trained, poorly supplied, and indifferently equipped regular was still essentially an organization man, representing law and order. The impression he made upon the Indian mind was an abiding one, and for good or ill it colored Indian-white relations throughout the half-century following the Civil War.

If the dominant mood of the 1865–1900 Gilded Age was that of a great barbecue as described by Vernon Louis Parrington in *Main Currents in American Thought*, the Regular Army was America's western grounds keeper and game beater for the festivities. The regulars were unbidden to the feast, except as servants. The doctrine of the times cast government in the role of provider and safeguarder of opportunities for wealth, and it followed that its military service must remove any Indian barriers to dreamed-of wealth in lands and minerals, break the way for great railroad land speculations, and provide whatever services and communications were needed for the immediate opening and exploitation of the post-Civil War West. To the regulars was allotted the task of spearheading the great work, without receiving even crumbs of recognition or appreciation in the doing, as was forcefully pointed up when Congress neglected to appropriate money for the pay of the army in 1877.

Giantism bestrode the land after 1865. Great areas of virgin plains and mountains awaited the plow, pick, and railroad—once the Indians were removed. The Black Hills could be a second Ophir, if the Sioux were confined to less favored areas. The gears and flywheels of mighty factories were turned by drive belting tanned from the hides of millions of buffalo. To hasten it all, a thin line of army blue was marched across the West, and the regulars did what was ordered of them to facilitate American digestion of the last great continental frontier, the culmination of the "manifest destiny" drive, implemented by men and animals straining for "forty miles a day, on beans and hay."

In New York, Boston, Washington, St. Louis, pyramided wealth was focusing on its self-appointed goals of developing and exploiting the most promising economy the world had yet seen; much of which drew its potential and material sustenance from the West. Jim Fisk, Jay Gould, Leland Stanford, Jim Hill, Philip Armour, and other financial giants of the age set the pace and tone of American life in the eastern half of the country. Massive industrialization and the accompanying crowding of workers in production centers resulted in an urbanization unequaled in previous American history, holding out to its participants the promise of what was essentially a culture based almost exclusively on the most self-seeking kind of materialism.

A thousand miles to the west, almost forgotten units of the Regular Army established crude forts and cantonments as outposts of government, broke passable roads to connect them one with another and with the towns and settlements and railheads that were burgeoning, and carried out innumerable patrols, campaigns, surveys, escorts, and communications details to make the virgin land available. Not for them were the gaslights of Broadway and the flashy overpadded women, gaudy in taffetas and velvets; nor the oyster and champagne suppers at Delmonico's; nor the extravaganza displays such as the great Philadelphia Centennial of 1876. But in a sense the men of the Regular Army were a cross section of what the nation represented in that era—its continental drives, restlessness, buoyant optimism, carelessness, cockiness, and the drive for agricultural and industrial power.

Destiny is never unmixed. The expansion that swept Indians into reservations, overseen by the army, dealt a cruel fate to a free people, whose right to half a continent in the West was based on first possession. That this was their inevitable fate is incontestable, and that a thin line of army regulars made it so is now a part of history. But the moral shock to them, and the moral loss to white America, cannot be denied either. The half-century from 1840 to 1890 was inadequate time for such a major readjustment in the lives and cultures of Stone Age peoples, and the sudden opening of so vast an agricultural and mineral resource to white culture produced attitudes and outlooks that today, nearly a century away in time, are slow in dying.

The thin line that seized and finally held the plains, the mountains, and the western littoral was not a new manifestation. Ragged, inadequate troops under Washington had set a precedent that in the nineteenth century, and even in the twentieth, was to prove enduring. Power in the nineteenth-century Indian wars was a little understood principle—although the Civil War foundation for it was clear enough.

A massive deployment of troops will be sought in vain in these

352

crucial years of American expansion. Power was in other forms—in the thrust of ambitious farmers and grazers from east of the Mississippi towards the immense expanses of free land in the West; in the masses of small shopkeepers, artisans, and financiers, who could win stakes in the less restricted social terrain of the West; in the railroad and steamboat developments which would ultimately make American agriculture the supplier of Europe and displace even Polish wheat in England's economy of industrial expansion.

Until the end of the nineteenth century, United States troops played a major part in keeping many of the western Indians on the reservations to which they had been assigned, to make way for a flood of development. Indian police and scouts were used to handle routine law enforcement, but in serious cases strong detachments of soldiers were called upon to enforce the *pax Americana* among the more restless Indians. Government often used the troops temporarily to counteract the rapaciousness of illegal white squatters, cattlemen encroaching on Indian lands, and prospectors hungry for gold known to exist on Indian lands.

The last war whoop was answered by rifle fire generations ago. The telegraph lines, wagon roads, surveys, and other services created and developed by soldier efforts in the West have long since been abandoned or replaced by modern facilities. Seventy years have wrought great changes in the West since the last major Indian campaign. The American army has likewise gone through many transitions since that time. Perhaps the men who make up the army have not changed so much. Certain it is that the older regular's better qualities of perseverance, endurance, initiative, loyalty, and courage are of timeless value.

From the shadow realms of the "Indian Wars," mixed legend and fact, the frontier regulars emerge as flesh-and-blood men. Neither always saints nor always sinners, they were average American soldiers of an earlier time confronted with different conditions, whose service did so much to shape the development of the trans-Mississippi West.

Bibliography

BIBLIOGRAPHIC DESCRIPTION OF SOURCES

Enlisted Regular Army life on the post-Civil War frontier has been presented, wherever possible, in the terms of and by the men who served in the ranks. The questionnaires, diaries, photographs, letters, and other material so generously provided by surviving frontier soldiers and their relatives have served as the basis for most of the directly quoted statements made in the text. Other quotations, used but not cited in footnotes, originated in hundreds of fragmentary comments culled from the old *Winners of the West* newspaper and a large volume of correspondence from the files of the United Indian War Veterans.

1. Unpublished and Manuscript Sources

Allen, Clarence H. "My Experiences in the Seventh Cavalry, Known as Custer's Regiment." Allen was a private in the Seventh Cavalry from 1887 to 1891, when he was medically discharged. His unpublished manuscript was lent to the author in 1954.

Bald, William. Diary of Private William Bald, C Troop, First Cavalry, 1893. Lent for research use by the diarist. Most of the entries concern Bald's service at Fort Grant, Arizona.

Bates Collection. Custer Battlefield National Monument, Crow Agency, Montana. Charles Francis Bates was General Edward S. Godfrey's son-in-law. Most of the papers in this collection are manuscripts written by Godfrey about his Seventh Cavalry experiences in the Indian Wars, including such items as "Jimmy Winn," a profile of an enlisted professional regular; "Recollections of the Medicine Lodge Treaty Conference, October, 1867"; "General Sully's Expedition Against the Southern Plains Indians, 1868"; and many letters written to Godfrey by former Indian Wars officers and soldiers. Of special value to this study is the anonymous Diary of a Seventh Cavalry Enlisted Man, January 1 to December 29, 1869.

Benteen-Goldin Letters. Gilcrease Institute Museum, Tulsa, Oklahoma. These letters, between Brigadier General Frederick W. Benteen and former Seventh Cavalry Private Theodore Goldin, were written in 1896. Benteen wrote very frankly, but with discernible bias and prejudice, about many aspects of Seventh Cavalry history, including the personalities of several officers and soldiers and controversial facets of the Battle of the Washita and the Battle of the Little Bighorn.

Bingham, Wallace E. "Early Days on the Frontier." The author was a private in the Twenty-third Infantry, 1880–85, serving in the Indian Territory and on campaign against the Utes in southern Colorado. His unpublished service account was lent by Mrs. W. E. Bingham.

Burt, Elizabeth J. "Forty Years in the U.S. Regular Army, 1862–1902." Mrs. Burt wrote this account of her travels and experiences during the forty years she accompanied her husband, General Andrew S. Burt, from diaries accumulated over the years. She makes some mention of the enlisted men in her account of life at Fort C. F. Smith and other frontier posts. Her lengthy, typewritten manuscript was lent by her son, Brigadier General Reynolds J. Burt, and is now in the Library of Congress.

Burt, Brigadier General Reynolds J. "Boyhood Data, 1874–1890." Written, at the request of the author, by a retired officer who spent his youth at a succession of western forts and camps. Very detailed, and many of the incidents described can be verified.

Carr, Brigadier General Eugene S. Letter of recommendation regarding a former sergeant. The General states that Sergeant Daniel McGrath killed the Cheyenne war leader Tall Bull, at the Battle of Summit Springs, Colorado, July 11, 1869. The letter is on file with the Registrar, Nebraska Soldiers' and Sailors' Home, Grand Island, Nebraska, among papers regarding Mrs. Josephine Mc-Grath.

Coon, Homer. "The Outbreak of Chief Joseph." On deposit in the William R. Coe Collection, Yale University Library, New Haven, Connecticut. This manuscript was written by a Seventh Infantry soldier, detailing his participation in the 1877 Nez Percé War.

———. "Recollections of the Sioux Campaign of 1876, as I saw it From the Viewpoint of an Enlisted Man." William R. Coe Collection, Yale University Library.

Custer, Elizabeth B., Collection. Custer Battlefield National Monument, Crow Agency, Montana. A large collection of all types of manuscript materials, including letters by former Seventh Cavalry enlisted soldiers and such items as Captain Winfield Scott Edgerly's account of the Battle of the Little Bighorn.

Custer Battlefield National Monument Files. Crow Agency, Montana. The research files contain originals and copies of orders and letters regarding Custer and the Seventh Cavalry, some of which were written by enlisted men. Individual items are cited in various footnotes.

Dose, Trumpeter Henry C. Letter to his wife, written June 8, 1876, reflecting his desire to return to Fort Lincoln and get the campaign over with. Dose was killed June 25, 1876, at the Little Bighorn. This letter is in the possession of Mrs. William Boland, Sturgis, South Dakota.

Dustin Collection. Custer Battlefield National Monument, Crow Agency, Montana. Fred Dustin began assembling information on the Battle of the Little Bighorn, the Indian Wars service of the Seventh Cavalry, and the 1876 Sioux campaign long before 1900. His collection of books, manuscripts, maps, and pictorial material is one of the most complete private collections on the subjects ever assembled. Individual letters from this collection are cited in several footnotes.

Flynn, Richard. Diary, August, 1876–August, 1877. The author was an enlisted soldier, but his name is not mentioned in the diary. Mr. Flynn, of Blair, Nebraska, is the present owner of the diary. Of special interest are the entries detailing General Crook's "starvation march" campaign in the late summer and fall of 1876.

Gale, Lieutenant George H. G. Letters, to his sister "Susie," written in 1882, concerning campaign operations against Apaches. Lent by Mrs. Mary Barr.

Gibson-Fougera Collection. Custer Battlefield National Monument, Crow Agency, Montana. Captain Francis Gibson, father of Mrs. Katherine Fougera, was an officer in the Seventh Cavalry during the 1870's and 1880's. Of special interest in this study is a letter written to Gibson in 1890, by First Sergeant Emil Walker, M Troop, Seventh Cavalry.

Godfrey, Brigadier General Edward S. Manuscripts Division, Library of Congress. Includes a collection of letters, reports, and other manuscript materials written by Godfrey or concerning events in which he was interested.

Goodin, Private B. C. Diary of Private B. C. Goodin, C Troop, First Cavalry, January 31, 1893 to July 14, 1893. Lent by William Bald, an army comrade of the diarist.

Hardin, Lieutenant Edward E. Diary of Second Lieutenant Edward E. Hardin, Seventh Infantry, 1874–1878. Lent by Mrs. J. J. McEwan, the author's niece. Hardin makes several references to enlisted soldiers of his regiment, while serving in Montana Territory.

Hardin, Lieutenant Colonel Edward E. Untitled manuscript on army life in the frontier West. Lent by Mrs. J. J. McEwan.

Hotchkiss, Samuel. Interview with Don Rickey, Jr., Miles City, Montana. The subject was a civilian army teamster in 1890, and had firsthand experience with regular soldiers as a cowboy, from 1885 to the 1890's.

Indian Wars Veterans Questionnaires, Service Accounts, and Personal Letters and Interviews. Over three hundred former Indian Wars regulars were contacted, mostly during the summer of 1954, and requested to furnish information on life in the ranks. The material provided by these men, then-living veterans of western service, from 1876 to the early 1890's, was essential to this study, as the work could not have been undertaken without it. All questionnaires are in the possession of the author. Sixty-four separate individuals are cited in footnotes throughout the study, documenting soldier attitudes, beliefs, and reactions.

Indian-Pioneer Papers, Phillips Collection. University of Oklahoma, Norman, Oklahoma. Typed Interviews with Oklahoma pioneers, including a few who had come to the area as soldiers in the Regular Army prior to 1889. Example: "Antonio Frascola, 5th Cavalry, 1884–89."

Koch, Peter. Letters of Peter Koch, written from Fort Ellis, Montana Territory, in early 1871. Letters describe post life, and Koch's views on the army. Koch was a clerk in the post sutler's store. In possession of Dr. Carl B. Cone, University of Kentucky, Lexington, Kentucky.

Lester, Private Charles, Company H, Fourth Infantry. Letters to his sister, Mrs. Lucy O. Stanley, 1867–69, written from several frontier camps and stations. On deposit at Fort Laramie National Monument, Fort Laramie, Wyoming.

McAnulty, Private George W., Company C, Ninth Infantry. Letters to Miss Lillian Moore, 1878. On deposit at Fort Laramie National Monument, Fort Laramie, Wyoming.

Miller, Colonel William H. "Incidents of the Modoc War." Miller served through the Modoc War, 1872–73, as a lieutenant. This manuscript was lent by Captain Charles F. Humphrey.

National Archives, Old Army Section. Nearly all of the material bearing on regular enlisted men found in these collections was written about rather than by the men themselves. Some valuable information can be obtained in the form of officer opinions on various enlisted problems. Individual reports, General Orders, and other manuscripts will be found cited in various footnotes. Record Group 94 contains considerable material reflecting post life and enlisted activities, such as the various Medical Histories of Posts, and the Consolidated Sioux War Files.

O'Donnell, I. D., Collection. Custer Battlefield National Monument, Crow Agency, Montana. O'Donnell was interested in Custer, the Seventh Cavalry, and Montana Indian Wars history in general. Much of the manuscript material in this collection is in the form of verbatim notes from conversations with John Burkman, a Seventh Cavalry soldier for ten years.

Order of Indian Wars Files, Order of Indian Wars of the United States. Washington, D. C. These files contain a modest volume of material, but it is almost all firsthand information, and includes many letters and other manuscripts from the Indian Wars era. Example: Lieutenant Harry D. Moore, Letter to his Family, April 29, 1873, from "Camp in the Lava Beds . . . ." during the Modoc War, wherein he gives eyewitness descriptions of action conditions, and says some blunt things about cowardice and heroism. The Order of Indian War Files are administered by the American Military Institute.

Paulding, Dr. Holmes Offley. Diary. Office of the Chief of Military

History, United States Army, Washington, D. C. Paulding was a surgeon with Colonel John Gibbon's column during the Sioux Campaign in the summer of 1876.

Ricker Collection. Nebraska State Historical Society, Lincoln, Nebraska. Judge Ricker recorded his interviews with Sioux warriors and former army scouts on pencil tablets, before 1910. This collection contains a wealth of fine material on all the Sioux and Cheyenne campaigns, mainly from the hostile viewpoint.

Schlosher, Harry. Interview with Don Rickey, Jr., April 29, 1957, Miles City, Montana. Schlosher was a cowboy in and around the Miles City area from 1882 to the early 1900's. He saw a great deal of the regulars stationed at nearby Fort Keogh, and supplied information on citizen-soldier relations and attitudes.

Seventh Cavalry Collection. Custer Battlefield National Monument, Crow Agency, Montana. This material consists of muster rolls, casualty and enlistment records, courts-martial cases, and post and regimental order books as well as many other manuscript items related to the history of the regiment, from its creation in 1866 through the early 1900's. Individual items are cited in many footnotes.

Snyder-Ronayne Collection. Custer Battlefield National Monument, Crow Agency, Montana. Diaries of Simon Snyder, Captain and Major, Fifth Infantry, from 1866 through the 1880's, and his account and order books and personal letters to his mother from this valuable collection.

Swayne, Robert E. Letter to Don Rickey, Jr., January 4, 1954, transmitting the service record of William A. Magee, from the Civil War through the Spanish-American War, including almost continuous service in the interim.

Tonamichel, Jake. Interview, March, 1957, Medora, North Dakota. The subject lived at Fort Laramie as a boy, where his father was post hospital steward. He recalled several aspects of life at the post, from which he ran away, to become a horse wrangler, about 1884.

United Indian Wars Veterans Files. San Francisco, California. This collection contains more material about enlisted service during the Indian Wars than any other single collection.

White, William, Second Cavalry. Diary of William White, Second Cavalry, 1876. In possession of William Watt, Crow Agency, Montana. White's company participated in the 1876 Sioux Campaign.

Wilkinson, Major William Grant, Private, Eighth Cavalry, 1886–91. "The Death of Sitting Bull, the Sioux Indian Chief." Lent by author. Wilkinson's Eighth Cavalry troop was drawn up just outside Sitting Bull's village, on Grand River, South Dakota, when the chief was killed in the early morning of December 15, 1890. Wilkinson, as an advance skirmisher, was one of the first soldiers in the village as the hostiles withdrew.

———. "Four Months in the Saddle, the Cross-Country March of the 8th Cavalry, from the Mexican Border to the Canadian Border." Lent by author. This march was made in 1888, to exchange stations with the Seventh Cavalry. The account is an enlisted man's view of the march.

———. "The Sioux Campaign of 1890–91." The author went to college after discharge in 1891, and, becoming educated, later wrote out his accounts with far greater clarity than most former enlisted men could demonstrate.

2. Printed Documents

Office of the Adjutant General, United States Army. *Decorations of the United States Army, 1862–1926.* Washington, Government Printing Office, 1926. A compilation of decorations awarded, including all the Certificates of Merit and Medals of Honor issued for exceptional bravery and outstanding service during the Indian Wars. A brief description of the basis of each award is included.

Headquarters, Department of the Missouri, United States Army. *General Courts Martial Orders, 1869.* St. Louis, Missouri, Government Printing Office, 1870. These orders include accounts of crimes and breaches of regulations, sometimes in detail, and list the punishments imposed.

———. *General Court Martial Orders, 1870.* St. Louis, Missouri, Government Printing Office, 1871. Same type of material as in preceding compilation.

General Orders No. 43, Headquarters of the Army, Adjutant General's Office, July 11, 1868. This Order provides schedules of fines to be assessed against enlisted men "loosing" government rifles.

General Courts Martial Orders, No. 19, Headquarters of the Army, Adjutant General's Office, March 26, 1879. The court-martial of Captain Thomas French, revealing a long list of military crimes and moral aberrations.

Goodenberger, Private Charles, Ninth Infantry. "Marksmanship Certificate No. 1140, Headquarters, Department of Arizona, Office of the Inspector of Rifle Practice, Los Angeles, California, July 31,

1888." These certificates were awarded for various levels of proficiency, and recorded the scores shot by the holders.

Heitman, Francis B. *Historical Register and Dictionary of the United States Army, 1789 to 1903*. Vol. I. Washington, Government Printing Office, 1903.

Hershler, N. *The Soldier's Handbook*. Washington: Government Printing Office, 1884. Contains Regulations and Articles of War specially applicable to enlisted men, and short chapters on guard mount, care of public animals, pay, and other topics of interest and value to the rank and file. The soldier's marksmanship and clothing records were kept in special sections of the *Handbook*.

Ludington, Colonel M. T. *Uniforms of the Army of the United States, from 1774 to 1889*. Washington, Quartermaster General's Department, 1889. A folio collection of detailed color plates and itemized listings of uniform regulations and alterations.

Military Division of the Missouri, United States Army. *Outline Description of the Posts in the Military Division of the Missouri, Commanded by Lt. General P. H. Sheridan*. Chicago, Illniois, Military Division of the Missouri, 1876. Each fort, depot, and camp is concisely described—including size of buildings, materials used in construction, and weather and supply factors. A diagram of each station is included.

Pendell, Lucille H. and Bethel, Elizabeth (compilers). "Preliminary Inventory of the Records of the Adjutant General's Office." Washington, National Archives, 1949. This inventory provides short descriptions of various categories of material and illustrates with specific cases.

Surgeon General's Office, United States Army, Assistant Surgeon George A. Otis (compiler). *A Report of Surgical Cases in the United States Army, 1865–1871, Circular No. 3*. Washington, Government Printing Office, 1871. Contains an extensive section on arrow wounds and the circumstances and treatment of many other wounds incurred in frontier service.

U. S. Congress, House of Representatives, D. B. Sackett, *Protection Across the Continent, House Executive Document No. 23, 39th Cong., 2nd Sess*. Washington, Government Printing Office, 1867. A discussion of the inadequacy of the small Regular Army to control the western tribes, and the low quality of arms, material, and training provided.

U. S. Congress, House of Representatives. *The Reorganization of the Army. House Report No. 354, 44th Cong., 1st Sess*. Washington,

Government Printing Office, 1876. Testimony gathered in hearings and letters in the Military Affairs subcommittee investigations aimed at providing the basis for revamping the Regular Army, during the early spring of 1876.

U. S. Congress, House of Representatives, Committee of Military Affairs. *Reorganization of the Army. House Miscellaneous Document No. 56, 45th Cong., 2nd Sess.* Washington, Government Printing Office, 1878. The second and more extensive investigation, including much material on army shortcomings, as revealed at the Little Bighorn and the Battle of the Big Hole. Contains considerable material on enlisted men. After 1878, the army underwent many changes, as a direct result of the findings in this report and the earlier one begun in 1876.

War Department. *Revised United States Army Regulations of 1861, and . . . Articles of War, to . . . June 25, 1863.* Washington, Government Printing Office, 1863. The regulations embodied in the 1863 edition remained standard until the extensive revisions undertaken in the 1880's.

———. *Annual Report of the Secretary of War, for the Year 1876.* Vol. I. Washington, Government Printing Office, 1876. Includes discussion of desertion and other enlisted problems, and summations of many army problems for the years 1865 through 1876.

———. *Annual Report of the Secretary of War, for the Year 1891.* Vol. I. Washington, Government Printing Office, 1892. This report contains recapitulations of army affairs since the end of the Civil War, and a great deal on desertion, pay, enlistments, and other matters pertaining to the rank and file, from 1865 through 1891.

3. Periodicals and Newspapers

Barnes, Sergeant Will C. "The Battle of Cibicue," *Arizona Highways,* March, 1936.

Bisbee, Brigadier General William H. "Items of Indian Service," *Proceedings of the Annual Meeting and Dinner of the Order of Indian Wars of the United States, Held January 19, 1928.* No place or publisher, 1928. This material is drawn from the author's 1866 to 1868 diaries of service in Wyoming and Nebraska.

Billings Post, July 15, 1882, Billings, Montana Territory. A news story relating a Fourth of July riot at Miles City involving soldiers from the Fort Keogh garrison.

———, June 12, 1884, Vol. III, No. 20. Under local items, a story about a private from Fort Custer who invested money in Billings real estate while on pass.

Bozeman [Montana Territory] *Avant-Courier,* September 27, 1877. News article on the privations suffered by the Seventh Cavalry while pursuing Joseph's Nez Percés down the Clark's Fork River and across the Yellowstone for a few miles up Canyon Creek, where a small fight developed between the soldiers and the Nez Percé rear guard.

Brown, Colonel William C. "The Sheepeater Campaign," *Winners of the West,* Vol. V, No. 12 (November, 1928). The author was a participant in this 1879 campaign.

Burns, Richard T., Second Infantry, 1890. "Campaign of 1890–91," *Winners of the West,* Vol. XV, No. 3 (March, 1938).

"Comrade Rev. Chas. S. Winans," *Winners of the West,* Vol. XIII, No. 11 (October, 1935). Winans served as an enlisted man in the Apache campaigns of the 1880's, and later became a lawyer and a Protestant minister.

Cox, John E., Sergeant, First Infantry. "Soldiering in Dakota Territory in the Seventies: A Communication," *North Dakota History,* Vol. VI, No. 1 (October, 1931).

Craly, Major General E. T., Adjutant General, United States Army. "Letter to Mr. George Arrington, Ex-Sergeant, 24th Infantry," *Winners of the West,* Vol. XIV, No. 3 (February, 1937). The letter relates to the issuance of the Distinguished Service Cross in lieu of the Certificate of Merit awarded to Arrington during his frontier service.

Damn, William, Third Cavalry, 1879. "The Meeker Massacre and Ute Jack's Death," *Winners of the West,* Vol. XIII, No. 9 (August, 1936).

"Diary of George S. Howard, Co. E, 2nd C.," *Winners of the West,* Vol. XIV, No. 3 (February, 1937). Howard's unit was part of General Crook's 1876 column sent against the Sioux and Cheyennes in Wyoming, Montana, and South Dakota.

"Diary of Sgt. James B. Kincaid, Co. B, 4th Cav., August 5, 1876 to 1881," *Winners of the West,* Vol. XVI, No. 6 (July, 1939). The diarist was a member of General Ranald S. Mackenzie's famous regiment, and participated in the fall campaign against the Sioux and Cheyennes in Wyoming, including the Dull Knife Fight.

Dubois, Sergeant George B., F Troop, Eighth Cavalry. "Letters to George Thomas," *Winners of the West,* Vol. XII, No. 4 (March, 1935). The letters describe Dubois' participation in the events surrounding the death of Sitting Bull. They were written December 3 and December 18, 1890.

"84-Year-Old Veteran Remembers Buffalo Bill," *The Happy Harvester*, Vol. VII, No. 3 (September, 1951). Service account of Indian Wars veteran Jacob Markert, who was stationed at Fort Custer, Montana, and participated in the 1890 Sioux Campaign.

Elmo. "Livingston Resident with Reno at Time of Custer Massacre," *Rocky Mountain Husbandman*, May 12, 1938.

"The Experience of Major Mauck in Disarming a Band of Cheyennes on the North Fork of the Canadian in 1878," *Proceedings of the Annual Meeting and Dinner of the Order of Indian Wars of the United States, Held January 19, 1928*. No Place or Publisher, 1928.

Flynn, Andrew M. "Looking Back Over Forty-Nine Years," *Winners of the West*, Vol. XVI, Nos. 10 and 11 (November and December, 1939). The author was an enlisted man in the Sioux Campaign of 1890 and 1891.

Godfrey, Major Edward S. "Cavalry Fire Discipline," *Journal of the Military Service Institution*, Vol. XIX, No. 83 (September, 1896). The author cites examples from his wealth of combat experience against Indians, 1868 through the Battle of Wounded Knee in 1890.

———. Brigadier General, United States Army Retired. "Battle of Wounded Knee," *Winners of the West*, Vol. XII, No. 2 (January, 1935).

Hardin, Major Charles B. "The Modoc War," *Proceedings of the Annual Meeting and Dinner of the Order of Indian Wars of the United States, Held January 24, 1931*. No Place or Publisher, 1931. Hardin participated in the Modoc War, 1872–73, as a First Cavalry enlisted man.

Hauser, C. R. "Meeker Massacre and Colonel Merritt's Record Ride," *Winners of the West*, Vol. XI, No. 2 (January, 1935). Hauser was an enlisted man during the Ute War, 1879–80.

Hettinger, August. "Personal Recollections of the Messiah Craze Campaign, 1890–91," *Winners of the West*, Vol. XII, Nos. 1, 2, and 3 (December, 1934, January and February, 1935).

Hoekman, Steven H. "The History of Fort Sully," *South Dakota Historical Collections and Reports*, Vol. XXVI (1952). A well-written and researched Master's thesis, containing good material on enlisted life at a frontier fort.

"How E. M. Locke Saved Command of Captain Clark From Massacre [1879]," *Rocky Mountain Husbandman*, January 29, 1942. Relates incidents of a summer campaign in north central Montana, with mentions of beer and liquor traders catering to soldiers in the field.

Hudnutt, Dean (editor). "New Light on the Little Big Horn [*sic*]," *The Field Artillery Journal*, Vol. XXVI, No. 4 July–August, 1936). This is a series of letters written by Surgeon Holmes O. Paulding, a member of Colonel John Gibbon's Column, during the 1876 Sioux summer campaign. Paulding had small regard for the campaign and combat readiness of the average soldier.

Hutchins, James S. "The Seventh Cavalry Campaign Outfit at the Little Bighorn," *The Military Collector and Historian*, Vol. VII, No. 4 (Winter, 1956). The best article, based on very extensive research, on a very complicated subject.

"Interview With George App [Company D, Third Infantry, 1873–78]," *Bridgeport* [Connecticut] *Post*, July 27, 1933. App served at Camp Supply, Indian Territory, in 1874 and in Montana in 1878.

Jett, W. B., Fourth Cavalry, 1884. "Engagement in Guadeloupe Canyon," *Winners of the West*, Vol. XIV, No. 9 (August, 1937). An extremely well-written account of a small but bloody action with Apaches.

Johnson, Roy P. "Bismarck Man, Nearing 94, Recalls Custer, Indian Wars," *Fargo* [North Dakota] *Forum*, August 29, 1948. Results of interviews and long time acquaintance with Jacob Horner, Seventh Cavalry, 1876–81.

———. "Jacob Horner of the 7th Cavalry," *North Dakota History*, Vol. XVI, No. 2 (April, 1949).

"Joseph Sinsel of Butte, Member of Gibbon's Command in 1876," *Billings* [Montana] *Times*, April 30, 1925. An interview, including many direct quotes, with a Seventh Infantry soldier of the 1870's.

Kellogg, Mark, "Mark Kellogg's Diary," *North Dakota History*, Vol. XVII, No. 3 (July, 1950). Kellogg was a newspaper correspondent, killed June 25, 1876, at the Battle of the Little Bighorn. His diary and other personal effects were with the regimental pack train, and were not captured by the Indians.

Kurz, Corporal Frederick C., Eighth Cavalry, 1883–88. "With the 8th Cavalry," *Winners of the West*, Vol. XV, No. 11 (December, 1938).

"Lieutenant Fountain's Fight With Apache Indians at Lillie's Ranch, Mogollon Mountains, December 5, 1885 and at Dry Creek, N. M., December 19, 1885," *Proceedings of the Annual Meeting and Dinner of the Order of Indian Wars of the United States, Held January 19, 1928*. No Place or Publisher, 1928.

Lovell, Frank, Fifth Cavalry, 1872–77. "Indian Fighter Recalls Eventful Days of the Frontier," *Winners of the West,* Vol. XVI, No. 7 (August, 1937).

"Major George Ford Dies at 91," *Winners of the West,* Vol. XVI, No. 7 (August, 1939). Obituary of a Negro Ninth Cavalry soldier, who became superintendent of several Negro National Cemeteries and served as a major of Kansas Volunteers during the Spanish-American War.

Mattison, Ray H. (editor). "The Diary of Surgeon Washington Matthews, Fort Rice, D. T.," *North Dakota History,* Vol. XXI, Nos. 1 and 2 (January–April, 1954). Matthews served at several frontier posts during the late 1860's.

–––. "Old Fort Stevenson," *North Dakota History,* Vol. XVII, Nos. 2 and 3 (April–July, 1951). A well-documented short history of this Missouri River frontier port.

McBlain, John F. "With Gibbon on the Sioux Campaign of 1876," *Cavalry Journal,* Vol. IX (June, 1896). The author was a Second Cavalry enlisted man in the middle 1870's.

McClernand, Brigadier General Edward J. "With the Indians and the Buffalo in Montana," *Cavalry Journal,* Vol. XXXV, No. 145 (October, 1926). The author was an officer in Montana during the 1870's, and took part in the Sioux Campaigns of 1876.

McCormack, George R. "Man Who Fought With Custer," *National Republic,* Vol. XXI, No. 11 (March, 1934). This is the story of Jacob Adams, a participant in the Reno-Benteen aspect of the Battle of the Little Bighorn.

Meyers, Augustus, Second Infantry, 1857. "Dakota In the Fifties," *South Dakota Historical Collections,* Vol. X (1920). The author served in the ranks of the Second Infantry at Fort Randall, Dakota Territory, during the late 1850's. His account of regular soldier life prior to the Civil War provides some interesting contrasts and similarities to enlisted life in the post-War years. A detailed account of punishment by flogging is of special interest.

Nixon, John R., Seventh Cavalry, 1890. "Memoirs," *Winners of the West,* Vol. XV, No. 7 (July, 1938).

Nugent, William D. "Thrilling Experiences of William D. Nugent, A Troop, 7th Cavalry, Near Custer Battlefield [1876]," *Winners of the West,* Vol. III, No. 2 (February, 1926). Nugent survived the Battle of the Little Bighorn, as a member of the Reno-Benteen contingent.

Palmer, Captain H. E. "History of the Powder River Expedition of

1865," *Transactions and Reports of the Nebraska State Historical Society,* Vol. II (1887).

Parker, Brigadier General James. "The Geronimo Campaign," *Proceedings of the Annual Meeting and Dinner of the Order of Indian Wars of the United States, Held January 26, 1929.* No Place or Publisher, 1929.

Parker, Sergeant Joseph, Thirteenth Infantry, 1871. "Indian War Veteran Recalls Past," *Winners of the West,* Vol. XVI, No. 7 (August, 1939).

Parker, William Thornton, M. D. "A Soldier's Plea For Justice," *Winners of the West,* Vol. XI, No. 3 (February, 1934). Parker served as an enlisted man in the late 1860's, and studied medicine after discharge.

Proceedings of the Annual Meeting and Dinner of the Order of Indian Wars, Held February 23, 1935. No Place or Publisher, 1935. Copies of all the printed annual meeting proceedings are now extremely rare, as only enough were printed to provide each member of the Order with a copy, and the membership, limited to officers, and descendents of officers, who served in the Indian Wars, was never more than a few hundred. The impromptu after dinner remarks on combat heroism, cowardice, and the Medal of Honor made by General David L. Brainerd are included in the 1935 publication. Brainerd served as an enlisted man in the middle 1870's.

Remington, Frederick. "Our Soldiers in the Southwest," *Harpers Weekly,* Vol. XXX, No. 1548 (August 21, 1886). The author was employed as *Harper's* special correspondent during the Geronimo Campaign. His article makes detailed mentions of several individual soldiers he became acquainted with.

Robinson, Brigadier General Frank U. "The Battle of Snake Mountain," *Military Affairs,* Vol. XIV, No. 2 (Summer, 1950). This account relates material on the transportation and care of the wounded, after the hard-fought, successful attack on a strong band of Arapaho hostiles, July 4, 1874, in northwestern Wyoming.

Russell, Don. "Veteran Madsen," *Winners of the West,* Vol. XXI, No. 2 (February, 1944). The story of Chris Madsen, famous Indian Territory and Oklahoma Peace Officer, stressing his two enlistments in the Regular Army during the 1870's.

Russell, Mrs. Hal. "Memoirs of Marion Russell," *Winners of the West,* Vol. XXI, No. 3 (March, 1944). Recollections of an enlisted soldier's wife.

Ryan, Sergeant John, Seventh Cavalry, 1866–76. "Custer's Last

Fight," *Billings* [Montana] *Times,* July 5, 1923. This long article bears mainly on the title subject, but includes material on many aspects of Ryan's ten years in the Seventh Cavalry. The original manuscript of the article is on deposit in the Custer Battlefield Museum, Custer Battlefield National Monument, Crow Agency, Montana.

Schenck, Martin D. "Early Experiences of Martin D. Schenck," *Winners of the West,* Vol. XI, No. 4 (March, 1934). A first person article by a regular veteran of frontier service.

Schrieber, Philipp. "My Twelve Years in the United States Army," *Winners of the West,* Vol. XIV, No. 9 (August, 1937).

"Sergeant James A. Richardson," *Portland* [Maine] *Sunday Times,* June 27, 1909. Richardson spent thirty years in the Regular Army in the West, and was a veteran of the Battle of the Little Bighorn.

Shields, Alice Mathews. "Army Life on the Wyoming Frontier," *Winners of the West,* Vol. XXI, No. 5 (May, 1944). The wife of a soldier, Mrs. Shields and her husband settled at Laramie, Wyoming in the late 1870's, after he was discharged from Fort Laramie.

Slaughter, Private William J. "Some Recollections of Wounded Knee," *Winners of the West,* Vol. XIV, No. 5 (April, 1937).

Smith, Mrs. George W. "Captain Geo. W. Smith," *Proceedings of the Army of the Cumberland, 14th Corps, 1894, 1895, 1896, 1897.* Columbus, Ohio, Press of John L. Trauger, 1898. The author praises the courage and loyalty of the Negro regulars who continued to fight against a large body of Apaches after Captain Smith was killed, and who brought his body in to post to save it from mutilation by the hostiles.

Stewart, Edgar I. (editor). "Letters from the Big Hole," *Montana Magazine of History,* Vol. II, No. 4 (October, 1952). The letters were written immediately after the battle, in August, 1877, by Lieutenant Charles A. Woodruff, Seventh Infantry.

Thomases, Jerome. "Fort Bridger: A Western Community," *Studies on War.* Washington, *Infantry Journal,* 1943. A short article describing many facets of life at the isolated frontier forts, stressing the self-sufficient aspects of the western posts.

Walker, Reverend James F. "Old Fort Berthold As I Knew It," *North Dakota History,* Vol. XX, No. 1 (January, 1953).

Weir, Lieutenant W. B. "Infantry Equipments, Ordnance Notes No. LXVII," *Ordnance Notes, Nos. 4–67, 1877.* A discussion of suggested modifications in uniforms and equipments used in western campaigning.

Winners of the West, 1922 to 1944. The official publication of the National Indian War Veterans, from the organization's National Headquarters, St. Joseph, Missouri. Each of the monthly issues contains articles relative to Regular Army service in the post-Civil War Indian Campaigns, most of which were written by Indian War veteran participants. In addition to titled articles, the letters to the editor, from hundreds of former frontier regulars, provide one of the outstanding sources of information on enlisted service in the West.

4. Books

Ashburn, P. M. *A History of the Medical Department of the United States Army.* Boston, Houghton Mifflin Company, 1929. Valuable to this study because of the firsthand accounts of frontier service included, and some remarks on the medical services provided for western regulars in the years from 1865 through the early 1890's.

Association of the Graduates of the U. S. Military Academy. *Twelfth Annual Reunion of the Association of the Graduates of the United States Military Academy, at West Point, N. Y., June 9, 1881.* East Saginaw, Michigan, E. W. Lyon, 1881. A short obituary of each member of the association who had died since the previous reunion is included in the annual publication. The obituary of Second Lieutenant Samuel A. Cherry relates his assassination by one of his enlisted men.

Beyer, W. F., and Keydel, O. F. (editors). *Deeds of Valor,* Vol. II. Detroit, Michigan, The Perrier-Keydel Company, 1907. Volume II of this two-volume compilation contains a section on Medals of Honor awarded during the Indian Wars.

Brown, Mark H., and Felton, W. R. *The Frontier Years; L. A. Huffman, Photographer of the Plains.* New York, Henry Holt & Company, 1955. Some of the Huffman photos are of Fort Keogh, Montana.

Carrington, Frances C. *My Army Life and the Fort Phil. Kearney* [*sic*] *Massacre.* Philadelphia, J. B. Lippincott Company, 1910. The author was the second Mrs. Carrington. In 1866, she was the wife of Lieutenant Grummond, who was killed with Fetterman, December 21, 1866, outside the fort. She married Colonel Henry B. Carrington several years later. Her own story includes several references to the enlisted soldiers, and the verbatim accounts of Sergeant Gibson and Private S. S. Peters, who served at Fort Phil Kearny, are excellent sources of information.

Carter, Captain R. G. *The Old Sergeant's Story.* New York, Frederick H. Hitchcock, 1926. The "Old Sergeant" is Sergeant John B. Charlton, who served under Carter in the 1870's. The book is largely a compilation of letters written to the author by Charlton, who furnishes an enlisted man's view of several significant events.

David, Robert Beebe. *Finn Burnett, Frontiersman.* Glendale, California, The Arthur H. Clark Company, 1937. Burnett was a sutler's employee in the late 1860's, and was in close touch with the rank and file of the frontier army along the Bozeman Trail and the forts built to guard it. He was a survivor of the Hay Corral Fight, outside Fort C. F. Smith, Montana, August 1, 1867.

Department of the Army. *American Military History, 1607–1953.* Washington, Government Printing Office, 1956. A textbook survey of the whole of American military history. Lacking in detail, the book at least provides a broad framework for the subject.

Finerty, John F. *War-path and Bivouac.* Chicago, M. A. Donohue & Company, 1890. The author was a war correspondent with General George Crook's 1876 column, from Fort Fetterman, Wyoming, to southern Montana. He did his best to report in a factual and unvarnished style, and his book has become a standard reference on the subject of the 1876 Sioux Campaign. Finerty was popular with most of the officers and with the rank and file, and earned the sobriquet of "Fighting Irish Pencil Pusher" for his participation in combats with the hostiles.

Forsyth, Brigadier General George A. *The Story of the Soldier,* Vol. I. (Builders of The Nation Series.) New York, The Brampton Society, 1908. Written by an Indian Wars officer, who served in the West from the 1860's through the 1890's. The section on the Indian Wars is drawn from his wide experience with the frontier rank and file, both white and colored, and reveals Forsyth to have been an officer of more than average perception.

Ganoe, Major William A. *The History of the United States Army.* New York, D. Appleton and Company, 1924. Ganoe's history was a pioneer study in the field, and has been dated for several years. He relates little material about the enlisted man, but provides information on over-all army policies and developments.

Hein, Lieutenant Colonel O. L. *Memories of Long Ago.* New York and London, G. P. Putnam's Sons, 1925. Hein served as a company officer in the West during the 1870's and 1880's.

Kimball, Maria Brace. *A Soldier-Doctor of Our Army.* Boston, Houghton Mifflin Company, 1917. The author relates considerable material about post life in the 1870's and 1880's, but mainly in connection with surgeons and officers, with some sidelights on the rank and file.

King, Captain Charles. *Campaigning With Crook and Stories of Army Life.* New York, Harper & Brothers, 1890. King left the army in the early 1880's, and became the most popular novelist and story writer publishing contemporary fiction and articles on the Regular Army in the West. He became a brigadier general of volunteers during the Spanish-American War. This book relates King's participation in the 1876 Sioux Campaign with Crook, and the "stories" included are purely fictional.

Larson, James. *Sergeant Larson, 4th Cavalry.* San Antonio, Southern Literary Institute, 1925. Larson enlisted just before the Civil War began, and most of his book relates to his service during the war. He took his discharge in 1866, and closes his book with some candid comments on the recruits being taken into the regulars after the Civil War ended.

Libbey, Orin Grant (editor). *The Arickara Narrative of the Campaign Against the Hostile Dakotas, June, 1876.* Bismarck, North Dakota, The Torch Press, 1920. The Arickara scouts who accompanied Lieutenant Colonel George A. Custer's Seventh Cavalry were interviewed at great length, and the information they provided forms one of the classic references to the study of the Battle of the Little Bighorn. They made some mentions of the enlisted men in their accounts.

Lockwood, James D. *Life and Adventures of a Drummer-Boy.* Albany, N. Y., John Skinner, 1893. The author served through most of the Civil War in a volunteer regiment, and enlisted in the Regular Eighteenth Infantry in 1866. He wrote very candidly about his experiences in the West, the other men in his unit, officers, and the Indians he encountered. He served at Fort C. F. Smith, on the Bozeman Trail, until the post was abandoned in August, 1868. Very few copies of his book were ever circulated, though it contains a wealth of material on the Indian campaign in Wyoming and Montana, 1866–68.

Mills, Anson. *My Story.* Washington, D. C., Press of Byron H. Adams, 1918. The author served in the Civil War and on the frontier after the war. He developed the Mills woven webb cartridge belts and accouterments, left the army and became very wealthy. At the

Battle of Slim Buttes, Dakota Territory, September 9, 1876, he captured much Indian loot and Seventh Cavalry articles taken by the Indians from Custer's men six weeks earlier.

Mulford, Ami Frank. *Fighting Indians in the 7th United States Cavalry.* Corning, N. Y., Paul Lindsley Mulford, 1879. Mulford joined the Regular Army as a "Custer Avenger" in the summer of 1876. His book was written during a long convalescence, after he was medically discharged following an injury received during the Nez Percé War, in the fall of 1877. The book contains more material on rank and file life in the West than does any other, and includes excerpts from his diaries and letters written during his service.

Portrait and Biographical Album of Otoe and Cass Counties, Nebraska. Chicago, Chapman Brothers, 1889. A run-of-the-mill subscription book. The section on "W. H. Pickens" relates the after-discharge history of a Fifth Cavalry sergeant following his leaving the army in 1878 to settle and help develop the area in and around Plattsmouth, Nebraska. By 1888, he was a prominent contractor and builder.

Quaife, Milo H. (editor), and Will, George F. (translator). *Army Life in Dakota, Selections from the Journal of Phillippe Regis de Keredern de Trobriand.* Chicago, Lakeside Press, 1941.

Schmitt, Martin F. (editor). *General George Crook, His Autobiography.* Norman, University of Oklahoma Press, 1946. Crook makes some interesting mentions of the enlisted men, and especially the hardships suffered in the course of the 1876 "starvation march."

Spotts, David L. *Campaigning With Custer and the Nineteenth Kansas Volunteer Cavalry.* Los Angeles, Wetzel Publishing Company, 1928. Spotts was one of the Kansas ninety-day volunteers in 1868. His observations on the treatment of enlisted regulars in the Seventh Cavalry are quite significant.

Summerhayes, Martha. *Vanished Arizona.* Salem, Mass., Salem Press Company, 1911. The author was the wife of an Eighth Infantry officer during the 1870's and 1880's. She makes many mentions of enlisted soldiers, and writes very frankly about life in the frontier regulars.

Wagner, Glendolin D. *Old Neutriment.* Boston, Ruth Hill, Publisher, 1934. "Old Neutriment" was John Burkham, a ten year regular and Civil War veteran, who served as one of Custer's orderlies. The book contains several factual inaccuracies about the Battle of the Little Bighorn, but reflects much light on enlisted life in the 1870's.

Webb, George W. *Chronological List of Engagements Between The*

Bibliography

Regular Army of the United States and Various Tribes of Hostile Indians, Which Occurred During the Years 1790 to 1898, Inclusive. St. Joseph, Missouri, Wing Printing and Publishing Company, 1939.

Wheeler, Colonel Homer W. *Buffalo Days.* Indianapolis, The Bobbs-Merrill Company, 1925. The author secured a direct commission in the middle 1870's, for his scouting and combat service against hostile Indians in Kansas.

Zogbaum, Rufus F. *Horse, Foot, and Dragoons.* New York, Harper & Brothers, 1888. A comparison of French, British, German, and American Armies in the middle 1880's, with some first hand observations on the rank and file. The author considered himself of the officer caste.

Index

Index